THE CHURCH OF ENGLAND
1688–1832

This book is a wide-ranging new account of a key period in the history of the Church in England, from the 'Glorious Revolution' of 1688–89 to the Great Reform Act of 1832. This was a tumultuous time for both Church and State, when the relationship between religion and politics was at its most fraught. *The Church of England 1688–1832* considers the consequences of these important events and the rapid changes it brought to the Anglican Church and to national politics.

Aspects of the social history of the Church are discussed, including the role of the Church in eighteenth-century culture and the development of nationhood. Anglican attitudes to European Protestantism and Methodism are also evaluated.

Drawing on a wide range of contemporary sources, *The Church of England 1688–1832* presents evidence of the widespread Anglican commitment to harmony between those of differing religious views and suggests that High and Low Churchmanship were less divergent than usually assumed. This is both a detailed history of the Church in the eighteenth century and a fresh and stimulating re-evaluation of the nature of Anglicanism and its role in society.

William Gibson has written widely on the eighteenth- and nineteenth-century Church and society. He is currently a senior manager at Basingstoke College of Technology and a Hartley Fellow of Southampton University.

THE CHURCH OF ENGLAND 1688–1832

Unity and Accord

William Gibson

London and New York

First published 2001
by Routledge
11 New Fetter Lane, London EC4P 4EE

Simultaneously published in the USA and Canada
by Routledge
29 West 35th Street, New York, NY 10001

Routledge is an imprint of the Taylor & Francis Group

© 2001 William Gibson

Typeset in Garamond by Steven Gardiner Ltd, Cambridge
Printed and bound in Great Britain by
TJ International Ltd, Padstow, Cornwall

British Library Cataloguing in Publication Data
A catalogue record for this book is available from the British Library

Library of Congress Cataloging in Publication Data
Gibson, William, 1959–
The Church of England 1688–1832: Unity and Accord / William Gibson.
p.   cm.
Includes bibliographical references and index.
1. Church of England – History. 2. England – Church history. I. Title.
BX5070   G53 2000
283′.42 – dc21   00-036635

ISBN 0 415 24023 9 (pbk)
ISBN 0 415 24022 0 (hbk)

CONTENTS

PREFACE AND ACKNOWLEDGEMENTS

It is one of the luxuries afforded the author of a book to anticipate the criticisms that reviewers will make. Doubtless one of these will be that this book is wide-ranging and broadly-woven. This is undoubtedly the case, and necessarily so. For if the argument presented in this book is valid (that the unity and accord which characterised the Church of England in the eighteenth century has been neglected and overlooked by historians) then it needs to be considered in a range of contexts. Indeed in an earlier version the typescript of this book was significantly longer than its present length. The reader will therefore find that from time to time this book 'rides two horses at once': establishing a sufficient narrative framework for a study of over a century and secondly developing the central argument.

This book has had something of a chequered history, having first been commissioned by UCL Press, before its acquisition by Taylor and Francis, and before the latter had absorbed Routledge. I am therefore in the rare position of having a number of editors to thank: Stephen Gerrard and Aisling Ryan at UCL and at Taylor and Francis, and Heather McCallum and Vikki Peters at Routledge. I also owe a debt of thanks to three colleagues who were generous enough with their time to read and comment on the book in manuscript: Professor Jeremy Black of Exeter University, Dr Grayson Ditchfield of the University of Kent, and Robert Ingram of the University of Virginia. All three made valuable and incisive comments, but the responsibility for the errors and weaknesses in this book remain my own. I also wish to record my gratitude to the University of Wales Guild of Graduates for supporting a visit to the Ransom Research Center at the University of Texas, Austin, and to the Hartley Institute at Southampton University for appointing me to a fellowship for 1999–2000 in support of this project.

William Gibson
Chandlers Ford
February 2000

INTRODUCTION

Less than twenty years ago historians bemoaned the absence of studies that would place the eighteenth-century Church in a clearer and truer perspective. Today that imbalance has largely been corrected with a number of studies of the Church between 1689 and 1832. In fact Boyd Hilton has suggested that the rehabilitation of the eighteenth-century Church 'is now almost a commonplace'.[1] For ecclesiastical historians of the eighteenth century that proposition is surely true; but it is less of a cliché for writers who consider the eighteenth-century Church from other perspectives.[2]

Almost without exception the recent studies of the eighteenth-century Church have redressed the traditional view of bishops, clergy and laity. However most of these works have viewed the Church from within a traditional framework, which assumes that the eighteenth-century Church was irrevocably divided and fractured by controversy. Yet a thorough reading of the work of churchmen of the century suggests that divisions between them have been exaggerated. Certainly the division between High and Low Churchmen of the eighteenth century was narrower than that between Laud and the Puritans and the Tractarians and Low Churchmen of the nineteenth century. Moreover the historical attention given to the fleeting moments of controversy in the eighteenth century has masked the widespread and profound commitment to peace and tranquillity among both the clergy and the laity. The same applies to divisions between Anglicans and Dissenters; not only did most live in peace with one another, but in many ways they did not see themselves as separate and discrete.

The unity of the Church stemmed from the Glorious Revolution. While the Revolution was the cause of the departure of the Non-jurors from the Church, it also established a providentialism that was a corner-stone of eighteenth-century Anglicanism. For the most part the Revolution of 1688 ensured that unity of the Church by emphasising the continuity of the monarchy and ecclesio-political doctrines like that of the divine right of kings. In turn the Church ensured that the Revolution was in Steven

Pincus's words 'a national revolution'.[3] But the Revolution of 1688–9 also demonstrates the inadequacy of the categories of churchmanship that historians have, for the most part, been happy to use. High Church and Low Church were not exclusive categories of thought and churchmanship. They were blurred and broad streams within Anglicanism that often merged, overlapped and coincided. The mistaken assumption that these were hard and fast categories helped to construct an appearance of division and disunity. As a result, moments of controversy and division have become archetypes for the Church in the eighteenth century. Instead of seeing the Convocation, Sacheverell and other episodes as untypical, transitory moments, historians have seen them as symptomatic of divisions that reached from the top to the bottom of the Church. Yet there is little evidence for this; and far more that the political relationship between Church and State pacified and united society. The alliance between Church and State under Robert Walpole and Edmund Gibson neutralised Jacobitism, and by the second half of the century militant High Church-manship had evolved into a movement for doctrinal orthodoxy that was mobilised to defend the State from Dissent and radicalism.

In part the ecclesiastical commitment to unity and peace was a response to the Toleration Act, which created competition in worship. Clergy walked a narrow path between attracting worshippers to the Church and correcting the behaviour of their parishioners. But it also created higher and uniform standards of pastoral care, better training for the clergy, sustained moral regulation and a buttress for orthodoxy in the universities. One of the ways in which the Church gave effect to its commitment to unity and peace was its participation in culture. The engagement of the Church in both popular and elite cultures suffused society in the Anglican values of politeness, civic humanism and social reconciliation. The Church's doctrine of unity was also reflected in its commitment to the unity of Protestant Christendom. Anglican leaders were instinctively attracted to unity with foreign Protestants; and they felt an equally strong call to co-operation and amity with Dissent. The same is true between Anglicanism and Methodism – indeed paradoxically the antagonism between the Church and Methodism arose from a hatred of schism and separateness.

National identity in eighteenth-century England was also indivisible from Anglicanism: government was a religious construct and Anglicanism was welded into the structure of the establishment. This identification of religion and national identity was both a potent cause and a consequence of national conflicts abroad. The effect was that in most shared national experiences – worship, lore, education and charity – Anglicanism was ever-present. Its gift to national identity was to drench nationhood in tradition and in the Anglican values of moderation and restraint.

The aim of this book is to take a slice through the eighteenth-century Church to recover a neglected theme. The theme is the sense of unity and accord that pervaded the Church in the eighteenth century and which has been largely neglected by historians. Eirenicism, the doctrine of peace and unity within the Church, was a powerful presence in much of the eighteenth century. Indeed Stillingfleet's *Irenicon* was the motivation for Wesley's attempt to remain within the Church of England. The flight from the damage of the ecclesiastical and political divisions of the seventeenth century is a recurring theme in the sermons and treatises of the period, and church-men repeatedly sought strategies that would avoid divisions and schism. Yet historians have tended to focus on the moments of furious controversy and division, indeed a recent discussion has asserted that 'the Church of England was bitterly divided' after 1689.[4]

If as J. H. Hexter claims, history, and particularly ecclesiastical history, is divided into 'splitters' and 'lumpers' this book is clearly a work of lumping.[5] But it does not assume that Anglicanism was a universal solvent in the eighteenth century. Undoubtedly there were divisions in the Church, the question is how profound were they and did they blight the effectiveness of Anglicanism. Was the principal identity and instinct of Anglicanism toward division or unity? This work seeks to advance the view that division was not the principal feature of the eighteenth-century Church; peace and unity were stronger forces in the minds of churchmen.

Notes

1 B. Hilton, 'Apologia pro Vitis Veteriorium Hominum', *Journal of Ecclesiastical History*, 1999, vol. 50, no. 1, p. 119.

2 Though the *Daily Telegraph*'s series *AD 2000 Years of Christianity* asserted of the eighteenth century that 'the Church was by no means ineffective in the parishes' and on the clergy 'the evidence of Bishop's Visitations indicates a generally high standard'. *AD 2000 Years of Christianity*, Part 5, 1999, p. 29. In contrast, John Brewer's recent book *The Pleasure of the Imagination*, London 1997, fails to see the significance of religion in the eighteenth century. And Frank O'Gorman recently claimed that the spiritual needs of the people 'were not being met'. F. O'Gorman, 'Eighteenth Century England as an *Ancien Regime*', S. Taylor, R. Connors, C. Jones (eds.), *Hanoverian Britain and Empire, Essays in Memory of Philip Lawson*, Woodbridge, 1998, p. 32.

3 S. Pincus, ' "To Protect English Liberties": the English Nationalist Revolution of 1688–9', T. Claydon and I. McBride (eds.), *Protestantism and National Identity, Britain and Ireland, c.1650–c.1850*, Cambridge, 1999, p. 102.

4 K. Robbins, *Great Britain, Identities, Institutions and the Idea of Britishness*, London, 1998, p. 113.

5 J. H. Hexter, *On Historians*, Cambridge Mass., 1979, pp. 241–3. I owe this reference to Robert Ingram of the University of Virginia. Hexter wrote: '. . . Instead of noting difference, lumpers note likenesses; instead of separate-ness, connection . . .'.

1

HISTORIANS AND THE EIGHTEENTH-CENTURY CHURCH

If the mantra of the post-modernist historian is 'history is theory, theory is ideology and ideology is material interests', a study of the eighteenth-century Church, superficially at least, is a model of postmodernist history. The historiography of the eighteenth-century Church is profoundly ideological: Victorian historians defended their class, professional and intellectual interests, and diverted attention from the need to change, by consciously depicting their predecessors as incapable of reaching Victorian standards. Even the most restrained critic of the Victorians conceded that what they wrote of the eighteenth-century Church was myth: 'self-confident and self-assertive, they [the Victorians] developed a mythology about their Georgian predecessors, and this mythology has held sway since then'.[1] Like a wilful child jealous of a sibling, the Victorian ecclesiastical establishment attracted attention to the achievements of its own age and intentionally suggested that the Georgians were hopelessly divided and turbulent. The Victorian view is particularly ideological since many nineteenth-century historians were clerical adherents of the Tractarian and Evangelical movements, which assailed their opponents as bitterly as any political party. Consequently there was more at stake than just an account of the past; the Victorians were writing a history which would defend their own ideology and the construction of their own religious establishment. It was as if Margaret Thatcher was writing the history of the post-war consensus.

To suggest that only postmodernist 'interest' conditioned the Victorian response to the eighteenth-century Church would however be an inadequate explanation. The Victorian world was one in which the sciences had come of age, and in which the changes engendered by urbanisation and industrialisation had effected an intellectual and cultural transformation. What Victorians did not recognise was that a judgement of the eighteenth century that did not acknowledge these changes was anachronistic. The core of the difference between the eighteenth-century world view and that of the Victorians was the collapse of hermeneutics and the division of knowledge.

To the eighteenth-century mind, philosophy, science, religion, and politics could still be treated as a unity. As Thomas Sprat's *History of the Royal Society* (1663) indicates, reason and unreason, mysticism and rationalism, had not formed into clear and discrete realms. Hence Isaac Newton was a brilliant physicist, but was also committed to notions of alchemy, millenarianism and the mysticism of freemasonry. Other scientists of the early eighteenth century, such as Boyle and Keill, moved easily between mysticism, natural religion and science. For Newton, Boyle and their contemporaries, the quantitative forces of a modern economy had not emerged, nor had its social instruments. Eighteenth-century concepts of education, advancement, merit and professional duty were largely those inherited from the Tudors and Stuarts. When Gladstone criticised the clergy of the eighteenth century for being 'secular in their habits'[2] he lapsed into anachronism by suggesting a division between the secular and the spiritual that had not emerged in the eighteenth century. In the eighteenth century there was no organised scepticism and no coherently developed sense of secularity, there was no division between the values and behaviour of laity and clergy. As a result, for example, bishops of the eighteenth century, among them Henry Compton, Gilbert Burnet, George Fleming, and Thomas Herring, saw no conflict between their role as clergy and taking to military service in 1689, 1715 and 1745 respectively. Bishop John Robinson of London saw no incongruence between service to the State as a diplomat at the Treaty of Utrecht and his episcopal status; nor did Francis Atterbury, who was intended for a ministerial post if the Hanoverian succession had been averted in 1714; or Edward Willes who was Decypherer to the King and bishop successively of St David's and Bath and Wells. William Warburton was rare in regarding Church and State as in an alliance rather than a single entity, but many churchmen did not see the difference between religious and political matters in the way that Victorians had divided them. In Georgian England, as much as in the seventeenth century, politics was a branch of theology.

Brian Young has recently suggested the eighteenth century was an era in which society was only gradually becoming secularised, but the Victorian emphasis on progress intrinsically attacked it.[3] The Victorian historian J. A. Froude's attack typifies this:

> the bishop, rector or vicar of the established Church in the eighteenth century is a byword in English ecclesiastical history. The exceptional distinction of a Warburton or a Wilson, a Butler or a Berkeley, points the contrast even more vividly with the worldliness of their brothers on the bench. The road to honours was through political subserviency. The prelates indemnified

themselves for their ignominy by the abuse of their patronage, and nepotism, and simony were too common to be a reproach.[4]

For Froude, everything was black: the eighteenth-century clergy were lazy and 'low' in matters of doctrine, they were unversed in theology, class-ridden, debased and tolerant of abuses. He was anxious to promote the Whiggish idea of the progress of society from the depths to the sunny uplands; after all, the enlightenment of his own century could only mean that its precursor was inadequate and unworthy.

What gives the lie to the Victorian position is that even the reformers and apparent dissenters from the established ecclesiastical order in the eighteenth century were decried. Radical proponents of Church reform like Hoadly and Watson were attacked by Charles Abbey and John Overton as men in 'want of spiritual depth'.[5] Deists, Non-jurors, evangelicals and all shades of churchmen in between were excoriated for their views or actions. Consequently Young suggests that the Victorians were engaged in 'present-centred history', formulating prescriptions for their own age by a coloured view of the past:

> in the process, history was inevitably distorted: heroes and villains were identified and religious and philosophical movements were measured against the requirements of the times. . . . In attempting to understand eighteenth-century thought, the late twentieth-century scholar has to engage with the . . . [Victorians'] prejudices and blindspots. . . .[6]

The Victorian age produced historians of widely differing perspectives: Leslie Stephen, Thomas Macaulay, Thomas Carlyle, W. H. Lecky, Mark Pattison, James Froude, W. H. Hutton, John Overton and Charles Abbey. These historians crossed a broad spectrum of political views, Tory and Whig; of religious views, Tractarian to agnostic; and of intellectual disciplines, historians, philosophers and theologians. But as laymen or clerics they shared a view of their own religious ideology as progressive and overcoming an inadequate system. They blamed the churchmen of 1689 and 1714 for much, including the failure of the Church and State in 1829 to defend an establishment which had united the two institutions. It was as if churchmen like Benjamin Hoadly had consciously sought to divide and marginalise the Church of England in order for it to become a single denomination among many a century later. As Tractarians and sceptics looked into the blazing flame of ritualist controversy, it affected their vision when they looked outward to the apparent darkness of the eighteenth century.

There is no doubt that this engendered a view of the past which was shrouded in a mythology, and which exaggerated the conflicts and disputes of the eighteenth century. High Churchmen viewed Charles I as an unavenged 'King and Martyr', they saw the Non-jurors as the lost tribe without which the Church wandered into error, and the churchmen of the eighteenth century as quarrelsome betrayers of their birthright.[7] Sometimes historians like John Overton and Charles Abbey recognised this as mythology, and in flashes of perception suggested greater intellectual cohesion than they otherwise allowed. Thus in *The English Church in the Eighteenth Century* (1878) Abbey and Overton made the suggestion that Benjamin Hoadly and Thomas Sherlock were men of the same church-manship. It was a view that they eradicated in the condensed single-volume edition of their work in 1887.[8]

In the same way, historians credulously treated Deism, Arianism and Socinianism as part of a Low-Church Anglican spectrum, which stretched into heresy and imported division and disagreement into the Church. They ignored the supreme driving belief in unity and accord which led Samuel Clarke to refuse two mitres to avert a division in the Church, and over-looked the staunch defence of orthodox Anglican doctrines by the leaders of the eighteenth-century Church, such as Wake, Gibson, Butler and Secker. Instead Overton treated William Law, the Non-juror, as the lost leader of eighteenth-century Anglicanism.[9]

Overton also advanced the muddled myths of the ritualists. In *Life in the English Church 1660–1714* (1885) Overton seemed to point the finger of blame for the ills of the Church on the defining moment of 1714. Of the Anglican Church in the Commonwealth of the 1650s he wrote: 'never was her life more vigorous than when she was spoken and thought of as dead and buried'.[10] The Caroline Church and its divines were advanced as models of Anglican piety and even under Anne the popularity of the Church was noted. The implication of the book was clear: the rot set in during 1714, decline occurred under the house of Hanover.

Of course this further exposes the Victorian myth. In reality the Hanoverian succession changed very little in the Church, which was as immersed in politics before 1714 as after. The roots of Latitudinarianism were laid well before this date. Toleration of Dissent had been granted by the royal prerogative before 1688, and the Toleration Act was a result of the Glorious Revolution, not of the Hanoverian succession. Moreover the philosopher John Locke had suggested that the Church was a voluntary society well before 1714. The strengths of the Church – its scholarship, its growing status as a profession, its pastoral work and the support it attracted from the people – were all features that remained and broadened after 1714. On no rational grounds could 1714 be judged as a watershed for the

Church. But Overton was not judging the history of the Church on rational grounds. The preface to *Life in the English Church 1660–1714* indicates that some of his inspiration came from 'Wednesday evening congregations at Epworth Church', and one suspects that Overton sought to use his book to paint in the monochrome palate of religious edification and mortification.

The question is, why did the Victorian analysis of the eighteenth-century Church hold sway for so long? The question is especially pertinent, given the availability of opposing views. The Victorian position was undoubtedly challenged, and fairly quickly. John Wickham Legg's *English Church Life from the Restoration to the Tractarian Movement* (1914) and Aldred Rowden's *Primates of the Four Georges* (1916) were both admirable attempts to present balanced evidence of the eighteenth-century Church without the overlay of Victorian censoriousness. Both historians sought to judge the eighteenth-century Church by its own standards and to avoid anachronistic judgements. They also presented little-known evidence of the conscientiousness of churchmen of the period and their efforts to discharge their duty; both books have been unjustifiably neglected.[11]

Without doubt, Norman Sykes made the greatest contribution to the rehabilitation of the eighteenth century Church this century. Sykes's study of *Edmund Gibson* (1926) and of *Church and State in England in the Eighteenth Century* (1934) developed a new view of the eighteenth-century Church. Both books were overtly sympathetic to the eighteenth-century Church, and sought to explain and understand the difficulties under which it laboured. In his later biographical study of *William Wake* (1957) Sykes also portrayed the Church as an institution in which clergy and bishops successfully discharged their duties. The strength of Sykes's work is that it drew on a wide range of manuscript sources to defend the Church from the suggestion that it ignored reform and slumbered. The problem with Sykes's biographical studies of Gibson and Wake, however, was that they were open to the imputation that their subjects were presented as exceptional rather than representative bishops. Moreover Sykes's modesty and wide range of historical interests prevented him from founding a school of historians to promote his work. Even his pupil G. V. Bennett, whose biographical studies of White Kennett and Francis Atterbury[12] followed in Sykes's footsteps, recognised the limitations of Sykes's influence. Sykes's revisionism was also limited by the marginalisation of religious history and its separation from political and social history. In the sphere of political history the work of Sir Lewis Namier placed an emphasis on political structures, careers and patronage networks which underscored the Victorian analysis of the Church and did not connect with Sykes's revisionism. It would have been impossible for historians of the sixteenth and seventeenth century to divorce religion from politics; but historians of the eighteenth century were able to effect this separation without challenge.

Other historians of the eighteenth-century Church did not take up the opportunities afforded by Sykes's revision. Edward Carpenter's *Thomas Sherlock* (1936), his biography of *Thomas Tenison* (1948) and his study of Bishop Henry Compton[13] appeared to rehabilitate their subjects, but did not promote the revision of the Church as whole. Similarly A. T. Hart's work eroded Victorian attitudes but was not explicit in its claims for the eighteenth-century Church.[14] R. N. Stromberg's study of religious liberalism in the eighteenth century claimed that the theology of the Church was 'weak-kneed' in the face of Arianism, Socinianism and unorthodoxy.[15]

The decade in which ecclesiastical historians at last grasped the implications of Sykes's work was ironically the period which witnessed a further set-back for the study of the eighteenth-century Church. During the 1960s and 1970s R. W. Greaves, Norman Ravitch, G. V. Bennett, and others promoted a more positive view of the eighteenth-century Church.[16] But, elsewhere in the discipline historians such as Edward Thompson, Eric Hobsbawm, Christopher Hill, and Lawrence Stone encouraged a radical, and sometimes Marxist, view of the eighteenth century. They viewed religion in general and the Church in particular as instruments of opposition to progress and change. Paradoxically they also advanced a view of the Church as intellectually enfeebled and sleepy. The contradiction between an institution effective enough to oppress but weakened in ideas is one that was never resolved. Like the Victorians, radical and Marxist historians had their own agenda. 'Present-centred history' was revived to advance the view of an oppressed people, enslaved by eighteenth-century religion and capitalism. Frank O'Gorman has also argued that 'social and economic historians were predictably unhappy with the *ancien regime* model [of English society] because it appeared to ignore many of the modernising elements upon which their careers depended: industry, capitalism, commerce and new patterns of consumption'.[17] Moreover, the separation of religious history from the 'mainstream' of political and social history affected the ability of the revision of the eighteenth-century Church to influence the trend of historical writing.

A renewal of the revisionist impetus has occurred in the 1980s and 1990s as a result of the work of a range of ecclesiastical historians like Jeremy Gregory, Arthur Warne, Albion Urdank, Jeffrey Chamberlain, John Guy, Viviane Barrie-Curien, Jan Albers, Donald Spaeth, and William Jacob.[18] At the same time political and social historians have recognised the need to incorporate religion in their work. Linda Colley's *Britons*, for example, emphasised the importance of Protestantism in the development of a sense of British nationhood in the eighteenth century, though perhaps she failed to identify differences between Protestants.[19] Eveline Cruickshanks and Jeremy Black have also restored religion to a central place in the study of Jacobitism and the wider history of the century. The most significant re-evaluation of the role of the Church of England and religion in the ideology and politics of the eighteenth century came in Jonathan Clark's *English Society 1689–1832* (1985).

Clark's contribution to eighteenth-century ecclesiastical history has been to restore it to a central place in the study of the period. His stated aim in *English Society 1689–1832* was

> to re-integrate religion into an historical vision which has been almost wholly positivist; to discard economic reductionism, to emphasise the importance of politics in social history, and to argue against the familiar picture of eighteenth century England as an era of bourgeois individualism by showing the presence of the *ancien regime* until 1828–32, and the autonomous importance of religion and politics in its final demise.[20]

Clark's target was those Marxist social historians, such as the Webbs, Tawney, Cole, and E. P. Thompson, who had developed a view of English society in the eighteenth century which resonated with the reductionist view of the era. Indeed what Clark exposed was a rich irony: that the Victorian view and the Marxist view of the eighteenth century had been mutually sustaining. Both asserted that eighteenth-century institutions were corrupt, divided and in need of reform. It was essentially a positivist view and one which drew on economic reductionism to suggest the primacy of material life. They suggested that Lockean ideas of utilitarianism started a process which culminated in the reform of parliament and society in the nineteenth century. To this Whiggish interpretation the socialist historians of the 1960s added the view that forces of reaction and capitalism defended the *ancien regime* in England and resisted reform in Church and State in the eighteenth century. Rationalism, linked with greed and class interest, had created an abhorrent regime.

In contrast, Clark took the view that eighteenth-century English society was 'Anglican, aristocratic and monarchical' and that the eighteenth century was not an era of bourgeoisie individualism; nor was the decline of the *ancien regime* inevitable as historians have assumed. He excoriated earlier historians for allowing prejudices about the Church, aristocracy and monarchy to affect their views of the eighteenth century. It was a revolutionary and complex argument, and one which deserves some detailed examination.

For Clark, the Glorious Revolution changed the monarchy, but it did not alter ideas of patriarchalism, order, hierarchy and stability. The three pillars of eighteenth-century society remained Church, King and nobles. The legitimacy and stability of the regime rested on ideas of social permanence with deep historical roots, hence the broad preoccupation with antiquity, including the attempt of Archbishop James Ussher of Armargh to date events back to the Bible. It was also reflected in the claims of the Convocation, the Church's legislative body, in 1705 to possess ancient privileges. It is with this powerful sense of stability and cohesion in the Church that this book is concerned.

An essential element in Clark's view is that rationalism gained less ground in the eighteenth century than historians hitherto thought. Clark argues that the quick rationalist victory of Locke over traditional ideologies of mysticism, deference and paternalism has been overstated; in reality the older values persisted into the eighteenth century. Moreover, Locke was less important than other historians have assumed and the Whigs were less bound to revolutionary and republican principles, a point with which Peter Nockles agrees.[21] The Whigs tended to focus more on the legitimacy of the doctrine of resistance to the established authority (which had been challenged by the Revolution of 1689) than the idea of an 'original contract' between ruler and ruled, and which some claimed James II had broken. But far from being the beneficiary of the revolutionary or even liberal principles of resistance and of a contract, the Church of England after 1689 was dominated by comparatively conservative ideas.

Clark argues that most people in the country were in a dependent position, either as servants, women, employees or journeymen; and most people were also deeply imbued with faith:

> The salient fact for the social historian of eighteenth-century England is that Christian belief is initially almost universal, a belief calling attention to the history of a chosen nation conceived as a family or group of families with a Holy Family as its culmination; a faith whose established Church taught obedience, humility and reverence to superiors with unanimity and consistency down the decades. . . .[22]

Christianity and its moral code were the 'common possession' of all strata of society. It was a moral code linked to economic success – a notion to which even Thomas Malthus subscribed. Anglicanism erosion by Dissent was not an intellectual defeat, but one of the sheer number of dissenters. But the triumph of Dissent should not be too quickly anticipated in the years before 1828: as late as 1802 William Cobbett said that from the top of any hill he could look down on England and see the spires of churches all over the country.

For Clark, Anglicanism was also inextricably linked with the State: the patrician class were Anglicans, Anglicanism defined the elite, and non-Anglicans were excluded from exercise of power in the State. Therefore the collapse of the *ancien regime* was sounded by the repeal of the Test and Corporations Acts in 1828. It was this measure that ended the Anglican hegemony and the idea of assimilation into an elite by conforming to its religious tenets. Thus for many historians Clark's thesis was the most powerful confirmation of the legitimacy of the idea of the 'long eighteenth century'.

At the centrepiece of Clark's view that traditional values survived the Revolution of 1689 is his assertion that the divine right of kings remained strong in the dynastic doctrines of the State after 1689. The Church's preoccupation with issues of submission or resistance to the ruler itself was evidence of the survival of the concept. Clergy preached the doctrine under both William III and Anne. The theory evolved into a view that the successions of William, Anne and George I were divinely ordained and the conquest by William and the dynastic failure of Anne were expressions of it. Paradoxically, the Jacobites also clung to the idea of the divine right of kings, and up to 1750 Non-jurors sought to promote a model of a Stuart monarchy which God would restore to absolute authority. The survival of the theory of the divine right, whether in its pure or providential form, is one of the pillars of the Church's commitment to unity and accord in the eighteenth century.

The dynastic principle was underscored by the celebration of anniversaries of the martyrdom of Charles I, the Restoration of Charles II and the Glorious Revolution. The notion of the divine right was also exhibited by the occasional royal touching for the king's evil, which persisted into the reign of Anne. Such superstition was an integral element in what Clark saw as traditional religion:

> Too little weight is often given to the immense continuity, and vast inertia, of popular and rural sentiment, especially in the case of England. Not least has this reflected the polemical denigration within the 'Whig interpretation' of the Church as somehow at once somnolent, or ineffectual, and the advance guard of modern rationalism.[23]

Whilst the indefeasible notion of the divine right of kings was killed off by the Jacobite defeat of 1745–6, Clark argues that religious ideas of monarchy survived into the late eighteenth century in four key ideas. First was a providential divine right. Secondly the idea of a 'Patriot King', developed under George II and III, which seemed to be confirmed by military successes of the country and which upheld liberties and the constitution. Thirdly there was a sentimental attachment of the King to the social structure, which seemed to sanctify both. Finally even radicals like Thomas Paine, author of *The Rights of Man* (1790), built on the principle of the divine right by extending it to all men. Whatever the nature of the religious ideas of civil authority after 1760, the religio-monarchical consensus between Whig and Tory after 1760 prevented civil strife and supported the hegemony of the Church.

What England had rejected in 1688 was not the notion of a divinely-ordained monarchy, but a Catholic one with the dogmatic right of interference in people's lives. The nature of the established Church was especially important to Clark:

> The nature of the Church establishment was therefore of consider-able importance, and conventional caricature of it as somnolent, corrupt and unthinkingly subservient to the civil power is particularly distorting. Even Low Churchmen of the eighteenth century sought, as their ideal, not a subordination of the sacred to the secular but a purposeful identity, a close connection between Church and State which would take as its motto George Lawson's words: 'Politics are from God. . . . Hence it is that politics, both civil and ecclesiastical, belong unto theology; and are but a branch of the same'. Under the first two Georges, just such an alliance was sustained between the Whig political establishment and the bishops.[24]

To Clark, accusations of Erastianism were particularly erroneous because the Church was responding to the needs of the people in identifying the Church with the State. The Whig alliance with the Church under George I and II gave just such a purposeful identity to the altered circumstances of 1689. In the parishes this was translated into the alliance between the parson and the squire, and in the nation between bishops and ministers. It was a strategy that was successful. The decision to abandon the Whigs' agenda of the comprehension of Dissent in favour of Edmund Gibson's defensive alliance with them ensured that moderate High Churchmen dominated the Church after 1727. Bishops such as Wake, Gibson, Potter, Secker and Sherlock were able to assert High Church values and above all they ensured that the Test remained unchallenged.

Clark also argued that late eighteenth-century Britain was not dominated by ideas of democracy and representation, but by ideas of allegiance and sovereignty of the Church and State – indeed this was so in America and France as well as Britain. The Tory intellectual position strengthened after 1760 as they succeeded the Whigs as the party of the Church. The Tories asserted that the establishment represented not simply mindless authoritarianism, but a position which had intellectually defeated radicalism. Tories like William Blackstone, the eighteenth-century jurist, sought to raise the monarchy above party strife and reinforce High Church ideas by defending the Test Act and denying Dissent a legitimate role in the State. His view was that Dissent was illegal, and that the Toleration Act of 1689 was merely a suspension of that illegality. In opposition to these ideas, the Whigs found themselves increasingly sympathetic to Dissent. Predictably for a Church committed to the preservation of peace and stability, the clergy were in the forefront of defence of the State from these attacks. High Church Whig and Hutchinsonian clergy, such as Horne, Paley and Warburton, placed royal authority alongside Trinitarianism and the apostolic succession. Inevitably the religious analysis of government was intensified by the French Revolution and Horne re-asserted the ancient doctrine of passive resistance. Without the king he claimed there would be no Church and therefore the French Revolution threatened religion as much as the political establishment. Similar doctrines were advanced by the moderate bishops Horsley, Hallifax and Pretyman; they asserted that the ordination of the King at the coronation and the oaths sworn to him demanded the allegiance of the people.

Clark suggests that the success of this High Church defence of the State can be seen in the response of Methodism. Methodists joined Anglicans in supporting the status quo and turned against the radical clamour. Wesley's defence of royal paternalism was so strong that he was accused of Jacobitism. The French Revolution also enabled Wesley to add an anti-popish flavour to his defence of the establishment. Whilst local Methodists embraced radicalism, the Methodist Conference remained strongly conservative until the 1830s. This is not surprising, given the conservative antecedents of Methodism which included Non-jury. Even Burke was won for the establishment by the French Revolution; by 1792 he advanced a defence of Anglicanism which treated the Church and State as a unity. He did so in the teeth of ideas of the 'rights of man' and Jacobinism which he associated with English Dissent. For Burke, however, duties, including religious duties, were not voluntary. Anglican political ideology also dominated thinking at the turn of the century because of the radical reactions to it. Radicals, such as Heywood, advanced a contractual view of royal authority. During the Napoleonic War they attacked aristocratic systems of government, but, following the royalist resurgence after the war, they turned their attentions to the Church. As late as 1820 therefore bishops such as William Van

Mildert were defending the Church in the same terms as they had defended the State twenty years earlier.

Just as the establishment could be defined in terms of the orthodox Anglican monarchical ideology, Clark argues that radical opposition was rooted in anti-Trinitarianism and religious heterodoxy. Their target became the State:

> the agency of the State which confronted him [the radical opponent] in his everyday life was not Parliament, . . . elections were infrequent, contests less frequent still, the franchise restricted. . . . The ubiquitous agency of the State was the Church, quartering the land not into a few hundred constituencies, but into ten thousand parishes, impinging on the daily concerns of the great majority, supporting its blackcoated army of a clerical intelligentsia, bidding for a monopoly of education, piety and political acceptability.[25]

Thus for any radical, reform had to mean reform of the Church as much as the State. Clark effectively reformulated eighteenth-century radicalism as a religious rather than a secular movement. The decision to exclude Unitarians and Socinians from the benefits of the Toleration Act of 1689 established a group of radicals who would always be beyond the pale. Thus opposing the State was always a religious act.[26] Throughout the eighteenth century radicalism was a religious expression: Arians were excluded from office in the State, the Blasphemy Act of 1697 was specifically aimed at Unitarians, and in 1723 Archbishop William Wake himself obtained the secretary of state's warrant to destroy the galleys of a Socinian printer.

Clark suggests that ultimately both Church and State were ineffective in stamping out heterodox radicals: the role of the Church courts of the eighteenth century declined, acts of general pardon undermining them by annulling their penalties. Moreover the preferred remedy against heterodoxy for High Churchmen was Convocation, hence the conflicts in Convocation between 1701 and 1717, but Convocation was silent from 1717. For many radical republicans numerous divisions distracted them from the national stage before 1760. Thus in the years after 1714 the Church was less seriously threatened by heterodox republicans, than by the 'Venetian Oligarchy' to which they were allied. The repeal of the Schism Act, the repeal of Occasional Conformity Act, the Close Vestries Bill, attempts to repeal the Test Act, the Act for the Quieting and Establishing of Corporations, the Quaker Affirmation Bill, the Tithe Bill, Church Courts Bill, the Church Rates Bill, the Mortmain Bill and the Quaker Tithe Bill seemed to assault the Church with Whig anti-clericalism. It was the Quaker Tithe Bill that destroyed the alliance. The rebuilding of the relationship with the State after 1736 was the work of bishops like Thomas Secker and moderate High Churchmen. When the State again needed the support of the Church after 1760 High Churchmen responded to a refocused heterodox onslaught from John Wilkes, and his Unitarian supporters, and from heterodox elements within the Church itself: Edmund Law, John Jebb, and John Disney, all of whom advocated a doubtful view of the Trinity. Indeed threats of heterodoxy from within the Church animated orthodox defenders most strongly of all. The rejection of the Petition in 1772 and its successor in 1774 committed the Church to orthodoxy and led a cadre of heterodox clergy to leave the Church, including Jebb, Lindsey, Tyrwhitt, Wakefield, and Disney.

After 1760, Clark argues, the real threat to the Church came from a more assertive form of Dissent. Before 1760 men like Thomas Secker, Joseph Butler, John Potter and Isaac Maddox left Dissent for Anglicanism, and in many parishes across the country Dissenter and Anglican lived on good terms; after 1760 prominent Dissenters were less willing to sacrifice their views, and sought equality with Anglicanism in the State. The focus of the Dissenters' attack was the Test Act. Whilst annual Indemnity Acts after 1727 had in effect suspended the Act, permitting Dissenters into office, they felt disadvantaged by the Test Act. Moreover, after 1774 the Dissenters added demands for parliamentary reform. This was part of a broader movement for political change. In the wake of the American War of Independence (1775–83), Paine's *Rights of Man* savagely attacked the monarchy, the aristocracy and the Church – especially revealed religion and the Bible as a tool of enslavement.

By 1820 the Tories sought to weld the Church and King together against the three challenges – the repeal of the Test Act, Catholic emancipation and parliamentary reform. The Whigs had attracted religious dissenters: Holland an atheist, Lansdowne a Unitarian, Brougham a Deist, and their platform became freedom of conscience. By 1820 Whig votes were increasingly reliant on Dissenters. They were not influenced by nascent ideas of democracy but by the need to respond to their electoral supporters. Urbanisation led to a growth of the dissenting view that the constitution needed to be unshackled from the Church. The decline of Anglicanism in these areas was not a matter of its intellectual integrity, but of growth in numbers of urban Dissenters. They faced a Tory party divided over reform, and Catholic emancipation in particular, whose Anglican base was declining.

In stark contrast to the Victorian view, Clark argues that the passage of Catholic emancipation and repeal of the Test Act in 1828–9 was a consequence of the broken will of the Tories and the bishops. The ultras and bishops in 1829 shared the same views as Wake and Gibson who had defended a Protestant constitution, but they lacked their resolution and betrayed the alliance of Church and State from within. The monarchy, aristocracy and the Church were eclipsed by the forces of parliamentary reform which were unleashed by the reforms of 1828–32. The Whigs' reform of the Church in the 1830s dismantled the Church as an ally of the State because the Church had been a scapegoat for the reformers. In 1689 the nation chose the Church and Protestantism over the monarchy, in 1829–32 it chose a reformed parliamentary monarchy over the Church. For the eighteenth-century historian 1829–32 ended the ancien regime; for the Victorian historian it established the start of a new social order.

English Society 1689–1832 had a dramatic impact on the historiography of the eighteenth century, and provoked wide-ranging discussion. Clark's conscious decision to emphasise the role of the monarchy, Church and aristocracy attracted responses from historians who see the commercial classes, women and the industrial working classes as features of the eighteenth century he neglects.[27] There has been a reaction to Clark's perception of the self-confidence of the Church in the second half of the eighteenth century. James Bradley suggested that Anglican sermons in the 1770s and 1780s betray an anxiety and concern and the clergy's staunch orthodoxy may have been a response to the pressure they felt the Church was under. He also emphasised that a gulf was developing between clergy and people.[28] Moreover, John Phillips suggested that the relationship between clergy and parishioners in later Georgian England was decaying into one of declining deference born of a conditional response to the parson, determined largely by individual qualities.[29] Clark's response to this has been to further define the concept of a 'confessional state' in the eighteenth century as one in which a moral critique of society and a providential view of politics was sustained, and he asserts that these characteristics applied to Georgian England. It was an intellectually sophisticated view and drew on a wide range of material. He also claimed that the notion of a 'confessional state' did not imply universal orthodox Anglicanism, but suggested an absence of secularism and atheism and that there was a broad support for Anglicanism.[30] Frank O'Gorman's response has been that popular culture was as much secular and pagan as Anglican. He also dismisses Clark's claim of a society 'imbued with the orthodox religion of the State' and that Anglicanism was 'the social cement which was the foundation of a deep-seated ideological consensus' as a view that 'trembles on the verge of ecclesiastical nostalgia.'[31]

Clark also stimulated debate on the culture of eighteenth-century England. His view is clearly that its political and religious culture was directly inherited from the seventeenth century. Hence Clark's emphasis on continuity leads him to place most accent on anti-rationalist thinkers such as George Horne, as representative of eighteenth-century thought. It is an emphasis Clark advances again in selecting Samuel Johnson, a Tory-Jacobite and Non-juror, as a central figure of eighteenth-century thought and enlightenment.[32] In contrast, Paul Langford and Roy Porter view the eighteenth century as an era of the growth of new ideas and the enlightenment.[33] Clark has an ally in Owen Chadwick, who has suggested that in England, unlike much of the rest of Europe, the process of enlightenment and secularisation was largely a nineteenth-century phenomenon.[34]

Clark's thesis has not found universal acceptance, in part because his subsequent work *Revolution and Rebellion: State and Society in England in the Seventeenth and Eighteenth Centuries* appeared to attack an 'old guard' of historians who had held back the study of the period and appeared to have sustained the Whig historical tradition.[35] A more fruitful critique of Clark's work is his view that the 'long eighteenth century', 1688 to 1832, forms a coherent historical period. The disadvantage of the view is that, ironically for a historian arguing frequently for the continuity of English history, it over-states the effect of the repeal of the Test and Corporations Acts and of Catholic emancipation. Undoubtedly these events had a significant impact on the relationship between Church and State; but the impact was that of a change in the relationship rather than a cessation of it. The reforms of 1828–9 may have made the Church of England into one of a number of Christian denominations – though this in itself was not new – but it remained the predominant denomination, *primus inter pares* perhaps, by virtue of the enduring Anglican links with the establishment. The monarchy, the coronation oath, the exclusion of Catholics from the succession, Church patronage and the use of Anglicanism as an instrument of the State ensured that the Church of England remained the State religion after 1829.

The emphasis on 1828–33 as a watershed also distorts the issue of reform in the Church. Edmund Gibson sought reform from the 1720s and gradually reform in pastoral care emerged in the 1740s. From the 1770s there were a number of statutes that sought to promote ecclesiastical reform in clerical residence, church building, the extension of parishes and the provision and payment of curates.[36] Thus the ecclesiastical reforms of the 1830s were the culmination of a longer period of reform, and of an accommodation of change established in the second half of the eighteenth century, rather than a stark contrast with the 1820s. They were also the culmination of a period of toleration both of Dissent and Catholicism, which grew from the Anglican sense of charity and moderation. Moreover, the motives that conditioned the Duke of Newcastle's exercise of Church patronage and attitudes to the role of the Church in society had far more in common with Disraeli and Gladstone than Clark's stark divide in 1828–33 permits.[37] Paradoxically, by creating a historical divide in 1829 the essential continuity in the Church's relationship with the State has been erased, and

Clark has unconsciously promoted an historical division which encourages the Victorian interpretation of the history of the Church. Moreover, Peter Nockles's emphasis on the complexity of continuity of the High Church strands in Anglicanism from Horne, Jones and Horsley to Tractarianism raises questions about Clark's sharp divide at 1829.[38]

Intellectual historians have also taken Clark's ideas forward. Brian Young's work has advanced a view of the eighteenth-century Church which accords with Clark's in many ways, but from a different foundation.[39] Young's view of the eighteenth-century enlightenment goes beyond Pocock's claim that it was essentially clerical and intellectually conservative. Young suggests that the clerical culture of the eighteenth century was committed to fruitful intellectual controversy. Anglicanism was marked not by the deadening rationalism of traditional history, but by a richness and diversity of intellectual activity. Indeed the richest debates were not between atheist free-thinkers and churchmen, but between churchmen themselves. Like Roy Porter and David Spadafora, therefore, Young places the eighteenth-century English enlightenment squarely into the realm of piety and religion. In doing so, Young achieves a synthesis between Paul Hazard,[40] who argued that reason and religion were in conflict, and Clark, who suggests that the Anglican hegemony was a continuing feature of eighteenth-century society.

Young argues that intellectual debate was endemic in eighteenth-century Anglicanism. But the principal focus was subscription to the Thirty-Nine Articles, the Church's legal and canonical statement of doctrines including Trinitarianism. For the Latitudinarians, subscription was regarded as an attempt to circumscribe freedom of conscience and it was this Locke-inspired tenet that drew 'anti-dogmatists' such as Edmund Law, Samuel Clarke and Francis Blackburne together. For Locke, toleration had established the legitimacy of individual conscience and this idea influenced Tillotson, Burnet and Hoadly. Young accepts that the onslaught of Waterland and other orthodox 'dogmatists' defeated the Lockean anti-dogmatists by the 1740s; but asserts that the works of John Jortin and David Hartley ensured the survival of anti-subscription ideology into the Cambridge circle of Law, Blackburne and the later eighteenth-century anti-dogmatists such as Paley.

In fact the arguments employed by Blackburne against the insistence on orthodoxy of churchmen like Thomas Secker were the same as those of Hoadly and Clarke: freedom of conscience and the fallibility of man-made doctrines. Blackburne's *Confessional* argued that artificial constraints, such as the Thirty-Nine Articles, excluded men of good conscience from the Christian service of the Church. In contrast, the cadre of orthodox clergy introduced into the Church by Secker and other bishops were prepared to accept the choice between 'subscribe or starve'. Moreover there were those like John Randolph who argued that parsons were public teachers and therefore required to avoid false teaching through subscription. Burke took this a stage further by asserting that, as a pillar of the State, the Church needed doctrinal foundations that were firm, and these were the Thirty-Nine Articles. To men of this ilk, the defeat of the anti-subscription petitions was not just a victory for the Church but security for the State.

Young confirms Clark's thesis in arguing that, while the rationalist-empirical ideas of Newton and Locke lay behind the anti-dogmatists' views, the contextualist argument that they were prominent largely because they were allied to the Whigs is mistaken. Indeed the monolithic nature of the Newtonian–Lockean–Latitudinarian connection is largely demolished by Young. Not only were there disagreements between rationalists like Locke and Newton, but both were inclined to build their arguments on metaphysical foundations. Moreover, the successors of Newton and Locke were far from united: Clarke and Law were engaged in controversies on the nature of God and the universe which derived from the rationalism of Locke and Newton. Young also argues that the opponents of Locke and Newton derived a scepticism from them, which encouraged the mysticism of Law, Wesley, Waterland, the Moravians, Horne and Hutchinson. Just as Newton built science on metaphysics, so Hutchinson argued that God caused all movement in the Universe. The orthodox-dogmatists were as divided and prone to controversy as the rationalists: Hutchinson, William Law, Wesley and Horne were unable to agree with one another on issues such as the nature of matter, emotion, and the relative merits of faith and works for salvation. Moreover, rationalism and revelation were not exclusive or immutable; Martin Greig has shown that Gilbert Burnet could be both a rationalist and reject intellectualism.[41] And Edmund Gibson could sustain a close co-operation with the State – the fruits of a Whig-rationalist stance – and assert to the people of his diocese:

> be not persuaded to part with revelation under pretence of relying on natural reason as your only guide. For reason without the assistance given it by revelation has in fact appeared to be a very insufficient guide.[42]

Thus the dichotomy of antidogmatic-rational-Whiggery in conflict with dogmatic-Hutchinsonian-Toryism is a false one; the epistemology of the eighteenth-century enlightenment is far more complex than hitherto recognised.

In this complex and fragmented picture of two inter-connected but opposing religious traditions, Young argues that Bishop William Warburton stands out as a neglected enlightenment cleric of European influence.

Bishop Richard Hurd claimed that Warburton's work defeated unbelief, and that Warburton's *Divine Legation of Moses Demonstrated* (1738–41) advanced the clearest historical view of the way in which the Old Testament and the Mosaic tradition prepared the way for the New Testament. For Young, Warburton was an intellectual leviathan, whose work easily outstripped Hume and the other free-thinkers. Young's conclusion is that when the writers of the late eighteenth century spoke of an enlightenment they meant the theological renewal that Warburton and others had effected. Though in Europe his ideas were brought into secular thinking by Condillac and Lessing, by 1800 Samuel Horsley – the representative of the orthodox counter-enlightenment – was able to use Warburton's arguments to defend the Whig thinkers of the mid-eighteenth century. Though Young's ideas are predicated on the concept of an eighteenth-century enlightenment, there is also a theme that supports Clark's thesis. The survival of ideas of the supremacy of the scriptures, and the debate on the nature of the soul after death, from the seventeenth century into the eighteenth century suggests the continuity of Anglican intellectualism, and that seventeenth-century ideas were still potent a century later. Young asserts a view of England as the intellectual legatee of the *ancien regime*, as firmly as Clark locates it institutionally in the *ancien regime*.

Young's overarching argument – the intellectual vitality of the Church – is one to which contemporaries subscribed. William Powell's charge to the archdeaconry of Colchester in 1769 considered the nature of the religious controversies besetting the Church in a strong and positive light. Powell, in a series of epigrams, asserted that intellectual challenges to the Church were 'beneficial':

> When the city is in security, the watchman slumbers, when an universal agreement removes all apprehension of danger to religion its guardians are often inattentive or indolent. Few inquire where all assent. . . . Truth always appears in the greatest lustre when its adversaries have cast a shade around it.

For Powell, Protestantism and Anglicanism were born from religious debate and therefore he regarded sincere and well-founded religious inquiry as positive and helpful to understanding and knowledge.[43]

Young's most recent work presents a theme with which this book takes issue: the relative unity of the eighteenth-century Church. In an essay on the role of the Church in developing national identity, Young argues that:

> England may have been a Protestant nation, but its national
> Church harboured variations, both Catholic and Proto-unitarian,

which led its members to identify with things and places other than and beyond England. It is perhaps testimony to the strength of the idea of the Church of England, and to the comparative weakness of Dissent (including Roman Catholicism) that it maintained the allegiance of so many disparate members.[44]

Young is right that the eighteenth-century Church was astonishingly broad, able to encompass Hoadly and Atterbury within the same liturgy, but his claims that: 'Anglicans were to be rent asunder by arguments on the status of patristic authority . . .', that 'disputes over the Trinity were endemic to the Church . . .' and that 'not only was the Church divided, it was fractured along a bewildering variety of faults, all cutting across each other . . .' are misleading.[45] Some of the 'divisions' he cites are actually important evidence of the inadequacy of traditional interpretations of divisions in the Church.[46] The fact that Robert Nelson and others returned from Non-jury to the Church, which at that time also encompassed Samuel Clarke and William Whiston, suggests an instinctive and emotional attachment to the Church that was more important than absolute and rigid doctrinal uniformity. Certainly a number of historians have recently argued that there were many 'streams' within the Church in the eighteenth century. Martin Fitzpatrick has identified the survival of Latitudinarianism; Anthony Waterman has traced a Cambridge school of moderate churchmen and Jeffrey Chamberlain, Peter Nockles and Fred Mather have argued that High Churchmanship was strong.[47] Most eighteenth-century churchmen and laity accommodated the breadth of the Church in the way that Whitman was able to do: 'Do I contradict myself? Very well then I contradict myself. I am large, I contain multitudes.' Moreover breadth was of course a precondition to unity. Young also suggests that the intellectual position of High and Low Churchmen was blurred and often contradictory: 'patterns of political partisanship and ecclesiastical identity were not automatically obvious'.[48] This is an assertion which this book seeks to examine in some detail. However, whilst controversy existed in early eighteenth-century England, there was a large measure of agreement on both the form and content of Anglicanism.

The work of Young and Clark has created a new synthesis in eighteenth-century thought. Clark's thesis places the Church in a central role in eighteenth-century society and regards it as a largely conservative force; indeed towards the end of the eighteenth century the Church was the bulwark of the status quo, and as a result the lightning conductor of radical agitation. Young adds a re-evaluation of the nature of the eighteenth-century intellectual world, questioning the easy divisions of the ideologies that historians have long taken for granted.

A number of other historians have also suggested that there was greater unity within the Church than hitherto conceded. Jan Albers's study of Lancashire argues that as the century progressed there was a 'deterioration' of party conflict within the Church, 'the Church parties were becoming a more united front, acting as a government party rather than as the guardians of partisan animosities'.[49] Stephen Taylor's study of mid-eighteenth-century relations between Church and State also asserts that 'the dominant themes of eighteenth-century religious thought were eirenicism, charity and a desire to avoid controversy'.[50] It is a view that he further developed, with John Walsh, in the introduction to *The Church of England c.1689–1833 From Toleration to Tractarianism.*[51] In asserting that 'the centripetal forces within the Church were still vastly more powerful than the centrifugal', Walsh and Taylor recite the evidence of the contributors to the volume: that the SPCK was the product of High and Low Church founders; that some High Churchmen were tolerant to Whig Low Churchmen; that Tillotson the Latitudinarian died supported in the arms of Nelson the Non-juror; and that Anna Larpent read, and William Cleaver recommended, both High and Low Church sermons.

The rise of unity can be ascribed to a number of factors: a reaction to the seventeenth century, the gradual abatement of party conflict as the eighteenth century progressed, the fact that the Whig hegemony denied the opportunity for disunity, and the growth of a sense of security as the threat of Dissent declined. Moderation was the product of a new generation of clergy untrammelled by Jacobitism and Non-jury, of the government exercise of patronage in favour of moderate churchmen and of a self-consciously developed temperate identity. This concept drew on the need to develop a path between the poles of Catholicism and deism, and on the developing consensus that bound the clergy to the doctrines of the Church. 'Such eirenicism did not prevent religious conflict from disturbing the peace of the Church. Yet not all of these were disruptive of its stability. . . .'[52] Other historians have also argued that eighteenth-century society was less divided than has hitherto been recognised: 'recent studies have argued that these periods were far less stormy, much less revolutionary, and inherently more stable than orthodox interpretations had suggested'.[53] Jeremy Black's claim that 'it is possible to emphasize the general success of the eighteenth-century political system in preventing civil conflict, rather than to stress the divisions within it' is one that can be extended to other social institutions, including the Church.[54] John Bossy's study of the role of the Church as a peace-maker between individuals in Europe suggests that far more effort was directed by churches to this end than historians have hitherto conceded. Bossy suggests that the maintenance of peace between individuals was a 'moral tradition' that survived from the Reformation into the eighteenth century.[55]

The work of these historians has created a matrix into which this study fits. It builds upon this work to argue that the orientation of the eighteenth-century Church was principally and profoundly towards unity and moderation. Much has been made of the Church in the eighteenth century as riven with disputes and controversies. But this view only considers moments of controversy: 1689, 1705, 1710 and 1717; it ignores the dominant instincts of the clergy and the overwhelming direction of the Church's institutional momentum. The unity and accord that lay at the heart of eighteenth-century Anglicanism survived the Revolution of 1689, and flourished in the years after 1700. Clerical attitudes converged onto a series of beliefs such as that of providential divine right and, with the exception of a handful of absolutely uncompromising Altitudinarians or Latitudinarians, they incorporated elements of both intellectual strands.

Notes

1 P. Virgin, *The Church in an Age of Negligence*, Cambridge, 1989, p. iv.
2 W. Gladstone, *The Gleanings of Past Years*, London, 1879, vol. 5, pp. 7–8.
3 B. W. Young, 'Knock-Kneed Giants: Victorian Representations of Eighteenth Century Thought' in J. Garnett and C. Matthew (eds.), *Revival and Religion Since 1700*, London, 1993.
4 J. A. Froude, 'On Progress' in *Short Studies on Great Subjects*, London, 1878–83 vol. 2, pp. 351–64.
5 C. J. Abbey and J. H. Overton, *The English Church in the Eighteenth Century*, London, 1878, vol. 1, p. 15.
6 B. W. Young, *op. cit.*, p. 93.
7 See for example, J. A. Froude, 'The Oxford Counter Reformation' in *Short Studies in Great Subjects*, London, 1883, vol. 4, pp. 247–8.
8 C. J. Abbey and J. H. Overton, *The English Church in the Eighteenth Century*, London, 1878, vol. 2, pp. 229–31. *Ibid.*, 1887 edn, p. 113.
9 J. H. Overton, *William Law: Non-juror and Mystic*, London, 1881.
10 J. H. Overton, *Life in the English Church 1660–1714*, London, 1885, p. 3.
11 For a detailed examination of the historiography of the eighteenth-century Church see W. Gibson, *The Achievement of the Anglican Church, 1689–1900: The Confessional State in Eighteenth Century England*, Lewiston, 1995, Chapter One.
12 G. V. Bennett, *The Tory Crisis in Church and State 1688–1739*, Oxford, 1975.
13 E. Carpenter, *The Protestant Bishop*, London, 1956.
14 A. T. Hart, *Some Clerical Oddities in the Church of England from Medieval to Modern Times*, Bognor, 1980; *William Lloyd 1627–1717*, London, 1952; *The Eighteenth Century Country Parson*, Shrewsbury, 1955; *Ebor*, York, 1986; *Clergy and Society 1600–1800*, London, 1968; *The Country Priest in English History*, London, 1960; *The Curate's Lot*, Newton Abbot, 1971; *The Country Clergy in Elizabethan and Stuart Times, 1558–1660*, London, 1958;

The Life and Times of John Sharp, Archbishop of York, London, 1949; *The Man in the Pew 1558–1660*, London, 1966; *Country Counting House*, London, 1962.

15 R. N. Stromberg, *Religious Liberalism in Eighteenth Century England*, Oxford, 1954, p. 93.

16 N. Ravitch, *Sword and Mitre*, The Hague, 1966; G. V. Bennett, *White Kennett, 1660–1728*, London, 1957; *idem, The Tory Crisis in Church and State, 1688–1739*, Oxford, 1975; *idem*, with J. Walsh (eds.), *Essays in Modern Church History in Memory of Norman Sykes*, London, 1966 which includes essays by Greaves and other Church historians.

17 F. O'Gorman, 'J. C. D. Clark *English Society 1688–1832* . . . Reappraised' in *Reappraisals in History* Institute of Historical Research, London Web-site 1998, http://www.ihr.sas.ac.uk/ihr/reviews/frank.html

18 V. Barrie-Curien, *Clergé et Pastorale en Angleterre au XVIIIe siècle, Le diocese de Londres*, Paris, 1992; J. Gregory (ed.), *The Speculum of Archbishop Thomas Secker*, Church of England Record Society, vol. 2, 1996; J. R. Guy, *The Diocese of Llandaff in 1763*, South Wales Record Society, 1991; D. R. Hirschberg, 'A Social History of the Anglican Episcopate, 1660–1760', Michigan University PhD thesis, 1976; W. M. Jacob and N. Yates (eds.), *Crown and Mitre*, Woodbridge, 1993; W. M. Jacob, *Lay People and Religion in the Early Eighteenth Century*, Cambridge, 1996; J. Jago, *Aspects of the Georgian Church: Visitation Studies of the Diocese of York 1761–1776*, London, 1997; S. Taylor, 'Church and State in England in the Mid-Eighteenth Century: The Newcastle Years 1742–1762', Cambridge University, PhD thesis, 1987; A. Urdank, *Religion and Society in a Cotswold Vale, Nailsworth 1780–1865*, Los Angeles, 1990; J. Walsh, C. Haydon and S. Taylor (eds.), *The Church of England c.1689–1833*, Cambridge, 1994; W. R. Ward *Religion and Society in England, 1790–1850*, London, 1972; *idem, Georgian Oxford*, Oxford, 1958; *idem* (ed.), *Parson and Parish in Eighteenth Century Surrey: Replies to Bishops' Visitations*, Surrey Records Society, vol. XXXIV, 1994; *idem* (ed.), *Parson and Parish in Eighteenth Century Hampshire: Replies to Bishops' Visitations*, Hampshire Records Series, vol. 13, 1995; A. Warne, *Church and Society in Eighteenth Century Devon*, Newton Abbot, 1969.

19 J. Black, 'Confessional State or Elect Nation? Religion and Identity in Eighteenth-Century England', T. Claydon and I. McBride (eds.), *Protestantism and National Identity: Britain and Ireland c.1650–c.1850*, Cambridge, 1998.

20 J. C. D. Clark, *English Society 1689–1832*, Cambridge, 1985, pp. ix–x.

21 P. B. Nockles, *The Oxford Movement in Context: Anglican High Churchmanship, 1760–1857*, Cambridge, 1994, p. 46.

22 Clark, *op. cit.*, p. 87.

23 *Ibid.*, p.165.

24 *Ibid.*, pp. 136–7.

25 *Ibid.*, p. 277.

26 *Ibid.*, p. 283.

27 K. Sharpe, 'Symposium: Revolution or Revisionism', *Parliamentary History*, 1988, vol. 7, no. 2. See also the Introduction to L. Davison, T. Hitchcock, T. Keirn and R. Shoemaker (eds.), *Stilling the Grumbling Hive: The Response to Social and Economic Problems in England, 1689–1750*, Stroud, 1992.

28 J. E. Bradley, 'The Anglican Pulpit, Social Order and the Resurgence of Toryism During the American Revolution', *Albion*, 1989, vol. 21, no. 3.

29 J. A. Phillips, 'The Social Calculus: Deference and Defiance in Later Georgian England', *Albion*, 1989, vol. 21, no. 3. Doubtless Eric Evans would add tithes to this conditional response: E. J. Evans, *The Contentious Tithe, the Tithe Problem and English Agriculture 1750–1850*, London, 1976.

30 J. C. D. Clark, 'England's Ancien Regime as a Confessional State', *Albion*, 1989, vol. 21, no. 3.

31 F. O'Gorman, 'Eighteenth Century England as an *Ancien Regime*' *op. cit.* p. 32.

32 J. C. D. Clark, *Samuel Johnson, Literature, Religion and English Cultural Politics from the Restoration to Romanticism*, Cambridge, 1994.

33 P. Langford, *A Polite and Commercial People*, Oxford, 1989, and R. Porter, 'Georgian Britain: An *Ancien Regime?*', *British Journal for Eighteenth Century Studies*, 1992, vol. 15.

34 O. Chadwick, *The Secularisation of the European Mind*, Cambridge, 1975.

35 For the debate on J. C. D. Clark's *Revolution and Rebellion: State and Society in England in the Seventeenth and Eighteenth Centuries* see 'Symposium: Revolution and Revisionism', *Parliamentary History* 1988, vol. 7, part 2.

36 R. E. Rodes Jr, *Law and the Modernization of the Church of England: Charles II to the Welfare State*, Indiana, 1991, pp. 23–52. See also F. O'Gorman, *op. cit.*

37 See for example, W. Gibson, 'Disraeli's Church Patronage 1868–1880' in *Anglican and Episcopal History*, vol. 61, no. 2, 1992, and *idem*, ' "A Great Excitement": Gladstone and Church Patronage' in *Anglican and Episcopal History*, Sept. 1999.

38 P. B. Nockles, *op. cit.*, *passim*.

39 See for example: B. W. Young, *Religion and Enlightenment in Eighteenth Century England: Theological Debate from Locke to Burke*, Oxford, 1998 and B. W. Young, ' "The Soul-Sleeping System": Politics and Heresy in Eighteenth Century England', *Journal of Ecclesiastical History*, 1994, vol. 45, no. 1.

40 P. Hazard, *The Crisis of the European Mind, 1680–1715*, London, 1953.

41 M. Grieg, 'The Reasonableness of Christianity? Gilbert Burnet and the Trinitarian Controversy of the 1690s', *Journal of Ecclesiastical History*, 1993, vol. 44, no. 4. Robert Cornwall has also denied the usual alignment of Anglicans as supporters of the union of Church and State and dissenters as separatists, see R. D. Cornwall, 'Advocacy of the Independence of the Church from the State in Eighteenth Century England: A Comparison of a Non-juror and a Nonconformist View', *Enlightenment and Dissent*, 1993, vol. 12.

42 E. Gibson, *Bishop Gibson's Three Pastoral Letters to the People of his Diocese; particularly to those of the two great cities of London and Westminster in defence of the Gospel Revelation . . .*, London, 1820, p. 7.

43 W. S. Powell, *Discourses on Various Subjects*, London, 1776, pp. 293–303.

44 B. Young, 'A History of Variations: the identity of the eighteenth century Church of England', T. Claydon and I. McBride (eds.), *Protestantism and National Identity: Britain and Ireland: c.1650–c.1850*, Cambridge, 1998, p. 128.

45 *Ibid.*, pp. 111, 113, 115.

46 Examples of these divisions are: the Sussex High Churchmen, who were also Whigs; the fact that Joseph Butler was a High Churchman and also a Whig; the fact that some of Hoadly's opponents were Whigs, and that the orthodox Waterland was a Whig.

47 M. Fitzpatrick, 'Latitudinarianism and the Parting of the Ways: A Suggestion', J. Walsh, C. Haydon and S. Taylor (eds.), *The Church of England c.1689–1833*,

Cambridge, 1994; A. M. C. Waterman, 'A Cambridge 'Via Media' in late Georgian Anglicanism', *Journal of Ecclesiastical History*, 1991, vol. xlvii; J. Chamberlain, 'Portrait of a High Church clerical dynasty in Georgian England: the Frewens and their World', J. Walsh, C. Haydon and S. Taylor (eds.), *op. cit.*, P. B. Nockles *op. cit.*, F. C. Mather, 'Georgian Churchmanship reconsidered: some variations in Anglican Public Worship', *Journal of Ecclesiastical History*, 1985, vol. xxvi.

48 Young, *op. cit.*, p. 115.

49 J. M. Albers, 'The Seeds of Contention: Society, Politics and the Church of England in Lancashire, 1689–1790', Yale University, PhD thesis, 1988, vol. 2, p. 326.

50 S. Taylor, *op. cit.*, p. 216.

51 See the introduction to J. Walsh, C. Haydon and S. Taylor (eds.), *op. cit.*

52 *Ibid.*, p. 59.

53 L. Davison, T. Hitchcock, T. Keirn and R. Shoemaker (eds.), *op. cit.*, p. xii.

54 J. Black, *The Politics and Culture of an Aristocratic Society*, Charlottesville, VA, 1999, p. 8.

55 J. Bossy, *Peace in the Post-Reformation*, Cambridge, 1998, *passim*.

2

THE ANGLICAN
REVOLUTION

True Englishmen drink good health to the mitre
Let our Church flourish though her enemies spite her[1]

On 12 December 1688, some Kentish sailors and fishermen watched what they supposed were Catholic priests, wearing dark clothes with long cloaks drawn close around them, on a boat which had stopped on the Thames estuary to pick up ballast. The fishermen thought – given the alarms of the moment – that they should stop the priests from making their escape, and capture them. Immediately they recognised Sir Edward Hales as one of the supposed priests and in wonderment found the second figure was King James II. The discovery of James's escape was described by Gilbert Burnet as a turning point in history:

> here was an accident that seemed of no great consequence; yet all the strugglings which that party have made ever since that time to this day, which from him were called afterwards the Jacobites, did rise out of this: for, if he had got clear away, by all that could be judged, he would not have had a party left: all would have agreed that here was a desertion, and that therefore the nation was free, and at liberty to secure itself.[2]

But there could be no desertion with the King incarcerated after his capture by the fishermen. Eventually, James was deliberately left so poorly guarded that he was able to escape to France and not present further problems to his son-in-law, who assumed power in London. The factionalism of Jacobites and Non-jurors has led historians to highlight the divisions created by the Glorious Revolution. But for the Church the intellectual and religious consequences of the Revolution were marked more by unity than division.

The dissatisfaction that burst forth in the reign of James II had been a long time in the making. In 1680–1 the attempt to exclude James from the throne on account of his Catholicism had failed. His brother Charles II pursued a largely Catholic foreign policy, favouring Louis XIV and antagonising the Protestant Dutch in matters of trade; and at home he demonstrated no sympathy for the Covenanters in Scotland. Catholicism was regarded as a threat by most of the Anglican clergy: Thomas Tenison, rector of St Martin's in the Fields, published *A Discourse on Idolatry* (1687) which exposed and denounced Catholic practices as mere superstition and a distraction from the true meaning of Christianity.[3] However, Tenison was careful to avoid the iconoclasm of the Dissenters, and spoke from the position of a moderate Anglican whose instinct was to be loyal to the crown. Tenison's moderate Anglicanism attracted support for his book, which as late as 1697 was recommended by Thomas Bray,[4] he spoke for a good many Anglicans who found it difficult not to associate the absolutism of the Catholics with the intolerance of the Puritans during the Commonwealth.

Increasingly, the forces that might have moderated the growing Catholic policy under Charles were restrained. In reaction to the Rye House plot, Oxford University in its 'judgement and declaration' decreed that all students should be instructed in the high Anglican doctrine of passive obedience to the King, 'submitting to every ordinance of man for the Lord's sake, teaching that this submission and obedience is to be clear, absolute and without exception of any State or order of men'. This 'necessary doctrine' was claimed to be a central teaching of the Church. Furthermore, the revision of city charters, which began in May 1684, sought to dismantle Whig control of municipal corporations. Essentially Charles II had set the nation on its course of militant Erastianism before his death. What saved Charles from the fury unleashed on his brother was the lack of an overtly doctrinaire spirit, and the emotional attachment of people who continued to hold Charles in affection for restoring the Church and monarchy. Paradoxically and astutely Charles also supported a series of laws which reflected popular attitudes to Anglicanism. In 1678 a law on the observance of the sabbath imposed fines on those who did 'worldly labour', even including the use of boats.[5] Acts of parliament in 1662 and 1663, which restored the Church, imposed penalties on parsons who failed to read the Common Prayer at least once a month.[6] And in 1664 a law secured closed vestries as an Anglican monopoly by requiring vestrymen to make a declaration of conformity to the liturgy of the Church of England.[7] Charles, in other words, was happy to ride two horses at the same time: Catholic in polity, Anglican in popular practice. With the result that he did not offend the Anglican hierarchy or popular support for the Church. It was a contradictory mixture that a man of Charles's latitude could encompass, but it was one his brother's character could not sustain.

The attempt by James to reintroduce Catholicism to England was misguided, badly misjudging the Protestant character of the English. Popular Protestant clergy such as Thomas Tenison and John Sharp were subject to the disapproval of the court, and Sharp was even suspended from the rectory of St Giles in the Fields for an anti-Catholic sermon in 1686. The refusal of Bishop Compton of London to suspend Sharp led to his own suspension from episcopal functions, and Steven Pincus has argued that the action against Sharp and Compton led churchmen to 'redefine their commitment to loyalty'.[8] Nevertheless, James was more astute in some of his policy than he has often been allowed. His *rapprochement* with the Dutch encouraged William to dismiss the Duke of Monmouth from his court, and forced the Duke into a desperate bid for the throne in the Western Rising of 1685. According to Henry Sacheverell in 1710, on the day before his execution the Duke had been urged to admit that, since the Church of England was committed to the doctrine of non-resistance, he had fallen into sin by his rebellion. He was urged to embrace the doctrine by Thomas Tenison, who later asserted that resistance to James was legitimate.[9] The Monmouth rebellion was a set-back to the opposition to James; the Church momentarily drew back from support for resistance to the King and there were renewed expressions of the doctrine of non-resistance.

However, James failed to capitalise on his advantage. The attempt to convert his daughter Mary, the princess of Orange, to Catholicism could not have been more misjudged, since it drew attention to the alternative Protestant court at the Hague and was publicly rebuffed by the princess. Equally James's attempts to woo the Dissenters, by suggesting that they could obtain religious liberties in the wake of Toleration of Catholics, collapsed when William and Mary published a pamphlet entitled *Their Highnesses the Prince and Princess of Orange's opinion about a General Liberty of Conscience*, which was widely distributed in England and which indicated that William and Mary would ameliorate the Test Act with a wider Toleration of religious observance. Similarly the Three Questions, issued by James in 1687, which lords lieutenant and mayors were required to ask of parliamentary electors and candidates, backfired spectacularly.[10] Even the Imperial ambassador in London regarded the Questions as a grave miscalculation, which only drew attention to the fact that James's policies flew in the face of popular opinion.

The nation stubbornly supported the Test Act, and its moral legitimacy was almost universally accepted. When in the autumn of 1687 James gleefully installed Dissenters as lord mayor and aldermen of London, expecting that he could drive a wedge between the Anglicans and the

Protestant Dissenters, he was appalled to find that they had sworn the oaths required by law, and had attended Anglican services at the Guildhall Chapel. The idea of a dispensing power was regarded with horror. In a well-chosen analogy, Bishop Henry Compton in the House of Lords likened the suspension of laws to removing the dykes in Holland. The sea of Catholicism would inundate the nation. In short, the core of James's policy which alarmed his subjects was his attack on the Anglican monopoly.

The Anglican clergy were critical opinion-formers during the last months of James's reign. Steven Pincus claims they were conscious that the Revolution was a national movement in which a free people were choosing their own form of government.[11] In April 1688 James issued the Declaration of Indulgence for Liberty of Conscience, which re-asserted his insistence on tolerance for Catholics, and demanded that it be read in all churches on the successive two Sundays. The seven bishops who refused to order the reading of the Declaration – High and Low Churchmen alike – became heroes for the people of London. Influential London clergy such as Simon Patrick, Thomas Tenison, William Sherlock, Edward Stillingfleet and John Tillotson, successfully drew public opinion over to the seven bishops. On 17 May Simon Patrick listed seventy London clergy, of all theological hues, who supported the decision not to read the Declaration. The decision to have the Declaration read two weeks earlier in London than in the rest of the country was a fatal error, permitting militant London clergy to lead the opinions of their provincial brethren. For Edward Stillingfleet, who had preached the duty of obedience and the sinfulness of rebellion as recently as February 1687, the Declaration of Indulgence was a vital moment providing a taste of defiance of the King.[12] A bruising interview between James and the seven bishops emphasised that the bishops did not regard themselves as disloyal or as triggering a rebellion. The bishops protested that they were not in revolt against the King and that they 'never preached any such things, but only obedience and suffering when they could not obey'. Thomas Ken, the saintly Bishop of Bath and Wells, was especially pained by the accusation, asking James of the Monmouth rising, 'Did I not go down to suppress a rebellion?' The King scorned his question and brought charges against the bishops to stand trial.[13] On 20 May 1688 only Thomas Sprat, the pliant dean of Westminster, read the Declaration in London, though his congregation refused to listen and walked out. A fortnight later the clergy in the rest of the country were almost unanimous in refusing to read it. Some, like Samuel Wesley, even preached against it.[14]

The trial and acquittal of the seven bishops excited enormous popular support for the Church and much feeling against James. More significantly, the birth of a son to the Queen boded ill for Protestants in the longer term.

On the day of the acquittal of the seven bishops the invitation to William of Orange was issued and Thomas Tenison ominously warned Simon Patrick to take his money out of the capital. James saw the reality of the situation too late, and informed Bishop Mews of Winchester of his intention to take the Church of England under his protection on 22 September. But even when they were so close to the precipice, James and his followers were capable of folly. The King's promise of a free parliament and the grant of a general pardon, issued on 29 September omitted mention of the clergy. The next day a Catholic preacher at the Savoy made an open attack on the Church of England. James also imposed a new bishop on the diocese of Oxford in the face of the refusal of the canons of Christ Church to elect him; even the compliant Sprat had been pushed too far and resigned his seat on the Ecclesiastical Commission rather than discipline the recalcitrant canons.

Thus between James's accession and the Glorious Revolution a profound change was wrought in the hearts of the English clergy and people. Dorothy Woodforde, in July 1685, wrote of the Monmouth rebellion as 'a horrid treason' and concluded her journal entry: 'may all that ever rise up against our lawful King and the Church be brought to shame in this world'.[15] But by 1688, when James put the seven bishops on trial for failure to read the Declaration, she asked God to 'make good thy promise to them, and give them a mouth which all their and our enemies may not be able to gainsay nor resist'. Similarly, when William and Mary were proclaimed King and Queen, she rejoiced but prayed that 'our late King [James]' would have his eyes open to the truth.[16] Such was the dilemma of a Protestant who adhered to the doctrine of the divine right of kings. Another diarist, Isaac Archer, a doubting Anglican ever-ready to ponder defection to Dissent, found his reaction to the 'late King' was influenced by James's flight to, and succour from, France, where the persecution of the French Protestant Huguenots seemed to presage what was happening in Britain. On Christmas day 1688 Archer wrote in his diary: 'because he [James] may stir up the French, I begged that the Lord would repel foreign force and settle us'. Three months later he recorded that James had gone to Ireland 'and which is said to be given up to the French', Archer prayed for William's victory and for him to be strong.[17] For the Presbyterians and other nonconformist groups, the issue sometimes appeared to be irrelevant to them. Nevertheless, Thomas Jolly, the presbyterian minister of Altham spoke of William's invasion:

> it was strange to us who were altogether unacquainted with the thing and with the grounds of it, yet we might hope that such men had good grounds for what they did and we must needs wish well to them as Protestants.[18]

Perhaps the most eloquent expression of the dilemma facing the people was that of William King, the Irish Anglican churchman. In his autobiography he wrote:

> On the one hand my fealty to the King remained, and the oaths which at the bidding of the law I had taken . . . I was indeed sufficiently convinced that these were not established with the purpose of giving the King absolute power over laws or over his subjects, or of changing the constitution and form of the commonwealth; but a doubt arose as to whether this could be prevented in any other way than by a war against the King . . . If, therefore, I stood by the King I perceived that I should further the enslavement of the country, the overturning of religion, and the destruction of liberty; if I abandoned the King's side I would assent to these depositions, which I thought I ought not to do . . . I considered therefore carefully what I should do . . . But when [under James] I saw the whole constitution of the commonwealth overthrown by the repeal of the Acts of Succession and Explanation (by which the inheritance of the Protestants was secured to them) . . . I had no longer any doubt but that it was lawful for me and others to accept that deliverance which providence offered by the prince of Orange . . . and to submit to him as King and liberator, especially since I had contributed nothing either by deed or writing towards the deposition of King James or the promotion of William to the crown. For [I had no doubt] that it was lawful to submit to him to whom such power had been given by all orders of the entire commonwealth and by Divine providence. . . .[19]

Some clergy were quicker than William King to change their allegiance. In October 1688, the chapter of Durham was still loyal to James and the dean contributed one hundred pounds and the chapter members fifty pounds each to raise cavalry for his defence. Later that month, the Earl of Bath tried to get the chapter to make an address of loyalty to James, which they refused. Within a month, the loyalist dean, Granville, fled to Edinburgh and then to France to join James in exile. Granville was an exception, the majority of the clergy followed William King. The relative ease with which most clergy shifted was a consequence of the events of James II's reign. Mark Goldie argues that during James's reign the clergy developed, 'a considered case for resistance . . . those who resisted James regularly claimed to be standing upon conscience, upon the laws of God, rather than the laws of the land.'[20]

In the last moments of his reign, James desperately hoped the bishops would be a source of pacification of the nation in the face of William's military advance from Torbay. The archbishop and senior bishops were called to Whitehall on 2 November 1688 to be met by James and Lord Preston, holding a copy of William's declaration which claimed that he had been invited to invade England. The King asked the bishops whether they were party to the invitation to William, the answers were in the negative, though some, such as Compton, carefully evaded a direct answer. To this, James said he felt that the bishops should publish their denial, and invited them to print such a statement. The bishops knew they had tacitly supported William's military actions. For those present who later became Non-jurors this was a difficult moment. The attempt by James to extract a letter of support from the bishops came to nothing. They kept him waiting for four days, then replied that they could not support him; they suggested that the best way they could help him would be in the House of Lords in a freely elected parliament. Instead of writing to support James, Bishop Compton took a brace of pistols and escorted Princess Anne's coach out of London in an obvious declaration of support for William. The Imperial ambassador reported to the Emperor Leopold that the clergy were the principal group James had ranged against him. It was undoubtedly the Church that was uppermost in the minds of those who left James for William. Lord Cornbury, James's nephew, deserted the royal army with his cavalry troop, which Cornbury sought to hearten by asking them whether they would fight for William to save the Church of England.

The flight of James in December seemed to imply an abdication, but his subsequent attempts to regain the throne by his invasion of Ireland suggested that he had not willingly deserted or abdicated the throne. Nevertheless, the bishops were in agreement up to 11 December 1688 that James had vacated the throne, and that William was *de facto* either King or *custos regni*. Led by Archbishop William Sancroft, bishops Turner of Ely, Lake of Chichester, Thomas of Worcester, White of Peterborough, Ken of Bath and Wells, Lloyd of Norwich and Frampton of Gloucester gradually decided that they could not accept William as *de jure* King while James was still alive. After elections were held, Sancroft refused to attend the Convention parliament which met on 24 January 1689. The Convention was in no doubt that James was not to be recalled, but was divided between those who regarded James as incapable of exercising his kingship and there-fore a regent was required to act for him, and those who wanted to set James aside entirely and replace him with William. The vote for a regency was lost by forty nine votes to fifty one, although a majority of bishops voted for it, thirteen favouring a regency to just two (Compton and Trelawny) who advocated the unqualified accession of William. Gilbert Burnet, newly raised to the see of Salisbury, said it would be an invidious position to maintain the fiction that James was King. Would new oaths be sworn to James, or to the government carried out in his name by others? What would be the legal position of the members of the new government if James returned? Could they be convicted of treason, even though they were acting on the authority of parliament? There were other problems. The Commons wanted to proclaim that James had 'abdicated', the Lords were less happy with such a word. The issue of the succession was also muddled. If James had abdicated, his heir (assuming his new born son to be an impostor) was William's wife, Princess Mary; on what grounds would William assume the throne? By March 1689, a way forward was agreed. The throne was declared 'vacated' and the succession settled jointly upon William and Mary. William had made it clear that he would not consider a regency nor a role as consort to Mary; he would be King or nothing. William held the whip hand, he took no part in the Convention parliament and hinted that he would return to Holland if necessary. The Whigs could not consider the return of James and were determined to establish a Protestant ruler. These were arguments that troubled Non-jurors and Tories, but even Archbishop William Sancroft was prepared to empower suffragans to undertake William's coronation.

The major problem arose from the oaths to be sworn to William and Mary. Every possible effort was made to incorporate as many into the new settlement as possible. The traditional oath to the 'rightful and lawful King' was set aside in favour of an oath simply to 'bear faithful and true allegiance' to the new monarchs. The Lords also made much of the precedent of Henry VII's reign that it was lawful for the people to obey a king in possession of the kingdom. The ingenious Bishop Lloyd of St Asaph claimed that William had made war on James in which he had called upon the decision of Heaven. For Lloyd, William's victory had been a judgement of providence, and though he had been simply the deliverer of the people, he had assumed the rights of James by conquest and was *de jure* king. Finally the Bill of Rights laid down that by virtue of James's departure, William and Mary 'did become . . . and of right ought to be by the law of this realm . . . King and Queen. . . .' But Sancroft and his seven colleagues could not accept the oath, and, after the expiry of the six months for them to consider their consciences, they, together with about four hundred clergy, were dispossessed of their bishoprics and livings.

Hard on the heels of the coronation and the Bill of Rights came the Toleration Act, which excused Trinitarian Dissenters from penalties for not attending Church and for holding their own services, but not those who denied the doctrine of the trinity such as the Unitarians. The Bill passed the Lords easily and was known to be strongly supported by King William. In the Commons, however, there was a demand from the Tories for a Convocation of the clergy, which attracted the King's disfavour. A second complementary bill, for the Comprehension of Dissenters into the Church by a change in the Anglican liturgy, failed to pass the Commons. This left the Toleration Act, originally intended only for those not comprehended within the Church, to apply to all Trinitarian Dissenters. The King established a commission ostensibly to draw up a list of matters to be referred to a Convocation of the Church, but in reality its role was to consider the means to effect the King's desire for a Comprehension, the inclusion of all Dissenters in the Church. Though the commission collapsed in a morass of argument on baptism, religious orders and other doctrinal matters, the King's position on the importance of the rights of Dissenters was clear. The passage of the Toleration Act without Comprehension left the Glorious Revolution incomplete as far as the Church was concerned. It created the possibility of division and controversy in the Church. What was extraordinary is that it did not condemn the Church to permanent internal strife.

Churchmen who felt that James remained the *de jure* king after 1688 had to choose between their principles and the expediency of events. Those who remained in the Church appeared to act out of expediency. After the departure of the Non-jurors, some ill-feeling between individual clergy arose from the earlier support for non-resistance among those clergy who took the oaths to William and Mary. George Hickes's attack on John Sharp and William Sherlock was motivated in part from his knowledge that, before 1688, they had agreed with him on the *de jure* nature of James's monarchy and he resented their acceptance of William and Mary.[21] Dodwell's attacks were similarly motivated. The doctrine of non-resistance had been a major strand in the ideology of the Church. Even Gilbert Burnet, William's staunchest supporter in the Church, had advanced it, though by the time of the execution of Lord William Russell in 1683 Burnet wrote 'the ill conduct of affairs has given me the bias rather in favour of resistance than against it'.[22] Hence Hickes's bitter letter to Sharp claimed that to suggest that the Non-jurors had left the Church was a nonsense:

> unless you will affirm that when a ship breaks from the shoar [*sic*] when she lies at anchor, the shoar removes from her not her from the shoar.[23]

Many of the debates between Non-jurors and those who accepted William and Mary drew on historical precedent, not just from the Bible and medieval period, but from the Reformation. Non-jurors, like Abednego Seller, in his *History of Passive Obedience since the Reformation* (1689), asserted that the principle of non-resistance had been advanced under Henry VIII to counter the papal power over England.

The doctrine of non-resistance did not enjoy universal acceptance in the Church. *Bishop Overall's Convocation Book*, written in 1606 but only published by Sancroft after the Revolution and after his Non-jury was proclaimed, laid down that a king *de facto* who was not also *de jure* could be accepted by the Church. Moreover the resurgence in Anglo-Saxon studies by Anglican scholars after 1660 identified that the early English monarchy was elective rather than hereditary. Therefore there could be an original contract with the people that could determine the character of kingship, and condition the terms of the loyalty of the people. Studies of the ancient coronation oaths taken by kings suggested that a promise to protect the people was part of the 'original contract' between James and his people. Gilbert Burnet strongly asserted that William the Conqueror's agreement to maintain the laws of Edward the Confessor was such a contract, and that it had been renewed throughout the medieval period. Biblical scholarship was also deployed to indicate that God had altered the royal succession in favour of David because of Saul's disobedience.[24] Indeed the prevalence of the idea of an original contract was such that two eighteenth-century Anglicans, Josiah Tucker and Benjamin Turner, decried its currency.[25]

The weakness of the Non-jurors' case was, in part, that they assumed the doctrine of non-resistance and passive obedience to be unlimited. For some churchmen, like William King, the doctrine was only valid while the King acted lawfully. King's *State of the Irish Protestants under James II* (1691) gave the clearest statement of the limit of the doctrine as he saw it:

> It is granted in the very first assertors of passive obedience, that if a King design to root out a people, or destroy one main part of his subjects in favour of another whom he loves better, that they may prevent it even by opposing him with force, and that he is to be judged in such a case to have abdicated the government of those whom he designs to destroy contrary to justice and the laws.[26]

Was the decision of the bishops to refuse publicly to deny their involvement in the Invitation to William (and thereby to implicitly support him) the application of such a limitation? During the eighteenth century, the nature of non-resistance gradually evolved into the right to resist within legal and constitutional bounds. Even Tory High Churchmen embraced the limited doctrine of constitutional resistance to the governing power. In 1769, Bishop Charles Moss of St David's preached the Charles I martyrdom anniversary sermon before the House of Lords. Moss was a ministerial Tory and a protégé of Thomas Sherlock, the moderate Tory son of William Sherlock. His sermon contained such a developed view of resistance:

if the constitution and frame of government be good, [but] administration of it be in bad hands; and the power committed to the magistrate for the protection of the subject may be employed for his destruction. And when governors either apply the powers they have to the oppression of their subjects, or assume new powers inconsistent with the constitution, and repugnant to the right of a free people, opposition to such encroachments become necessary. It is not only the right, but the duty of the subject to employ every reasonable and constitutional method of repelling evil'.[27]

Perhaps Moss and Hoadly would have parted company over the former's insistence on constitutional methods of resistance, but agreed on the principle of resistance to tyrants.

Naturally, the most important debate on the Revolution took place within the Church of England. It was the Church uniquely that could sanction the settlement of 1689 as legitimate, and the Church that could mobilise popular opinion in its support. Gilbert Burnet's *Pastoral Letter to the Clergy of His Diocese Concerning the Oaths of Allegiance and Supremacy to King William and Queen Mary* (1689) was an explicit attempt to draw the clergy to the side of the revolutionary settlement in the hope of leading the people to support it. The Church could mobilise its role as the *locus* of national commemoration and celebration to underscore support for William and Mary. Burnet's sermon preached before the House of Lords on 5 November 1689 – conveniently the anniversary of both the gunpowder plot and the landing of William at Torbay – used the happy coincidence to draw parallels between each as the rescue of Protestant England from Catholicism and tyranny.[28] As late as 1695 a sermon on the anniversary of the death of Queen Mary emphasised the importance of commending the settlement from the pulpit.[29]

The response within the Church to Non-jurors was varied. Gilbert Burnet, for example, conceded that 'there is a respect due to such as are willing to suffer for their consciences'.[30] But the militant Bishop Henry Compton was relentless in his determination to root out Non-jurors and excommunicate those he could not harry out of his diocese. Much of the ecclesiastical anger at the Non-jurors arose from a sense that they had been quiet during the Revolution and had only developed scruples afterwards; in short, that they inhabited a world of 'quixotic legalism'.[31] For the Anglicans who accommodated the oaths to William and Mary, Edmund Bohun's *History of the Desertion* (1689), was the best guide. Its theme was that the historic principles of the Church had not been violated. The issue was not whether the Church should abandon its obedience to the lawful king, but whether James *was* the lawful king. Equally, the Tory Bohun claimed, the divine right of kings was not abandoned, because the Church historically acknowledged the right of providence to determine the succession by a just war, and also because the Church held that the king was accountable to God, who could by an act of providence change the ruler. This providential doctrine became widely held.[32] It was advanced by Thomas Hayter in 1746 for the survival of the house of Hanover against the Jacobite Rebellion of the previous year as: 'a recent instance of such divine providence vouchsafed to our gracious sovereign in the suppression of an attempt to rob him of his Kingdom'.[33] Indeed Tony Claydon suggests that in 1689 Gilbert Burnet and a clique of court propagandists carefully fostered providentialism to legitimise William's rule. Burnet also developed 'a deeply Christian ideology which rested upon a set of Protestant and biblical idioms first developed during the Reformation of the middle of the sixteenth century'.[34] Thus, by emphasising the familiar Protestant nature of the new regime, there was a conservatism within post-Revolution Anglicanism which asserted that nothing had changed other than the identity of the ruler, and *that* had been effected by the will of God expressed through a just war. It was a profoundly unrevolutionary position. When Non-jurors claimed that passive resistance meant that a Christian should not rebel even against a prince who was acting wrongly, but should passively refuse to help him, Bohun held that this is exactly what most of England did in 1688; most people stood neither for James nor William but awaited the providential judgement of God. This was a response which emphasised that the events of 1688 were a second restoration rather than a revolution.

Although to modern eyes the oath occasioning the Non-jurors' schism was a modest one, to contemporaries the sacred nature of the oaths could not be ignored. But Edward Stillingfleet spoke for the ten thousand clergy who took the oath when he asserted that there was a difference between an oath which required a declaration of right by the swearer, and a simple oath of allegiance which required no such declaration. His *Discourse Concerning the Unreasonableness of the New Separation on Account of the Oaths* (1689) held that William's prior status as a prince qualified him to exercise authority and that if he fulfilled his duties as King he was owed allegiance. Stillingfleet also held that James had acted beyond the law. It was an *a posteriori* argument and open to the accusation of casuistry. But Stillingfleet also employed functionalist arguments: he claimed the Non-jurors attended too much to the *form* of the oaths and insufficiently to the *end* of the oaths. The general good occasioned by the Revolution, he claimed, enabled churchmen to maintain their undertakings to Church and nation. He claimed that if Non-jurors put oaths above these, they were blind to their other allegiances, and James would have turned Non-jurors' allegiance to bondage.

Both jurors and Non-jurors turned to the Bible in justification of their

views. Filmer's arguments on the patriarchal nature of monarchical government and the filial duty owed to it were derived from the Old Testament.
The Non-jurors were quick to argue that Chapter thirteen of St Paul's
Letter to the Romans was the basis of their actions.[35] It was not that those
who accepted the oaths rejected this injunction; but they regarded St Paul's
definition of power and authority only to apply to legitimate rulers. At the
core of the debate on oaths lay the issue of the origin of government. Every
pamphleteer and incumbent needed to decide exactly how God had laid
down that governments had been ordered. Bishop Lloyd of St Asaph warned
against too literal a reliance on the historical nature of the Bible, otherwise
it could be concluded that Roman rule in Palestine could have been
justified by right of conquest.[36] It seems unlikely that many clergy or laity
held exclusively to either side in the debate on the origins of government.
Even Gilbert Burnet accepted Filmer's idea of a patriarchal authority, but
held that if, like James, the ruler planned to destroy his people they had the
right to resist him.

The Bible also offered succour to those who held the view that rulers
exercised authority limited by a contract. The Old Testament Covenant
seemed to Hooker and Languet to presage the feudal idea of contractual
government. The disrepute that the contract gained from the events of the
Commonwealth and Republic did not prevent many from citing it as
a justification for the Revolution. After the Revolution, Peter Allix, a
Frenchman, described how the Britons

> chose themselves one King to reign over them, to govern God's
> people, and to maintain and defend their persons and their goods
> in peace and by rules of law. And at the beginning they made the
> King to swear that he should maintain the Christian faith with all
> his power, and govern his people by law . . .[37]

There were innumerable versions of the contract theory, including those
that allowed that permitted people to resign their contractual rights to
a sovereign. However for churchmen like Jeremy Collier, the idea of a
contract smacked of abhorrent ideas of democracy. To Collier, democracy
was madness and anarchy, with every man a ruler of himself. He conceded
that Englishmen possessed liberties allowed them by successive conquerors,
but these alone.[38] None of these arguments on oaths and contracts were
new, they were old debates applied to new circumstances. Yet the appeal of
both Non-jurors and Jurors to the Bible and to the historical idea of the
nature of government suggested that both took a conservative rather than a
progressive view of the Revolution.

The right of conquest had long been recognised as a legitimate means of assuming the throne in England; indeed the Tudor conception of government rested wholly on it. In addition to the general right of conquest, however, William added a concern for the Protestant succession and the liberties of the people. There were also arguments that the Revolution was a conquest to defend an hereditary right: Gilbert Burnet claimed that the Revolution was justified on the ground that William's invasion sought to secure the rights of his wife to succeed against James's pretended son.[39] Similarly the Whig Samuel Johnson, rector of Corringham, who had been a fierce opponent of James II, acclaimed William as 'one of the royal family' and therefore able to claim the throne by hereditary right.[40] Thomas Comber, Granville's successor as dean of Durham, observed that European peoples would be mystified by Non-jury, it being common for dynasties to change without difficulties over oaths. But many Whig writers commented on the similarity to the succession of Henry VII in 1485, even to the rule by Henry in spite of his wife's greater claim.[41] James likened himself to Richard II, wrongly deposed by a pretender with a tenuous hereditary right to the throne who ushered in the Wars of the Roses.

The intellectual processes by which these conflicting views could be resolved, and a king *de facto* become a king *de jure*, was illustrated by William Sherlock, who was initially suspended for Non-jury. However his reading of *Bishop Overall's Convocation Book*, at Sancroft's behest, led him to accept that a King by conquest could be accepted as the legitimate ruler. Sherlock felt that the evidence of the canons in *Overall's Convocation Book* showed that the doctrine of passive resistance did not exclude submission to a ruler by conquest. Sherlock's *Case of the Allegiance due to Soveraign Powers* advanced the view that there was in substance little or no difference between a king *de facto* and a king *de jure*. Kings *de facto* exercised plenary powers and protected the subjects 'when they are thoroughly settled in their thrones, they are vested with God's authority, and must be reverenced and obeyed by all'. Sherlock drew on Overall to develop a new definition of monarchy:

> a King is he who actually administers the government with a regal authority; not he who has a right to it but is kept from his right . . . when such a case happens it is not so unjust or unreasonable as to order the subjects to obey and stand by the King in possession: for the King has no right but by law and then the law may determine how far his right shall extend.[42]

In effect, Sherlock was moving Anglican ideology to an allegiance to the crown and the law rather than an allegiance to the person of the king. Of course the pro-revolutionary views of Burnet, Bohun and Sherlock left questions unanswered: particularly, what was the status of 'conquered' people, and what duty was owed to a usurped king seeking to restore his throne? Within a few months of his return to orthodoxy, however, Sherlock was rewarded with the deanery of St Paul's, a visible reminder to Non-jurors of the benevolence of the King to those who recanted their opposition to him as king *de jure*. The Lords resolved on 24 January 1693 that

> the assertion of King William and Queen Mary's being King and Queen by Conquest was highly injurious to their majesties, and inconsistent with the principles on which this government is founded, and tending to the subversion of the rights of the people.[43]

The discordance of the idea of William as a conqueror was replaced by the emollient view that he was legitimised as a king *de jure* by his providential role as restorer and deliverer of Anglicanism. This was an idea that could unite most Anglican clergy.

The notion of providence, emphasised within the English Church by Augustine, was held by Christians of the seventeenth century to be an immediate and literal force in the material world, and was invoked in 1693 by John Norris to defend the Glorious Revolution.[44] Gilbert Burnet, who wrote histories of the Reformation and the Revolution, justified *both* on the grounds of the direct action and sanction of divine providence. In the years after the Revolution, even Anglican Tories, like Atterbury, Sharp and Sherlock, regarded divine providence as a fundamental feature of historical Anglican doctrine, indeed it was the explanation for the defeat of the Armada, the discovery of the Gunpowder Plot, and the Restoration. In the battle against rationalism and deism, orthodox Anglicans regarded the doctrine of divine providence as the justification for, and evidence of, revealed religion and the basis for the requirement of faith in a personal, intervening God.[45] Providence explained not merely the triumph of William and the defeat of James but also the subsequent events which confirmed the legitimacy of the Revolution. In 1710 Edward Chandler, emphasising the providential nature of William's victory, drew attention to the smallness of William's forces, the size of James's army, the lack of bloodshed and damage to property.[46] The defeat of James's Irish venture in 1690–1, the growth of trade, and the resolution of European conflicts, all seemed to follow as a consequence of the providential sanction of William's regime.[47] Simon Patrick argued that divine judgement of governments was especially to be expected from providence

> if God demonstrates his providence in anything in this world, . . . he exercises it in the governing, defending, and protecting of publick persons and societies.'[48]

The attraction of the doctrine of providence was that it filled the void left by the doctrine of the divine right of kings. The events of 1649 and 1688 had shattered the purest sacramental form of the doctrine of divine right. But the Anglican notion of providence replaced it very swiftly. 'Providential divine right' continued to emphasise the ruler's responsibility to God and God's authority to install and dispense with rulers. Its highest expression was William Sherlock's *Case of the Allegiance due to Soveraign Powers* . . . :

> God governs . . . the world, removeth Kings, and setteth up Kings, only by His providence; that is then God sets up a King when by His providence he advances him to the Throne, and puts the sovereign authority into His hands; and He removeth a King, when by His providence He thrusts him from His Throne, and takes the government out of His hands: for providence is God's Government of the World by an invisible influence and power, whereby He directs, determines, overrules all events to the accomplishment of His own Will and Counsels . . .[49]

Men might propose a ruler, but God would dispose. The effect of the doctrine was to erode the difference between a ruler *de facto* and a ruler *de jure*. Some Anglicans, such as William Lloyd, were able to use the providential divine right as a means to attempt to reconcile the Non-jurors to orthodoxy: 'though no Christian ought to allow a rebellion of people against their prince, yet doth God never leave Kings unpunished when they transgress these limits'.[50]

Similarly Bohun's view that men proposed and God disposed was one which had the potential to square the circle with Non-jury:

> We are safe, if we do our duty, and submit to and pray for those powers that we do set over us, by men as instruments, by God as the dispenser of Crowns.[51]

The importance of this providential ideology was that Anglicans of all shades, and many Dissenters, could unite around this providential ideology, using the events of James II's reign to show God's providential involvement in the world. The 'Protestant Wind' – with all its analogies to the Armada – was one of numerous themes that emerged from the ideology. The immortalisation of the invasion in the tune *Lillibulero* confirmed the Revolution's place in popular culture and folklore. Stories circulated of Church bells ringing unpulled on William III's coronation day signalling God's sanction of the new King. The date of William's landing at Torbay joined the other powerful Anglican anniversaries, like that of Charles I's martyrdom and Charles II's Restoration, as one of the popular feasts in the Anglican calendar. William's rescue from the Turnham Green Plot in 1696 and the coming of peace with the Treaty of Ryswick in 1697 were also powerful evidence of divine approbation. The Anglican ideology of divine providence was therefore easily pressed into the popular consciousness in the service of the new regime. William's military actions against both James II and Louis XIV could take on the language and imagery of a crusade.

The Revolutionary doctrine of providential divine right survived the succession of 1714, and was alive well into the 'long into the eighteenth century'.[52] In 1710 the idiosyncratic John Asgill even made a claim that the pure form of the divine right of kings had survived.[53] In order to combat this in 1723 Thomas Trenchard devoted a whole issue of *Cato's Letters*, a Whig newspaper, to a denunciation of the providential divine right of kings.[54] Thomas Sherlock, reviewing the Revolution from the perspective of 1715, saw a succession of providential intervention which he warned his countrymen not to break. The strand started with James II, who

> imprisoned her [the country's] bishops, dispensed with her laws and broke down all the fences that were raised for her security; in which confusion she had utterly perished, had not the providence of God rescued her by means of a Protestant prince, happily allied to the crown of England by marriage and by birth. . . .[55]

During William's reign the providential theory of the divine right of kings was strengthened and traditional statements of it resumed, so that by 1701 William Binckes could liken Charles I's martyrdom to that of Christ.[56] William himself expected that the providential divine right entitled him to the passive obedience of his new subjects. Post-revolutionary Anglicans promoted passive obedience as a biblical doctrine in part to promote non-resistance to William among Jacobites and Non-jurors, who it was hoped could be persuaded to abandon military support for James II. Non-resistance to a divine monarchy was also broadened by the Church to include that parliamentary legislation which related to the Crown. This added legitimacy to the legislation for the succession, which, after the death of Mary in 1694, was a pressing matter since William had no children and did not re-marry. Moreover, as Gerald Straka has shown, William enjoyed all the prerogatives of the Tudor monarchy. Even William's portrait with allegorical figures, painted by Kneller in 1701, mimicked the early Stuarts in the suggestion of divine protection.[57] Under William, sermons on the anniversary of the martyrdom of Charles I continued unabated. William Wake likened William III to King David,[58] and even Francis Atterbury, the churchman who eventually defected to James's son's court, declared William to be 'a prince who hath happily join'd together the extremes of martial and political virtues; and knows as well how to govern a free people by their own laws and customs. . . .'[59] In 1701 George Hooper, the High-Church dean of Canterbury and later prolocutor of the Lower House of Convocation, also conceded William's title if it would induce him to call a Convocation.[60]

By the reign of Queen Anne, Thomas Sherlock, re-interpreted the doctrine of non-resistance. In the discourse 'Let every soul be subject unto higher powers', he advanced the view that St Paul asserted a doctrine of non-resistance and had warned that 'they who resist the power shall receive to themselves damnation'. But Sherlock argued that the circumstances were particular to the early Church; for the eighteenth century,

> the Scriptures are not to be tortured to speak in favour of one side or the other; for they stand clear of all disputes about the rights of princes and subjects: so that such disputes must be left to be decided by principles of natural equity and the constitution of the country.[61]

Historians have tended to assume that the Anglican defenders of the Revolution were predominantly Whig. In fact Tories, such as Sharp, Sherlock and Atterbury, wrote in defence of William largely because the Church successfully grafted the theories of providential divine right and of passive resistance onto the new monarchy. In 1702 the Tory Jonathan Trelawny defended the Revolution as legitimate, but was surprised that its detractors did not see the functional benefit of the settlement of 1689:

> I cannot therefore but wonder that of late years there should be suffered so many pamphlets against the settlement, nay [against] the very foundation of government and all religion. . . . For were the governors themselves meer atheists or unbelievers, were Christianity but a State policy . . . yet surely it must be common prudence to preserve the establishment of it, since there is no other notion can maintain any government long, but the sense of men's duty to be recompenc'd in another world.[62]

The belief in the providential legitimacy of the revolutionary monarchy survived the failures of William and Anne to provide heirs of their bodies, and took succour from the peaceful succession of their cousin George I, though the oath of non-resistance laid down by Charles II was repealed in 1719.[63] Nevertheless the Hanoverian monarchs continued to be designated by the Stuart invention of 'sacred majesty'. Well into the eighteenth century even Whigs promoted George I and George II as 'anointed by God' and sanctioned by heaven. In 1745 the new edition of *The Whole Duty of Man*, published under royal and episcopal licence, indicated the subject's relationship to the ruler:

> The King is the fount of authority, from whence all power descends upon lower magistrates . . . sovereigns are God's vice-regents, and do reign by his authority . . . they bear God's character, and do shine with the rays of his majesty: and consequently it is an affront to God's own majesty for subjects to contemn(sic) and vilify their sovereigns . . . [whose] commands are stamped with divine authority, and are thereby sacred.[64]

Published catechisms in the eighteenth century also continued to emphasise the divine origin of the King's authority.[65]

It has been easy for historians to characterise the political parties after the Revolution in stark colours. The Whigs seemed deep in Lockean contract theory and the Tories steeped in divine right theory. In fact, of course, there was no such easy division. As J. P. Kenyon and Jonathan Clark have suggested, Lockean ideas were far less prevalent than usually conceded by historians. The on-going debate on the Revolution engaged only marginally with Locke's work. For Lockean contract theory, unlike the work of Filmer and Hooker, seemed purely theoretical and un-biblical in foundation. Locke did not engage directly with Anglican or Dissenting theorists; nor did later historians engage comprehensively with Locke's views of the Revolution. For as Trevelyan wrote, 'the ultimate view that we take of the Revolution of 1688 must be determined by our preference for either royal absolutism or for parliamentary government'.[66] After the Revolution, as before, ideas of an hereditary monarchy, providential divine right and passive resistance crossed party boundaries. What defined emergent ideas of Whiggery and Toryism in the years after 1688 were religious responses to the Revolution. Tories in Church and State developed a view of the sacraments to justify the most contingent acceptance of William, closest to the *de facto* arguments. As a result they felt an affinity to the Non-jurors. Toryism clung to patriarchalism, and to historical precedents in the ordering of Church and State. In the Church this historicism was reflected in a dislike of the Toleration in William's religious policy and an assertion of traditional clerical privilege. In contrast, Whiggery was founded on government sanctioned by God, but operated by human agency in the interests of the society it governed. Providence for the Whigs justified the Revolution and the institutional unity of Church and State. In this particular, Whiggery developed spasmodically during William's reign; for some time, for example, the Whigs found the Charles I martyrdom sermons an embarrassment, since they rejected unadulterated divine right.[67] At their most reductionist, Whigs held that *vox populi* was *vox dei*, but in ecclesiastical terms this led to an embrace of Toleration and Comprehension of Dissent.

The proposed abjuration oath which followed the attempt on William's life in 1701 presented problems for Tories such as Nottingham and Halifax, since they were now required to deny the right of James II and his son to the throne. Only the swift death of William and the succession of Anne averted the enforcement of the oath. Abjuration was abandoned and a monarch was crowned who could lay claim to clear hereditary right as a Stuart in the direct line. Dynastic chance enabled the monarchy to raise a claim to the throne on a parliamentary, providential and also an hereditary basis, in a way that it could not do with William. For the Church, this raised the possibility that it might achieve a similar status; unshackled from contingent claims to institutional legitimacy it could reclaim ancient privileges.

It was not only in terms of Anglican ideology that the Revolution represented continuity with the past. The moral consequences of Anglican political and social attitudes remained unchanged and provided a focus for unity. The clearest illustration of this lay in attitudes to sin and vice. William was quick to show that he shared Charles II's response to vice. In a letter on 13 February 1689 he told the bishop of London and the archbishops that he held that

> a reformation of manners of all our subjects as being that which must establish our throne and to secure our people their religion, happiness and peace, all which seem to be in great danger at this time by reason of that overflowing of vice which is too notorious in this as well as neighbouring nations. . . .[68]

In the providential analysis there appeared to be an unassailable connection between the behaviour of the people and the blessings afforded to the nation by the political change. Consequently Queen Mary was especially anxious to prevent immorality, even writing to the Middlesex magistrates in 1691 to ask them to be diligent in prosecuting immorality – a measure urged upon her by Bishop Stillingfleet. Within six days of her public exhortation to the Middlesex justices, Queen Mary's father James was defeated in Ireland; it was greeted by Edward Stephenson as a divine blessing on Mary's actions.[69] The London Aldermen took their cue from the Queen and followed suit in pressing prosecutions for immorality. The endeavour was a Protestant rather than purely an Anglican one. The work of the Societies for the Reformations of Manners was a medium in which Anglicans and Dissenters could meet on equal terms. Benjamin Gravener, a Dissenting minister, called the

Societies for the Reformation of Manners 'the happiest omen to the nation next to the Revolution'.[70] For many Anglicans and Dissenters who strove to stamp out immorality, their work was a precondition for the continuity for the blessings of 1688. Indeed this was a view that William III himself held in 1698 when he warned that God might withdraw the benediction of the Revolution if vice and immorality were not combated by his new subjects.[71] Nevertheless the Societies for the Reformation of Manners were a means to enforce orthodox Anglican piety in society. Blasphemy, heresy, abuse of the sabbath and sexual vice were all forms of moral nonconformity that Anglicans called on the law to regulate, in the same way as the Test Act controlled religious nonconformity. Often members of the societies sought to prosecute heterodox religious works as well as immorality.[72] Samuel Bradford in 1709 suggested that Societies for the Reformation of Manners were examples of Christian unity, based on the primitive Church, because they embraced Dissenters and all shades of Anglican thought. He advanced the same argument of the unifying power for high and low Anglicans of the SPCK, the SPG, parochial libraries for poor clergy, charity schools and Queen Anne's Bounty. All these focused on the post-Revolutionary Church as an institution that acted as instruments of unity.[73]

There is no doubt that William, as a Presbyterian with experience of European religious intolerance, intended to grant as great a measure of Toleration as James. The only difference was William's intention to exclude Catholics, who were universally reviled in the wake of James's departure, and to sustain the Test Act. William's personal taste seems to have been in favour of wholesale Comprehension of Dissenters into the Church. Indeed William himself conformed to the rites of the Church of England at the Christmas services in 1688. But William was, above all, a pragmatist and recognised that decisions on Comprehension had to be left to the Church, in spite of the urgings of Gilbert Burnet to declare himself in favour of it. Tillotson's proposals for Comprehension were too much for the Church, which drew back from any wide measure of Comprehension, in spite of estimates that the proposals would bring two-thirds of Dissenters into the Church. Despite support for Comprehension from the unlikely quarters of Sancroft the Non-juring Archbishop and Baxter the Dissenter, the plan ran aground.[74]

However, Comprehension remained for many churchmen an enduring goal. Sancroft, the most vocal proponent, was lost to the Church; but there remained those who periodically raised the issue. Gilbert Burnet's *Exposition of the Thirty-Nine Articles* (1699) was 'a platform laid for Comprehension' which was fiercely prosecuted by Atterbury in Convocation in 1701 because it was seen as a means of comprehending Dissent.[75] Though Comprehension was lost in 1689, it was not forgotten; in the middle of the eighteenth century, some amiable but inconclusive talks were held between Doddridge and Chandler and Herring and Secker. For Hoadly the last major foray into publication was an attempt in 1734 to reconcile the Dissenters to the Anglican doctrine of Holy Communion. The failure of Comprehension in 1689 did not affect the Toleration Bill, introduced on the same day as the measure for Comprehension, by the Tory Earl of Nottingham. After a year, almost a thousand places of worship were registered by Dissenters, this undoubtedly alarmed parish clergy, but the bishops showed themselves sympathetic to Dissenters. Archbishops Tillotson and Sharp were both reluctant to prosecute Dissenters who failed to obtain the licences that the Act required; nor were they willing to stamp out Dissenting academies, which were opposed by the clergy on the ground that they fuelled the supply of Dissenting ministers.

Denied objection to the existence of Dissent, High-Church Anglicans resorted to opposition to the practice of occasional conformity to the Test Act by Dissenters who sought to qualify themselves for office. Equally the establishment was swift to scotch occasional attendance by Anglicans at Dissenters' meetings afforded by the Toleration Act. In 1704 Chief Justice Holt ruled:

> if a man be a professed churchman, and his conscience will permit him sometimes to go to [a dissenting] meeting instead of coming to Church, the Act of Toleration will not excuse him, for it was not made for such sort of people.[76]

There remained churchmen who regarded occasional conformity as a means to unite Church and Dissent. Thomas Tenison, in a speech in 1704 that infuriated Tories like Atterbury, commented on occasional conformity that

> . . . I think the practice of occasional conformity as used by Dissenters so far from deserving the title 'a vile hypocrisy', that I think it the duty of all moderate dissenters upon their own precepts to do it. . . .[77]

For many historians the divisions over Toleration and occasional conformity typified the apparent fissure within the Church which seemed to emerge within a few months of the Revolution. But even in the nineteenth century the simple division into High and Low Churchmanship proved an inadequate description.[78] The vague indices of churchmanship included: political views, doctrinal principles, personal piety, historical opinions and pastoral values. But these are inadequate for bishops such as William Lloyd,

Gilbert Burnet, William Wake, Edmund Gibson and numerous other churchmen who cannot be so comfortably labelled. Historians have often been unclear in defining Low Churchmanship or Latitudinarianism, concluding that it varied from a vaguely liberal Anglicanism to a set of rigid principles including an emphasis on biblical authority, the importance of conscience, a simplicity of doctrine, a reliance on natural religion over revelation, faith in the practical nature of Christianity, a sympathy for Dissenters and a suspicion of claims to sacerdotalism.[79] Martin Griffin has argued that in the late seventeenth century Latitudinarians were also the articulate opponents of the enemies of Anglicanism.[80] William Spellman has advanced a view of Latitudinarianism that suggested a commitment to a comprehensive Church of England based on orthodox Anglican theology.[81] In the eighteenth century it is possible to find examples of all these features in Latitudinarianism.

The foremost leaders of Latitudinarianism in the post-revolutionary Church were John Tillotson and Edward Stillingfleet.[82] During the eighteenth century Tillotson's claim to leadership of Latitudinarianism lay in part in the huge popularity of his sermons, which were published in vast numbers and used across the country by parish clergy. In the *Spectator* (1710), Sir Roger de Coverley recorded that his chaplain read Tillotson's sermons, and later in the century the surgeon in Henry Fielding's *Joseph Andrews* claimed that he had been raised on Tillotson's sermons as a boy and consequently knew how to get into heaven. Tillotson, who did not regard collects, liturgy, re-ordination and the rest as important enough to stand between him and Dissenters, made his sermons a model of natural religion. The principal criticism of his sermons was that they rarely mentioned Christ, to which Tillotson replied that Christ was always present when his teachings were spoken. John Bradman, a pupil of Tillotson's at Clare College, Cambridge, wrote that Tillotson had told him

> that Christianity, as to the practical part of it, was nothing else than the religion of nature or pure morality, save only praying and making all our addresses to God in the name and through the mediation of our Saviour, and the use of the two sacraments of Baptism and the Lord's Supper.[83]

The natural and moderate character of Christianity was a central element of Latitudinarianism and lay at the core of Tillotson's views.

It should not be overlooked, especially given the later popularity of some High Churchmen, that Latitudinarian churchmen were often hugely popular. Edward Stillingfleet, while dean of St Paul's, narrowly escaped assassination in the Popish Plot in 1678 and found that on the following

Sunday forty citizens with staves formed a spontaneous escort for him to go to Church. In 1699, on his monumental inscription, Richard Bentley hailed him as 'Ecclesiae Anglicanae Defensor Semper Invictus'. Even Thomas Hearne was outraged to find that Stillingfleet's library had been sold after the bishop's death, rather than saved for the nation. The Latitudinarian William Talbot was equally popular. In spite of replacing the Non-juror, George Hickes, as dean of Worcester, Talbot was met on his arrival in the city by thirty horsemen, the mayor and aldermen, a peal of bells and a volley of shots from the militia.[84]

To examine Latitudinarianism in detail it is worth examining the thought of Gilbert Burnet, William's first episcopal appointment. His *Discourse of Pastoral Care* (1692) gives an insight into the character of Latitudinarianism. The *Discourse of Pastoral Care* was hugely influential, it was used by generations of students of divinity, and recommended for their use well into the nineteenth century, by bishops such as Henry Bathurst.[85] Burnet's book places Latitudinarianism in a clearer focus than many second-hand accounts. Mark Goldie suggests that Burnet wrote the *Discourse* as a response to the Toleration Act, which ended the Anglican monopoly over pastoral care. Indeed Tillotson asked Burnet to write a new 'catechism for the post-Revolution pastorate'. Burnet sought a replacement for the coercive–punitive model of pastoral care. Certainly, as Jeremy Gregory indicates, the new circumstances of the 1690s placed far greater emphasis on pastoral duties.[86] Burnet saw his work as an attempt to produce a pastoral manual which would translate the moral renewal of the Society for the Reformation of Manners into Anglican parish activity but without the element of prosecution and coercion. At the core of Burnet's work lay an insistence that pastors needed to be moral and spiritual leaders, a critical issue if the Church were to compete with Dissent. Burnet had some harsh words for those clergy whose 'manners and labours' were inadequate. He also attacked the problems of simony, pluralism and non-residence – often the issues on which Latitudinarians were regarded as 'soft' – and held that richer clergy should encourage and support those in worse circumstances. Moreover, Burnet did not conform to the caricature of the Latitudinarian by suggesting that clergy could be 'moderate' and liberal in the moral and spiritual demands they made on their parishioners. He wrote at length on the value and benefit of the 'secret labors' of the clergy, the unseen visiting of homes and of the sick. He also wrote of the importance of parishioners preparing themselves rigorously and properly for Holy Communion, and of the importance of the clergy dispelling superstitious attitudes to the sacrament. Preaching, for Burnet, was an opportunity for clergy to lead their congregations and an opportunity to focus on purity of behaviour rather than debates on the doctrinal divisions in the Church. Low Churchmen, as

Burnet confessed himself, were 'cordially and conscientiously zealous for the church'.[87] Burnet was also concerned at the standards of training for the clergy. 'Literates', or non-graduate clergy, were often ill-educated and graduates were often only superficially educated in theology.

None of these were welcome messages for the clergy, and Burnet was bitterly attacked on the publication of the third edition of the *Discourse* (1713), though the motive may have been political.[88] In effect, Burnet's *Discourse* suggests that Latitudinarianism was very different from the usual depiction of Low Churchmanship. It was a rigorous, demanding and aspirational ideology, requiring extraordinary dedication and commitment by the clergy and laity. Burnet, and other Low Churchmen of the eighteenth century, are the embodiment of John Spurr's argument that historical interpretations of Latitudinarianism are problematic, and there was in reality little that was distinctive in Latitudinarian pastoral values, fuelling the view that the divisions between High and Low Churchmanship may be an chimera.[89]

There were other eighteenth-century churchmen for whom traditional models of High and Low Churchmanship were inadequate. For example, Henry Compton was a staunch Protestant, with all the credentials of a Low Churchman. He had been tutor to Princesses Anne and Mary, a conspirator against James II – who had suspended Compton as bishop – and had acted as a regimental colonel during the Revolution. Compton was a staunch proponent of the accession of William, and easily accommodated the concept of the abdication of James – even acting under commission for Sancroft at William and Mary's coronation. He also voted for the Toleration Act. Yet Compton was a Tory and a High Churchman. He consistently voted against the Whig administrations of William III's reign and entered more protests than any other bishop. Under Anne he even voted for the acquittal of Sacheverell at his trial.[90] Edward Stillingfleet, often identified as an archetype of Latitudinarianism, was undoubtedly a rationalist who was keen to make Christianity 'reasonable', and strongly supported the Comprehension of Dissent. However Stillingfleet had a long-running clash with Locke, over the latter's heterodoxy; and he asserted the validity of miracles and of the 'mysteries' of Christianity as a means to propagate faith.[91] John Wallis, the Savillian Professor of Geometry at Oxford and a staunch Whig and Low Churchman, also presents a conundrum. Wallis's Whig Erastianism led him to act as decipherer to William III and his work on differential calculus placed him at the forefront of the rationalist movement of the late seventeenth century. Nevertheless Wallis was a stout defender of Chalcedonian Trinitarianism. In 1691 alone he published *An Explication and Vindication of the Athanasian Creed* and followed it with *Three Sermons concerning the Sacred Trinity* and *A Fourth Letter concerning the Sacred Trinity.*[92] John Sharp was born of a Calvinist Puritan father and an Anglican mother. Throughout his career however he was thought of as a High Churchman: he supported the divine right of kings and was a Tory. But he accepted the oath to William and Mary, he forbade attacks on Dissenters from the pulpits of his diocese and advocated intercommunion with foreign Protestant churches.[93] Conversely, William Talbot, like Stillingfleet, was the embodiment of Latitudinarianism, and a zealous Whig and upholder of the Glorious Revolution. Talbot was the successor to the Non-juror Hickes as dean of Worcester, an opponent of Atterbury, a supporter of the Arian Samuel Clarke and a defender of the heterodox Thomas Rundle. Yet Talbot also expressed one of the principal High Church doctrines in his charge to the clergy of Salisbury when he succeeded as their bishop in 1715; he advanced a high view of the sacraments and sought to urge his clergy to 'bring your people frequently to the sacraments'.[94] Daniel Waterland, the oft-cited ultra-orthodox Trinitarian, was in many ways a High Churchman; his attitude to the sacraments, to the Church as the body of Christ and to the importance of episcopacy all placed him squarely in the High Church tradition. Yet Waterland was a Whig, antagonistic to Non-jurors, sympathetic to Dissenters and suspicious of mysticism and revelation, all of which aligned him with Low Churchmen.[95] Similarly, Waterland's immediate contemporary William Whiston was a Latitudinarian and rationalist of an extreme sort, crossing to Arianism, which views secured his expulsion from Cambridge and the censure of Convocation. Yet he expressed sympathy with Non-jurors and in 1693, when considering ordination, asserted

> I had no mind to apply myself to a bishop, how excellent so ever, who had come into the place of any who were not satisfied with the oaths to King William and Queen Mary, and so had been deprived for preferring conscience to preferment.[96]

Even Samuel Clarke, a churchman often portrayed as beyond the bounds of Trinitarianism, has been recently re-evaluated, suggesting that he was by no means an Arian and probably closer to Trinitarianism than previously thought.[97] In short, Latitudinarianism was not a party or a faction in the Church, but a cluster of values and ideas which were often held alongside Altitudinarian tenets.

Just as Latitudinarianism has been misrepresented by historians, so High Churchmanship has been reduced to a series of doctrines, distorting its breadth. Emphasis on a sacerdotal priesthood and episcopacy, the sacraments, apostolic succession and the claims of the Church to institutional equality with the State were all strands in High Churchmanship. But it is too simplistic to assert that these doctrines were those of the Non-jurors, and that the Church was denuded of its High-Church leadership after 1689. In reality Altitudinarian attitudes remained strong in the Church after the Glorious Revolution in two forms. First, High-Church attitudes remained a major feature in the thought of many clergy in the eighteenth century, not least in the doctrine of providential divine right and in the attitudes to the sacerdotal status of the clergy.[98] Secondly, High Churchmen were much in evidence in the eighteenth century, though in many cases their reputations in other spheres have obscured their doctrinal views: Atterbury, Gibson, Jane, Trelawny, Sharp, Wilson, Kennett, Wake, Potter, Sherlock, Secker, Horne and Horsley were all High-Church clergy. Indeed the High-Church bishops of the century were among the most influential and active.[99]

Following the departure of the Non-jurors, the High-Church movement was certainly not without leaders: Sharp went to York and led High-Church opinion together with bishops Crewe of Durham, Mews of Winchester, Trelawny of Exeter and Compton of London. They sat uneasily while parliament deprived their brother bishops who refused the oaths. It was an action that most felt was unprecedented and uncanonical, since they rejected the right of parliament to depose bishops or to replace them. But what discredited the Non-jurors in the minds of many High Churchmen was the decision in 1692 to establish a Non-juror succession of bishops, which in turn required them to obtain the approval of James now installed at Versailles. For many orthodox High Churchmen unity was so highly prized that it was this desertion that drove a wedge between them and Non-jury. Jacobitism and schism were united in William Sancroft's appeal to James for approval to consecrate Hickes.[100]

Within a short time of the Revolution, moreover, High Churchmen turned their attentions away from Non-jury. The themes around which the High Churchmen rallied were the assertion of clerical privilege and the determination to defend incursions into orthodox doctrines of the Trinity. A spate of disputes over the character of Christ took place after 1689. Arthur Bury's *The Naked Gospel* (1690), which seemed to question the orthodox doctrine of the Trinity, was the subject of a violent visitation of Exeter College, Oxford, where Bury was the rector and High-Church Trelawny the visitor. Eventually Queen Mary urged the vice-chancellor to quieten the dispute that had engulfed the University. Worse was Stephen Nye's *Brief Notes on the Athanasian Creed* (1688), which appeared to question Christ's divinity. Again a High Churchman, this time William Sherlock, responded with his *Vindication of the Doctrine of the Holy and Ever Blessed Trinity and the Incarnation of the Son of God* (1691). The controversy spilled over into Oxford until William issued 'A Letter of Direction to the archbishops and bishops for the preserving of unity in the Church and the Purity of the

Christian Faith concerning the Holy Trinity'.[101] This was an injunction to bishops and clergy to desist from theological argument. Whilst this quietened debate briefly, the High Churchmen were determined to defend orthodoxy and Sherlock's *Distinction between Real and Nominal Trinitarians* (1696) and George Bull's *Discourse on the Doctrine . . . concerning the Blessed Trinity* (1697) indicated the intellectual tenacity of the High-Church party.

During William's reign a principal thrust of government policy toward the Church was to dampen division between High and Low and even episcopal appointments were made to effect this.[102] But this obscures the intellectual similarities between the two. Both parties shared much in common and adopted a similar historical approach to the Church. Indeed rational and historical justifications were not the exclusive preserve of Latitudinarianism or High Churchmanship.[103] High Churchmen were as quick to find explanations and understanding of the issues facing the Church and society in historical scholarship as Low Churchmen. Atterbury, Wake, Gibson, Kennett, Nicolson, Hickes and Hearne were High-Church historians who developed claims for the clergy and the Church from their historical research, rather than simply relying on the sacerdotal claims usually advanced by High Churchmen. There was moreover a strong commitment to rationalism among the High Churchmen: Atterbury's commitment to the claims of reason led to his assertion that the Church of England 'desires nothing more than to be tried at the bar of unbiased reason, and to be concluded by its sentence'.[104] William Sherlock held that the principal division between Papists and Anglicans was that the former relied on priestly guides 'without reason and understanding', whereas Anglican priests 'inform our judgements that we may be able to understand for ourselves'.[105] Equally historians have been quick to grant High Churchmen a monopoly on revealed religion and miraculous faith, and to ignore the mysticism in the intellectual inheritance of the Latitudinarians. For example, the utopian mysticism of the seventeenth-century political theorist James Harrington, mixed rational ideas of a 'Godly republic' and Erastianism with revelation and faith in divine intervention.[106]

There was moreover a contemporary deprecation of the divisions in the Church, Hooper in the House of Lords decried the separation of High and Low.[107] Linda Colley has argued that the 'striking feature in the religious landscape [was] the gulf between Protestant and Catholic'; if this is so, how much narrower were the fissures between Protestants, she asks.[108] But the argument can be pressed further: if the gap between the various forms of Protestantism were relatively slender, how much more so were the distinctions between High- and Low-Church Anglicans? In reality, as Robert Cornwall has shown, the principal fissures between High and Low

Churchmen were those over the form of the Church, its visibility and authority. Yet on the substance of the doctrines there was striking agreement: the primacy of scripture and of the *sola scriptura*, the necessity of the sacraments, the importance of preaching, the pastoral example of the priesthood. In short the matters on which churchmen agreed were far more significant than those on which they differed.[109] The same applied, in some fields, to the other denominations. George Hickes argued that all Christians were part of the same family and likened the differing sects as

> apartments of the same house, as wards of the same city, as towns, hundreds, shires, provinces of the same spiritual kingdom, under one ecclesiastical economy and administration whereof Christ is the author as well as sovereign lord and head.[110]

The SPCK sought specifically to avoid distinctions between High and Low Churchmen. Its membership from the very beginning brought High Churchmen, like Robert Nelson and Sir Humphrey Mackworth, together with Low Churchmen, like Simon Patrick and Henry Shute, and even comprehended Grey Neville MP, before his departure to Nonconformity in 1709.[111] Certainly clergy in country parishes disliked the apparent divisions, and most refused to enter into such disputes in their parishes, 'on the contrary, instead of bandying the terms of "high" and "low", he strove to live peaceably with all men, teaching them how to resist evil. And the pithy sentence of Bishop Hall's was constantly in his mouth, "out-face sin, out-preach it, out-live it." '[112]

In matters of worship and practical piety also there were similarities in the position of many High and Low Churchmen. They shared a belief in the importance of catechising the young, which leaders of both parties urged on the clergy and laity.[113] Indeed catechising provides evidence of the proximity of High and Low Church traditions inherited by eighteenth-century Anglicanism. Ian Green's study of catechising concludes that from 1530 to 1740 there was a high level of doctrinal continuity and uniformity in published catechisms. The core doctrines imparted by the creeds, the Decalogue, the Lord's Prayer and the sacraments were the common heritage of all Church of England catechisms.[114] There was also agreement between High and Low Churchmen that doctrinal unity was important for the Church. Bishop Edward Fowler's *Principles and Practices of Certain Moderate Divines* (1670) underwent a revival in the 1690s in part because it included the view that 'we do not suffer any man to reject the Thirty-Nine Articles . . . neither do we oblige any man to believe them, but only not to contradict them'.[115] What was unacceptable to both High and Low was the replacement of scriptural faith with opinion and interpretations of the Bible that were not sanctioned by the *Book of Common Prayer* or the Thirty-Nine Articles. Historians who emphasise Church divisions neglect the unanimity of Anglican support for the Act of Uniformity of 1662 and the requirement that public Anglican worship should conform to the *Book of Common Prayer*. Moreover, historians have been credulous in their reading of some of the polemicists of the eighteenth century. Dean Swift may have advanced the false syllogism: 'some Whigs are atheists, Gilbert Burnet is a Whig, therefore Gilbert Burnet is an atheist'. But no High Churchmen truly believed that Latitudinarians such as Burnet were atheists. Dr Johnson asserted it in his *Dictionary*, but again rhetoric triumphed over sincerity. In spite of Johnson's public assertion of Non-jury, and his explicit belief in the divine right of kings, his theology remained predominantly that of an orthodox Anglican.[116]

The assumption of an intellectually coherent division between High and Low Churchmanship has been effectively demolished by Brian Young. His examination of the inter-relationship between the rationalists who followed Locke and Newton and the metaphysicists who inspired Hutchinson and Law suggests that there was a fragmented patchwork of views within the High and Low Church traditions.[117] Individual churchmen also illustrate the fluidity of these traditions: Simon Patrick, for example, was in many respects a model Latitudinarian, but he strongly opposed Comprehension. Similarly George Stanhope, dean of Canterbury from 1704, a chaplain to Queen Anne and prolocutor from 1713, was considered to be a moderate Tory.[118] His sermon before the House of Commons on the anniversary of the martyrdom of Charles I in 1704/5 however presented a mixture of ecclesiastical views.[119] After railing against faction and the death of Charles I he presented some standard High-Church views: he endorsed the need for a reformation of manners, he advanced the duty of submission to superiors, he embraced Trinitarianism, and acclaimed Anne as 'the best of Queens'. But his sermon also included some of the key features of Low Church ecclesiology: an attack on Catholicism, a horror of the disputes and factions within the Church, praise for the 'condescension' of William, and warnings not to indulge in experiments to change the settlement of 1689. In short, Stanhope's sermon bridged the widest possible spectrum of ecclesiastical thought and appealed for unity. It demonstrated that the division between High and Low Churchmanship was above all a contextualist construct.

The fluidity of the position of Latitudinarianism and High Churchmanship can also be seen in Gilbert Burnet's shifting views on the doctrine of passive obedience. Initially, Burnet held that evidence supported the idea of a divine sanction of government and monarch. He believed that this was inherent in the Old Testament Mosaic ordinance of government and in the assumption of royal powers by English kings before their coronations. In essence his position was that of Filmer and those who advocated the divine right of kings. It was a widely expounded view, evidenced in many of his early works, including *The Modest and Free Conference* (1669); his 1672 Charles I martyrdom sermon; his *Vindication of Church and State in Scotland* (1673) and his *Life of Bedel* (1685). Gradually, however, Burnet changed his mind. Two ideas were paramount in this: first that of self-preservation and the right to defend oneself and one's property, even against lawful authority; and secondly a belief that a madman in authority would have to be restrained, and that the idea of a regency indicated this was legitimate. By analogy, royal power could be limited. From this it was a short step to his justification of William's invasion, published on the eve of the invasion, *An Enquiry into the Measure of Submission to the Supreme Authority . . .* , which explicitly jettisoned his earlier position. Both Leslie and Hickes resented Burnet's abandonment of his earlier position; but it demonstrated it was possible to migrate between the two intellectual positions.[120]

Among the parish clergy too there were examples of the fluidity of the High Church–Latitudinarian divide. The correspondence of Richard Wavell, rector of St Maurice, Winchester with his friend Thomas Woolls, vicar of Fareham, between 1744 and 1778, indicates how Latitudinarians moved easily between Low and High Church views. Wavell and Woolls were both Hoadly's appointees who shared books and sermons and bore all the hallmarks of Latitudinarianism. Their correspondence shows their esteem for Isaac Newton, Thomas Chubb, Arthur Sykes, Thomas Balguy and others of the rationalist, Hoadlyite persuasion. Moreover Wavell was the son of a Presbyterian, who retained a dissenter's horror for idolatry and sympathised with persecuted Presbyterians. In matters of doctrine their correspondence shows evidence of Low Churchmanship: Wavell viewed both miracles and justification by faith with some suspicion. But there is much in their letters which suggests that they leavened their Low Church-manship with some Altitudinarian views. Wavell regarded heterodox divines, often including those he approved of, as 'Satan's decoy ducks'; he regarded himself as 'an Old Testament man' and showed great interest in comparisons between Old Testament theology and Pauline Christianity, and he held that Bishop Thomas Newton's book on prophecies had proven the existence of revelation in Christianity. All these were marks of High Churchmanship. For men like Wavell and Woolls the hard delineation of categories of Low and High Churchmen was inadequate.[121]

In some cases the features of High and Low Churchmanship have been so blurred as to make the terms meaningless. In 1758 William Powell was attacked by Francis Blackburne for defending subscription to the Thirty-

Nine Articles as a cynical means of promoting greater Comprehension.[122] To be attacked on these grounds by Blackburne, himself an avowed Latitudinarian, suggests that Powell was located deep in Hoadleanism. Admittedly Powell was a Whig, a tutor to Charles Townshend and a friend of Thomas Balguy; his Charles I martyrdom sermon in 1766 denounced the divine right of kings and those politicians who 'flatter the monarch's lofty notions of his own authority, and persuade his subjects to surrender to him their liberties. . . .'[123] But Powell's *Discourses*, based on his sermons whilst Master of St John's College, Cambridge, suggest that to allot him a place among the Latitudinarians would be an inadequate definition. His 1765 Whitsun discourse on 'the authenticity of the books of the New and Old Testament' and subsequent discourses on 'the credit due to sacred historians', 'the insufficiency of Mr Hume's objection to the credibility of miracles', 'the use of miracles in proving the divine mission of our saviour and his apostles' and 'the evidence arising from the prophecies of the Old Testament' indicate that he also reached deep into the theology of High Churchmanship. His defence of the miraculous and attacks on Hume's rationalism denied some of the central tenets of natural religion and would have done credit to the staunchest High Churchman. His charge to the clergy of the archdeaconry of Colchester in 1772 on 'the use and abuse of philosophy in the study of religion' advanced the view of 'how weak and yet how dangerous all our reasoning is when it would correct the doctrines of revelation'; and he denounced the attempt to rationalise religious mysteries as 'fruitless'.[124] Powell emerges from much of his writing as an orthodox Anglican, with whose opinions Horne, Warburton, Butler and Horsley would have been comfortable. Where then in the Anglican spectrum should Powell be located? A Latitudinarian, or a High Churchman; a rationalist or an adherent of divine revelation? Powell demonstrates how meaningless ecclesiological labels became during the eighteenth century.

Jeffrey Chamberlain's study of the Latitudinarian Thomas Curteis, rector of Wrotham, Kent, shows how historians need to revise their views on the differences between High and Low Churchmen. Thomas Curteis was a Whig and a Low Churchman, who was appointed to his living in 1716, and zealously supported the Duke of Newcastle's Whig electoral bloc in Kent and Sussex. He brought up his sons to believe that the church's 'ennobling Latitude' made it more effective than other national churches. Like many Latitude-men he was tolerant toward Dissent, believed in freedom of conscience and encouraged charitable attitudes to all men. He even suggested that Bishop Gibson of London should consider another stab at revision of the liturgy to comprehend Dissenters into the Church. In all this, Curteis might appear to be an archetype of a Low Churchman, who eroded Church unity and embraced Dissent. Yet Curteis was as rigid and unbending as any High Churchman in denouncing deism and infidelity – publishing three books on their dangers. He attacked Tindall and Collins and insisted that heterodoxy had no place in religious discourse. He clung to Old Testament proofs of the revealed nature of Christianity. In effect, Curteis used all the arguments and strategies to combat deism and atheism that High Churchmen employed. Moreover Curteis was just as happy to exclude the heterodox from politics as High Churchmen, and saw their influence as destructive of Church and State. Though High Churchmen denounced Curteis as a traitor and Curteis responded with accusations of rigidity, in reality all that divided them was a charitable response to men of different Protestant conscience.[125] Similarly Chamberlain's study of the High-Church Frewin family suggests that such people could be tolerant of Whig Latitudinarians.[126]

At the core of High and Low Churchmanship there was a measure of agreement. The Latitudinarian Bishop Edward Stillingfleet in the 1690s advanced the view that the Church and its various mechanisms, tithes, liturgy and administration, were established by law – ancient and sacred law maybe – but not by the Bible. This might appear to have been a red rag to the High Church bull. But some High Churchmen, like Hugh Davis, agreed that the liturgy and *Book of Common Prayer* were legal constructs for the purpose of promoting peace and unity among Christians. Stillingfleet's erastian claim was that the Church was subject to the law, and therefore it was lawful for William to deprive bishops and silence Convocation. It was a view that was confirmed by Edmund Gibson's monolithic High Church canonical study *Codex Juris Ecclesiastici Anglicani* (1713), which asserted that the Church was subject to the law because of its extensive temporal role.[127]

Historians, including some revisionists such as Jonathan Clark, have also implied that we can divide the eighteenth century into periods: 1689–1702 the rise of Latitudinarianism; 1702–1714 the triumph of the High Church; 1714–1740 Latitudinarianism again riding high followed by a slow decline until the latter half of the century when High Churchmanship again rises to dominance. In reality such suggestions simply reflect the trend of historians to pay attention to, or to neglect, the various churchmen of the age. There is no evidence that churchmen of either 'party' were in greater or lesser numbers during these periods, only that they carried greater or lesser weight from time to time, and attracted more or less attention in the eighteenth-century presses and consequently among historians. Certainly John Gascoigne has shown that Latitudinarianism remained a vibrant theological and political concept during the latter half of the eighteenth century when many historians assume that Latitudinarians faded.[128] By 1790, Bishop Samuel Horsley of St David's told his clergy:

everyone is a High Churchman who is not unwilling to recognise so much as the special authority of the priesthood – everyone who, denying what we ourselves disclaim, anything of a divine right to temporalities acknowledge however in the sacred character some-what more divine than may belong to the mere servants of the State or of the laity, and regards the sense which we are thought to perform for our pay as something more than a part to be gravely played in the drama of human politics. My reverend brethren, we must be content to be High Churchmen according to this usage of the word, or we cannot be churchmen at all.[129]

By these terms even Benjamin Hoadly's three charges to the clergy of Salisbury and Winchester would qualify him as a High Churchman.[130]

What can we make of the Revolutionary Church? The Revolution of 1688–9 was an Anglican Revolution: inspired by popular and elite fears for the Church of England's security under James; with disobedience led by the bishops and clergy, and a pre-eminent desire to re-assert Anglican dominance under William and Mary. In this sense the Church was the progenitor and midwife of the Revolution of 1688. In spite of, or perhaps because of, the schism of Non-jurors, mainstream Anglican ideology swiftly accommodated the Revolution, with only subtle changes in the civil doctrines of the Church. The Church could still sustain an Anglican monarchy of sacerdotal character, worthy of the anointing and consecration that was maintained in eighteenth-century coronations. Handel's anthem 'Zadok the Priest' drew on St Dunstan's ancient formula which emphasised the divine origin of royal authority in the eighteenth century as much as in Old Testament times.[131] In this respect Jonathan Clark's assertion that the Glorious Revolution 'was not a bid for a weak monarchy, but for a Protestant monarchy' is correct.[132] Though in the State there may have been those who sought a parliamentary monarchy, in the Church a strongly Anglican monarchy was both the objective and the achievement of 1688. The Bill of Rights, which is usually cited in support of the enthronement of a parliamentary monarchy, also endorsed the Anglican nature of the Revolution. It excluded Catholics from the throne, and ensured that William and Mary, Anne and the Hanoverians commanded a dynastic and popular sanction in Church and State that James II had not enjoyed.

The immediate turbulence of the post-Revolution months, with the departure of the Non-jurors, the consternation over Comprehension and the passage of the Toleration Act, has masked for historians the dramatic success of the Revolution for the Church. The achievement of the Revolution for the Church was the near-universal acceptance of the concept of an Anglican establishment in Church and State. The price of the achievement was a rejection of Comprehension and the maintenance of conservative Anglican ideology. The reaffirmation of the Test Act and the willingness of William to settle the Church on the basis of the revolutionary establishment of 1689 provided short-term reassurance for Anglicans and ensured the broadest base of support for the Revolution. Tony Claydon indicates the degree to which the architects of the Revolution consciously sought to lower the ideological temperature in the decade after 1688.[133] But while the breadth of Anglican support for the Revolution may have met the objectives of William and the Church leaders in 1688–9, it also created a number of problems for the Church. The Toleration Act essentially replaced James's broad religious indulgence with a narrower Protestant Trinitarian indulgence. Inevitably toleration of Dissent changed the Church's image of itself and its role. The broad consensus at the heart of Anglicanism lay in the growing importance of the Church's pastoral role to sustain its position as the established religious institution. The aspirations of the Post-revolutionary Church were two-fold: first the definition of orthodoxy, with attendant debates on the trinity and the privileges of the Church and clergy; and second the hankering for a broader Comprehension which would resolve the dangers of Toleration. However in reality the expressions of these aspirations in the Church were modest during the reign of William because of the absence of Convocation and the determination of William and Mary to pacify and quieten the Church. But the danger for historians remains in the tendency to exaggerate the divisions between High and Low Church views, and to neglect those potent forces of unity that dominated the Church.

For many churchmen, as well as politicians like Somers, Churchill and Godolphin, the Revolution was primarily directed at reducing the divisions and fissures in the state that James II had created. Gilbert Burnet looked to the reign of Elizabeth I as a model of Anglican ecclesiastical unity to which William and the Revolution aspired.[134] Like Elizabeth, William avoided faction at home, through the Toleration Act, in order to fight Popery abroad. William's suppression of Convocation to avoid institutionalised faction in the Church did not prevent churchmen from forming different expectations, and framing different views of Toleration and the relationship between Church and State. However, the Non-jurors 'lost' to the Church were frequently the clergy most vexatious and prone to dispute, like Leslie and Dodwell, and of the handful of Non-jurors of any calibre, most, like Robert Nelson, returned to the Church.

The ideological achievement of the Revolution for the Church was for James to depart across the English Channel and the waters of providential divine right and passive obedience to close over his head, as if he had been legitimately succeeded. In the short term this ensured that the Non-jurors were numerically small and relatively uninfluential, in the long term serious factionalism in the Church was eroded and averted. The Church had ensured the widest possible support for the Revolution and allegiance to William. It captured Nottingham, Danby, Godolphin Sharp and Sherlock and other High-Church Tories for the new regime. The Church had convinced them that William's rule was only marginally less sacred than that of James. The arguments of Burnet and Lloyd 'had the most universal effect on the greater part of the clergy',[135] and old Tories like Sir John Bramston read and were convinced by Sherlock's arguments.[136]

The effect of the Anglican ideology was to emphasise the unity of the Church and State longer than it might have otherwise, and certainly for the duration of the eighteenth century. From 1688 each political act could not avoid also being a religious act. George Fleming's arguments even carried the union of Church and State as far as to suggest that military ventures and diplomacy were directly overseen by God. The impetus of the Anglican ideology and the consensus of 1689 enabled a Cartesian view of progress to be adapted by Whigs into one which bridged the age of absolutism with that of enlightenment. The Revolution, often regarded as a source of division in Church and State, was a source of unity and cohesion.

Notes

1 Anon., *Verse on the defiance of the Seven Bishops, 1688*, Manuscript Collection, Brotherton (Library, Leeds University, Lt q 52, Record No. 4485.
2 G. Burnet, *History of My Own Time*, London, 1838, p. 505.
3 T. Tenison, *A Discourse on Idolatry*, London, 1687, pp. 4–6. It was a theme that Tenison returned to in his sermon *'Concerning Discretion in Giving Alms'. A Sermon Preached before the Lord Mayor of London . . .* , London, 1681.
4 T. Bray, *Bibliotheca Parochialis*, London, 1697, pp. 52–3.
5 29 Car. 2, c. 7.
6 13 & 14 Car. 2.
7 15 Car. 2, c. 2 & 5.
8 S. Pincus, ' "To Protect English Liberties": the English Nationalist Revolution of 1688–9', T. Claydon and I. McBride (eds.), *Protestantism and National Identity: Britain and Ireland, c.1650–c.1850*, Cambridge, 1998, p. 90.
9 H. Sacheverell, *The Loyal Catechism*, London, 1710, p. 24.
10 The Three Questions were 1. If chosen to sit in the next parliament will you vote for the repeal of the Test Act and of the penal laws? 2. Will you give your vote to candidates favourable to those repeals? 3. Will you support the declaration for liberty of conscience by living peaceably with Christians of a different creed to your own? To enforce the questions, James had to remove ten lords lieutenant who refused to put them and replaced them with court-appointed Catholics. Worse still, when the questions were put, only twenty-six per cent of respondents in England and twenty-two per cent of respondents in Wales supported the King's policies.

11 Pincus, *op. cit.*, p. 88.
12 R. T. Carroll, *The Common-Sense Philosophy of Bishop Edward Stillingfleet, 1635–1699*, The Hague, 1975 (International Archives of the History of Ideas, vol. 77), p. 32.
13 S. Patrick, *Autobiography . . .* , Oxford, 1839, p. 135.
14 Wesley's text for his sermon was from the book of Daniel: 'Be it known unto thee O king, that we will not serve thy gods, nor worship the golden image which thou hast set up'.
15 D. H. Woodforde (ed.), *The Woodforde Diaries*, London, 1932, p. 13.
16 *Ibid.*, pp. 17, 21.
17 M. Storey (ed.), *Two East Anglian Diaries 1641–1729*, Suffolk Record Society, 1994, vol. 36, p. 176.
18 H. Fishwick (ed.), *The Notebook of the Revd Thomas Jolly 1671–1693, Extracts from the Church Book of Altham and Wymondhouses . . .* , Chetham Society, 1894, vol. 33, new series, p. 91. Later in 1689, when asked to swear the oath of allegiance, Jolly was 'glad of an opportunity to testify to the world that we are not dissenters from the Church of England . . . wherein it is Protestant'. *Ibid.*, p. 95.
19 Quoted in G. T. Stokes, *Some Worthies of the Irish Church*, London, 1900, p. 168.
20 M. Goldie, 'The Political Thought of the Anglican Revolution', R. A. Beddard (ed.), *The Revolution of 1688*, Oxford, 1991, pp. 112, 117.
21 G. Hickes, *An Apology for a new separation . . .* , London, 1691, p. 1.
22 Though Burnet's *Vindication of the Authority, Constitution and Laws of the Church and State of Scotland . . .* , in 1672 added the condition that passive obedience was limited when 'the magistrate be furious or desert his right, or expose his kingdom to the fury of others . . .'. T. E. S. Clarke and H. C. Foxcroft, *A Life of Gilbert Burnet . . . with an Introduction by C. H. Firth*, Cambridge, 1907, pp. 198, 110. Overton lists numerous Whig clergy who had supported the doctrine, including Stillingfleet, Patrick, Kennett, Beveridge. J. H. Overton, *The Non-jurors*, London, 1902, p. 5.
23 Hickes, *op. cit.*, p. 4.
24 Bishop James Gardiner of Lincoln, quoted in W. C. Watson 'The Late Stuart Reformation: Church and State in the First Age of Party', University of California, Riverside, PhD thesis, 1995, p. 31.
25 C. Robbins, *The Eighteenth Century Commonwealthman*, New York, 1968, p. 63. Contract theory was often expressed subtly, as William Bradshaw argued in 1730, princes ordained by God behaved generously to their people, 'while governors thus act they become public blessings and are justly entitled to that esteem . . . which is required to be paid by inferior subjects'. W. Bradshaw, *A Sermon Preached before the Lords Spiritual and Temporal in Parliament Assembled in the Abbey-church at Westminster January 30th 1729/30*, London, 1730, p. 19.
26 W. King, *State of the Irish Protestants under James II*, London, 1691, p. 6.
27 C. Moss, *A Sermon before the House of Lords on 30th January 1769 . . . on the Anniversary of the Martyrdom of King Charles I*, London, 1769, pp. 6–7.
28 G. Burnet, *A sermon preached before the House of Lords November 5th 1689 . . . being Gun-powder Treason Day as Likewise the Day of His Majesty's Landing in England*, London, 1689.

29 Anon., *A Defence of the Archbishop's Sermon on the Death of her Late Majesty* . . . , London, 1695, p. 2.

30 G. Burnet, *Reflections upon a Pamphlet* . . . , London, 1696, p. 63. In 1710, it was to Gilbert Burnet that the staunch Non-juror Henry Dodwell turned when he sought baptism within the church of England for his children. C. F. Secretan, *Memoirs of the Life and Times of the Pious Robert Nelson* . . . , London, 1860, p. 75.

31 A historical view that survives in G. M. Straka, *The Anglican Reaction to the Revolution of 1688*, University of Wisconsin, Madison, 1962, p. 29.

32 See W. C. Watson, *op. cit.*, Chapter One.

33 T. Hayter, *A Sermon preached before the Honourable House of Commons at St Margaret's Westminster, being the anniversary of his Majesty's happy accession to the Throne*, London, 1746, p. 16.

34 T. Claydon, *William III and the Godly Revolution*, Cambridge, 1996, pp. 5, 18.

35 'whosoever resisteth the power, resisteth the Ordinance of God . . .'.

36 W. Lloyd, *A Discourse of God's Ways of Disposing of Kingdoms*, London, 1681, pp. 8–15.

37 P. Allix, *An Examination of the Scruples of those who refuse to take an oath of Allegiance* . . . , London, 1689, p. 3.

38 J. Collier, *Vindicae Juris Regii*, London, 1689.

39 G. Burnet, *Pastoral Letter to the Clergy of His Diocese Concerning the Oaths of Allegiance and Supremacy to King William and Queen Mary*, London, 1689, p. 20.

40 S. Johnson, *An Argument proving that the Abrogation of King James by the People of England from the Royal Throne, and the promotion of the Prince of Orange, one of the royal family, to the throne of the Kingdom in his stead, was according to the constitution of the English government and prescribed by it, in opposition to all the false and treacherous hypotheses, of usurpation, conquest, desertion, and of taking the powers that are upon content* . . . , London 1691, p. 1. In 1705 a broadsheet entitled *The Union of the Houses of Lancaster and York* . . . showed Queen Anne's descent from the Plantagenets.

41 Anon, *A Friendly Conference Concerning the New Oath of Aliegiance to King William and Queen Mary, Wherein the objections against taking the oaths are impartially examined* . . . , London, 1689, p. 2. Anon, *Reflections Upon Two Books, the One intitled The Case of Alliegiance to a King in Possession, the Other, An Answer to Dr Sherlock's Case* . . . , London, 1691, pp. 38–44.

42 W. Sherlock *The Case of the Allegance due to Soveraign Powers*, London, 1691, pp. 7, 65.

43 Quoted in G. M. Straka, *op. cit.*, p. 63.

44 J. Norris, *Discourses Concerning Submission to Divine Providence* . . . , London, 1693.

45 W. Fleetwood, *Essay on Miracles*, London, 1701.

46 E. Chandler, *A Sermon Preached at the Cathedral Church of Worcester* . . . *Being the day appointed for the General Thanksgiving for the Glorious Campaign of the Arms of Her Majesty*, Worcester, 1710, pp. 9–10. The providential nature of William's victory is fully explored in T. Claydon, *op. cit.*

47 Equally, the earthquake that affected London in 1692 drew dark warnings from some as evidence of Heaven's displeasure. R. Fleming, *A Discourse on Earthquakes as Supernatural and Premonitory Signs to a Nation*, London, 1692.

48 S. Patrick, *A Sermon Preached on the 5th November*, London, 1696, p. 27.

49 W. Sherlock, *op. cit.*, p. 12.

50 W. Lloyd, *A Discourse of God's Ways of Disposing of Kingdoms*, London, 1681, pp. 22–3. Providential divine right continued to be an expression of the clergy's attitude to the monarchy as late as 1817, when on the death of princess Charlotte, the Revd C. J. Hoare, vicar of Blandford Forum, preached and published a sermon entitled *Silent Submission to the Divine Will* which advanced essentially the same providential view of the treatment of royalty by God.

51 E. Bohun, *History of the Desertion*, London, 1689, p. 361.

52 R. Cornwall, *Visible and Apostolic: The Constitution of the Church in High Church Anglican and Non-Juror Thought*, London, 1993, p. 12.

53 J. Asgill, *The Assertion is that the title of the House of Hanover to the Succession of the British Monarchy is a title hereditary and of divine institution*, London, 1710.

54 *Cato's Letters* No. 132, 8 June, 1723.

55 T. S. Hughes (ed.), *The Works of Bishop Sherlock with some account of his life . . .* , London, 1830, vol. 3, pp. 334–6.

56 G. M. Straka *op. cit.*, p. 83.

57 *Ibid.*, p. 90.

58 William Wake, *A Sermon Preached before the House of Commons . . . 5 June 1689*, London, 1689, pp. 27 *et seq.*

59 Francis Atterbury, *The Wisdom of Providence manifested in the Revolution of Government: A Sermon preached before the House of Commons at St Margaret's Westminster, May 29th 1701*, London, 1701, p. 268.

60 G. Hooper, *A Sermon Preach'd before the Honourable the House of Commons at St Margaret's Westminster on Friday the 4th day of April 1701, being the day of publick fast and humiliation*, London, 1701, p. 22.

61 T. S. Hughes (ed.), *op. cit.*, vol. 3, pp. 219, 234. Ironically it was Sherlock himself in 1716 who attacked the rebels against the house of Hanover: 'where did they learn that rebellion is the proper remedy . . . ? The Church of England has no such doctrine; & if they cannot govern their passions, yet, in justice to her they ought not to use her name in a cause which she ever has and will disclaim . . .'. *Ibid.*, p. 364.

62 J. Trelawny, *A Sermon Preached before the Queen and both Houses of Parliament at the Cathedral Church of St Paul's, Nov. 12 1702, being the day of Thanksgiving for the signal successes vouchsafed to Her Majesties Forces by sea and land . . .* , London, 1702, p. 11.

63 The oath of non-resistance was required by Car. II. s 2, c 1; and repealed 5 Geo. I. c. 60.

64 R. Browning, *The Political and Constitutional Ideas of the Court Whigs*, Baton Rouge, 1982, pp. 198–9. *The Whole Duty of Man*, London, 1745; though the new edition of the *Whole Duty of Man* included some conditional elements, it asserted that a ruler had a right for his commands to be obeyed 'while he commands all things lawful'.

64 I. M. Green, *The Christians ABC: catechisms and catechising 1530–1740*, Oxford, 1996, p. 451. One of the first catechisms to explicitly deny the doctrine of the divine right of kings was Thomas Secker's, which in his lecture on the fifth commandment asserted that rulers were also bound by the laws of the land. T. Secker, *Lectures on the Catechism of the Church of England with a discourse on Confirmation*, London, 1826, p. 207.

66 G. M. Trevelyan, *The English Revolution 1688–1689,* London, 1956, p. 245

67 J. P. Kenyon, *Revolution Principles: the Politics of Party, 1689–1720,* Cambridge, 1977, p. 74.

68 H.M. *Letter to the Bishop of London,* London, 1689, p. 4. William showed his determination to stamp out vices by passing laws against them in 1694, 1695 and 1697. 6 & 7 William III, c 11 and 9 William III, c 35.

69 E. Stephenson, *The Beginning and Progress of a needful and hopeful Reformation,* London, 1691, p. 7.

70 B. Gravener, *A Sermon Preached to the Society for the Reformation of Manners,* London, 1705, p. 54.

71 *A Proclamation for Preventing and Punishing Immorality and Profaneness,* 24 Feb. 1698. The proclamation was re-issued 9 Dec. 1699.

72 S. Burtt, 'The Societies for the Reformation of Manners: Between John Locke and the Devil in Augustan England', R. Lund (ed.), *The Margins of Orthodoxy: Heterodox Writing and Cultural Response 1660–1750,* Cambridge, 1995, pp. 149 *et seq.*

73 S. Bradford, *Unanimity and Charity, the Character of Christians: A Sermon Preached . . . at St Sepulchre's Church June 16 1709,* London, 1709, pp. 15 *et seq.*

74 E. Cardwell, *Synodalia . . . ,* Oxford, 1842, vol. 2, pp. 40 *et seq.*

75 M. Greig, 'Heresy Hunt: Gilbert Burnet and the Convocation Controversy of 1701', *Historical Journal,* 1994, vol. 37, part 3.

76 R. E. Rodes, Jr, *Law and the Modernization of the Church of England: Charles II to the Welfare State,* Indiana, 1991, p. 89.

77 E. Carpenter, *Thomas Tenison,* London, 1948, p. 118.

78 C. J. Abbey and J. H. Overton, *The English Church in the Eighteenth Century,* London, 1878, p. 113.

79 C. Haydon, J. Walsh and S. Taylor (eds.), *The Church of England c.1689–1833,* Cambridge, 1993, pp. 36–7. W. Spellman, *The Latitudinarians and the Church of England 1660–1700,* Athens, Georgia, 1993.

80 M. I. J. Griffin and L. Freedman, *Latitudinarianism in the Seventeenth Century Church of England* (Brill's Studies in Intellectual History, vol. 32), 1992.

81 Spellman, *op. cit.*

82 J. Marshall, 'The Ecclesiology of the Latitude-men 1660–1689: Stillingfleet, Tillotson and Hobbism', *Journal of Ecclesiastical History* 1985, vol. 36, no. 3.

83 T. Birch, *The Life and Works of Archbishop Tillotson,* London, 1753, vol. 1, p. cxix.

84 J. Nankivell, 'Edward Stillingfleet, Bishop of Worcester 1689–1699', *Worcester Archaeological Society,* 1945, vol. XXII, *passim.*

85 C. L. S. Linnell, *Some East Anglian Clergy,* London, 1961, p. 143.

86 M. Goldie, 'John Locke, Jonas Proast and Religious Toleration, 1688–1692', and J. Gregory, 'The Eighteenth Century Reformation: the Pastoral Task of Anglican Clergy after 1689', both in Haydon, Walsh and Taylor, *op. cit.*

87 G. Burnet, *Discourse of Pastoral Care,* London, 1713, third edition, preface.

88 See for example George Sewell, *The Clergy and the Present Ministry Defended Being a Letter to the Bishop of Salisbury, occasioned by his Lordship's New Preface to his Pastoral Care,* London, 1713.

89 J. Spurr, 'Latitudinarianism and the Restoration Church', *Historical Journal,* 1988, vol. 31, pp. 61–82.

90 E. Carpenter, *The Protestant Bishop*, London, 1956, *passim*.

91 Carroll, *op. cit. passim*. J. Locke, *A Letter to Edward, Lord Bishop of Worcester, concerning some passages relating to Mr Locke's Essay of Humane Understanding*, London, 1697.

92 Wallis also defended the nature of faith and revelation over rationalism in *The Life of Faith in Two Sermons*, Oxford, 1684.

93 P. Avis, *Anglicanism and the Christian Church*, Edinburgh, 1989, p. 89. I am grateful for this reference to Robert Ingram.

94 C. J. Abbey, *The English Church and its Bishops 1700–1800*, London, 1887, vol. 1, pp. 158–9. W. Talbot, *The Bishop of Sarum's Charge to the clergy of his Diocese at his Primary Visitation, 1716*, London, 1717, p. 4.

95 R. T. Holtby, *Daniel Waterland 1683–1740. A Study in eighteenth century Orthodoxy*, Carlisle, 1966, pp. 206 *et seq*.

96 W. Whiston, *Memoirs of the Life and Writings of Mr William Whiston*, London, 1749, p. 30.

97 T. C. Pfizenmaier, *The Trinitarian Theology of Dr Samuel Clarke (1675–1729). Context, Sources, and Controversy*, New York (Studies in the History of Christian Thought), 1997, *passim*.

98 William Powell was something of a rarity in 1766 in denouncing the divine right of kings in his Charles I martyrdom Sermon. W. S. Powell, *Discourses on Various Subjects*, London, 1776, pp. 43–9.

99 F. Mather, *High Church Prophet: Bp Samuel Horsley*, Oxford, 1992; P. B. Nockles, *The Oxford Movement in Context*, Cambridge, 1994. For the view that the Church of England was dominated by high churchmanship see R. Sharp, 'New Perspectives of the High Church Tradition: historical background 1730–1780', G. Rowell (ed.), *Tradition Renewed*, London, 1986.

100 G. D'Oyly, *The Life of William Sancroft*, London, 1840, p. 296.

101 E. Cardwell, *Documentary Annals of the Church of England*, London, 1844, vol. 2, pp. 389–391.

102 G. V. Bennett, 'King William III and the Episcopate', G. V. Bennett and J. Walsh (eds.), *Essays in Modern English Church History in Memory of Norman Sykes*, London, 1966.

103 R. K. Webb, 'The Emergence of Rational Dissent', R. Haakonssen (ed.), *Enlightenment and Religion: Rational Dissent in Eighteenth Century Britain*, Cambridge, 1996, pp. 12–42. I. Rivers, *Reason, Grace and Sentiment: A Study of the Language of Religion and Ethics in England 1660–1780*, Cambridge, 1991, vol. 1.

104 T. Moore (ed.), *Sermons of Francis Atterbury . . .* , London, 1734, vol. 3, p. 29.

105 W. Sherlock, *A Short Summary of the Principal Controversies between the Church of England and the Church of Rome*, London, 1687, pp. 10–11.

106 M. Goldie, 'The Civil Religion of James Harrington', A. Pagden (ed.), *The Languages of Political Theory in Early Modern Europe*, Cambridge, 1987.

107 C. J. Abbey, *op. cit.*, vol. 1, p. 132.

108 L. Colley, *Britons*, New Haven, 1992, pp. 18–19.

109 R. Cornwall, *op. cit.*, pp. 45 *et seq*.

110 G. Hickes, *Two Treaties on the Christian Priesthood and on the Dignity of the Episcopal Order*, Oxford, 1845–7, vol. 1, p. 297.

111 C. Rose, 'The Origins and Ideals of the SPCK, 1699–1716', J. Walsh, C. Haydon and S.Taylor (eds.), *op. cit.*, pp. 173–6.

112 C. Oldacre, *The Last of the Old Squires*, London, 1854, p. 101.

113 George Bull, Peter Hewitt, Henry Bonwicke, Richard Kidder, Edward Wells and Joseph Harrison published works encouraging clergy to undertake catechising as a vital element for the church between 1700 and 1718.

114 I. M. Green, *op. cit.*, pp. 565–7.

115 E. Fowler, *The Principles and Practices of Certain Moderate Divines of the Church of England . . .* , London, 1670, pp. 191–2.

116 J. C. D. Clark, *Samuel Johnson: Literature, Religion and English Cultural Politics from the Restoration to Romanticism*, Cambridge, 1994, pp. 126–139.

117 B. W. Young, *Religion and Enlightenment in Eighteenth Century England: Theological Debate from Locke to Burke*, *op. cit.*

118 He was instrumental in quashing debate over Hoadly sermon in 1717 and silencing convocation.

119 His text was the pregnant verse from Psalm 44: 'Shall the throne of Iniquity have fellowship with thee who frameth mischief by a law?'

120 H. C. Foxcroft, *A Supplement to Burnet's History of My Own Time, derived from His Original Memoirs, His Autobiography, His Letters to Admiral Herbert and His Private Meditations, all hitherto unpublished*, Oxford, 1902, pp. 516–17.

121 Hampshire Records Office, Copy/605/1–118 *passim.*

122 B. W. Young, *op. cit.*, pp. 45–8.

123 W. S. Powell, *op. cit.*, p. 58

124 *Ibid.*, pp. 349 *et seq.*

125 J. S. Chamberlain, 'The Limits of Moderation in a Latitudinarian Parson: or High Church Zeal in a Low Churchman discover'd', R. Lund, *op. cit.*, pp. 195 *et seq.*

126 J. Chamberlain, 'Portrait of a High Church clerical dynasty in Georgian England: the Frewens and their world', J. Walsh, C. Haydon and S. Taylor (eds.), *op. cit.*

127 R. E. Rodes Jr, *op. cit.*, pp. 4–6.

128 J. Gascoigne, 'Anglican Latitudinarianism and Political Radicalism in the Late Eighteenth Century', *History*, 1986, vol. 71.

129 Quoted in F. C. Mather, *op. cit.*, p. 200.

130 J. Hoadly (ed.), *The Works of Benjamin Hoadly DD*, London, 1773, vol. 3, pp. 475–89.

131 The opening lines are 'Zadok the Priest and Nathan the Prophet, anointed Soloman King'.

132 J. C. D. Clark, *Revolution and Rebellion: State and Society in England in the Seventeenth and Eighteenth Centuries*, Cambridge, 1986, p. 89.

134 G. Burnet, *A Sermon Preached before the King and Queen at Whitehall on the 19th October*, London, 1690, pp. 34–6.

135 G. Burnet, *History of My Own Time*, London, 1838, p. 523.

136 J. Bramston (ed.), *The Autobiography of Sir John Bramston*, Camden Society, 1845, vol. 32, pp. 372–3.

3

THE DEVELOPMENT OF
THE CHURCH'S RELATIONS
WITH THE STATE

From the Convocation controversy to
Catholic emancipation

The Church's relations with the State were profoundly influenced by the Glorious Revolution. In one form or other toleration and comprehension of Dissent and the doctrine of passive obedience were themes that ran through it. They were the causes of divisions within the higher reaches of the Church, but the majority of the clergy were not engaged in these debates. Of greater significance to the clergy as a whole is the success of the Church in accommodating the Hanoverian succession. By 1760 the Church had overcome concerns of political heterodoxy and turned its attention to theological orthodoxy. By the turn of the eighteenth century this lesson was not lost on Dissent. From 1689 to 1829 the Church achieved a transformation: religious controversy was not permitted to spill into civil unrest, theological debates did not effect schisms, and political disagreement did not taint churchmen with treason.

The Convocation controversy had been brewing for years before the Glorious Revolution. Archbishop Gilbert Sheldon's surrender of the right of the clergy to tax themselves in 1664 and the inclusion of the taxation of the clergy in parliamentary money bills had raised the issue of the status of Convocation. Moreover, under both Charles II and James II Convocation met rarely since, like William III, they feared its disquieting effect on the Church and clergy. The archbishops prorogued Convocation between the formal licences which accompanied the calling of Parliament. William III continued this policy and the Convocation controversy arose directly from the unwillingness of William III to permit Convocation to meet between 1689 and 1700. His dislike of factionalism, and distrust of the predominantly Tory clergy, persuaded William it was better that the clergy sit on their hands than pursue potentially divisive debates in Convocation. He contented himself with the appointment of Whig bishops, who helped to pacify the Church. Gilbert Burnet claimed 'little good is to be expected from the synodical meetings of the clergy; there is so much ambition, presumption and envy among them, that they may do much mischief'.[1]

Francis Atterbury's *Letter to a Convocation Man concerning the Rights, Powers and Privileges of that Body* (1697), sponsored by a High-Church cabal of bishops Compton and Trelawny and Lord Rochester, questioned William's policy. The *Letter* drew heavily on the views of Non-jurors for expressions of High-Church sacerdotalism and on the grievances of the clergy, and was to some extent an attempt to influence the Church by those who had chosen to leave it.[2] Atterbury's *Letter* challenged whether rulers since Henry VIII had the right to control and to licence the meetings of Convocation. He argued that the canons of the Church alone required royal permission, but Convocation did not need such permission to meet, deliberate, or pass resolutions. Explicit in Atterbury's thesis was that the Church was equal to the State both in institutional terms and in terms of divine sanction.[3]

Atterbury's *Letter to a Convocation Man* made three claims that went straight to the heart of the Kings' unwillingness to call Convocations. The first was that a calling of a Convocation was necessary to respond to the contemporary challenges of immorality, anti-Trinitarianism and deism (a popular argument among the parish clergy). Second, Atterbury claimed that whilst it was arguable whether the King could summon and dismiss Convocation of his free will, he was certain that the primates had no power to adjourn the houses of Convocation. Atterbury made much play of the writs of *praemunientes*, summoning the bishops to Parliament, in which the King also asked the bishops to bring with them the representatives of the clergy in the Lower House of Convocation. Once summoned, Convocation, like a free Parliament, had a right to free debate and resolution. Third, Atterbury claimed that the canons and decisions of Convocation did not need further confirmation or approval by Parliament provided they did not 'impugn common law, statutes, customs or prerogatives'.[4] In short, Convocation, claimed Atterbury, was an estate of the realm, like Parliament, but unlike MPs, peers and the bishops who sat in Parliament, the lower clergy had been wrongly disenfranchised and denied a voice for too long.

The arid years of the reigns of Charles, James and William had turned the Convocation issue into tinder, onto which Atterbury's *Letter* fell like a spark, and popular clerical opinion was mobilised in support of Atterbury's *Letter*. Within weeks of the publication of the *Letter*, at the behest of Archbishop

Tenison, William Wake published a book on which he had been working for some time, *The Authority of Christian Princes over Their Ecclesiastical Synods Asserted.* . . . It was a massive response to Atterbury, running to over three hundred pages. Characteristically, Wake drew precedents from the early Church, the European Protestant churches and from the Church of England since the Reformation. Wake based many of his arguments on the Act of the Submission of the Clergy to Henry VIII of 1536 in which the King expressly ordered Convocation to sit only during his pleasure.[5] Wake exposed Atterbury's failure to distinguish between an ecclesiastical synod that engaged the clergy in ecclesiastical debate, and a parliamentary Convocation that was limited by royal authority. Wake also corrected Atterbury's claims for the writ of *praemunientes*, indicating that it was an ancient formulaic writ which was accompanied by the calling of provincial synods. Convocation writs, Wake asserted, were sent only to archbishops. Addressing Atterbury's contemporary theme, Wake denied that Convocation had a right to meet, and argued that such regular meetings as there were of parliament would be a burden not a privilege to the clergy.

Thus were the lines drawn: Atterbury sought a Convocation of almost unlimited authority and privilege to quash the advance of Dissent and heterodoxy; Wake demanded that Dissent be dealt with by the law and that the Church rest on William's desire for peace, rather than indulging in damaging rehearsals of the debates over Toleration, which it was widely perceived Atterbury wanted. For many churchmen, whilst Atterbury's claims were too high-flown, Wake's denials of clerical privilege were inflammatory. Indeed the reaction to Wake's *Authority of Christian Princes* was so vehement that he devoted most of 1698 to writing *An Appeal to all true members of the Church of England on behalf of the King's Ecclesiastical Supremacy*, in which he argued that his position was the long-held, traditional Anglican view of the Church's leaders, including Whitgift, Bancroft, Hooker, King James I and most other authorities. Atterbury in turn responded with a six hundred and fifty page tome *The Rights, Powers and Privileges of an English Convocation stated and vindicated* (1700). It included an *ad hominem* attack on Wake, and, in a significant inversion of ideologies, attacked Wake for defending royal authority on the lines that James II had also asserted it. The nature of the Convocation debate was such that Atterbury and Wake alternated in their adherence to traditional High Church regard for sacerdotal kingship as their arguments required. Atterbury also returned to the writ of *praemunientes* and claimed that for four hundred years the writs had called Parliament and Convocation at the same time. In a clever move, Atterbury claimed that Convocation might meet apart from, and less often than, parliament but remained part of it; and with skilful footwork he claimed that Henry VIII had simply removed the discretionary power of the archbishops to call and dismiss Convocations and had vested these powers in the King. Once again, whatever the rights of the case, Atterbury had gained the popular ground by championing the causes of the clergy; whereas Wake appeared simply to defend the status quo.[6] Atterbury's supporters were exultant when Lord Rochester prevailed on William III to call a meeting of Convocation in 1701, and the shortcomings of Atterbury's arguments were forgotten in his apparent victory in the cause of the clergy.

In spite of the calling of a Convocation, Wake's High-Church allies responded to his clarion call and to Tenison's fear that Wake's polemical work was being produced too slowly and was too abstruse for many. Even before the opening of the 1701 Convocation, White Kennett entered the fray with *Ecclesiastical Synods and Parliamentary Convocations in the Church of England Historically stated*, which reached deep into Anglo-Saxon and Norman History to defend Wake. Nicolson, Tanner and Gibson also responded to Atterbury before Wake himself published *State of the Church and Clergy of England in the Councils, Synods, Convocations, Conventions and other public assemblies. . . .* (1703), a work of over seven hundred pages. It was a magisterial study which dealt a mortal blow to Atterbury's arguments, but by that time the focus of the debate had moved on. The appointment of Atterbury to the archdeaconry of Totnes in January 1701 brought him into the Lower House of Convocation, in which Wake sat as dean of Exeter. Atterbury attracted a significant following in the elections to the Lower House, the Revd Thomas Naish being among those who publicly detached himself from Bishop Gilbert Burnet's party to join Atterbury's supporters.[7] The elections to the Lower House of Convocation were inevitably dominated by debates over Atterbury's and Wake's books, but, by its first meeting Atterbury's supporters had gained a majority in the Lower House.[8]

The meeting of the Convocation of 1701 was tense. Atterbury was determined to advance the rights of Convocation and to restore the authority of the Church; conversely the bishops – led by Archbishop Tenison – were adamant that no business should disquiet the Lower House. At the first meeting on 25 February, Tenison's writ of prorogation met with defiance as the Lower House appointed committees to investigate the heresies in various publications, including Toland's *Christianity Not Mysterious* and Bishop Burnet's *Commentary on the Thirty-Nine Articles*. Gradually, Tory politicians sensed that the Lower House of Convocation was out of control. The prolocutor, George Hooper, was in the hands of Atterbury and throughout March the bishops watched in horror as the Lower House piled up a series of censures and grievances against the post-Revolutionary governments. On 18 April Atterbury went a step further in marching at the head of the clergy to confront Tenison, who furiously demanded that the

Lower House submit to his prorogation. The Lower House's continued defiance was marked by a request to Oxford that the University confer a Doctorate of Divinity by diploma on Atterbury, to which the University assented. The meetings of the Lower House also continued to attack irreligion and Latitudinarianism, and ignored the bishops. Eventually in June William III was forced to issue a writ dissolving the Convocation. It was increasingly difficult for Tenison and the bishops to see the Whigs and Latitudinarians as other than their natural allies against the inflammatory views of radical High-Church clergy like Atterbury, and historians have tended to see the Convocation controversy as simply a battle between High Church and Latitudinarian thinking.

The shifting position of many clergy at this time is illustrated by Thomas Naish, sub-dean of Salisbury. Naish reluctantly took the oath to William and Mary on the last day permitted by law in 1689. However, Naish came under the influence of the Whig Bishop Gilbert Burnet, accepting £30 a year from him to finish his education, and later his nomination to St Edmund's Salisbury and the subdeanery of the cathedral. Naish was sufficiently reconciled to the Revolutionary settlement to be commended by Burnet for preaching a sermon in Salisbury cathedral in 1696 on the thoroughly Whiggish text 'to him that overcomes will I grant to sit with me on my throne'.[9] In the same year Naish joined Burnet and fifty-six other Salisbury clergy in signing an 'association' against the Fenwick plot on William III's life. However, Naish experienced growing disquiet at the 'feuds and distractions' of the Dissenters in his parish. In 1701 Naish opposed the pro-Dissent Whig Parliamentary candidates at the election, and his relationship with Burnet began to cool when the bishop failed to appoint Naish to a prebend he had expected. Naish also supported pro-Atterbury candidates for Convocation and was encouraged by others to resent the bond that Burnet had forced him to sign on accepting the subdeanery, in which he undertook to resign it if he took a living outside the diocese. Having broken with Burnet, Naish accepted the rectory of Corton in Bath and Wells diocese, where in 1708 he was elected as a representative in Convocation with the support of the High-Church diocesan, George Hooper.[10]

William's death in 1702 brought a sense of relief to the High Churchmen of Naish's kidney, particularly since he was succeeded by Queen Anne, a staunch Anglican Tory. But Anne was no prisoner of dogma and her political friends were principally moderate Tories and Whigs. The elections to parliament and Convocation strengthened Atterbury's hand. High-Church demands to act against the growth of Dissent grew apace, and some Tories saw their allies in the Church as a useful stick to beat the Whig government. But there was disquiet among ambitious Tories, such as

Edward Harley. Through the offices of Harley, who made vague promises to Atterbury, Convocation met and elected Dean Aldrich of Christ Church, a moderate Tory, to the prolocutorship. But the attempt to manage Convocation came too late; the Tory MPs for Oxford and Cambridge, Bromley and Annesley, introduced an Occasional Conformity Bill into the House of Commons, seeking to outlaw those Dissenters who occasionally conformed to the Church to qualify for an office under the Test Act. To Atterbury's disgust Harley, alarmed at the speed of events, allowed the Bill to be destroyed in the House of Lords. However, the Queen signalled her approval of the Bill at the end of 1702 by the subtle measure of evicting its chief opponent, Bishop Burnet, from his grace and favour apartment at St James's Palace.

Much of 1703 was taken up with attempts to prepare the way for a second Occasional Conformity Bill. Atterbury strongly supported the Bill, which in December 1703 easily passed the House of Commons and was lost in the House of Lords, this time by just twelve votes, with all but two bishops voting against it. In opposing it, Simon Patrick felt that he was expressing the eirenicism of the Church:

> I looked upon it [the Bill] as making a manifest breach upon the act of indulgence, which had made great peace, quiet and love among us. For it struck at the very best of the nonconformists; who, looked upon us as good Christians that had nothing sinful in our worship, [and] thought they ought upon occasion to communicate with us. . . .[11]

In frustration, Atterbury again led the Lower House in listing clerical grievances, to which he now added the wilful negligence of the bishops. But Harley was determined to use Atterbury to quieten the turbulent ecclesiastical debates, and in July 1704 appointed him to the deanery of Carlisle.[12] Harley's persuasion gradually worked, he convinced Atterbury that the interests of the Tories and the High Church party in the long term meant that they had to show that Tory High Churchmen could be trusted not to disturb the Queen's government. Such was Harley's success that in the Convocation of 1705 sarcastic comments were made that the northern air had moderated Atterbury's mood.[13] His hard-line Tory allies in the House of Commons tacked the Occasional Conformity Bill onto a Land Tax Bill, but it was a tactical error, infuriating back benchers who defeated the proposal in November. For Atterbury the greatest humiliation of his alliance with Harley came when Wake was preferred to the important diocese of Lincoln.

The 'Convocation crisis' abated in 1705 as quickly as it had arisen.

Ironically for the self-proclaimed opponent of Erastianism, Atterbury had been 'managed' by Harley and the government into moderating his zeal for the rights of the clergy in Convocation. It remained the paradox of Atterbury's position that the champion of the party which sought the independence of the Church from the State was so active in the systems that ensured the interdependence of the two. In the election of 1705 the Whigs stormed into power, and Atterbury's hopes for an Occasional Conformity Bill, which had largely superseded the claims of Convocation as his goal, were dashed. For some disillusioned Tory High Churchmen, like Trelawny, the Convocation affair had speeded their path to an accommodation with moderate Whigs, and, whilst Trelawny remained a Tory in politics, he disassociated himself from Atterbury and the High Churchmen.

The final act in the Convocation drama indicated the desire of the government for peace in the Church. In October 1705 Convocation met, and the bishops sent the Lower House a provocative motion asserting that those who, during and after the election of 1705, had argued that the Church was in danger were acting from motives of prejudice and ambition. The High Churchmen in the Lower House naturally sought to amend the motion; but Tenison told them that they could only accept or reject it. The Lower House erupted at what they saw as a calculated insult by the archbishop. Atterbury abandoned Harley's policy of caution and spoke vehemently against the archbishop. The government was appalled by the renewed conflict: when Godolphin and Marlborough joined the Whig junta they agreed to quieten the Church, and asserted that ecclesiastical patronage could only go to those who paid due respect to their Queen and their ecclesiastical superiors. On 1 March 1706 the Queen herself promised to take action to maintain her supremacy and 'due subordination of presbyters to bishops'. On hearing the Queen's statement in the Jerusalem Chamber Atterbury lost his composure. He grabbed the prolocutor's sleeve and called to his brethren of the Lower House to return to their own chamber; by the time they got there, they found that Convocation had been prorogued.[14] The 1706 session of Convocation was so cowed that the Lower House accepted the bishops' motion without demur. The Queen was also determined that the Lower House should not defy her. When, in 1707, the Lower House made modestly critical noises about the Act of Union with Scotland, Tenison called the Lower House before him, pronounced the prolocutor contumacious and read a stern letter from the Queen expressing her jealousy that Convocation should gainsay her prerogatives. In the wake of the crushing of Atterbury, moderate churchmen of both parties gained advancement: Trelawny to Winchester while Blackhall and Dawes were consecrated bishops.

What is the significance of the Convocation controversy? Perhaps it was as insignificant as the 'Phalaris controversy' of 1694–5 between Richard Bentley and Charles Boyle.[15] In some respects the Convocation controversy might be described as simply dissension and scholarship. Other than for the participants in the debates, the immediate matters at stake were arcane and obscure. Maurice Wheeler claimed 'the poor country parsons that know nothing of the matter, were instructed to vote for such as would assert their rights against the usurpation of the bishops'.[16] In such circumstances the likelihood of sustaining the controversy for long were low. It is equally unlikely that many of the country clergy supported Atterbury's intellectual position. Most clergy probably shared Wake's view of kingship, but supported Atterbury from a vague sense of grievance and concern at the rise of Dissent. The clergy had also been unsettled by the abandonment of censorship in 1695, which permitted attacks on the Church as much as on the monarchy and government; and the clergy felt aggrieved at the weight of taxation to pay for the war with France that they felt fell upon them disproportionately. It also seems implausible that the controversy can be claimed to have clarified the divisions between High and Low Churchmen. In reality, the arguments over Convocation were between High Churchmen of different hues. Atterbury represented clergy who resented Toleration and sought to advance clerical claims by making the Church independent of the State. Wake represented High-Church canonists who sought to elevate the rights of the Church in law by binding it tightly to the State. A number of Wake's supporters were also churchmen who came close to the Non-jurors' view in supporting an Anglican model of monarchy which emphasised the sacerdotal nature of kingship, and the rights it gave the King over the Church.

The true voice of early eighteenth-century Anglicanism is probably represented by Sir William Dawes, Queen Anne's favourite chaplain and bishop of Chester from 1708. From 1696, as the Convocation controversy developed, Dawes preached a series of sermons before William III and Queen Anne calling for moderation and quiet. His sermon on 'a wounded spirit who can bear?' argued that a distracted mind destroys 'true peace and tranquillity' and makes men 'turbulent and vexacious'. That on the beatitude 'blessed are the poor in spirit' Dawes took to mean blessed are those without conceit or pride which engendered anger and controversy. That on 'a good conscience [is] a pledge of future happiness' raised restraint as a seminal quality for Christians. Finally his sermon on 'the danger of talking too much and the wisdom of the contrary' argued that churchmen should not give offence with their tongues, and 'he that restraineth his lips is wise'. These tenets which assured Dawes three reprints of his collected sermons between 1708 and 1711, represents the true spirit of Anglicanism more than the abstruse arguments of the Convocation controversialists.[17]

Within a few years the Convocation controversy was supplanted in the minds of High and Low Churchmen. From 1705 Benjamin Hoadly and Francis Atterbury had engaged in a squabble from their respective London pulpits, reviving the Revolutionary debate on the legitimacy of resistance to rulers. Sermons and letters were published over the three years which followed that alternately advanced and denounced the High-Church doctrine of passive obedience. On 5 November 1709, however, Henry Sacheverell preached a sermon on the text 'in perils among false brethren'. It was the rehearsal of an earlier hectoring sermon against Dissent and Toleration and a vicious denunciation of Hoadly and Godolphin. Its core was a re-statement of the absolute submission of subjects to their rulers, which implicitly impugned the legitimacy of the Revolution. Its peroration parodied the Latitudinarian position as:

> to assert separation [by Dissenters] from her [the Church's] communion to be no schism, or that schism is no damnable sin, that occasional conformity is no hypocrisy, but rather for the benefit of the Church, that a Christian may serve God in any way or congregation, as well by extempore prayer as by a prescribed form of liturgy. . . .[18]

It was a statement of the High-Church agenda.

For the ministry, Sacheverell's sly denunciation of the Whigs as little better than Dissenters and atheists was intolerable. Unwisely, the government impeached Sacheverell, guaranteeing him a public performance for his views, and a thorough re-examination of his views on the legitimacy of the Revolution of 1688. Worse still, Sacheverell's impeachment in the House of Lords was avowedly political rather than judicial, allowing High-Church clergy to defend him from a political 'persecution'. While Sacheverell was being cheered on his daily processions around London, Hoadly and Atterbury poured out their views in print. Atterbury, and Sacheverell's shrewd lawyer Simon Harcourt, managed Sacheverell's publicity campaign brilliantly, distributing over forty thousand copies of his sermon. His opponents tried to attack him as a pawn of the French and of Catholicism, but without great success in the face of popular support for Sacheverell.

At the impeachment of Sacheverell in March 1710, the Whigs tried to drive a wedge between High-Church ideology and the establishment by claiming that he had impugned the Queen's title to the crown, that he had questioned the legal toleration of Dissent and had called down factionalism on the Church and State. Harcourt's defence was that of a David facing the Whig Goliath. However, to show Sacheverell's harmlessness, Harcourt abandoned the more extreme positions adopted in the sermon. He claimed Sacheverell had merely preached the historic doctrine of the Church, and he had not intended to promote a slavish passivity, such as might be advanced by Jacobites. Glibly and implausibly, Harcourt even claimed that Sacheverell had intended the passivity he had supported to include obedience to Parliament. A day was spent inflaming popular opinion by reciting attacks on Toland and Blount, and suggesting that Sacheverell was seeking to defend the Church from them. Whatever the Whig cause, the mob refused to see Sacheverell as other than a defender of the Church and Queen, and failed to see the logical inconsistencies of his position.[191]

Inherent in the articles of impeachment was the assertion that Sacheverell had disturbed the peace of the Church and the unity of the kingdom. Nicholas Lechmere asserted that the Queen's support for the Church was 'a fundamental and essential part of the union of the two kingdoms'. It was this security that Sacheverell had violated. Whig politicians stepped forward to denounce Sacheverell's disturbance of the peace. Walpole stated that Sacheverell's arguments were injurious 'to the peace and quiet of the kingdom'; Sir John Hawles cited as a model the silence of the apostles during the reigns of Vespasian and Trajan, and Stanhope pointed out that

> had the Doctor, my Lords, in the remaining part of his sermon, preach'd up peace, quietness, and the like; and shewn how happy we are under Her Majesty's administration; and exhorted obedience to it, he had never been called to answer a charge at your lordships' bar.[20]

Sergeant Parker claimed that Sacheverell was an incendiary intent on causing 'passion, heat and violence'. He was shocked that Sacheverell had stripped himself of a priest's 'peaceful and charitable temper, which the Christian religion requires of all its professors . . .'. To Parker, Sacheverell was

> one [who] should inflame the mob to such a degree of rage and mistaken zeal, as to forget the spirit of the Gospel and to believe it their duty to serve God by breaking the public peace, and to support his Church by pulling down all meeting houses and rifling the houses of all dissenters. . . .[21]

In his speech during the trial, Gilbert Burnet argued that the consequences of clergymen behaving like Sacheverell was that the laity might emulate turbulent priests and disquiet the country.[22] In short, the underlying theme of Sacheverell's trial was his disturbance of the unity and peace of the Church and State.

In the vote in the House of Lords the bishops were divided: Burnet, Cumberland, Fleetwood, Moore, Talbot, Trimnell and Wake voted for Sacheverell's guilt; Crewe, Compton, Dawes, Hooper, Sharp and Sprat voted for his acquittal.[23] Sacheverell was found guilty, but his punishment of three years' suspension from preaching and the public burning of his sermon by the common hangman, was seen to be so mild as to be a vindication; it represented the failure of the Whig will to exact a greater penalty in the face of overwhelming public support for Sacheverell.

While the government had gambled on the trial of Sacheverell and lost, much of the public, especially beyond the metropolis, was bemused by the matter. After the sermon had been published the *Observator* commented of it,

> I can't see how those men can be called Christians, who are so void of charity to Dissenters and moderate churchmen as to damn them. . . . They that have one Lord, one faith, and one baptism are of one body, as the Apostle tells us, Eph. 4.4.5. And that the Church of England and Dissenters have the same Lord, the same faith and the same baptism, is evident by their subscription to the same doctrine according to the Toleration Act. . . .[24]

The trial of Sacheverell, together with the loss of the Queen's support, sounded the death knell for the Whig government. In the election of 1710 the Tories were returned to power; but otherwise the significance of the trial lay in the illustration it provides of the intellectual weakness and inconsistency of the militant High-Church position. During his trial Sacheverell proclaimed his loyalty to Queen Anne, though all his dogma hinted at Jacobitism. His statements on passive obedience in the civil sphere sat uneasily with Atterbury's denunciation of Erastianism and, if applied to the Church, made the High-Church position over the Convocation crisis one of marked inconsistency. The flawed foundations of the militant High-Church position was one of the causes of its collapse after 1714. The real significance of the trial lay in the fact that political and religious leaders focused on the issue of unity, and the consequential fear of a disunited nation. Equally the trial highlighted the continuity of an ill-defined sense of unease and unrest among the Anglican clergy and laity over the growth of Dissent. It was a concern that was soon addressed by the new Tory government.

It would, however, be an error to assume that the Sacheverell affair was other than a passing trauma for the Church. Perhaps the growing concern over the health of Queen Anne attracted attention to the stark choice of a Protestant succession or a Catholic restoration. The fury that divided those of opposing views cooled quickly; even the bishops reported a swift decline in partisanship.[25] In Bristol there were differing approaches, the trial of Sacheverell did not appear to disturb the even tenor of the Church's desire for greater unity with the Dissenters.[26] Nevertheless, the electoral consequence of the Sacheverell trial was that the Church and its interest appeared to possess the power to mobilise voters toward the Tories who claimed to represent the High-Church movement, and away from the Whigs. In Salisbury, when in May 1710 Bishop Burnet rebuked the corporation of the city for rejoicing at Sacheverell's deliverance in a sermon, the mayor and corporation rose and left the cathedral.[27] The new Tory administration predictably sought to reward the Tory churchmen for their support. It seemed as if there was a Tory–High Church resurgence. Atterbury was again elected prolocutor of the Lower House of Convocation and busied himself on motions to advance the rights of the clergy, even at the cost of impugning Tenison's metropolitan authority as president of Convocation.

Undoubtedly Atterbury saw the Convocation of 1710 as the start rather than the end of a Tory–High Church resurgence, and even seemed intent on re-asserting the power of Church courts. However, as in 1705, Harley had no intention of permitting an uncontrolled High-Church backlash. Atterbury was marginalised by Harley and his ecclesiastical ambitions failed.[28] A key element in the restraint of Tory–High Church triumphalism was Queen Anne's refusal to give way to factionalism. During the trial of William Whiston in Convocation for heterodoxy Queen Anne deliberately mislaid the papers twice.[29] In frustration, Atterbury resorted to drawing up lists of books to be denounced for heterodoxy, including *A Historical Preface to Primitive Christianity* by William Whiston, and Samuel Clarke's *The Scriptural Doctrine of the Trinity* for which he secured Clarke's dismissal as a royal chaplain. The savagery with which Whiston was censured by the Convocation of 1710–11 even engaged moderate Whigs like White Kennett who said of Whiston: 'if we have any discipline left I hope it may be exercised upon one who has more than once subscribed our articles'.[30] But Atterbury's real goal was to influence the House of Commons. The first proposal of Convocation was universally acceptable and was carried into legislation in 1711 as the Act for the Building of Fifty New Churches, which sought to inaugurate a renaissance in London's church-building and religious life, paid from a duty on coal. The advancement of Atterbury to the deanery of Christ Church, Oxford indicated the government's support for the attempts of the Lower House.

While Atterbury raised dust in Convocation, other voices argued in favour of promoting unity within the Church. Daniel Whitby, precentor of Salisbury and former chaplain to Bishop Seth Ward, was one of those who had urged the Caroline Church to co-operate with Dissent in his *Protestant*

Reconciler (1672). In 1714 Whitby rose again to urge unity on the Church in *A Dissuasive from Enquiring into the Doctrine of the Trinity.* . . . Whitby recognised that the clergy would be asked 'shall I not be permitted fully to understand my creed?' But his response was that an easy explanation of the doctrine of the Trinity had defeated men of the calibre of Sherlock, Bull, South, Cudworth and others and there were numerous books on the subject including Clarke's censured work. Whitby's answer was to 'hold fast the orthodox faith, and live in expectation of a full, clear and ample confutation of all the Doctor [Clarke] hath or can say against it'.[31] Whitby also asserted that Church doctrines should be beyond discussion, and accepted by the people as simply as the Ten Commandments, the catechism and the sacraments. For Whitby, the danger was that 'you will be got into a dark and endless labyrinth' of theology. Whitby preferred to 'look upon this, as the generality of Christians do, as a great mystery, rather to be adored than curiously enquired into . . .'. Whitby also urged his readers to charity towards those who did question the doctrine, citing Tenison's claim that there could be no fault where there was no wilful transgression of Church doctrine. The core of Whitby's case was that enquiry into doctrine profited no one.[32] For Whitby peace and tranquillity in the Church was best achieved by a simple acceptance of the orthodox and traditional doctrines of the Church.

Similarly there were those who were vigilant in defending the Church from divisive Sacheverellite High-Church views. William Fleetwood's *Letter to an Inhabitant of the Parish of St Andrew's Holbourn about New Ceremonies in the Church* (1717), was occasioned by some parishioners of Henry Sacheverell at St Andrew's Holborn, who were concerned at his introduction of a rule that the congregation should rise and stand at the reading of the gospel. Fleetwood reassured the parishioners that Sacheverell could not enforce his request 'people are much at their liberty in their family or closet devotions, but must not innovate in congregations'. But his objection to Sacheverell was more profound; divisiveness and treason went hand in hand.

> What if, after all, these innovations of standing up at the reading [of] the second lesson . . . be not sincerely intended for greater decencies sake and shewing more reverence, but merely to start up a new distinction and make a farther difference betwixt those who come to the public worship in the same place and at the same time, with one another, but who are of different parties with respect to the King and State affairs? You know in what sort of people they are who chiefly promote these innovations, and are most forward to distinguish themselves by little ceremonious observances; and you also know what King it is they incline to.[33]

The Tories in Parliament were less impressed by such arguments for peace than the clergy. During 1711 they introduced an Occasional Conformity Bill, which secured an easy passage in both Houses. The Occasional Conformity Act, though it reaffirmed the terms of the Toleration Act, offended many: Dissenters who were well-affected to the establishment; Whigs who were attracted to ideas of freedom of conscience; and Latitudinarian Anglicans who, like Hoadly, still hankered for a greater Comprehension of Dissent into the Church. Most Dissenters, reassured by statements from the Whigs and the representative of the Electress Sophia that they would repeal the Act following the Protestant succession, remained in their offices and reluctantly conformed to the Church. The London Alderman Sir Thomas Abney made the required public conformity, but employed Isaac Watts as his household chaplain for private dissenting worship.[34]

The Tory government also enacted the Schism Act in 1714, a more pernicious piece of legislation. It was based on the punitive Clarendon Code of the seventeenth century and inspired by Sacheverell's sermon, which had attacked Dissenters' schools for promoting irreligion and disunity. It required all schoolteachers to hold an episcopal licence, and to conform to the Church. The Act was far more damaging to Dissent that the Occasional Conformity Act, since it struck at the academies, the nurseries of Dissent. Where the Whigs sought to encourage it, the Tories were unashamed in their desire to force Dissenters to conform to the Church. During the debate on the Schism Bill, Bromley, the High-Church Tory leader in the House of Commons, was explicit in offering to drop the Bill if the Whigs would agree to disenfranchise Dissenters. The attempts by Dissenters to appeal to the bishops, to Harley (himself the product of a Dissenting education) and even to the Queen came to nothing, though the bishops led by Wake opposed the Bill in the House of Lords. Only the death of Anne on the day of the enactment left the Schism Act as a hollow piece of legislation.

The death of Anne was potentially as great a crisis for the Church as her accession was a triumph; it was as if the clock had been turned back to 1688. For, like William III, George I was a Protestant but not an Anglican and therefore likely to be more sympathetic to Toleration than Anne. In such circumstances it was sometimes difficult to remember that the succession of George I was a means of safeguarding the Church of England. The Jacobites who sought a restoration of the Stuarts planned that, if successful, Atterbury would have a ministerial post, but the moderate Tories and Whigs secured the succession of the Hanoverians. The new regime refused to implement the Schism Act, and gradually loosened the ties that Atterbury had used to bind the Church and State. The accession of George I in 1714 alarmed many but roused few to action. The new king made his position clear after the Jacobite rising:

> the endeavour to persuade my people that the Church of England is in danger under my government has been the main artifice in carrying on the design [of the uprising]. This insinuation after the solemn assurance I have given, and my having laid hold of all opportunities to do everything that may tend to the advantage of the Church of England is both unjust and ungrateful.[35]

George I and his new administration understood the need to demonstrate their affection for the Church. The new king conformed to the Church of England at services in the Chapel Royal, and he appointed largely moderate bishops. Wake was promoted to Canterbury and new bishops embodied a variety of moderate churchmanship, including John Wynne, Richard Willis, William Talbot, Edmund Gibson, Edward Chandler and John Potter; though, just as the Tories had advanced Atterbury to Rochester in 1713, so the Whigs appointed Hoadly to Bangor in 1715. In December 1714 George I re-issued the directions to the archbishops and bishops on the dangers of clergy meddling in the affairs of the State, and he also promised to call a meeting of Convocation. Unlike Queen Anne, however, George I indicated the issues he wished Convocation to consider, among them regulating of marriage licences, consecration of churches, qualifications for orders and rules for confirmation.

The Church Whigs, led by William Wake, were hopeful of an accommodation with the new Whig-dominated administration elected following the Hanoverian succession. The appointment of Wake to the primacy in 1716 reassured the Whig bishops, and Wake's easy conversation with George I – in French – also boded well. However, Wake was worried by one of the first piece of legislation proposed by the new regime, the Close Vestries Bill, which threatened to remove the incumbent and churchwardens from dominance of parish administration. The Bill passed the House of Commons and was only abandoned in the House of Lords after Wake had spoken powerfully against it. It was a move that brought Wake the approbation of Tory bishops like Smalridge, but their support was to damage rather than benefit him.[36]

Where the Tories sought to bring Dissenters to the Church by closing their academies, the Whigs hoped to woo them by making the Church more accessible. Bishop Benjamin Hoadly's sermon 'My Kingdom is not of this World' (1717) suggested that Christ had not laid down an absolute form of Church government. The implication was that there was no single ecclesiastical order, like episcopacy, that could exclude any Protestants from the Church of England, and that Comprehension was therefore both biblical and proper. The sermon seemed to echo Toland's call for friendship between Low Churchmen and Dissenters. Most people assumed that Hoadly was flying a kite for the new regime, to Test the response to the idea of comprehending Dissent in the Church. Most of his fellow bishops were appalled. Some shared the view, fulsomely expressed by High Churchmen, that Hoadly was undermining the whole basis of the Church and episcopacy. Wake was more pragmatic, and realised that the dismissal of two royal chaplains who attacked Hoadly, and the silencing of Convocation, which was inflamed with anti-Hoadlean feeling, indicated the court's support for him. Hoadly's subsequent appointment as a privy counsellor and dean of the chapel royal was further evidence that he had captured the feeling of the new regime.[37]

The court's public support for Hoadly preceded the Whig observance of its promise to repeal the Occasional Conformity and Schism Acts. The difficulty for Wake was that some Tory bishops had become comfortable with these laws, and Wake himself was convinced that they had become a bulwark for the Church by pressing Dissenters to conform. Some of his brethren however felt that the repeal of the Acts would ward off greater danger. Edmund Gibson, bishop of Lincoln, wrote to Nicolson that Archbishop Wake,

> will not come into anything with regard to the Dissenters; though his four friends here (Worcester, Exeter, Lichfield and myself) are unanimous in our opinion that there is a necessity of something to be done in order to prevent a Tory Parliament and to keep a good understanding among the friends of the present establishment.[38]

Throughout 1717 the ministry tried to gain Wake's support for the repeal. But in 1718 Lord Sunderland's impatience to aid Dissenters prompted the government to abandon Wake and introduce a repeal Bill. In the House of Lords Wake opposed it, largely on the ground that it would alarm Anglicans and would not fully satisfy Dissenters. Nevertheless the repeal measure passed easily through both houses – Gibson arguing that it was a measure that promoted unity among the king's Protestant subjects, and thereby strengthened the 'Protestant government'.[39]

The putative understanding between Wake and the Whigs fell apart, leaving the government feeling betrayed by their new primate. Moreover, Wake's relations with his closest allies, Gibson, Blackburne and Trimnell, were irreparably damaged. The subsequent introduction of a Blasphemy Bill by Lords Willoughby de Broke and Nottingham proved a further disappointment to the ministry. Though Wake had grave misgivings he supported the Bill, but failed to bring a majority of the episcopal bench with him. The failure of the reform of the universities, and of Lord Sunderland to achieve a repeal of the Test Act, reflected an element of division within the Whigs. Radical Whigs, such as Sunderland, sought a progressive policy to support Dissent, whereas moderate Whigs, like Walpole, were anxious not to fuel anti-clericalism. The Whig majority stood in the mainstream of the orthodox establishment of 1689: it opposed a weakening of the Test Act, but didn't support the unbridled Anglicanism of the Blasphemy Bill of 1721. Minor concessions such as the Quieting of Corporations and the Quaker Affirmation Acts, which respectively permitted unchallenged Dissenters to retain municipal office and relieved Quakers of the obligation to swear oaths, were comparatively uncontentious, but divided the bishops, and therefore passed with ease. But the death of Stanhope and Sunderland in 1721 and 1722 respectively deprived the radical Whigs of their leaders, to be replaced by the moderate Walpole and Townshend who were determined to preserve the status quo for as long as possible in alliance with the Church.[40]

The experience of the quarter century after the Glorious Revolution suggested that the period of greatest calm in the Church had been in the early years of William III's reign. This was not lost on Walpole. By 1723 Walpole sought another ecclesiastical leader, one less accommodating to the Tory bishops than Wake, who would help the Whigs in the House of Lords and would usher in a return to tranquillity and calm in the relationship between Church and State. Gibson's rise coincided with Atterbury's fall. In 1723 Gibson succeeded to the diocese of London, and Atterbury's clandestine correspondence with the Pretender was revealed first in the Secret Committee and later in the House of Lords. Atterbury's treason was laid bare in deciphered correspondence and, stripped of his bishopric, he was banished to France.[41] The bitter lesson of Atterbury's treason not only re-affirmed the authority of the post-Revolutionary State to deprive a bishop of his office, but also suggested that only moderate churchmen were likely to be politically reliable because militant High Churchmen were tarred with the Jacobite brush.

After the death of Bishop Charles Trimnell of Winchester – Sunderland's protégé and ecclesiastical adviser – the advancement of Gibson to leadership of the Church was confirmed by the extraordinary series of nine episcopal appointments that he filled in the summer of 1723, Walpole accepting all his nominations. Indeed the confidence of Carteret, Townshend and Walpole in Gibson was such that he eclipsed Wake, and other senior bishops, such as Willis, in dominance of the Bench's relations with the government. As Newcastle wrote to Townshend of Gibson 'he is and must be our "pope" '.[42] In May and June 1723 the value of Gibson as the Whig pope was seen when he led twenty-two fellow bishops into the lobby in defence of the ministry over the South Sea inquiry. The government survived by five votes.[43] Gibson's credentials for such a role were unimpeachable. His early career had been spent in historical research, and later as an aide to Archbishop Tenison. In this position he had seen the damage caused by the Convocation controversy to both Church and State. He had written the monolithic *Codex Juris Ecclesiastici Anglicani* (1713), which was to be the principal work of canon law for the next two centuries, and which epitomised the status of the Church in relation to the State. He was a High Churchman, dedicated to strict rule of the Church by canon law and to the defence of the Church's position against Dissent by efficient ecclesiastical administration; he was orthodox in ends and Whig in means. He was to establish thirteen years of relative tranquillity in the Church's relations with the State and to achieve a remarkable reconciliation of the Tory clergy to the succession of 1714. His strategy was:

> that there is noe way to preserve the Church, but by preserving the present establishment in the State; and that there is far greater probability that the Tories will be able to destroy our present establishm't in the State, than the Dissenters will be able to destroy our establishm't in ye Church.[44]

The goal Gibson set himself was the neutralisation of the Tories, who posed a far greater danger to the Church than Dissent. Many Tory clergy were sympathetic to Jacobitism and this raised the question of whether the Church justified its privileged position in the State. Gibson's concentration on the Tories distracted him from the claims of the Dissenters and, in time the Whigs found their demands irresistible.

Gibson hoped to be able to win over the Church and clergy to an accommodation with the Whigs, and saw a means to do it in the emollient use of preferment. Gibson's schemes to establish Whitehall preacherships for eminent clergy in the two universities and to found the Regius professorships of Modern History and of languages at Oxford and Cambridge were successful attempts to harness the influence of the universities to the Hanoverian regime, in stark contrast to Sunderland's heavy-handed attempt at reform. Gibson's attempt to pacify the clergy at large was also determined by patronage: he proposed that all livings in the gift of the Crown should be conferred upon the clergy within the diocese in which the vacancy occurred. Loyalty to the house of Hanover would follow the routine appointment of diocesan clergy to vacancies, as well as the expectation of it. The schemes were approved by the government and on

6 May 1724 the King issued a proclamation to its effect to all archbishops and bishops. However, the proposal for the preferment of the clergy failed when Lord King succeeded as lord chancellor in 1725 and refused to accept any surrender of his patronage to diocesan bishops. Walpole and Townshend blanched at the prospect of losing a lord chancellor and acquiesced in the face of his intransigence. Gibson, though disappointed, reconciled himself to the failure of this part of his plan after receiving assurances that he would play the major part in the nominations to vacant dioceses. In this last also, Gibson hoped to be able to promote loyalty to the house of Hanover by advancing bishops to the bench on the basis of seniority and loyalty. In this, as in the scheme for diocesan patronage, Gibson was adopting strategies that had been considered and discussed under both William III and Queen Anne, and had been associated with the pacification of the Church by advancing proven moderate churchmen.

Gibson's first controversial decision on episcopal preferment was to deny Francis Hare's nomination to Bath and Wells in 1727. Hare was a staunch Whig, a former protégé of Marlborough but was too partisan and controversial for Gibson, who also held that new bishops should not be leap-frogged over their seniors for the best bishoprics. Consequently, the moderate Whig John Wynne was advanced from St Asaph to Bath and Wells and Hare succeeded him at St Asaph. By and large, Gibson's preferments went to moderate men like Richard Willis, John Green and John Leng. But Gibson also triumphed over Archbishop Lancelot Blackburne of York in 1726 in nominating Samuel Peploe, a staunch Whig, to Chester over the claims of Blackburne's nominee, the thirty-three year old John Gilbert.

The succession of George II in 1727 brought new influences into the contest for nominations to sees: Queen Caroline and Lady Sundon. In 1727, however, Gibson vanquished the new Queen's attempt to foist the Arian Samuel Clarke onto the bench of bishops and in 1730 he blocked Hoadly's preferment to Durham. He saw both as attempts to promote heterodox divines within the Church. But Gibson did not control all appointments. He could not prevent Caroline from advancing Thomas Sherlock, a moderate ministerial Tory, to Bangor in 1728 and on to Salisbury in 1734, or the preferment of Hoadly to Winchester in 1734, or the appointment of Robert Butts to Norwich in 1733. Nevertheless in 1731 Sydall's appointment to St David's, and translation to Gloucester, Tanner's appointment to St Asaph, Claggett's appointment to succeed Sydall at St David's and Chandler's promotion to Durham were all Gibson's nominations.

Though it is easy to present the pact between Gibson and Walpole as a passing convenience, and one which fell apart in acrimony, Walpole and Gibson were firm friends up to 1736.[45] And though Gibson remained enormously frustrated at the confinement of the agreement to the exercise of patronage, because he had hopes of leading a religious reformation, their pact secured for the Church a critical period of calm and tranquillity. It was in defence of the *status quo* that Gibson expended his credit with Walpole. Gibson had indicated his commitment to the pact in 1731 when, in his visitation charge, he had made clear that his clergy owed a debt of loyalty to the Whig administration for defending them from a Bill recently introduced to relieve Dissenters of tithe payments.[46] But the alliance was subject to intolerable strains from radical Whigs who supported the desire of Dissenters for religious and political freedom. The elections of 1727 brought an infusion of support for radical Whigs to the House of Commons. Worse still, for Gibson, in 1730 Townshend left politics, removing a stalwart Anglican from the ministry.

In February 1730 a Bill was advanced to prevent suits for tithe payments which had not been made for some years, and would therefore be regarded as lapsed. The measure passed a first reading but was crushed by Walpole in March. In the same month a proposal was made to prevent episcopal translations, again the government intervened. During 1733, however, it was Gibson who protected Walpole by leading his brethren in the House of Lords to prevent a re-opening of investigations into the South Sea Bubble affair. A popular ballad – the Knight and the Prelate – depicted Walpole calling to Gibson 'help Lords or I perish'. In the same session a proposal was made to strip Church courts of their powers. It passed the House of Commons, but was abandoned in the House of Lords through government influence. Another simultaneous proposal, to take Church rates out of the hands of the churchwardens and place it in the control of JPs, was also killed off by the government. Gibson's disquiet was not simply that these anti-Church measures came from Walpole's own party, but that they sought to undermine the establishment of 1689. Gibson regarded the Church, the Protestant succession and the limited Toleration of 1689 as pillars of the settlement that were mutually supportive, and feared that to remove or weaken one would imperil all. But Gibson's ability to appeal to Walpole was marred by the Rundle affair. In 1733 Thomas Rundle was proposed to succeed to the vacant see of Gloucester. Rundle was a Latitudinarian and Gibson suspected him of heterodoxy, but he had the backing of Lord Chancellor Talbot and the court. Gibson announced that he would even refuse to consecrate him if appointed. Walpole, torn between Gibson and the court, left the see of Gloucester vacant for a year for the elections to pass and then appointed Martin Benson to it in 1734. Gibson was triumphant, but it was difficult to avoid the public perception that his influence with Walpole was too great, and that he was an over-mighty subject. Walpole certainly resented having to choose between his lord chancellor and his 'pope' which lost him the support of Talbot, and further imperilled his majority as Talbot's son William abandoned Walpole in the House of Commons.

In March 1736 the Protestant Dissenting Deputies proposed a repeal of the Test Act, a reward for electoral support for the Whigs that they felt was long overdue – especially after Walpole was returned in the 1735 election with a narrow majority. In spite of Walpole's request that they leave the matter to rest the Dissenters pressed on, and he was forced to block the proposal in the House of Commons, at the risk of imperilling Whig unity. Gibson had already expressed his views on the repeal of the Test Act in *The Dispute Adjusted: About the Proper Time of Applying for a Repeal of the Corporation and Test Act, by Shewing that no time is proper* (1732), whose title encapsulated its argument.

In March 1736 however, two radical Whig bills were introduced into the House of Commons: the Mortmain Bill, which would prevent endowment of the Church, and the Quaker Tithe Bill, which would exempt Quakers from some legal actions for payment of tithes. Whilst these bills were the culmination of the anti-clericalism evident from 1730, Walpole viewed them as an opportunity to re-align the Whig factions. He may also have regarded them as different in character to the earlier ecclesiastical proposals, which struck at the constitution and the institutions of the Church. In contrast the Mortmain and Quaker Tithes Bills were more modest measures to defend dying men from priestly solicitations and to relieve Quakers from often ineffective and costly suits to enforce tithe payments. The debates on these bills were the opportunity for the expression of strong anti-clerical feeling in the House of Commons. The Mortmain Bill passed into law and Walpole appeared to be unable to resist pressure from his supporters to accept the Quaker Tithe Bill, but he did not consult Gibson before finally agreeing to support its passage. It may be that the bills were an attempt by Walpole to divide opposition Whigs and Tories by picking measures which would force a wedge between them.[47] Either way, on the bench of bishops there was consternation and Thomas Sherlock wrote pamphlets opposing the Quaker Tithe Bill, which won over Queen Caroline. As a last resort Gibson broke with the ministry and went into open opposition to Walpole, circulating a request to his clergy to write and petition in opposition to the bills, and opposing the measure in a circular letter to the bishops. The request yielded over forty petitions to the House of Commons against the Bill. At the last minute Walpole threw his policy into reverse and opposed the Bill, requiring the lord chancellor and Lord Hardwicke to vote against it. In the vote in the House of Lords, Gibson marshalled fifteen bishops and six proxies – enemies as well as friends – against the Quaker Tithe Bill which fell by 54 votes to 35.[48] However Walpole felt furiously aggrieved by Gibson's open opposition and his resort to extra-Parliamentary action.

The clergy of London voted thanks to Gibson at Sion College. In contrast there were harsh words at court and after a chilly exchange of letters the alliance between Gibson and Walpole was over. Gibson asked

> Can the bishops go on to support the Whig cause with such unanimity and zeal and justify their doing so to themselves and the clergy, unless some restraint be laid upon the lay Whigs . . . ?[49]

William Wake's death in January 1737 brought an opportunity for the ministry to punish Gibson by refusing him the primacy.[50] Subjected to much abuse for ambition and pride, Gibson gained nothing personally from the alliance with Walpole.

It has been easy to misrepresent the pact between Gibson and Walpole as a piece of corrupt Erastianism. In reality it was an attempt to sustain the settlement of 1689 intact. For Gibson this meant making orthodox appointments and defending the Church, the Protestant succession and a limited Toleration. His hopes to go beyond that, and build a reinvigorated Church had been dashed. But Gibson's alliance with Walpole, judged a failure by historians, was in reality a success. Gibson's aim had been to win over the clergy for the establishment in Church and State and there is evidence from a number of recent studies to suggest that this policy had a significant impact beyond Fulham Palace and the Cockpit. Jeffrey Chamberlain's study of Sussex High Churchmanship suggests that Tory High Church opposition to the Hanoverian regime underwent a dramatic decline between 1714 and 1745.[51] Many Tory High Churchmen were reconciled to the House of Hanover in part because of the perception that the Whigs had changed their position:

> the Whigs offered their protection, benefaction and patronage for the Church, and parsons responded with gratitude and respect. The result of this was that High Churchmen came to trust the Whigs politically and began to align with them rather than the Tories . . . clergymen had lost their fear and distrust for the Whigs.[52]

Whilst Chamberlain's study is focused on Sussex, his thesis is one that applies nationally.[53] Gibson's achievement was to demonstrate to the clergy that those Church-Whigs attached to the house of Hanover were no threat to the Church. Indeed his defence of the Church from the anti-clericalism of radical Whigs in the 1730s had an impact in the minds of clergy across the country. This was uppermost in his mind during the breach of 1736; writing of the union between the Whigs and the bishops, Gibson asked has not the great means of maintaining that union been on the one hand the steady adherence of the Whig bishops and clergy to the lay Whigs . . . and on the other hand a readiness on the part of the lay Whigs to act in such a manner as shall leave the Tory clergy no reasonable ground to accuse the Whig bishops and clergy of joining in measures with the enemies of the Church?[54]

The most convincing evidence of Gibson's reconciliation of the clergy to the Hanoverian establishment came in December 1736, as the dust of the Quaker Tithe debates settled, when Walpole declared to his supporters that 'the clergy were not to be attacked' as they had been in 1736. Radical Whigs were subjected to the same restraints they had been during the Gibson–Walpole pact to prevent the clergy from being driven back into the arms of the Tories.[55] The achievement of the pact was seen in electoral terms in Yorkshire where, between 1710 and 1742, there was a huge shift of clerical votes from the Tories and to the Whigs.[56] Whilst its true that in Cheshire clerical Toryism remained unaffected for the first half of the eighteenth century, the particular circumstances of a strong cadre of Tory grandees meant that the clergy were more resistant to persuasion than they were elsewhere.[57] Other studies have assumed, perhaps wrongly, that the dramatic shift in clerical votes from Tory to Whig after 1714, such as that in Lancashire, was simply a response to the exercise of patronage.[58] But whilst patronage might have achieved electoral advantage for the Whigs it would not have effected the profound cultural change in clerical sentiments suggested by Chamberlain.

An element of success in Gibson's alliance with Walpole was the decline of Latitudinarianism, Dissent and deism. From 1705 to the 1720s Benjamin Hoadly, the standard-bearer of Latitudinarianism, advanced the causes of the comprehension of Dissent, of the right of resistance to rulers and of the radical principles of the Revolution, he also befriended the heterodox Samuel Clarke. Gibson, however, restrained the Hanoverian court's instinctive support for Hoadly and Latitudinarianism. Whilst he was not able to prevent Hoadly's advancement, he had been able to slow it. From 1730, Hoadly was a spent force on the national stage: he lived until 1761 but his ecclesiastical and intellectual influence was gone and, with the exception of a study of the Eucharist in 1734, he published little. He remained a rare Low-Church bishop on a bench composed largely of moderate High Churchmen – though Latitudinarianism remained strong in some dioceses, and Hoadly enjoyed some success in attracting Dissenters to the Church in Winchester.[59] The decline of Latitudinarianism coincided with the defeat of deism. Daniel Waterland, George Berkeley, Joseph Butler, William Law and John Wesley effected an onslaught onto deism from which it did not recover. Deism lacked a coherent theology, and existed largely as an attack on the Church. John Jackson believed that by 1744 that deism had been defeated, and that the Church was stronger and more vibrant as a consequence.[60] Moreover by 1740 there was evidence that Dissent was also in decline. In Winchester diocese in the eighteenth century support for Dissent crumbled. As Chamberlain claims for Sussex:

> Dissent – the most significant impediment to High and Low Church solidarity – had markedly diminished in the years after the Hanoverian succession. As nonconformity faltered, the number of clergymen who decried Whig governance and patronage plunged, because the alliance of Whigs and Dissenters was not nearly the threat to the Anglican Church it had once been.[61]

Nationally there was a decline in the registration of Dissenters' meeting houses from 1,260 in 1710 to 448 in 1740, and 'Dissent was in an advanced state of atrophy in 1740'.[62] Much of the collapse of Dissent was due to the erosion of its puritan cultural underpinning and the damage to the dissenting *raison d'etre* sustained at the Revolution. But it was also in part due to the perception of the Church that Gibson laboured to defend, complemented by the Test and Toleration Acts. The evidence of the success of Anglicanism in making itself accessible to Dissent lies in the records of the diocese of Winchester in the eighteenth century, in which ten former Dissenters received ordination.[63] In 1730 Strickland Gough and Philip Doddridge both agreed that in the wake of the decline of deism, Dissent was also perilously placed.[64] In effect therefore, while deism and Dissent declined, the Church subtly embraced Toleration, a piece of syncretism that enabled it to meet the challenge of rationalism and to play an important role within it rather than oppose it, as continental churches tended to do.

Another consequence of Gibson's co-operation with Walpole was Warburton's *Alliance Between Church and State . . .* (1736). The crisis of 1736 stimulated much debate on the Church's relationship with the State: Lord Hardwicke claimed during the debates on the Mortmain Bill that Gibson's *Codex . . .* had asserted a view of Church–State relations that bordered on divine right and high-flown sacerdotal claims for the Church.[65] Warburton's aim was to defend the *status quo*, but in doing so he produced a new description of Church and State as separate institutions in a mutually beneficial alliance. Warburton's analysis of the alliance was wholly unrepresentative of Anglican ideology, which held that the Church and State were united, or at least more tightly bound together than Warburton admitted. But the implication of the *Alliance . . .* in the context of the 1730s was that the State benefited more from the support of the Church than vice versa, and the relationship was one that was unequal and Erastian. The attention paid by historians to Warburton's work has popularised a view of the relationship between Church and State that was inaccurate and atypical of contemporary opinion.[66] Perhaps Gibson and Walpole's agreement misled Warburton, for Gibson himself was in no doubt that the Church and State, were indissolubly linked by the Church's legal control over spiritual and moral discipline and the position of the king as supreme governor of the Church.[67] Whatever Warburton's misapprehension, Gibson undoubtedly saw his work with Walpole in this light. When he recommended the scheme for Whitehall preacherships, or nominated to bishoprics, or threatened to refuse to consecrate a clergyman, or led a cadre of episcopal voters in the House of Lords, he was acting in the same relationship to the State as a Church court did in condemning and punishing adultery or fornication. His co-operation with Walpole was a means of promoting the spiritual integrity of the Church and of ensuring that the royal prerogatives over the Church were properly discharged.

After the collapse of the Walpole–Gibson alliance, successive ministries avoided reliance on a single episcopal leader. Lord Hardwicke's ascendancy in the governments of the 1740s and 1750s brought a force hostile to the Church to the counsels of the Whigs; but the Duke of Newcastle's growing standing also filled the vacuum left by Gibson's control of Church patronage with a more benevolent force. The Marriage Act of 1753 exemplifies the equivocal position that the bishops faced. Hardwicke sought to regulate marriage law to prevent abuses, and in this he was joined by the episcopate. The Act's creation of a virtual Anglican monopoly on marriage confirmed the Church's victory over Dissent; but the regulation of marriage by ecclesiastical courts was effectively ended by the Act, which appropriated matrimonial cases to the civil courts. This was an outcome that appalled Gibson, whose view of the relationship of Church and State was grounded on shared legal responsibility for the regulation of individual lives by ecclesiastical courts.

Newcastle's term as 'ecclesiastical minister' brought a largely secular influence to Church patronage. Much has been made of the effect of Newcastle's patronage on the Church, and it is usually characterised as wholly Erastian, creating a subservient episcopate, with an eye to preferment, and a willingness to march to Newcastle's drum in the House of Lords. There is no doubt that Newcastle recognised the political advantages that the appointment of Whig bishops could bring to the House of Lords, and he was temperamentally inclined to curry favour with patrons. But other factors entered Newcastle's calculations. He was a devout Anglican, and undoubtedly sought men of talent and ability for the bench of bishops; he was responsible for the advancement of clergy such as Butler, Conybeare, Hutton, Secker, Pearce, Trevor, Thomas, Drummond, Ewer, Newton and Osbaldeston. In 1750, having advanced Joseph Butler to Durham, John Conybeare to Bristol and Thomas Secker to the deanery of St Paul's, Newcastle rightly told Herring that he had made three appointments 'as great and as reputable promotions as ever were made at one time in the Church'.[68] The search for the best men led him to appoint the politically heterodox on occasion: Secker, whose independence on the bench was notorious;[69] Pearce a client of Lord Bath; Trevor, a High-Church Tory; and Sherlock, a moderate Tory.[70]

The silencing of Convocation in 1717 denied the Church a forum for debate for senior churchmen, leaving them only the House of Lords. The presence of lawyers and laity as well as churchmen made the House of Lords a symbol of the Church's relationship with the State. Though bishops used proxies regularly until the 1740s, and on a less frequent basis until much later, their visible presence in the House of Lords was important to the government, and ministers often nagged bishops to attend. As a result, the bishops continued to be an important group of voters in the House of Lords; though they were only 13.5% of its membership, they represented 18.5% of those who attended in the mid-eighteenth century.[71] Their voices were heard less frequently in debates than their temporal peers however. Though there have been attempts to portray the bishops as a disciplined and homogenous voting bloc, this view is difficult to sustain. While Gibson led his fellows into the Whig lobbies, on occasion nearly all of them as in 1733 when he defended Walpole, these were rare occasions. On the most highly-charged political occasions episcopal attendance tended to drop, and in the 1740s and 1750s, the era in which Newcastle has been regarded as building a disciplined and submissive episcopal bloc, bishops such as Secker, Benson, Maddox, Hayter, Smallbroke, Egerton and Reynolds were frequently wayward voters who abandoned the government in the lobbies. The idea that bishops were submissive clients who were preferred or translated in exchange for votes has been demolished without great difficulty.[72] Certainly the bishops did not see their role in the House of Lords to participate in party politics, though they were often invited to Newcastle's Whig caucus meetings. Nor did the bishops feel altogether comfortable in entering debates of a purely civil nature. Secker held that he had a legitimate role in the consideration of the Naturalisation of Jews and Spirituous Liquors Bills because of their ecclesiastical and moral consequences, but few bishops felt comfortable entering purely political debates.[73]

The best description of the episcopate's view of its role came from the politically independent Martin Benson, who wrote in 1738 that it is so necessary for supporting the interest of the Church, that the bishops should be present in Parliament, that it is our duty I think to appear there and if we take care to shew that it is not our private interest which brings us thither and rules us there, we may be able to do some good, or at least to hinder a good deal of mischief.[74]

Occasionally secular Bills with an ecclesiastical consequence were also the cause of episcopal rebellion: the bishops' opposition to the 1746 Bill to disarm the Highlands of Scotland was grounded on a clause which limited episcopal orders in Scotland, and even ministry loyalists like Herring voted against it with nineteen of his brethren. Of course episcopal opinion could be as equivocal and capricious as temporal views. In 1753 the Bill for the Naturalisation of Jews passed into law with the support of Thomas Secker, and the quiet ambivalence of many bishops. The popular reaction to the measure was an out-pouring of anti-Semitism so strong that the ministry in 1754 repealed the law, again with the support of Secker.[75]

While bishops in the 1740s and 1750s were prepared both to defend the regime and to oppose the governments of the day on individual pieces of legislation, there was an unwillingness to press issues of a political nature. This was exemplified by the issue of America. The sympathy of all shades of the episcopate to the cause of a bishop for America was overwhelming. In 1745–6 and 1748 respectively Archbishop Potter and Bishop Sherlock advocated the consecration of a colonial bishop. But the Whigs feared that it would be turned – in Horace Walpole's words – 'into a matter of controversy in the pulpits' by Dissenters, and a revival of Church strife as 'occasioned great mischief in this divided country in former reigns'. The ministry's terror of turning the clock back to the days of Atterbury, Sacheverell, and Hoadly was enough to convince it, and the episcopate, to drop the matter. Though some, like Secker, remained convinced supporters of the idea, the majority, like Bishop Green of Lincoln were content to 'submit . . . to the wisdom of the government' in this matter.[76]

After 1760 the growth of the peerage made the episcopate a less significant group in the House of Lords and, perhaps as a consequence, the bishops' attendance dropped.[77] The use of proxies declined also and there was an sharp increase in the number of bishops who regularly opposed govern-ments in the 1760s.[78] There were also occasions when the bishops flooded back to the benches and demonstrated their ability to react *en masse* to measures, such as the abortive 1765 Ecclesiastical Estates Bill and the proposals in 1772 and 1773 to grant relief to Dissenters. The episcopate's interest in the issue of a bishop for America gave them a particular concern for the Rockingham proposals to repeal the Stamp Act in 1766, and the bishops' votes proved decisive on a number of occasions. Moreover, continued episcopal involvement in the House of Lords was expressed in registered protests against the motions of the House of Lords. Before 1760 these were rare events, the last one having been in 1742, but in the five years after 1763 there were twelve episcopal protests.[79] From 1760 stronger Toryism made politics a patchwork of greater diversity than it had been under George II, though it did so against a backdrop of George III's claim that the Test Act was the palladium of the constitution. Newcastle's efforts to achieve the appointment of politically reliable and orthodox Trinitarian bishops gave way to a greater tolerance of heterodox political and religious opinions. McCahill's analysis of the activity of forty-four late eighteenth-century bishops identified sixteen who were regular or occasional opponents of ministers;[80] and Grafton's appointments in 1769 of Hinchliffe and Shipley brought Latitudinarianism akin to Hoadly's back to the bench, and Edmund Law's appointment to Carlisle gave it a dash of Socinianism.[81] There was, moreover, room for bishops like Percy and Yorke who in the 1770s actively sought a liberalisation of the Thirty-Nine Articles so as to comprehend Dissent.

Tory bishops like Charles Moss also came to regard Toleration as an unchallengable liberty. In his sermon on the anniversary of the martyrdom of Charles I in 1769 he suggested that:

> it was the Revolution that removed us from the opprobrium of Christianity, the spirit of intolerance, which had been avowed and exercised by every sect of Christians; and recognised the Dissenters from the established Church as fellow-Christians and fellow-subjects.[82]

In a modest way, government policy in the 1770s also became more liberal toward Dissent. While the Dissenters Relief Bills of 1772 and 1773 failed with overwhelming episcopal opposition to them – in part because they encouraged the view of Dissent as motivated by agitators and rebels – by 1779 a similar measure passed easily, allowing Dissenting ministers and schoolmasters exemption from subscription to the Thirty-Nine Articles.[83] The roots of the success of the 1778 Catholic Relief Act and the Dissenters Relief Act of 1779 lay in the lessons of overseas conflicts, which demonstrated the need for the solidarity of all Trinitarian religious groups, permitting Catholics to serve in the army while balancing it with a strengthening of the Protestant Dissenting interest. As Jeremy Black has pointed out, the interests of the State militated against religious division: states needed resources from all people, irrespective of faith, to fight wars and thus endowed Toleration with a political and military rationale.[84] High Churchmen, such as Horne, opposed both measures but the majority of bishops responded to the circumstances of the moment. While there were signs that Dissent was allied to political radicalism and agitation, when it was prepared to be harnessed to the interests of the nation it was not turned away.[85] Similarly ecclesiastical attitudes were moderating. Thomas Secker wrote in February 1768 to the Bishop of Derry regarding the position of Catholics. Secker proclaimed himself the friend of toleration of all religious opinions that were not dangerous to the state, but argued that 'a Protestant State hath no security against papists' but that the State should use the gentlest methods to defend itself. He advocated the repeal of the severer laws against Catholics, but recognised that English bishops could not appear to be the friends of leniency to Rome.[86]

The rejection in 1772 of the Feathers Tavern Petition for liberalising clerical subscription to the Thirty-Nine Articles and of a Bill to relieve Quakers of tithe payments suggested an element of intolerance that is perhaps unjustified. Prosecutions of Quakers for non-payment of tithes were low, and attitudes to Dissent were sympathetic to the idea of greater freedom of conscience. Catholics also benefited from this growing liberalisation – perhaps conditioned by the signal defeat of Jacobitism. The Quebec Act of 1774 which permitted Catholic worship and civil law in Canada, and the 1778 Catholic Relief Act suggested tolerance for Trinitarian nonconformity, though George III was hooted when he granted his assent to the Quebec Act, and the Gordon Riots suggested that popular anti-Catholicism could be easily excited.

Thus while some social and political forces operated in favour of tolerance of religious diversity, within the Church the insistence on a strictly limited Toleration and Anglican orthodoxy remained unaltered, and the liberal bishops remained silent. The gravitational pull of the doctrinal orthodoxy was strong in the Church. As Nigel Aston has shown, occasional attempts, such as that of Bishop Clayton in 1753 to revive an Arianism akin to that of Toland and Clarke, were strongly rejected. Clayton's book *An Essay on Spirit* stimulated some of the strongest re-statements of Athanasian Trinitarianism, including Randolph's *Vindication of the Doctrine of the Trinity*, William Jones's enormously popular *Essay on the Trinity* and Scott's *Doctrine of the Trinity*. Clayton's later abortive attempt to reform the liturgy and a further foray into dogmatic theology, *Vindication of the Old and New Testaments*, blocked opportunities to pursue Latitudinarianism in theology or liturgical reform. The most fruitful avenue to pursue for Latitudinarians was a relaxation of clerical subscription.[87]

The origins of an attempt to relax clerical subscription to the Thirty-Nine Articles, the Feathers Tavern Petition, lay in Francis Blackburne's

Confessional (1766), which argued that no Protestant minister should be required to subscribe to the Thirty-Nine Articles, and that a general assent to the scriptures was sufficient.[88] It was a view advanced by Hoadly in the early eighteenth century and Strickland Gough in the 1730s.[89] But the Feathers Tavern Petition was not widely supported. Blackburne, with Lindsey and Disney, only managed to get two hundred and fifty Anglican clergy to sign it. Methodists opposed it and Lady Huntington formed a counter-petition. Burke's opposition to it was a model Anglican response to heterodoxy:

> these gentlemen complain of hardships: let us examine a little what that hardship is. They want to be preferred clergymen of the Church of England as by law established; but their consciences will not suffer them to conform to the doctrines and the practices of that Church. . . .[90]

The distinction between subscription to doctrine and to scripture was an important one to the two hundred and seventeen MPs – Gibbon called them 'worthy champions' of the Church – who easily defeated the seventy-one supporters of the petition. The difference between adherence to doctrine rather than to scripture defined the contrast between those who could explicitly affirm to Anglican orthodoxy, and those whose commitment was simply to biblical Christianity, a position that could encompass all Christians from Unitarians to Jesuits. The defeat of the petition demonstrated this as Jebb, Disney and Lindsey left the Church to become Unitarians. Their departure contrasted strongly with the Church earlier in the century, which had encompassed men of similar sympathies: Stephen Nye, Samuel Clarke, John Jackson, Edward Evanson and William Chambers. Indeed the position advocated by Francis Blackburne was essentially the same as Bishop John Williams of Chichester, who urged that the Thirty-Nine Articles should be treated

> as articles of peace and not articles of doctrine. The meaning of which was that they were articles which all men were bound to acquiesce in and not to contradict, but were not bound to believe. . . .[91]

The inability of Jebb, Lindsey and Disney to remain within the Church reflected their stiffening conscience, and the realisation that they championed a lost cause within the Church.[92] For after 1760, largely through Thomas Secker's influence, orthodoxy became the dominant instinct of the Church. Even churchmen sympathetic to Latitudinarianism, like William Powell, found abandonment of subscription unacceptable. He had held that to abandon subscription

> would give occasion to perpetual changes; and every change to fresh disputes. For who shall fashion our new systems? Where are the men who have no favourite notions to inculcate, no hated heresy to condemn?[93]

Similarly, Josiah Tucker asserted that the abandonment of subscription would mean anarchy:

> one clergyman would read one part of the service, and another would read another, and both perhaps would add something peculiar of their own; whereas a third might read no part at all but launch out extempore effusions. Some would mangle and curtail the service through one motive and some through another and the passions and prejudices of all would be greatly inflamed . . . the warm, the bigoted or enthusiastic would be split into sects and furious factions.[94]

Even Archdeacon Thomas Balguy, the inheritor of the mantle of Hoadly's Latitudinarianism at Winchester, was acclaimed by Warburton for having crushed the Feathers Tavern Petition in his Charge of 1772.[95] Clergymen also rejected relaxing the subscription to the Thirty-Nine Articles for fear of the example of the seventeenth century. John Butler, later bishop of Oxford and of Hereford, wrote to George Onslow in November 1771 revealing a fundamental resistance to abandonment of subscription:

> One thing is certain, whatever their merit is, the moment they are altered, a party will arise up in favour of the old articles. It must needs be that parties arise, and old and new articles known or unknown will inflame men like old and new wine. A religious war will consume much of both and may in time turn the wine to blood.[96]

As Martin Fitzpatrick has shown, Blackburne and the Latitudinarians found their constituency eroded by growing High Church and Evangelical movements in the Church and the tendency of the clergy toward a more orthodox and conservative position. By the end of the century Richard Watson was perhaps the sole episcopal successor of Bishop Hoadly's radical heterodoxy.[97] Even among Hoadly's closest followers there was a strong reaction against the liberalisation of subscription.[98]

The forces for change in the religious establishment were also met with powerful arguments for maintenance of the settlement of 1689. Even liberal Whigs found themselves defending the establishment when it was threatened. In the 1760s Edmund Pyle, Hoadly's Latitudinarian protégé, regarded the radical politician John Wilkes as 'a Whig Sacheverell in a red coat'. This description showed how far Hoadlyanism had come, in 1717 Whig Latitudinarians might have welcomed Wilkes's obstinate support for liberty and an original contract, but by the 1760s Wilkes was regarded as an enemy of the establishment even to the successors of Hoadly.[99] Similarly, the Hoadleian Parson Richard Wavell wrote to his friend Thomas Woolls, vicar of Fareham in 1778, 'between friends at this time of day I question whether it be safe to write or preach in defence of what Bishop Hoadly, Dr Sykes, etc. would have called religious liberty'.[100] In Jonathan Shipley's charge to the clergy of St Asaph of 1774 he commented that Dissenters' calls for relief were 'a direct attack upon our church'. His rejection of calls for relief were grounded on the argument that 'it is certainly [in] the interest and wisdom of the State to chuse such as may be teachers of virtue and good morals to their fellow citizens . . .'; thus they justified a privileged position in the State, and thus the Dissenters were denied it by the liberal Shipley.[101]

The response from conservative churchmen was even more inflexible, though grounded on less pragmatic premises. George Horne's response to the pressure to revise subscription to the Thirty-Nine Articles and to tolerate Arianism was that 'orthodoxy and heterodoxy are but other terms for right and wrong'.[102] The determination of Horne, Horsley, Jones, Porteus, and other High Churchmen to defy the 'enlightenment' of Priestley indicates the resolute vitality of orthodox Anglicanism and its determination to challenge radical religious thinking. Inspired by John Hutchinson's emphasis on biblical revelation, Horne and his fellow High Churchmen were satisfied by the sufficiency of Anglican doctrine and liturgy as a means to promote faith in the way that Priestley was not. Horne held that the purpose of philosophy was to aid faith and Anglicanism, whereas for Priestley it was an instrument for scepticism. Nigel Aston asserts 'Horne . . . saw the Church of England as an unblemished witness of a Christ-centred doctrine handed down to it by the Fathers of the Church, and his task was to hold on to it . . .'.[103] Horne preached the Bampton lectures in the 1780s in which he rejected Hume's idea of a natural religion. He also rejected Priestley's Socinianism, which struck at the tap-root of orthodox Trinitarianism and underpinned the anti-subscription movement. In a devastating attack on Priestley's *Free Enquiry*, Horne questioned whether Priestley believed in anything fixed and whether he could lay any claim to be called a Christian.[104] Horne's elevation to the episcopate and old age denied him further onslaughts on Priestley, but the French Revolution hastened the intellectual union of orthodox Christianity with the political survival of the State. Priestley and heterodox Christianity were vanquished as the forces of the establishment of 1689 rallied to the defence of the country against French Jacobinism.[105] The Hutchinsonian victory was to inspire a generation of High Church conservative bishops well into the nineteenth century and to ensure the survival of anti-rationalist doctrines.[106] Equally the victory of orthodox Trinitarianism was undoubtedly also due to the dogged determination of its champions. Archdeacon George Travis of Chester, for example, wrote *Letters to Edward Gibbon Esq* . . . in 1784. It was a methodical and exhaustive refutation of the aspersions Gibbon cast on the scriptural basis of the Trinity. By 1794 the book has run through three editions, each one enlarged and incorporating copious replies to criticisms made of previous editions. The third edition ran to over five hundred pages and was published by Travis himself.

The notion of subscription by the clergy to attest to orthodoxy naturally became connected with that of the Test for lay conformity to the doctrines of the Church. The most popular enquiry into the validity of the Test was William Paley's *Principles of Moral and Political Philosophy* (1785) which was widely read. Paley argued for Toleration on utilitarian grounds.[107] Gradually, however, Paley and his Cambridge intellectual circle found themselves troubled by Toleration. Paley himself shifted to a defence of an establishment founded on the vital social role of the clergy as public preachers.[108] Paley's friends, Balguy, Pretyman, Hay and Watson were members of the Cambridge intellectual circle that formed a *via media* to orthodoxy rooted in theological arguments. Hay, as the first Norrisian Professor, produced detailed arguments in support of subscription and Pretyman's *Elements of Christian Theology* drew together the major body of orthodox writers of the eighteenth century. The influence of these writers was widespread, dominating the thinking of Anglicanism for two generations.[109] Their contribution was to assert that it was possible to defend subscription as vital for Anglican integrity and the Test as a utilitarian requirement for the State, but also to argue for greater tolerance. Josiah Tucker advanced exactly this position in *Apology for the Present Church of England as by law Established occasioned by a Petition laid before Parliament for Abolishing Subscriptions* . . . (1772).[110] By the end of the eighteenth century therefore even those of liberal tendencies had been pulled by the gravity of orthodox Anglicanism to remain committed to the establishment of 1689.

The entrenchment of orthodox Anglicanism had consequences elsewhere. Some sermons of the period were marked by a greater emphasis on authoritarianism and on the doctrine of passive obedience.[111] Brownlow North's sermon to the SPG on the American imbroglio in 1778 is reminiscent of the Anglican responses to the 1688 Revolution:

it is not the part of Christian ministers or of Christian congregation to complain. I shall pass by the sufferings of both on this occasion, but I must in the spirit of charity lament the unhappy delusion of the peoples themselves, whose religious apprehensions have been raised by the political leaders for political purposes.[112]

Many High Churchmen, like Samuel Horsley, drew a correlation between support for the government, even on issues like America, and High Churchmanship.[113] Similarly, William Jones's sermon in June 1778 in defence of the established order and against political reform could have come from the pen of a Non-juror in 1689.[114]

The defeat of Britain in North America momentarily fuelled arguments to repeal the Test Act. It was no coincidence that Henry Beaufoy's proposal to repeal the Test Act in March 1787 were presented to Parliament a month after the consecration at Lambeth of Bishops White and Provoost as bishops for America. The consecrations, resonant with overtones of the defeat in America and the establishment of a separate Anglican hierarchy, gave an important impetus to radicalism and to Dissent. Beaufoy's argument for repeal of the Test was grounded on what he saw as the absurd disqualification under which he, as a Quaker, laboured. The Test Act of 1678 allowed him to be elected an MP, but he was barred from being a member of a municipal corporation or a company director. His ally, Charles James Fox, argued on the broader principle that to penalise minorities by reason of their consciences, and highly respectable and moral ones at that, was unjust. The opposition of Pitt was based on his desire not to provoke hostility in the Church by removing penalties that were not in themselves very harsh. Archbishop Moore had been consulted by Pitt and reported that an overwhelming majority of bishops opposed the repeal of the Test Act. The argument advanced against the repeal was that the Test Act did not exclude all Dissenters from office, but it did exclude those whose doctrines were so far at odds with orthodox Anglicanism as to refuse to communicate with it. It was the same argument that Henry Pelham had used in 1753 for the naturalisation of Jews.[115] It was an argument that, after seven hours of debate, won the day in the House of Commons by a majority of seventy-eight votes.[116]

Two years later the majority against another attempt at repeal dropped to just twenty votes. But the French Revolution was decisive: in March 1790 Fox's third attempt failed by almost two hundred votes. Relief for Unitarianism was similarly rejected: petitioned by Dissenters, a Bill was proposed by Fox in 1792 that sought to grant them the same rights as Trinitarian Dissenters under the Toleration Act of 1689. Pitt opposed the

Bill, but found it difficult to counter the argument that if Unitarianism was akin to sedition the law should pursue and punish their political acts. But he found it easy to point to Priestley and Unitarians as dangerous political radicals at a time of national emergency, and he held that Unitarians could disband as a group and worship as individuals. The Bill was lost by seventy-nine votes.[117]

One recent writer has suggested that the Church of England at the end of the eighteenth century was influenced by the ideas of democracy from the American and French Revolutions.[118] In fact, the counter-acting forces of the reaction to these events had a far greater impact. The Church moved to conservatism in religious and political values. Bishops like Samuel Horsley found the Catholics – especially after their abandonment of ultra-montanism – preferable to Dissent and its radical Jacobin allies. He also preferred the closure of Sunday schools to the spread of literacy with its opportunities for religious and political sedition. The conservative–orthodox reaction in the Church and State was most evident in Lord Sidmouth's Bill of 1811 which sought to outlaw itinerant preaching. The Bill struck at the heart of Methodist circuits and other nonconformist connections, and sought to strengthen the Church against the growth of Nonconformity.[119] Archbishop Manners-Sutton of Canterbury found the measure unduly provocative and persuaded Sidmouth to withdraw it. However Manners-Sutton was prepared to take a combative approach to the growth of Dissent, rebuking the Duke of Kent in 1805 when he joined the British and Foreign Bible Society – which admitted Dissenters as well as Anglicans – with the words 'he that is not with us is against us.'[120]

Parliament, however, found some measure of Toleration difficult to resist. The Protestant Society for the Protection of Religious Liberty, established in 1811 in response to the Sidmouth proposal, was especially influential. In 1812 Liverpool's Tory government granted it an extension of the Toleration Act, by permitting groups of twenty Dissenters, rather than five, to meet together for unlicensed worship, and in 1813 the proposal of 1792 to extend the Toleration Act to include Unitarians was passed. These relaxations of Toleration served only to focus attention on the Dissenters' principal grievance, the Test Act. The Protestant Dissenting Deputies formed a campaign for the repeal of the Act including publication of the *Test Act Reporter*. Their campaign utilised the tactics of the evangelical–High Church Hackney Phalanx and the Clapham Sect, carefully making their movement respectable to MPs.

Nevertheless, Parliament demonstrated its commitment to the monopoly of the Church with the most significant weapon at its disposal. In 1812 four hundred thousand pounds was provided by the government in augmentation of Church livings and a further two hundred thousand pounds was committed to relinquish taxation on livings.[121] Six years later the Prince Regent's speech at the opening of Parliament proposed a grant of funds to make up the deficiency in Church buildings and accommodation, and a Bill subsequently voted funds for that purpose. In the debates for the allocation of funds, Liverpool openly declared the purpose of the measure was to 'remove dissent'.[122]

In spite of attempts to bolster the Church, the forces of relief for Dissent gained influential adherents: the Duke of Sussex and Lord Holland presided at meetings of the Protestant Society. The liberal Whigs undoubtedly saw themselves as successors of Somers, Halifax and Burnet, advancing comprehension through renegotiation of the status of Dissent and of Toleration.[123] The growing sympathy of Whigs for the repeal of the Test Act, the circumstances in Ireland and the threat from O'Connell and the Catholic Association were undoubtedly key factors in the repeal of the Test Act. However, less attention has been paid to another significant factor in the collapse of the Test Act: the unity and determination of Dissent. In March 1827 the Protestant Dissenting Deputies and the Protestant Society joined with the Unitarian Association, the Ministries of the Three Denominations and the Board of Congregational Ministers to intensify their demands for repeal of the Test Act.[124] Later in the month the group, chaired by William Smith, MP for Norwich, was joined by the United Associate Presbytery of London. Lord John Russell was charged with responsibility for piloting a Bill repealing the Test Act; and a new journal, *World*, was founded to support the campaign. The thoroughly constitutional methods adopted by Dissenters had a vital impact on the perceptions of the repeal campaign. By January 1828 the Common Council of London, like many other municipal corporations, joined in petitioning the House of Commons in favour of the Bill, as did Roman Catholics. Moreover the liberal Whigs did not mount a frontal assault on the Test Act. During his speech in favour of the measure in the House of Commons on 26 February 1828, Russell advanced an extraordinary and historic vindication of the Test Act. He denied that men had an absolute right to freedom of conscience in matters of religion, and argued that if the religious principles of any group incorporated political views that were hostile to the State they should be subject to a Test and disqualification from power. Thus far, Russell endorsed the integrity of the revolutionary establishment of 1689: 'the noble lord did not appear to see . . . that he was justifying all the penal statutes that had ever been passed against any body of religionists.'[125]

But the *coup de grace* of Russell's speech was that whilst in theory the Test Act could be so justified, it *was* an injustice in practice because the Dissenters were not disloyal to the State, nor did their religious or political principles threaten it. It was an argument that Sir Robert Inglis, the leading

High Churchman in the House of Commons, found impossible to counter; a quarter of a century earlier he might have been able to suggest that Dissent was connected to Jacobinism, but the argument could not be made of Catholicism in the circumstances of 1828. In the House of Lords, in character with a Church that had forged a new relationship with Dissent, the Archbishop of York and the bishops of Lincoln, Durham and Chester welcomed the repeal. Only Lord Eldon, in twenty amendments and thirty-five speeches, opposed the repeal Bill. The government of Peel and Wellington abandoned opposition to the Bill and it passed without a division. In the spirit of moderation that won the repeal, the *Test Act Reporter* thanked the bishops for their liberal and conciliatory response. At the root of the repeal, which Eldon defined as a separation of Church and State, lay a sense that religious division and strife were redundant.

> The principal characteristic of this last and successful struggle for the repeal of the Test and Corporation Acts was the friendly attitude assumed by members of the established Church towards Dissenters . . . the representatives of that Church had finally become convinced that the prostitution, for its own apparent protection, of one of the most sacred acts of religious worship for the purpose of obtaining public office . . . was detrimental to the interests of the Church. . . .[126]

At the core of this explanation was that between 1788 and 1828 the perception of Dissent and Catholicism both in the Church and State had changed from one which was politically radical to one which was no longer a threat to the State. The conscious decision of Methodists, Baptists, Presbyterians and Catholics to abandon their association with radicalism after 1800 brought them into a relationship with the Church and State that threatened neither. The Republican Commonwealthmen and Jacobites of the seventeenth and eighteenth centuries had not survived into the nineteenth, nor did the religious principles that placed them outside the establishment. The argument for a Test based on the security of the State – the notion that lay behind the Revolution of 1688–9 and which Secker had espoused in 1768 – could only have ever been a contingent one, as William Paley indicated in *Principles of Moral and Political Philosophy.*

> The State undoubtedly has a right to refuse its power and its confidence to those who seek its destruction. . . . But even here it should be observed that it is not against the religion that government shuts its doors, but against those political principles which . . . the members of the communion are found in fact to hold.[127]

It was the collapse of the second case that occurred in 1828–9.

In a selective account of the Church's relationship with the State in eighteenth-century England it is difficult to be anything other than illustrative. Nevertheless from events such as the Convocation controversy and the Sacheverell trial the Church emerged strikingly unscathed. No enduring Convocation or Sacheverell 'split' occurred; indeed the Church survived these episodes with ease. An element in this was the desire of Harley and others to avoid disputes in the Church from spilling over into the State. But once the leaders of the disputes were silenced – Atterbury by management, Sacheverell by sentence of Parliament – the Church returned to peace quickly enough. Militant Anglicanism lacked the intellectual rigour and consistency to survive. However the Church's eirenicism should not be mistaken for simple passivity or inertia. Gibson's alliance with Walpole demonstrates how eirenicism could be actively engaged by a policy of co-operation with the State. A combination of judicious patronage and the defence of the Church from Whig anti-clericalism convinced the clergy that adherence to the establishment of 1689 and 1714 was legitimate.

In the second half of the eighteenth century, though State policy dictated a more liberal response to Trinitarian Dissent, the Church's reaction was retrenchment to a reaffirmation of the Thirty-Nine Articles and a defence of the Test. The trend to orthodoxy was powerful enough to draw even the adherents of liberal thought away from a Hoadlyite position on freedom of doctrine. This conservative response was an attempt to assert the unity of the Church on a doctrinal basis; it identified unity with dogmatic homogeneity in a way that was absent in the first half of the eighteenth century. Rejection of heterodoxy and theological conservatism allied the Church to the Tories at a time when events in France also tended politicians and churchmen to resist new ideas.

Throughout the eighteenth century the Church benefited from the pragmatism of politicians: Harley, Walpole, Newcastle, North and Pitt were all keen to avoid religious strife. Peel and Wellington were no different. Driven by dint of circumstances, they responded to the events of 1828–9 in the same way that their predecessors would have, by insulating the State from religious division and by neutralising the source of the strife. The same instinct that closed Convocation in 1717 and threw votes into reverse in the Quaker Tithe Bill in 1736 led Peel to abandon the Test. Clark's assertion that 1828 was a failure of will is therefore unfair. Undoubtedly the eirenicism of the Church was connected to the Erastianism of the era. Throughout the eighteenth century the State sought political tranquillity. It often drew deeply on the Church to give effect to it; but when the Church was the cause of disturbance the State sought ways to prevent contagion.

Notes

1 T. E. S. Clarke and H. C. Foxcroft, *A Life of Gilbert Burnet . . . with an Introduction by C. H. Firth*, Cambridge, 1907, p. 274.

2 M. Goldie, 'The Non-jurors, Episcopacy and the Origins of the Convocation Controversy', E. Cruikshanks (ed.), *Ideology and Conspiracy: Aspects of Jacobitism 1689–1799*, Edinburgh, 1982.

3 R. E. Rodes Jr, *Law and the Modernization of the Church of England: Charles II to the Welfare State*, Indiana, 1991, p. 9.

4 F. Atterbury, *Letter to a Convocation Man concerning the Rights, Powers and Privileges of that Body*, London, 1697, pp. 63–4.

5 25 Henry VIII, cap 19.

6 See N. Sykes, *William Wake*, Cambridge, 1957, vol. 1, pp. 103–4.

7 D. Slatter (ed.), *The Diary of Thomas Naish*, Wiltshire Archaeological and Natural History Society, 1965, vol. 20, p. 43. This was one of the sources of disputes between Naish and Bishop Burnet which led eventually to a protracted legal dispute, and Naish's election to Convocation for the diocese of Bath and Wells. It is easy to overstate the majorities achieved by the Tories in the Convocation elections, they were 'never substantial' and most majorities were only marginal. W. C. Watson, 'The Late Stuart Reformation: Church and State in the First Age of Party', University of California, Riverside, PhD thesis, 1995, p. 289.

8 G. V. Bennett, *The Tory Crisis in Church and State 1688–1739*, Oxford, 1975, pp. 55–6.

9 Book of Revelation, ch. 3, v. 21

10 D. Slatter (ed.), *op. cit.*, pp. 24, 36, 43–4, 46.

11 S. Patrick, *The Autobiography of Symon Patrick*, Oxford, 1839, p. 185.

12 Nicolson, bishop of Carlisle, who had been Atterbury's opponent over the issue of the rights of Convocation, was appalled to find his diocese invaded by a dean of Atterbury's brand, and refused to institute him until he had appeared before the Bishop's court to explain himself. F. G. James, *North Country Bishop*, New Haven, 1956.

13 Bennett, *op. cit.*, p. 79.

14 *Ibid.*, pp. 82–5.

15 Swift dismissed the latter as 'the battle of the books' and one more recent view was that it was a debate of 'manners of scholarship'. W. G. Hiscock, *Henry Aldrich Christ Church 1648–1710*, Oxford, 1960, p. 55. Also J. H. Monk, *The Life of Richard Bentley DD*, London, 1833, 2 vols.

16 Christ Church, Oxford, Wake Ms 23, f 135.

17 W. Dawes, *Sermons Preached Upon Several Occasions Before King William and Queen Anne*, London, 1709, pp. 3, 167, 173, 196, *et seq.*

18 H. Sacheverell, *In Perils among False Brethren: A Sermon preached before the Lord Mayor of London . . .*, London, 1710, p. 11.

19 R. N. Stromberg, *Religious Liberalism in eighteenth century England*, Oxford, 1954, p. 133.

20 *The Tryal of Dr Henry Sacheverell before the House of Peers for High Crimes and Misdemeanours . . .*, London, 1710, pp. 38, 72, 90, 99, 109.

21 *Ibid.*, pp. 167, 430.

22 *The Bishop of Salisbury's and the Bishop of Norwich's Speeches in the House of Lords on the First Article of the Impeachment of Henry Sacheverell . . .*, London, 1710, p. 16.

23 E. Timberland, *The History and Proceedings of the House of Lords*, London, 1742, vol. 2, 277.

24 *Observator*, 9–12 November 1709, pp. 2–3.

25 W. C. Watson *op. cit.*, p. 240.

26 J. Barry (ed.), 'The Society for the Reformation of Manners 1700–1750', J. Barry and K. Morgan (eds.), *Reformation and Revival in Eighteenth Century Bristol*, Bristol Record Society, 1994, vol. XLV, p. 54.

27 Slatter (ed.), *op. cit.*, p. 68.

28 G. V. Bennett, 'The Convocation of 1710: An Anglican Attempt at Counter-Revolution', *Studies in Church History*, 1971, vol. 7.

29 H. D. W. Lees, *The Chronicles of a Suffolk Parish Church*, Lowestoft, 1949, p. 172.

30 E. Duffy, ' "Whiston's Affair": The Trials of a Primitive Christian 1709–1714', *Journal of Ecclesiastical History*, 1976, vol. 27, no. 2.

31 Though equally, Whitby claimed 'that Dr Clarke never denied the son to be really and truly God'. D. Whitby, *A Dissuasive from Enquiring into the doctrine of the Trinity . . .* , London, 1714.

32 It was a view he also expounded in *The Difficulties and Discouragements which attend the Study of the Scriptures in the Way of Private Judgement . . .* , London, 1714, which ran to five editions.

33 W. Fleetwood, *A Letter to an Inhabitant of the Parish of St Andrew's Holbourn about New Ceremonies in the Church*, London, 1717, second ed.

34 N. Sykes, *From Sheldon to Secker*, Cambridge, 1959, pp. 96–8.

35 Quoted in A. Plummer, *The Church of England in the Eighteenth Century*, London, 1910, p. 65.

36 N. Sykes, 'Archbishop Wake and the Whig Party 1716–1723: a study in incompatibility of temperament', *Cambridge Historical Journal*, 1945 vol. 8, no. 2.

37 After 1717, with the Convocation of the Province of Canterbury silenced, the Convocation of the University of Oxford and the Congregation of the University of Cambridge provided substitutes for expressions of clerical opinion and censure. Indeed if George I or II, or their ministers, considered permitting the Convocation of Canterbury to resume sittings they had only to glimpse the regular disputes in the universities to reassure them that they were wise to follow the policy of silence. With the additional fuel of boisterous young men, the universities had the making of hotbeds of contention and strife. The existence of *terra filius* at ceremonies at Oxford before 1713 (and as the title of a journal after 1721) provided plenty of opportunities to throw abuse at politicians and churchmen.

38 Bodleian Library, Oxford, Add. Mss. A269 f 70.

39 British Library, Stowe Ms. 354 f 195.

40 G. M. Townend, 'Religious Radicalism and Conservatism in the Whig Party under George I: The Repeal of the Occasional Conformity and Schism Acts', *Parliamentary History*, 1988, vol. 7 pt. 1.

41 W. Gibson, 'An Eighteenth Century Paradox: The Career of the Decypherer-Bishop Edward Willes' *The British Journal for Eighteenth Century Studies*, 1989, vol. 12, pt. 1.

42 British Library, Add. Mss. 32,686 f 353.

43 S. Taylor, ' "Dr Codex" and the Whig "Pope": Edmund Gibson, Bishop of Lincoln and London, 1716–1748', R. W. Davis (ed.), *Lords of Parliament, 1714–1914*, Stanford, 1995, p. 15.

44 Bodleian Library, Oxford, Ms Add. A. 269 ff 72–3.

45 N. Sykes, *Edmund Gibson*, Oxford, 1926, p. 144.

46 Public Record Office, SP Domestic, George II, B, 23.

47 S. Taylor, 'Sir Robert Walpole, the Church of England and the Quaker Tithes Bill of 1736', *Historical Journal*, 1985, 28.

48 Gibson also controlled six episcopal proxy votes. The non-voters were the elderly Wake and Hough, both of whom were too old to attend or vote, Hoadly the arch-Whig and Latitudinarian, and Wynne, whose absence had never been satisfactorily explained. S. Taylor, *op. cit.*, pp. 67–8. Hoadly later spoke at his 1736 visitation of Winchester that he had not intended by his absence 'not to have a tender concern for the support and creditable subsistence of my brethren in a lower station' but that he could not in conscience oppose the Bill nor in conscience support it. J. Hoadly (ed.), *op. cit.*, vol. 3, p. 492.

49 St Andrews University, Gibson Mss, VII. 13 quoted in N. Sykes, 'Edmund Gibson, 1669–1748 Bishop of London', Oxford University, D.Phil thesis, 1922, vol. 3, p. 767.

50 In fact it seems clear that Bishop Gibson had decided not to accept the primacy when Archbishop Wake died, even before the crisis of 1736. N. Sykes, 'Bishop Gibson and Sir Robert Walpole', *English Historical Review* 1929, vol. xliv.

51 J. S. Chamberlain, *Accommodating High Churchmen: The Clergy of Sussex, 1700–1745*, Chicago, 1997.

52 *Ibid.*, p. 166.

53 It was an argument that Tom Kendrick found convincing in 'Sir Robert Walpole, The Old Whigs and the Bishops, 1733–36: A Study in Eighteenth-Century Parliamentary Politics', *Historical Journal*, 1968, vol. 11, no. 3, p. 422.

54 St Andrews University, Gibson Mss, VII. 13 quoted in N. Sykes, 'Edmund Gibson, 1669–1748 Bishop of London', Oxford University, D.Phil thesis, 1922, vol. 3, p. 768.

55 T. J. F. Kendrick, *op. cit.*, p. 445.

56 P. Adman, W. A. Speck and B. White, 'Yorkshire Election Results 1734 and 1742: a computer analysis', *Northern History*, 1985, vol. 21.

57 S. W. Baskerville, 'The Political Behaviour of the Cheshire Clergy 1705–1752', *Northern History*, 1987, vol. 23.

58 J. M. Albers, 'Seeds of Contention: Society, Politics and the Church of England in Lancashire 1689–1790' Yale University, PhD thesis, 1988, vol. 2.

59 W. Gibson, ' "A Happy Fertile Soil which bringeth forth Abundantly": The Diocese of Winchester, 1689–1800', J. Gregory and J. Chamberlain (eds.), *The Church in its Local Identities, 1660–1800*, Woodbridge, 2000.

60 J. Jackson, *An Address to the Deists*, London, 1744, pp. 159–60.

61 Chamberlain, *op. cit.*, p. 91.

62 A. D. Gilbert, *Religion and Society in Industrial England 1740–1914*, London, 1976, pp. 32–4.

63 A. J. Willis (ed.), *Winchester Ordinations, 1660–1829*, Folkestone, 1964, vol. 1, *passim*.

64 Strickland Gough, *An Enquiry into the Causes of the Decay of the Dissenting Interest*, London, 1730 and P. Doddridge, *Free Thoughts on the Most Probable Means of Renewing the Dissenting Interest*, London, 1731.

65 R. Sedgwick (ed.), *Some Materials toward Memoirs of the Reign of King George II*, London, 1931, p. 536.

66 S. Taylor, 'William Warburton and the Alliance of Church and State', *Journal of Ecclesiastical History*, 1992, vol. 43, no. 2.

67 E. Gibson, *Codex Juris Ecclesiastici Anglicani*, London, 1713, vol. 1. It was a view that Joseph Butler shared: 'A Constitution of Civil government without any religious establishment is a chimerical project of which there is no example'. W. E. Gladstone (ed.), *The Works of Joseph Butler*, Oxford, 1897, vol. 2, p. 308.

68 British Library, Add. Mss. 32,722 f 5.

69 Above all, he had led an episcopal rebellion against the Spirituos Liquors Bill in 1743, which lowered duty on gin. But within a few months, Secker was being canvassed for Winchester if Hoadly were to die. L. W. Barnard, 'Thomas Secker and the English Parliament', *Parliaments, Estates and Representation*, 1992, vol. 12, no. 1, p. 50.

70 For examples of Newcastle's other heterodox appointments see S. Taylor, 'The Government and the Episcopate in the Mid-Eighteenth Century: The Uses of Patronage', C. Giry-Deloison and R. Mettam (eds.), *Patronages et Clientelismses, 1550–1750*, London, 1995, p. 195.

71 These statistics from S. Taylor, 'Church and State in England in the Mid-Eighteenth Century: The Newcastle Years 1742–1762', Cambridge University, PhD thesis, 1987, Chapter 8.

72 S. Taylor, 'The Government and the Episcopate in the Mid-Eighteenth Century: The Uses of Patronage' *op. cit.* W. Gibson, *The Achievement of the Anglican Church, 1689–1800: The Confessional State in England in the Eighteenth Century*, Lewiston, 1995.

73 Hoadly was unique – as usual – in being a Whig pamphleteer in the 1710 election and in contributing to the Whig press in the 1720s.

74 B.L. Add. Mss. 39,311 f 39.

75 W. Gibson, *Religion and Society in England and Wales, 1689–1800*, London, 1998.

76 For Walpole and Green see S. Taylor, 'Whigs, Bishops and America: the Politics of Church Reform in Mid-Eighteenth Century England', *Historical Journal*, 1993, vol. 36, no. 2.

77 This was the culmination of a long process: at the end of James II's reign, the bishops made up a seventh of the membership of the Lords. By the end of Anne's reign, her creations and the addition of the Scottish representative peers, meant that they made up an eighth of the house.

78 Though Newcastle's influence with a handful of bishops remained a factor for some years, even when he was in opposition.

79 J. E. Thorold Rogers, *A Complete Collection of the Protests of the House of Lords . . .* , Oxford, vol. 2, pp. 24–8.

80 M. W. McCahill, *Order and Equipoise: The Peerage and the House of Lords, 1783–1806*, London, 1978, pp. 146–7.

81 Law at Cambridge had been an avowed Unitarian.

82 C. Moss, *A Sermon Preached before the House of Lords Jan 30th 1769, op. cit.*, p. 18.

83 G. M. Ditchfield, 'The Subscription Issue in British Parliamentary Politics 1772–9', *Parliamentary History*, 1988, vol. 7, pt 1.

84 J. Black, 'The Confessional State or Elect Nation? Religion and Identity in Eighteenth-Century England' in T. Claydon and I. McBride (eds.), *Protestantism and National Identity: Britain and Ireland, c.1650–c.1850*, Cambridge, 1998, p. 70.

85 The arguments that Dissent and radicalism were in alliance can be found in essays by A. W. C. Waterman and John Gascoigne, K. Haakonssen, *Enlightenment and Religion, op. cit.* However, John Seed's essay in the same volume suggests that Dissent may have been more conservative that otherwise held.

86 Public Record Office of Northern Ireland, D2798/5/6, 25 February 1768. I am grateful to Robert Ingram for a copy of this letter.

87 N. Aston, 'The Limits of Latitudinarianism: English Reaction to Bishop Clayton's *An Essay on Spirit*', *Journal of Ecclesiastical History*, 1998, vol. 49, no. 3. Aston argues that the leadership of the Church was 'sadly compromised' by heterodoxy; alternatively it could be regarded as broadened.

88 Arguably Blackburne inherited the ultra-Protestant view from the Commonwealthman tradition of the seventeenth century. B. W. Young, ' "The Soul-Sleeping System": Politics and Heresy in Eighteenth Century England', *Journal of Ecclesiastical History*, 1994, vol. 45, no. 1.

89 S. Gough, *An Enquiry into the Causes of the Decay of the Dissenting Interest in a Letter to a Dissenting Minister*, London, 1730. *The Works of William Paley DD in one volume*, London, 1853, p. 45.

90 *Parliamentary Debates.*

91 H. C. Foxcroft, *op. cit.*, p. 507.

92 Though men like Charles Le Grice, George Dyer and William Frend were Unitarians who were persecuted when they remained within the Church. G. M. Ditchfield, 'Anti-trinitarianism and Toleration in Late Eighteenth Century British Politics: The Unitarian Petition of 1792', *Journal of Ecclesiastical History*, 1991, vol. 42, no. 1.

93 W. S. Powell, *op. cit.*, p. 42.

94 J. Tucker, *An Apology for the Present Church of England as by law Established occasioned by a Petition laid before Parliament for Abolishing Subscriptions in a Letter to one of the Petitioners . . .* , Gloucester, 1772, p. 79.

95 G. H. Blore, 'An Archdeacon of the Eighteenth Century, Thomas Balguy DD 1716–1795', *Winchester Cathedral Record*, 1951, vol. 20, p. 19.

96 Surrey History Centre, G173/2/1 f. 57, John Butler to George Onslow 21 November 1771.

97 M. Fitzpatrick, 'Latitudinarianism at the Parting of the Ways', J. Walsh, C. Haydon and S. Taylor (eds.), *op. cit.*

98 Hampshire Records Office, Copy/605/102. Nevertheless, Wavell felt that complete homogeneity in subscription was impossible. He joked to Woolls in 1775 that Dr Balguy's sermon in defence of the Thirty-Nine Articles contained material contrary to them, and concluded that 'every sensible divine is a sinner in this respect'. *Ibid.*, f 111.

99 A. Hartshorne (ed.), *op. cit.*, pp. 365–6.

100 Hampshire Record Office, Copy/605/118.

101 W. D. Shipley (ed.), *The Works of the Right Reverend Jonathan Shipley DD, Lord Bishop of St Asaph*, London, 1792, vol. 1, pp. 27–29. However, Shipley changed his views by 1779.

102 Quoted in N. Aston, 'Horne and Heterodoxy: The Defence of Anglican Belief in the Late Eighteenth Century', *English Historical Review*, October 1993, p. 897.

103 *Ibid.*, 902.

104 Though it must be admitted that Priestley, in embracing the Armenian doctrine that mankind was essentially pure and undefiled and denying the stain of original sin, shared some views in common with the mysticism of William Law. W. Wilberforce, *A Practical View of the Prevailing Religious System*, London, 1797, pp. 20–50; R. N. Stromberg, *op. cit.*, p. 169.

105 J. Hunt, *English Religious Thought from the Reformation to the End of the Last Century*, London, 1873, vol. 3; J. Gascoigne, *Cambridge in the Age of the Enlightenment: Science, Religion and Politics from Restoration to the French Revolution*, Cambridge, 1989.

106 E. A. Varley, *The Last of the Prince Bishops*, Cambridge, 1992, pp. 41–2.

107 W. Paley, *The Principles of Moral and Political Philosophy*, London, 1785, p. 145.

108 W. Paley, 'Sermon preached at the Consecration of John Law DD to the Diocese of Clonfert . . . 21 Sept 1782', *The Works of William Paley DD in one volume*, London, 1853, pp. 588–9.

109 A. M. C. Waterman, 'A Cambridge "Via Media" in Late Georgian Anglicanism', *Journal of Ecclesiastical History*, 1991, vol. 42, no. 3.

110 J. Tucker, *op. cit.*, pp.13, 51.

111 G. M. Ditchfield, 'Ecclesiastical Policy Under Lord North', C. Haydon, J. Walsh and S. Taylor (eds.), *op. cit.*; *idem*, 'The Subscription Issue in British Parliamentary Politics, 1772–9', *Parliamentary History*, 1988, vol. 7, no. 7; J. E. Bradley, *Popular Politics and the American Revolution in England*, Macon, 1986; W. Gibson, *Church, State and Society 1760–1850*, London, 1994.

112 B. North, *A Sermon before the Incorporated Society for the Propagation of the Gospel in Foreign Parts . . .* , London, 1778.

113 F. Mather, *op. cit.*, p. 223.

114 W. Jones, *Sermons: Practical, Doctrinal and Expository*, London, 1829, pp. 139–41.

115 'The Jews are in much the same case with the other dissenters from the Church of England: we ought not to look on them as enemies to our ecclesiastical establishment, but as men whose conscience will not allow them to conform to it; therefore we may, in charity we ought to, indulge them so far as not to endanger thereby our ecclesiastical establishment'. W. Gibson, *Religion and Society in England and Wales, 1689–1800, op. cit.*, pp. 221–4.

116 William Cowper in his *Expostulation* charged that Pitt had:

> . . . made the symbol of atoning grace
> An office-key, a pick-lock to a place
> That infidels may prove their titles good
> By an oath dipp'd in sacramental blood. . . .

117 G. M. Ditchfield, 'Anti-trinitarianism and Toleration in Late Eighteenth Century British Politics: The Unitarian Petition of 1792', *Journal of Ecclesiastical History*, 1991, vol. 42, no. 1. In fact the 1792 Unitarian petition was not the product of a mass movement, it only attracted between 1,600 and 2,000 signatures and was representative largely of affluent support rather than the *sans culottes*.

118 K. Hylson-Smith, *The Churches in England from Elizabeth I to Elizabeth II*, London, 1997, vol. 2, p. 199.

119 D. Hempton, 'Evangelicalism and Reform *c*.1780–1832', J. Wolffe (ed.), *Evangelical Faith and Public Zeal: Evangelicals and Society in Britain, 1780–1980*, London, 1995, pp. 26–7.

120 E. Neale, *The Life of the Duke of Kent*, London, p. 320.
121 *Parliamentary Debates*, xvii, p. 769.
122 *Ibid.*, xxxviii, pp. 710–12.
123 H. S. Skeats, *A History of the Free Churches in England*, London, 1869, p. 567.
124 *Test Act Reporter*, March 1827, p. 2.
125 Skeats *op. cit.*, p. 571.
126 Skeats, *op. cit.*, pp. 578–9.
127 *The Works of William Paley DD in one volume, op. cit.*, p. 146.

4

CHURCH LEADERSHIP IN THE AFTERMATH OF TOLERATION

The nature of the Church's leadership in society was varied. It was effected through, among others, the bishops' leadership of the clergy and laity, through the Church courts' regulation of morality and spiritual discipline, and through the Church's dominance of the universities. In these three fields ecclesiastical leadership was focused on doctrinal orthodoxy and pastoral uniformity. The nature of the Church's leadership was altered by the Toleration Act of 1689. For clergy, the urge to promote religious uniformity was intensified by Toleration; for many parishioners Toleration meant choice. For the first time since the Reformation nonconformist worship was legal and in consequence, as during the Reformation, the Church responded with a greater emphasis on uniformity of religious experience. Diversity in religion and disunity were regarded by Anglicans as a cause of Nonconformity and were to be avoided at all costs. As a result much of the work of eighteenth-century bishops and clergy, irrespective of spiritual complexion, focused on the development of ecclesiastical unity and the uniformity of worship and religious observance.

The Victorian historical confidence-trick, to which Clark and others have objected, reached its zenith in the consideration given to the leadership of the eighteenth-century Church. The bishops of the eighteenth century have rarely been considered in any broader context than of the criticism heaped upon them by nineteenth-century historians, and have been judged by standards never achieved in either the pre- or post-Reformation Church in England. Rosemary O'Day's study of the Elizabethan and Jacobean episcopates illustrates some of the problems they faced: low incomes, low standards of education, poor recruitment, administrative tasks which outstripped their experience or abilities, conflict with Catholics and Puritans, inadequate patronage and indiscriminate ordination. O'Day's conclusion is that for the most part, the Elizabethan episcopate faced enormous problems and attempted only *ad hoc* solutions, many of which were ineffective.[1] Similarly, the evaluation of the Stuart episcopate by

Kenneth Fincham sounds uncannily like Overton and Relton's view of that of the eighteenth century.[2] In short, there was no 'golden age' in the Reformation Church from which the episcopate of the eighteenth century had declined.

Moreover, Norman Ravitch's comparative study of the French and English episcopates places the eighteenth-century English episcopate in a European context. The English episcopate was drawn from a wider social spectrum than their aristocratic French counterparts, and was consequently better integrated into society. The English Church was not exploited for places for nobles as in France; nor did it develop the aristocratic mentality of the French Church.[3] Daniel Hirschberg's study of the eighteenth-century episcopate confirms that it developed some caste features. For example, it became increasingly dominated by recruits from the middle class – and especially clerical – families. The eighteenth-century Anglican episcopate was better educated, better prepared, trained in 'middle management', and populated by men of diverse and significant achievement more than at any earlier time.[4] Increasingly, the rising incomes of the bishops, their growing social status and achievements prior to consecration have been seen as advantages which overcame two centuries of an episcopate hamstrung by low incomes, low status and low levels of training.[5]

The plethora of published visitation returns and diocesan records demonstrates the gravity and conscientiousness with which these bishops exercised oversight of their clergy – a unique measure since visitation records are not complete for the seventeenth century and by the nineteenth century had changed in form.[6] In making evaluations of the leadership of the Church, historians have been distracted by individual bishops. Yet, of course, this is not the point. In all ages of English history there have been clergy and laity whose values and behaviour have exceeded or fallen short of the canons of the Church and the standards set for them by bishops. The measure of the leadership of the eighteenth-century Church is not whether in thousands of parishes across England and Wales pastoral perfection was achieved (even if it could be effectively assessed);[7] but what was the quality of leadership provided by the bishops, what were the standards established by the Church for the clergy and laity, and in what direction did the bishops lead them? The episcopate only exercised direct supervision of the clergy, lay discipline was loosened by the Toleration Act and the growth of secularity. Throughout the eighteenth century, the episcopate focused on doctrinal and liturgical unity as a critical objective, and high pastoral standards as the means to achieve it. Disunity had been the cause of religious and political strife in the seventeenth century, and was therefore to be avoided at all costs. Moreover, disunity opened the door for the competing denominations newly-legitimised by the Toleration Act. Through precepts for the life and work of the clergy, the bishops strove for unity and harmony. It is by these principles, clearly stated as general rules, that the episcopate should be judged. What is helpful to historians is that there is no lack of such principles laid down in the correspondence of bishops in the eighteenth century. Indeed the number of them is testimony to the bishops' determination to give explicit guidance to their clergy.

That eighteenth-century bishops, High Churchmen and Latitudinarians alike, took their duties of leadership seriously is undoubted. William Wake's view of the episcopate was expressed on his nomination to Exeter in November 1705: 'I have a high opinion of the work of it and know too well my own insufficiency for it'.[8] Gilbert Burnet held a similarly high view, and on the eve of his consecration composed a prayer for strength in discharging the heavy duties of the office.[9] He also set himself demanding targets, including annual visitations of his diocese.[10] White Kennett was equally anxious to lay down the affirming nature of the relationship between him and his clergy,

> let my clergy expect from me a paternal care, a brotherly love and a friendly reception upon all reasonable occasions of access or application to me: they shall find me ready to advise them, and as far as I am able, to instruct them in any duties of their office and functions; to protect them according to law in all their just rights and privileges. . . .[11]

But bishops were also rigorous and determined in calling their clergy to account. In 1700 Bishop Jonathan Trelawny told his clergy, with some conviction, that 'I will never fail of punishing an ill clergyman, I am always ready to support a good one, and will stand close by him against all the powers and factions on earth'.[12] Trelawny's view of the duty and blessings of episcopacy was that it established a focus of unity for the Church. In 1708, reflecting on the English Civil War, he identified the danger that 'each parochial Church had its particular faith and through the diversity of their opinions there was such a spawn of impious doctrines. . . .'[13]

Predictably in the search for uniformity of purpose, one of the bishops' principal concerns was the preparation and examination of candidates for orders. Bishop Gilbert Burnet asserted 'I looked on ordinations as the most important part of a bishop's care and that on which the law had laid no restraints . . .'.[14] White Kennett, Bishop of Peterborough, pointed out to the clergy in 1710 that they should take great care to provide testimonials for candidates for orders only to 'fit persons'. As he explained, 'I shall ordain none . . . but upon your testimonials, and your titles; and if you are not faithful and truly conscientious in them, I shall be mistaken . . .'. Moreover

Kennett weeded out unsuitable candidates, including one for 'being often in drink and talking very rudely', even though his 'title and learning were very sufficient'.[15]

The urge to establish and monitor high standards of pastoral care and the need to ensure doctrinal orthodoxy led the bishops to warn the clergy not to employ curates without the sanction of the diocesan, whose duty it was to license each parson in the diocese. Wake insisted of curates,

> I must take this occasion openly to declare that I do not allow, nay as much as in me lies I do inhibit them from preaching, unless they be first examined and approved by myself. . . .[16]

The duty of licensing clergy was one which bishops could use to attempt to diminish non-residence. In 1722 Archbishop Wake wrote to the clergy of his London peculiars with a resolution: 'I will not grant a licence to any person to be a lecturer in London who is already possessed of two cures of souls'.[17] Bishops were also keen to regulate the salaries of curates, though not simply in order to relieve their poverty. Samuel Horsley in October 1788 wrote,

> I should have felt but little satisfaction in my late regulation for augmenting the stipends of the curates throughout my diocese, had I not a further view to the encouragement it would afford to their better education. . . .[18]

If the examination and regulation of incumbents and curates was a precondition for the performance of their religious duty, so of course was residence. This was also a matter that bishops often drew to the attention of the clergy. Thomas Secker was especially keen to demand that his clergy reside:[19]

> it must not be pleaded that however necessary the residence of some minister may be that of a curate may suffice. For your engagement is, not merely that the several duties of your parish shall be done, but that you personally will do them.[20]

The duty of taking services was one which bishops would not allow the clergy to shirk. Thomas Secker was explicit in linking the need for performance of duty to the presence of non-Anglicans in a parish. James Martin incumbent of Heythrop received a warning from Secker in August 1738 that the smallness of your congregation ought not to hinder you from performing divine service in your Church twice every Sunday and that your having papist families in your parish makes it particularly requisite. . . .

The correspondence between Secker and Martin on the bishop's demands continued for some weeks, but Secker gave no quarter.[21]

Bishops like Thomas Secker were aware that one distinction between nonconformity and Anglicanism was the opportunity for Holy Communion offered by the Church. It was a weapon to be used in the contest with Dissent, and in emphasising the importance of doctrinal conformity of parishioners. Secker in his second charge advised his clergy that

one thing might be done at present in all your parishes, as, God be thanked, it is in most of them; a sacrament might easily be interposed in that long interval between Whitsuntide and Christmas; and the usual season for it, about the feast of St Michael (when your people having gathered in the fruits of the earth have some rest from their labours, and must surely feel some gratitude to the Giver of all the good) is a very proper time. And if afterwards you can advance from a quarterly Communion to a monthly one, I make no doubt but you will.[22]

Secker was following a trend established by Edmund Gibson who, while rector of Lambeth, published *The Sacrament of the Lords Supper Explained: or the things to be known and done to make a worthy communicant . . .* (1705). The book exhorted his parishioners to 'daily prayers and frequently receiving of the Holy Sacrament'. It also encouraged the parishioners to examine themselves in preparation for receipt of Holy Communion. The 'Heads of Examination' included one hundred and seventy-three questions that communicants should ask themselves to ascertain their suitability for the eucharist. These included the communicant's 'duty to God', 'duty to neighbour', 'duty to ourselves', as well as duties to children, parents, brethren, spouses, masters and servants.[23] In this way frequent Communion and doctrinal orthodoxy were encouraged to go hand in hand. In some areas regular Communions were established for entirely practical reasons. In 1743, Thomas Herring was told that at Holy Trinity, Hull weekly Communions had been held for fourteen years. Previously there had been monthly Communions but the vicar and curate could not deal with the hundreds of communicants, so the vicar had adopted weekly Communions as a way of dealing with the large numbers.[24]

Bishops were also insistent on the attendance of the clergy at their visitations, not least so that the clergy could follow the bishops' precepts. In 1750 Bishop Secker sent Mr Stockwood of Henley a stinging rebuke for failure to attend his visitation:

> Appearing before your Diocesan is somewhat more in the way of your profession than sitting upon appeals for the Land Tax: my citation, I conceive, carries somewhat more authority with it than the summons of a clerk: there are other commissioners of that tax, but only one rector of Henley, why then should you not rather have given notice to them, that you were obliged to be with me?[25]

The instructions and precepts laid down by the bishops did not only apply to clergy. In April 1740 Secker made churchwardens the object of his demands when he wrote to Dr Ward, rector of Cuddesdon with a list of instructions for the repair and decorations of the Church.[26] Archdeacons were also an important part of the oversight of ecclesiastical unity. William Wake in 1707 wrote to his archdeacons,

> I do therefore particularly desire you in your approaching visitation to press the clergy of your archdeaconry to a steady and regular observance of that part of the Act of Uniformity which relates to catechising . . . and that . . . they must expect to be answerable to God and their own consciences, as well as the laws ecclesiastical and civil of this realm for any ill consequence of their neglect. . . .'[27]

Catechising led to confirmation, and in this matter bishops were alert to the way in which it reinforced membership of the Church. Confirmation often placed burdens on bishops.

In contrast to traditional historiography, Benjamin Hoadly also set himself rigorous objectives. In his charge to the clergy at his primary visitation in the diocese of Winchester, he argued

> I have thought it much better to defer it [confirmation] for some time, than to mix it with the business of the visitation: but I shall take the first opportunity of confirming throughout my diocese, and shall afterwards, if God grant me health, frequently repeat that office in a regular course: of which due notices shall always be given you.[28]

The stringency of the discipline exercised by the bishops over their clergy had specific objectives: the effective operation of the Church through the proper selection and licensing of the clergy, their residence and professional standards of duty. But these were means not ends. The immediate purpose of the effective operation of the Church was to enable the discharge of the spiritual teachings of Christianity. But there were also goals which focused on popular adherence to the Church, on its unity, and the uniformity of worship and religious observance.

To achieve these goals bishops issued advice and instruction most frequently in the form of charges at visitations, and in pastoral letters. Bishop Henry Compton, for example, held regular conferences with his clergy during his tenure of the diocese of London from 1675 to 1713. In all there were twelve conferences on such matters as the liturgy, baptism, the eucharist, confirmation, extempore prayer and all manner of canons and pastoral activities. After each conference he published a pastoral letter encapsulating his view of the topic discussed.[29] But the guidance he provided went beyond matters of doctrine and religion. Compton's conference of 1692 focused on 'how they [the clergy] ought to behave themselves under a toleration'. Compton made clear his support for the Toleration Act and claimed that it afforded a 'repose' for Dissenters, and indicated his high hopes for co-operation between the Church and Dissent. His objective was for the Church and Dissent to live amicably together. Compton argued it would 'render charity triumphant over division . . . and make us one in spirit though of different minds'.[30] He also advocated that Anglican clergy and Dissenters should co-operate to seek out those who attended neither Church nor Chapel and enforce their attendance.

Compton was perhaps unduly optimistic in hoping that Toleration would become a matter of temperament as well as of law. Most of his fellow bishops thought Toleration established competition for the Church and some of their charges to the clergy reflected this. Up to the middle of the eighteenth century, when Dissent was prematurely declared dead, the charges of the bishops focused on the development and strengthening of those features of pastoral work of the Church which would act as a bulwark against Dissent. Leading bishops such as Thomas Tenison, John Sharp, White Kennett, Edmund Gibson, William Wake, William Lloyd and Thomas Sherlock exhorted their clergy to take great pains in catechising, in preaching, in providing a moral example to their congregations, in encouraging confirmation and in conducting daily prayers.[31] For these bishops the principal means to respond to the Toleration of Dissent was to develop those features of the Church which would attract parishioners away from Dissent, and to buttress the doctrines of the Church against Dissent. To improve the teaching of the people, to offer them greater opportunities to conform to the Church and to lead them by example seemed to be the most effective way to dispel the attractions of any alternative to the established Church.

Catechising especially concerned bishops as there was evidence that in the seventeenth century the practice had been displaced in some parts by an afternoon sermon.[32] Moreover catechising was the best opportunity for clergy to ensure the retention of the laity by the Church, and to underpin the uniformity and orthodoxy of their beliefs. John Tillotson moved catechising away from the traditional rigid form of question and answer, in which there were formal enquiries and responses on the doctrines of the Church. Tillotson argued that this system inhibited genuine knowledge and understanding of the doctrines and was not a method laid down by scripture. Bishops Simon Patrick and Gilbert Burnet were equally keen to abandon the old system of question and answer and replace it with a discourse between the pastor and the children of his parish.[33] Gilbert Burnet was also anxious that catechism and confirmation should be a carefully considered choice:

> I judged that nothing would be a likelier means to raise the spirit of religion . . . than the calling on persons to be confirmed not in their childhood upon their having the Church catechism by rote, but when they were coming to years of discretion. . . . I thought that this would likewise give the clergy the opportunity of going from house to house about their parishes.[34]

Bishops like William Wake, Edmund Gibson, Thomas Herring and Thomas Secker showed concern in their visitation enquiries that catechising should be undertaken.

As a result there is evidence of a significant revival of catechising in the eighteenth century. William Beveridge complained of the neglect of catechising in the seventeenth century and both he, and later Edmund Gibson, promoted the idea of catechising undertaken by parents at home. The eighteenth century also saw new catechising methods supported by the use of books which were divided into an introduction to the catechism and planned weekly readings and reflections. Ian Green's conclusion on catechising in the eighteenth century is that:

> despite the onset of a limited Toleration in 1689, catechising took place in a clear majority of parishes for at least part of the year and that in a number of parish churches and elementary schools there was also some second-level catechising in the form of exposition of what had been taught already. . . . There [was] also a shift away from stating that the laity did not *know* the basics, to saying that they did not *understand* them fully.[35]

Moreover Robert Cornwall has recently concluded that confirmation was an area of Anglican spiritual vitality in the eighteenth century. Cornwall identified over two hundred publications on the rite during the century, and suggests that bishops strove to impress its importance on the clergy.[36] Wake was to observe with some satisfaction,

> I do believe that confirmations have never been so regular throughout the kingdom as within the last thirty years, nor the episcopal visitation, and that by the bishop in person, so constant. . . .[37]

Toleration, in establishing a 'market' in religion, created a dilemma for the bishops, and a tension in matters of pastoral care. The laity could act as 'customers' of the Church, for which there were now alternative suppliers; but the Church still had demands to make upon both the clergy and the laity. In his visitation sermon and charge in 1708, Bishop George Bull of St David's indicated that the new environment of Toleration demanded renewed efforts by the clergy. His sermon laid down four qualities for his clergy: knowledge, prudence, exemplary holiness and responsibility for parishioners, and he exhorted his clergy to great effort:

> let us therefore, reverend brethren . . . from henceforth return to our several charges, zealously and industriously plying the great work and business that is before us. Let us think no pains too great to escape that greater judgement that otherwise attends us. Let us study hard and read much, and pray often and preach in season and out of season and catechise the youth. . . .[38]

Bull's charge also listed five duties of a parson: reading divine services, preaching, catechising, administering Holy Communion and visiting the sick.[39]

But Bull's high view of clerical duties did not exist in a vacuum. In both his sermon and charge Bull directly addressed the laity on the nature of ministerial care under Toleration. He wanted to defend the clergy from the Nonconformist intruders into parishes. In his sermon he reminded the laity that each clergyman had been trained in 'the schools of the prophets' and had been ordained after a long period of study. Therefore he asked

> how horrible is the confidence, or rather the impudence of those mechanics that have leapt from the shopboard or plough into the pulpit, and thus *per saltem* by a prodigious leap commenced [as] teachers! . . . It is a miracle that any such person should dare to

preach, or if he do than any man in his right wits should vouch-safe to hear him. . . .[40]

But while the dangers of Toleration were clear, they did not moderate Bull's strident tone with the laity in the duties they owed to the clergy among them to

> give honour and respect to your pastors for the Lord's sake, what-ever their personal defects may be . . . their character and office calls for this from you. . . .

He spoke equally sternly to churchwardens threatening them with the damnation of their own souls if they failed in their duties.[41] For bishops like Bull, Toleration might have created competition in the form of ploughboys who mounted the pulpit, but it did not diminish the demands he made on the laity for the respect and dues owed to the clergy.

Bishop Bull's inflexible sacerdotal view was not representative. For once, Hoadly was more typical of his fellows in encouraging clergy to embrace a high view of the priesthood without fostering rancour with Dissenters. Hoadly argued that clergy had chosen holy orders in the Church of England because it was the best form of Christianity, and they were therefore committed to its defence. In his charge to the clergy of the diocese of Salisbury in 1726 he wrote:

> we must consider ourselves as ministers in the Church of England . . . we have deliberately chosen, not merely conformity to this Church but the ministerial duty in it. And if we have acted sincerely in this . . . this choice must have been made because it appeared to us . . . to be the most unexceptionable and most excellent of all which have come within our view. . . . This there-fore we are obliged to defend by our arguments as persons always ready to give a reason for the choice we have made. . . . In all our defences of it [the Church] against those who differ from us . . . we must never forget the two considerations that we are Christians and Protestants.

For Hoadly the most effective means to combat Dissent was for the clergy to lead public worship:

> in a manner that may shew us to have a mind to preserve and to conciliate a respect and serious regard to them: behaving ourselves . . . with the utmost decency and gravity: reading the offices

with a distinct, deliberate and manly pronunciation; without the affectation of anything theatrical on one hand, or anything low, careless, dead and spiritless on the other.[42]

In his second charge to the clergy of Salisbury, Hoadly went even further. He praised the 'blessings' derived from the 'legal settlement of Christianity in this country', but asked his clergy what they sought to do with such an advantage: 'shall we spend our time cursing our enemies, in calling down fire from heaven upon them?' Hoadly's charge was that the clergy should employ themselves in learning and acquisition of knowledge.[43] In his third Winchester charge in 1736 Hoadly spoke of the nature of the priesthood. He took the words of the ordination service to develop the role of the clergy as 'watchmen, messengers and stewards' of the Church. It was a theme that allowed him to advocate evangelism, pastoralia and admonishment.[44]

It was not just nonconformity against which the bishops warned the laity in the first half of the eighteenth century. Another competitor to orthodox Anglicanism was deism. Bishop Edmund Gibson of London addressed this issue directed in his *Third Pastoral Letter to the People of his Diocese . . .* (1731). Gibson denounced deist writings as attacks on the New Testament. His advice to the laity of his diocese was to cleave to the teaching of the Church: that the four gospels contained the truth of the life of Christ and that the acts and epistles of the apostles laid down the scheme of Christianity to be followed. It was a thoroughly orthodox Pauline defence of the Church, founded on the assertion that the early Fathers accepted the apostles' teachings as a model for the Church. Gibson also attacked Locke's *Reasonableness of Christianity . . .* as rejecting the teachings of the apostles. The climax of the letter was an appeal to hold fast to the New Testament and reject novel writings that were inspired by 'profit or pleasure, pride or passion'.[45]

Under Toleration the nature of the advice and leadership offered by the bishops to their clergy responded to the circumstances in which they lived and this applied equally to the second half of the eighteenth century. By the end of the eighteenth century new dangers were reflected in episcopal charges and pastoral letters. The dangerous events in France were denounced in the 1790s, not least by Bishop Richard Watson of Llandaff.[46] Equally dangerous, claimed Bishop Pretyman of Lincoln, were millenarian ideas circulating in England.[47] But the most significant social change that faced the bishops and clergy was the growth of an industrial working class and a rural population that was susceptible to Dissent.

Bishop John Butler of Hereford's charge of 1792 compared the Church attendances evidenced by the visitation of 1747 with that in 1792 and was alarmed by the decline. Paradoxically, Butler claimed that the drop was due in part to the energy the clergy had spent on defending the doctrines of the Church; but Butler claimed that battle against heterodoxy was now won, and that the clergy had to turn their attention to their pastoral duties.[48] Even the arch-conservative Bishop Lewis Bagot of Norwich was shocked by the complacency of some of his clergy. In 1784 he excoriated those who seemed too quiescent, citing one who referred to 'the stated and occasional duty' of his cure:

> 'the stated and occasional duty'! Good God! Is this their care, their anxious concern for the souls of those of whom they are to give their account to their Redeemer?[49]

Bishops like Beilby Porteus and William Cleaver, both of whom learnt their lessons as successive bishops of Chester, made clear their determination to respond to the challenges of huge urban parishes which were growing in the great cities of the north.[50] For Porteus, the problem remained competition with nonconformity, and he returned to a theme comparable to the early eighteenth-century response to Toleration:

> It is a fact which admits of little doubt that when the itinerant preacher who goes forth upon his mission, he commonly looks out for those parishes where either the shepherd has entirely deserted his flock. . . . But in general he very prudently keeps aloof from those parishes where he sees a resident minister . . . ; watching over his people with unremitting care; grounding them early in the rudiments of sound religion; guarding them against the false glosses and dangerous delusions of illiterate and unauthorised teachers . . . into parishes so constituted the self-commissioned preacher seldom, if ever, enters. . . .[51]

Porteus's attack on non-residence was echoed in the charges of Buckner of Chichester, Horsley of St Asaph and Secker of Canterbury.[52]

In such circumstances, as in the first half of the eighteenth century, the bishops urged their clergy to action. Porteus emphasised the importance of residence to the clergy as the key to success and Sunday schools as a means to inculcate sabbatarianism among the young of the industrial cities.[53] Bishop Majendie of Chester asked his clergy to ensure that they enforced the 1802 Health and Morals of Apprentices Act as vigorously as possible to avoid godlessness among the poor.[54] Avowedly political concerns were increasingly apparent in charges and pastoral letters. The emphasis on the social conditions of the poor was born of the concern that the lower classes, if neglected by the clergy, were prey to Dissent. Bishop Fisher of Exeter claimed that Christianity was a gospel of 'social action' which he urged on his clergy in order to defend the interests of the poor.[55] More optimistic, perhaps, was Horsley's view that his clergy should emphasise that all people, whatever their station, could achieve salvation.[56] To effect this, and with one eye on revolutionary France perhaps, his fellow bishops were keen to encourage the clergy to act as agents of social reconciliation. In 1794, Pretyman told his clergy that their role was to promote a gospel of 'gentleness, forbearance and contentment' among the poor. Porteus held that the role of the clergy was to promote 'the peace, the morale, the good order, the welfare and the happiness of the community'.[57] Majendie was more concerned that the disaffection of the working classes would spread to the lower orders of the clergy. In 1804 he reassured the clergy that the new legislation against pluralism and for minimum stipends for curates[58] was a reward for the clergy for their exertions.[59] Bishops also felt that the Church's improvement lay in the hands of the wealthy. Barrington of Durham told his clergy that he hoped that the problem of church building might be resolved by the great landed magnates. John Randolph of London hoped that the wealthy areas of London could be encouraged to raise money for church building in Hackney and Marylebone.[60] But there were also bishops who sounded a warning, that unless the clergy showed themselves capable of reforming themselves, the Church would be reformed from without by 'ruder hands'.[61]

The pastoral leadership of the Church by bishops was complemented by the moral leadership in society provided by the Church courts. It has become an axiom of those who advance a pessimistic view of the eighteenth-century Church that it was too enfeebled to enforce spiritual and moral discipline.[62] In fact the spiritual and moral jurisdiction of the Church declined later than has hitherto been conceded, and then largely owing to external factors rather than to want of popular regard for spiritual discipline or the absence of a coherent Anglican culture. After the Restoration a statute of 1661 relieved defendants of the burden of having to give evidence on oath that might incriminate themselves.[63] The measure was an attempt to avoid repetition of the practices of the Commonwealth's High Commission, but it hit ecclesiastical courts hard, as they often relied on the sworn evidence of defendants. Moreover the cost of litigation in the Church courts increased dramatically after 1694 when a stamp duty of sixpence a page was applied to all legal documents.[64] There was also a strong argument that the Toleration Act of 1689 made Church courts an anachronism, especially if they were to pass judgement on people who might observe the doctrines of a different denomination. Moreover Toleration meant penitents could 'vote with their feet'. As William Wake wrote in 1715:

> if any person be admonished to come to Holy Communion or [be] threatened for that as for any other neglect, they presently cry they will go to the [Dissenters'] meetings to avoid discipline.[65]

There were also secular legal incursions into the work of the spiritual courts. During the eighteenth century successive civil judges accepted legal proceedings on tithe, debt, and charities in the Chancery courts, which had greater powers of enforcement than ecclesiastical courts. Gradually Chancery courts also took over actions on money suits arising from probate, and again circumvented ecclesiastical jurisdiction. In other areas judges in civil courts granted prohibitions against hearings by the spiritual courts, until a codification was established in 1776 by Lord Mansfield. It was no wonder that the Societies for the Reformation of Manners sought to prosecute vice and immorality in magistrates' courts, where justice was more quickly and securely administered; but it was also an irony that such organisations should so obviously undermine the Church courts.

As parliamentary legislation increased, the range of matters defined by statute and therefore reserved for the civil courts also grew; most famously traditional ecclesiastical jurisdiction over marriage was appropriated by Lord Hardwicke's Marriage Act of 1753 into the civil courts, and in consequence vast swathes of cases fell from the Church courts. Legislation on cathedral statutes in 1707, on the union of parishes in 1714 and 1733, on probate in 1692 and on curacies in 1713 provided the opportunity for prohibitions from civil courts to prevent ecclesiastical jurisdiction over them. Thus a clergyman in 1741 was found in contempt of a Chancery court for conducting the marriage of a ward without permission of the court.[66] As Edmund Gibson asserted of religious matters, 'after a temporal law has put the work into temporal hands, yet it [ecclesiastical jurisdiction] certainly loses its vigour and effects. . . .'[67] Gibson himself knew only too well the potency of civil law: in 1746 he resorted to the secular rather than spiritual courts to prosecute the racing of coaches between Tyburn and Watford on a Sunday.[68] Certainly studies of York and Exeter dioceses suggest that tithe disputes were particularly prone to transfer to the civil courts.[69]

A plethora of manuals on Church law was produced in the eighteenth century to respond to changes in ecclesiastical and civil law and the type of cases presented to the courts.[70] A further blow came in Lord Hardwicke's judgement in 1736 in the celebrated case of *Middleton v. Croft* which found that the canons of 1603 were not binding on the laity unless they were also confirmed by statute. By 1787 another constraint on Church courts was effected by an act allowing a statute of limitations on cases before them of eight months, to prevent the Church courts from prosecutions for ante-natal fornication.[71]

Explanations for the decline of the Church courts may also lie in the changing relationship between landlords and tenants, which made the courts redundant as an instrument of social control. Before enclosure there was perhaps a legitimate role for the spiritual courts in settling moral and religious matters between yeomen; after enclosure the discipline that land-lords could exercise over their tenants and employees was so monolithic and unquestionable, and largely dominated by a labour contract rather than moral obligation, that it superseded the need for spiritual jurisdiction.

Thus the legal framework within which the spiritual courts operated became both increasingly complex and loaded in favour of the civil courts. The proposal of the radical Whigs in 1733 further reduce to the Church courts of their powers was an easy way to attack the Church because legal constraints had grown up so much as to create a thicket of legal problems in some suits.[72] There was also political interference in the Whig governments' Acts of General Pardon in 1689, 1696, 1708, and on other occasions later in the century, which relieved those under sentence by the ecclesiastical courts for spiritual offences of their punishments. In the *Codex Juris Anglicani* Gibson held that the State had encroached too much on the jurisdiction of the Church courts and should return the responsibility for the suppression of vice to them.[73] However the authority of the civil courts to enforce spiritual discipline rigorously was evident in the 1750 assize sermon at Winchester, in which the preacher asserted that civil 'magistrates were appointed by God to punish vice'. Moreover civil courts could defend the Church more effectively than the ecclesiastical courts: in July 1756, for example, the assizes in Winchester sentenced a man to the pillory three times for transgressions of the Blasphemy laws.[74] In such circumstances, it is a wonder that the Church's spiritual jurisdiction operated after 1689 at all; certainly ecclesiastical lawyers and registrars found it harder to earn their fees.[75] However the eighteenth century saw expressions of the highest possible view of ecclesiastical jurisdiction: Edmund Gibson wrote that the Church had a 'divine right' to 'exercise spiritual discipline'.[76]

In fact the longevity of the Church's jurisdiction was greater than has been supposed: W. E. Tate discovered an example of public penance for defamation at Westbury-on-Severn, Gloucestershire as late as 1846 – nine years before the abolition of the spiritual courts' jurisdiction over defamation.[77] In some areas the role of the Church courts remained extremely strong throughout the eighteenth century. On the Isle of Man, for example, Bishop Thomas Wilson maintained the Church's spiritual jurisdiction with vigour, even drawing up forms for the use of his clergy for acts of public penance, for reconciliation and for excommunication. As a result of his leadership, the Manx Church courts were active and commanded widespread support in the population of the Island.[78] In London too, the Church courts were active, hearing four hundred and sixty-one cases in the first decade of the eighteenth century, by the middle decade this fell to two hundred and thirteen, but, by the final decade, this had stabilised at two hundred and eleven cases.[79] In Winchester diocese also Church courts were active and accorded popular assent.[80] There is circumstantial evidence of the activity of the Church courts in *The Compleat Parish Officer* (1734), which instructed churchwardens in their duties in the prosecution of 'adulterers, fornicators, drunkards, swearers, blasphemers . . .' etc. in the Church courts. It also came in the regularity with which the episcopal visitation enquiries asked whether such offenders were presented in the ecclesiastical courts.[81]

An insight into the compelling nature of prosecution in Church courts is evident in a letter from William Wake regarding Mr Draper, vicar of Stageden and Stevington, who had transgressed a spiritual injunction:

> this is a crime. . . . If the censures of the Church take effect upon him, he will be cast out of the ministry. . . . If otherwise, I do not see how we shall acquit ourselves either before God or men, of being partakers with him in his sins. . . . We have the eyes of many . . . upon us and which is much more, we have a God in Heaven to whom we must render an account of what we are now doing . . . for myself . . . I shall do it on that side which the glory of God and the honour of his Church . . . and the discouragement of vice and immorality all prompt me to err. . . .[82]

To do nothing to correct vice and immorality meant that parishioners were all partakers in the sin and as liable to punishment by God as the sinners themselves.

Mary Kinnear has shown that in Carlisle diocese after 1700 the assumption that the Church courts were moribund is 'premature'.[83] Presentations to the archdeacons' and consistory courts increased in Carlisle in the eighteenth century: they were made in about thirty per cent of the parishes in the diocese in the early eighteenth century, and in the period 1731–40 this rose to about sixty per cent of parishes. There was a sharp rise in the percentage of cases for sexual immorality: between 1704 and 1756 such cases rose from fifty three per cent of the total to ninety nine per cent of cases.[84] This appears to have been a national trend and may in part be due to external influences; in some dioceses, such as Oxford, midwives were required by their oaths to report illegitimate births to the Church courts. In London, where defamation made up a majority of cases for most of the century, it may have been due to a greater vigilance by parish authorities, such as that exhibited in St Luke's, Chelsea in the 1790s. Moreover popular opinion swung against 'bastardy', as evidenced by the Act of 1732 which permitted the imprisonment of fathers of illegitimate children until they paid the parish funds to support their children.[85] A further reason why the Church courts were increasingly active in sexual regulation is that it became of greater concern to parishioners. Eighteenth-century women were increasingly protective of their reputations, and actions for defamation were part of the growth of the defence of sexual reputations.[86] The rise of affective marriage may also lie behind an increase in cases for marriage within the proscribed degrees of kinship and affinity;[87] certainly the increase in cases of divorce and disputed marriage in London appears to have been the consequence of growing domesticity and affective ideas of marriage.[88]

Doubtless a further reason for the continued activity of Church courts was also the exhortations of bishops to their clergy to make presentations of offenders to the courts. In 1717, in his first charge to the clergy of Lincoln diocese, Bishop Edmund Gibson told his clergy that if admonition and reproof for immorality failed, 'there is one step further . . . and that is the presenting of offenders to the spiritual power to bring them to public shame, and to deter others from falling into the like practices'. Gibson also encouraged his clergy to act in cases of immorality, drunkenness and swearing.[89] Besides cases of immorality, presentations to the courts for administrative matters, such as the repair of churches, the enforcement of clerical residence and the provision of pews were common throughout the century. These are in some ways more compelling evidence of the credibility of Church courts, since many of these presentations were by parishioners who were anxious to ensure that they retained access to the spiritual comforts of the Church.

Jan Albers' study of Lancashire makes a strong assertion respecting Church courts in the eighteenth century: 'Lancashire deanery courts were far more effective for most of the eighteenth century than they had been in the aftermath of the Reformation'.[90] It is a view that William Jacob confirms for Norfolk – that the mid-eighteenth century Church courts were more active than those of the post-Reformation period.[91] Like Kinnear, Albers found that sexual offences made up an increasing proportion of the work of Church courts: from seventy one per cent of cases in the first decade of the eighteenth century to almost a hundred per cent of cases by the 1770s.[92] In other areas of the country the number of cases of defamation in Church courts increased as the century progressed: in the London Consistory court from 1780–83 there were fifty nine cases, a significant increase on previous years.[93] Moreover there was a marked growth in presentations to Church courts in north Lancashire from seven cases in 1710 to ninety cases in 1770 – which seems to further confirm the effectiveness of the determination of bishops like Samuel Peploe to prosecute vice.[94] Albers also suggests that a reason for the high number of presentations to the Church courts was the party strife between Whigs and Tories, which fuelled the willingness or otherwise of churchwardens to make presentations. In contrast to stereotypes of churchmanship, there was a strong correlation between high levels of presentation by Low-Church Whig clergy, and between low levels of presentation by High-Church Tory clergy. In the parishes in the east of the county, like Wigan, where Whig clergy and patrons predominated, presentations were frequent. In contrast, in those parishes dominated by Tory patrons and High-Church clergy, such as Standish, North Meols, Leyland, Croston and Leigh, there was a low level of presentation.[95]

Albers' explanations lie in the residue of Calvinism among Low Churchmen and close relations between High-Church clergy and Tory patrons. The former encouraged the correction of vice in a more thorough manner, the latter promoted a willingness to overlook vice. Neither of these explanations is entirely convincing; nevertheless such evidence suggests that the dichotomy between High-Church and Low-Church attitudes may be as meaningless in moral discipline as in so many other areas. Albers also suggests that the low levels of presentations by High Churchmen engendered popular allegiance to the Church by the laity – an argument which inverts the historiography of the Church more than most.[96] However, Albers also contradicts this suggestion: in the areas of Lancashire where the Church courts were most active there was a greater rather than lesser willingness on the part of defendants to appear in the courts (nearly two-thirds of defendants in north Lancashire, compared to a third in the south).[97] This suggests that active Church courts could achieve greater esteem and responsiveness to their demands than areas in which the operation of spiritual justice was lower.

In Lancashire seven per cent of presentations were of 'gentlemen', a higher proportion than this group comprised of the population as a whole, suggesting that active Church courts were also more willing to treat offenders of differing social classes equally. This was certainly the case with Bishop Robert Frampton of Gloucester, who in the 1680s found Lord Wharton had broken into and vandalised a Church in his diocese. Frampton, though painfully aware that he was the son of a farmer and Wharton a peer, was adamant that Wharton must submit to ecclesiastical discipline or risk excommunication. When Wharton sent a servant to plead his case to Frampton the Bishop told Wharton that if he did not submit to him when he next entered his diocese he would be sentenced. Wharton submitted, and the bishop allowed him to pay a handsome fine rather than make public penance.[98]

A consequence of a sentence of public penance and excommunication was that the Church required the sentence to be lifted before further ecclesiastical processes could be enacted. Neither probate nor marriage, for example, could be granted to an undischarged penitent. In 1766 a Worcestershire parishioner endured the embarrassment of discharging his penitence, robed in a sheet and holding a white wand, before he was allowed to marry. One account is that his bride waited outside the Church with her father while her groom discharged his sentence before the wedding ceremony could begin.[99] For those who did not resolve their contumacy, or minor excommunication, the sentence could be increased to major excommunication, and if undischarged in some places, such as Middleton in Yorkshire, the guilty party was recorded as spiritually dead. Sentences of spiritual death were proclaimed as late as 1792.[100] At Lowestoft in 1720 and 1727 excommunicates were 'laid into the ground without funeral service.'[101]

One critical function of public penance was the acknowledgement of a sin so that others might be warned against it. At Lowestoft a penitent, Margaret Newton, was recorded as standing in the Church 'clothed in white, a white wand in her hand, having a paper pinned on her breast describing her crime, performed penance, December 8 1751'.[102] A more important objective of the penance imposed by Church courts was that of reconciling a community to itself and pacifying the tensions within a parish. In cases of defamation or of practices that were against the community's moral code it was important that the divisions and fissures in the parish were healed. Public penance did not therefore focus entirely on blame and guilt but also on reconciling the penitent with the community.[103] In March 1777 at Pluckley, Kent, William Jones preached to the parishioners on the occasion of public penance by two women:

> my desire is to lead you to the proper use which ought to be made of the example we have before us this day in the Church; and to stop the mouths of those . . . who may forget their profession so far as to mock at the offence when they ought to be grieved for the offender.[104]

The effect of this sort of injunction was, in many cases, that the Church courts became an arbitration service, healing the divisions in the community and effecting social harmony as much as social control. This was the explicit view advanced in James Talbot's *Judicial Power of the Church Asserted* (1707). Talbot asked 'am I my brother's keeper?' and responded with a resounding 'yes', that Church courts were the last resort for communities concerned at the behaviour of individuals and which sought to broker a resolution between individual and community.[105]

The social legitimacy accorded to penance is evidenced by its widespread use in the eighteenth century. In the archdeaconry of Nottingham in the early eighteenth century the performance of thirty five public penances a year was not unusual, and twenty-five a year in the second half of the century.[106] Across the country there were numerous examples of public penance in the second half of the eighteenth century.[107] Yet prosecutions in the Church courts were not entered into lightly, and were regarded by some clergy as evidence of the failure of their pastoral care and encouragement to a moral life. Thomas Long, rector of Finmere, Buckinghamshire, responded to Bishop Secker's visitation queries in 1738 that he had a recalcitrant woman parishioner, who failed to attend Church services; but, he told the bishop: 'when I despair of the success of my own endeavours I will take care that she is presented either by myself or the churchwardens'.[108]

At the core of the Church's ecclesiastical jurisdiction was not merely a crude instrument of social control, but a means whereby local communities could collectively strive to achieve the spiritual aspirations of the Church. Thus in February 1706 the vicar of Birstall, Yorkshire, asked the registrar of the archidiaconal court to include in the schedule of penances for his parishioners a requirement that the penitents remain in Church at the end of the service on the Sunday of their penance 'because I design a discourse upon the occasion at which I would have them present'.[109] In this sense the Church had a means to enforce the confessional nature of eighteenth-century society. The Toleration Act undoubtedly weakened the foundations of this power, but the popular legitimacy of the Church's right to enforce moral discipline was unchallenged. Though clergy strove to avoid the failure that presentation at the archdeacon's court implied, both clergy and laity seem rarely if ever to have questioned the basis on which the Church claimed to enforce moral justice. In this way the moral legitimacy of the Church's jurisdiction remained intact, even though the growth of urban centres and other factors made its application difficult. The final decline of ecclesiastical jurisdiction at the end of the century was not due to a decline in popular assent but to practical difficulties in the administration of justice. It is perhaps no coincidence that the majority of examples of penance that survived into the nineteenth century occur in the south of England.

Evidence from Hexham in the early eighteenth century suggests that detailed knowledge of an area by ecclesiastical court officers and a good measure of moderation could play an important role in earning popular legitimacy for the courts. George Ritschel, curate and lecturer of Allenhead and a commissary of the Hexham peculiar court in 1718, employed tact and local knowledge to win back the co-operation of the churchwardens appearing before the court so that they paid overdue fees. Similarly Ritschel's sensitive handling in 1712 of the case of poor Dissenters who could ill-afford to pay their Church rates was a model of judiciousness. Ritschel cited them to appear before the court, but met them privately and was generous in accepting part-payment of the rates by the offenders. As Ritschel told the registrar of the court, if he was less generous 'people here about would exclaim and reflect on your court and myself'. Three years later, Ritschel permitted two women found guilty of fornication to make their penance in ordinary clothes apart from the other penitents, because the men with whom they had sinned had already done their penance, and he did not want to compound their offence. It was, Ritschel wrote, 'very satisfactory to the congregation and all that heard of it'. Ritschel's sensitive tactics bore fruit in the widespread pressure to present those who did not attend Church after 1714. Ritschel, aware that Hexham's harsh winters placed an extra burden on Church-going, delayed action against non-attenders until Whitsun 1714. Thereafter Ritschel's action appeared harsh: he cited non-attenders and threatened sentences of excommunication. But his intention was not to make the final declaration of the sentence until he had interviewed the offenders and showed them the writs of excommunication. The results were impressive, he told the registrar 'those presented, etc. for not coming to Church have promised and begun to reform and amend'. In the end only two of the sixteen offenders were so recalcitrant as to require a declaration of excommunication.[110]

Ecclesiastical discipline applied not only to the laity; clergy were also presented by the churchwardens for a number of faults including non-residence, non-performance of duty and immorality. In 1704 Bishop Stratford of Chester deprived Mr Burges, incumbent of Maghull, and degraded him from orders for frequenting alehouses, paying boys to write his sermons, organising horse races and consorting with whores. Two years later he deprived Thomas Proddy of his living for inveterate drunkenness. He was no less stern with the ill, suspending William Dennis of Doddleston for three years and sequestering his income because he was mentally disordered. Stratford even insisted on public penance from his clergy, including John Brand vicar of Ripon, though the law did not permit this punishment for clergy. Some bishops like Thomas Wilson, William Lloyd and Samuel Peploe were noted for the sternness with which they disciplined their clergy. Schoolmasters were equally liable to dismissal for misbehaviour, Mr Wilkinson, schoolmaster of Bedale, being dismissed for drunkenness and neglect in 1705. And churchwardens were themselves presented, often by their incumbents, for failure to repair the Church, often itself caused by their inability to extract the Church rate from the parishioners.[111]

Church discipline in the eighteenth century relied on close-knit communities of people who shared the Church's doctrines on moral regulation and were prepared to report instances of moral laxity, act as witnesses and support the churchwardens. It also relied on the adherence of the laity to the idea of the Church courts as the earthly agents of a divine order, and to a moral code that they accepted as the foundation of their lives. This may have been a counsel of perfection but it was a perfection for which the overwhelming majority of the population strove and upheld as their moral yardstick. The examples of voluntary confession of moral turpitude, which in Norwich diocese were sufficient to justify the production of a standard formula for court use, suggests that invariably and without compulsion the transgressors shared the standards that the courts enforced.[112]

There was clearly an element of collectivism in the discharge of spiritual justice that was likely to decline in effectiveness in an era of growing individualism. The concept of parochial moral justice, in which neighbours sought to evade the visitation of biblical justice for the collective sins of the community was likely to decline in an age of growing rationalism. After the middle of the eighteenth century, when there was less evidence of divine intervention in the world (at least in the forms of plagues, fires, and earthquakes) parishioners felt less personal concern at the effect of their neighbours' sin. Church discipline was a widely-accepted feature of eighteenth-century life; but it does appear to have been eroded by urban growth, in which communities were less able to police their own offenders. As Albers concluded, 'after 1750 the number of presentations began to go down . . . in roughly inverse proportion to rising population.'[113] Equally there were other forces eroding the effectiveness of the Church courts. William Jacob identified the decline of 'village tension' offences, such as witchcraft, because of the greater regulation of the poor by the wealthy and the growing demands of work and earning a living.

The execution of justice by the ecclesiastical authorities was not the only means by which the Church emphasised the shame of sin, reconciled God and sinner, and presented itself as the sole path to salvation. Criminal justice was also attended by the presence of the established Church, in the form of assize sermons and the attendance of clergymen at prisons and at the execution of prisoners. Prison visiting and providing solace for the condemned was by no means the monopoly of the Methodists in the eighteenth century. Indeed a glance at *The Newgate Calendar* confirms the emphasis placed by Anglicans on the redemption of the condemned. For example, Captain Kidd, executed on 22 May 1701, died 'professing his charity to all the world and his hope of salvation through the merits of his redeemer'. Richard Pain and his accomplices in deer-stealing died on 4 December 1723 having received the sacrament at Newgate and on the scaffold 'beseeching [God's] mercy, through the merits of Christ'. The notorious Jonathan Wild received the sacrament and questioned the chaplain of Newgate gaol closely on the sinfulness of suicide before making an unsuccessful bid to cheat the noose. The murderers James Welsh and Thomas Jones, executed on 6 September 1751, were attended by their parson, Dr Howard of St George's, Southwark. Even Lord Ferrers, executed on 5 May 1760 for the murder of a servant, after initially rejecting the chaplain's offer to pray, joined him in the Lord's Prayer and at the last called for God's pardon. The most fulsome expression of piety by a criminal was that of Dr Cameron on 7 June 1753, following his sentence for treason:

> I thank God I die in charity for all men . . . I die a steadfast, though unworthy, member of that Church in which I have always lived, the Church of England; in whose Communion, I hope, through the merits of my blessed saviour, for the forgiveness of my sins, for which I am heartily sorry.[114]

These and many other examples of gallows piety may, of course, simply be the embellishments of the authors of *The Newgate Calendar*. But even this suggests something of the expectations of the authors and readers. The role of the Church in criminal justice was both a solace for the condemned and a sanction of the system; but there was an equally important role in demonstrating to the public the sorrow and remorse experienced on the scaffold and the need for penitence for sins. Bishop Gibson in 1724 even used the repentance of the condemned as an explicit warning to people to defend Sunday observance; in a sermon at St Mary Le Bow he said:

> it is a common observation . . . that public criminals when they come to their unhappy end, and make their dying declarations to the world, frequently charge their sinful crimes in which they have lived to their neglect and abuse of the Lords Day as the first occasion of leading them into all other sorts of wickedness.[115]

The Church's emphasis on unity was also expressed through its dominance of the universities. The universities were places of potential dissension and division. Yet in the eighteenth century the Church's role in them was to moderate the divisions, and use them as a means to achieve greater doctrinal orthodoxy and unity. In the eighteenth century increasing numbers of clergy were graduates of Oxford or Cambridge and the vast majority of fellows of colleges were ordained. The Test applied to universities just as it did in the State: matriculants at Oxford were required to subscribe to the Thirty-Nine Articles and to take the oaths of allegiance and supremacy on graduation, while at Cambridge subscription to the Articles alone was required on graduation, but not on matriculation. The universities both imposed the so-called Stamford oath, which had been instituted in 1334 to prevent the establishment of a university there, but which prevented any graduate from teaching at another institution. Its use in the eighteenth century was to restrain graduates from teaching in Dissenting academies. As a result the universities were virtually untouched by the impact of the Toleration Act. Each university was also represented in parliament by two MPs, and their members carried especial weight in the House of Commons on ecclesiastical issues, as when Annesley and Bromley, members for Cambridge and Oxford, introduced the Occasional Conformity Bill of 1705. Moreover there were many bishops in the Lords who had built ecclesiastical careers as professors or heads of houses, including Atterbury, Sherlock, Gooch, Watson, Potter, Wynne, Horne, Mawson, Hough, Markham, Hallifax, Smalridge and Law. Thus both houses of parliament contained powerful Anglican representatives of the universities. It was not surprising that the Mortmain Bill of 1736, which threatened to prevent bequests to the Church and the universities, attracted such heavy Church opposition in parliament. Moreover crown patronage of key appointments in both universities provided opportunities to reward and prefer supporters.

In the universities, the opportunities for division existed as clearly as in the realm of politics. At Oxford the University was dominated by Tories, and the few leading Whigs – Gibson, Potter, Wynne, Kennett, Charlett and Wake – were beleaguered. Undergraduate Whigs, such as Edward Willes and John Conybeare, joined the staunchly Whig Constitution Club, whose activities occasionally spilled over into riots and violence.[116] These were all churchmen who later stoutly also defended Anglican orthodoxy. But Nonjury lived on in the universities, even though in the years after 1689 forty two fellows at Cambridge and fourteen at Oxford refused the oaths to William and Mary and were expelled from their colleges.[117] Of greater concern was Jacobitism, especially at Oxford, which was stubbornly rooted in the notion of the divine right of kings. In 1713 Young, a poet and fellow of All Souls, depicted Charles I at Christ's right hand in *A Poem on the Last Day*. As Queen Anne aged and ailed, every historic anniversary was the occasion for some pointed demonstration of Jacobite or Hanoverian celebration. The accession of George I sparked riots between Whigs and Jacobites in Oxford, which led to the passage of the infamous Riot Act, and also inevitably raised questions in the mind of the new regime about the loyalty of the University. Cambridge's address to George I on his accession, and Richard Bentley's sermon against Popery soon after, pleased the King sufficiently for him to make a gift of the six thousand pound library of

Bishop John Moore to the University; whereas Oxford's continuing unrest led to the despatch of a squadron of horse to quieten the city, and the imprisonment of the publisher of the *Evening Post*. Naturally invidious comparisons were made between the Hanoverian response to the two universities.

Even though some Anglicans in the universities were seriously divided there were churchmen anxious to effect the reconciliation of the university to the establishment. At Cambridge, besides Bentley, the leading advocate of reconciliation was Daniel Waterland, Master of Magdalene College.[118] Indeed Waterland presaged Gibson's achievement in drawing churchmen to an acceptance of the Hanoverian succession. As Eamon Duffy has argued,

> Waterland's real achievement in these years was to establish the compatibility of Whig political views with loyalty to the Church and its formularies and a vigorous defence of orthodox doctrine. . . . His collected writings on the Trinity represent the most sustained defence of Chalcedonian orthodoxy ever constructed in English . . . this theological work was a crucial part of the settling of moderate Whiggery as a viable option for loyal churchmen and therefore of establishing political and religious stability. . . .[119]

While Oxford Jacobites had little impact on events in the University or the State, their presence was a constant reminder of the potential threat the Hanoverian regime faced. The capture of a Christ Church undergraduate at Preston during the 1715 rebellion and the vain attempt of the Oxford Convocation to rule out certain seditious practices during the 1745 emphasised the threat from Oxford clergy. As late as 1748, in a celebrated case, Mr Blacow, a Whig, prosecuted seven Balliol undergraduates for toasting 'King James'; William King conceded that Jacobitism was dead only in 1761 and Theophilus Leigh, the Jacobite Master of Balliol, died in 1785.[120]

Nevertheless the universities assumed a vital role as the scrutineers and watchdogs of Anglican orthodoxy. The regular resolutions in the universities in the seventeenth century that passive obedience was an orthodox doctrine was a self-conscious regulation of Anglican education. Oxford's heads of houses also declared the teaching of the rationalist ideas of John Locke unacceptable in 1703. In 1690 Bishop Trelawney's crushing visitation of Exeter College, Oxford and the ejection of the rector, Dr Bury, was a response to his questioning of the miracles of Christ in *The Naked Gospel*.[121] Heads of houses throughout the eighteenth century expelled heretical students, as Shippen did at Brasenose.[122] The colleges and the universities regularly took formal action against the heterodox: in 1730 Magdalen

College, Oxford expelled three students for deism and in 1745 the Convocation of Oxford expelled Selwyn for blasphemy.[123] In 1779 George Mountsey, a fellow of Jesus College, Cambridge, was expelled for a drunken blasphemy.[124] Humphrey Prideaux, dean of Norwich, also proposed a revision of the divinity curriculum to prevent the dangers from

> atheists, deists, Socinians, Arians, Presbyterians, independents, Anabaptists and other adversaries and sectaries . . . set as a battle-array against us.[125]

Occasionally colleges uncovered surprising pockets of heresy, as when in 1728 a relative of the Tory Earl of Ailesbury committed suicide at Trinity College, Oxford; in his belongings was blasphemous material and evidence that he was a deist.[126] Even established scholars were subject to penalties. In 1710 William Whiston was expelled from his Chair at Cambridge for attempting to advance a scientific explanation for the Deluge, and Thomas Woolston's *Discourses on the Miracles of Christ* was prosecuted for heresy at Cambridge.

The highest expression of the universities' determination to defend orthodoxy was the expulsion of six students from St Edmund Hall, Oxford for Methodist practices in 1768.[127] Of the students, Dr Johnson said, 'a cow is a very good animal in the field, but we turn her out of a garden'. The expulsion released a flood of debate on the importance of academical subscription to the Thirty-Nine Articles on matriculation or graduation.[128] It also fuelled the national debate in the 1770s on clerical subscription that culminated in the Feathers Tavern Petition (1772). As a result subscription by undergraduates remained one of the principal issues that consumed the attention of the universities in the 1770s. Richard Watson at Cambridge led a campaign to abolish subscription and in 1772 the Senate conceded that graduates in Arts could replace their subscription to the Thirty-Nine Articles with a less stringent but no less binding declaration that they were *bona fide* members of the Church of England. At Oxford the Regius Professor of Divinity, Edward Bentham, also advocated liberalisation, and together with some heads of houses proposed a similar measure. In February 1773 the Convocation of the University met and a storm of opposition was brought down on the supporters of the proposal, which was rejected by two to one.

The opponents undoubtedly saw themselves as consciously defending Anglican doctrinal orthodoxy: George Horne, President of Magdalen, wrote to the Chancellor, Lord North, 'to you, My Lord, your orthodox University looks up . . . to preserve her dignity and her utility inviolate'.[129] Another attempt at compromise was advanced in March 1773 and in spite of the fact that North supported the liberalisation, the attempt failed. Oxford ended the century as strongly a bastion of support for the status quo in Church and State as it had been equivocal in 1714.

Orthodoxy was secured in the universities in part through the efforts of dedicated orthodox teaching. Even the most eminent scientists supported orthodox Anglicanism as Boyle's lectures on Christianity and Wallis's book on the Trinity demonstrated. Waterland and Bentley at Cambridge, and Conybeare at Oxford were among those distinguished for the effectiveness of their academic defences of Anglicanism from the ideas of Tindal, Toland, Collins and the rest. In 1716, Waterland was stern in warning that party disputes at the universities allowed heresy to grow:

> as divisions increase, Christian charity will decline daily, till it becomes an empty name or an idea only. Discipline will of course slacken and hang loose; and the consequence of that must be a general dissoluteness and corruption of manners. Nor will the enemy be wanting to sow tares to corrupt our faith as well as practice, and to introduce a general latitude of opinion. Arianism, deism, atheism, will insensibly steal upon us while our heads and hearts run after politics and parties.[130]

Waterland's *Advice to a Young Student*, used extensively in the forty years after it first appeared in 1706, encouraged undergraduates to use *The Whole Duty of Man*, Nelson's *Festivals*, Taylor's *Golden Grove* and *Prayers Used By King William* – all of which were High-Church orthodox safeguards against heresy.[131]

The issue of religious orthodoxy at the universities went to the core of the Church's relationship with the State in the final decades of the eighteenth century. Peter Nockles has pointed out that the term 'orthodox' was ill-defined, able to be interpreted in terms of dogma, philosophy, churchmanship or politics.[132] But this is a dilemma that did not face the universities, they knew what was heterodox: deism, Methodism and the attempt to loosen subscription. The debate on Anglican orthodoxy in the eighteenth century has concluded that it stood in the mainstream of Augustinian-Reformation doctrine, and it was to this, with the establishment of 1689, that the universities sought to act as bulwarks.[133]

The leadership of the Church in eighteenth-century English society was problematic; the Toleration Act meant that bishops and Church leaders had to undertake a careful balancing of interests in the way that previous clergy had not. In their injunctions to clergy and parishioners, bishops had to bear in mind the competition from Dissent. Similarly in the regulation of moral and spiritual discipline, the Church faced the need to sustain its correctional role when parishioners could legally worship elsewhere. Yet the Church did not abandon its role in providing moral leadership, indeed Toleration underscored the need for effective parish clergy. Church courts have been written off too hastily as dead by the end of the seventeenth century. Leadership in an age of Toleration also meant providing a standard of orthodox faith and defending it in parishes, courts and the universities, which were the nurseries of the clergy.

Notes

1 R. O'Day, *The English Clergy 1558–1640*, London, 1979, pp. 33–48.
2 K. Fincham, 'Episcopal Government', K. Fincham (ed.), *The Early Stuart Church 1602–1642*, London, 1993, pp. 92–3.
3 N. Ravitch, *Sword and Mitre*, The Hague, 1966, pp. 214–16.
4 D. R. Hirschberg, 'A Social History of the Anglican Episcopate, 1660–1760', Michigan University, PhD thesis, 1976, *passim*.
5 W. Gibson, *The Achievement of the Anglican Church, 1689–1900: The Confessional State in Eighteenth Century England*, Lewiston, 1995.
6 C. Annesley and P. Hoskin (eds.), *Archbishop Drummond's Visitation Returns, 1764*, vol. 1, Yorkshire A–G, Borthwick Texts and Calendars, vol. 21, 1997; L. A. S. Butler (ed.), *The Archdeaconry of Richmond in the Eighteenth Century*, Yorkshire Archaeological Society, vol. CXLVI, 1990; J. Gregory (ed.), *The Speculum of Archbishop Thomas Secker*, Church of England Record Society, vol. 2, 1996; J. R. Guy, *The Diocese of Llandaff in 1763*, South Wales Record Society, 1991; J. Jago, *Aspects of the Georgian Church: Visitation Studies of the Diocese of York 1761–1776*, London, 1997; H. A. Lloyd-Jukes (ed.), *Bishop Secker's Visitation Returns, 1738*, Oxfordshire Record Society, vol. xxxviii, 1957; M. Ransome (ed.), *The State of the Bishopric of Worcester 1782–1808*, Worcestershire Historical Society vol. 6, 1968; *idem* (ed.), *Wiltshire Returns to the Bishop's Visitation Queries, 1783*, Wiltshire Record Society vol. XXVII, 1972; W. R. Ward (ed.), *Parson and Parish in Eighteenth Century Surrey: Replies to Bishops' Visitations*, Surrey Records Society, vol. XXXIV, 1994; *idem* (ed.), *Parson and Parish in Eighteenth Century Hampshire: Replies to Bishops' Visitations*, Hampshire Records Series, vol. 13, 1995.
7 One of Wake's archdeacons, Kennett, making his annual archidiaconal visitation in 1706 was able to claim 'I rejoyce that his Lordship [Bishop Wake] will here find a very regular and creditable clergy discharging their respective offices with due care and conscience'. G. V. Bennett, *White Kennett, 1660–1728*, London, 1957, pp. 195–6. See also E. Carpenter, *Thomas Sherlock*, London, 1936, p. 134.
8 N. Sykes, *William Wake*, Cambridge, 1957, vol. 1, p. 157.
9 N. Sykes, *Church and State in England in the Eighteenth Century*, Cambridge, 1934, p. 92.
10 H. C. Foxcroft, *A Supplement to Burnet's History of My Own Time, derived from His Original Memoirs, His Autobiography, His Letters to Admiral Herbert and His Private Meditations, all hitherto unpublished*, Oxford, 1902, p. 329.
11 G. V. Bennett, *op. cit.*, p. 223.

12 M. G. Smith, *Fighting Joshua, Sir Jonathan Trelawny 1650–1721*, Redruth, 1985, p. 69.

13 J. Trelawny, *Sermon of Sir Jonathan Trelawny, Bishop of Winchester and Charge to the Clergy of that Diocese, 1708*, London, 1876, pp. 12–13.

14 Sykes, *Church and State . . .* , p. 106.

15 Bennett, *op. cit.*, pp. 228, 232.

16 *Bishop of Lincoln's Charge to the Clergy of his Diocese at his Triennial Visitation . . . 1709* in Sykes, *Church and State . . .* , p. 176.

17 Sykes, *William Wake, op. cit.*, vol. 1, p. 234.

18 F. C. Mather, *High Church Prophet: Samuel Horsley*, Oxford, 1992, p. 175.

19 A. P. Jenkins (ed.), *The Correspondence of Bishop Secker*, 1991, Oxford Record Society, vol. 57, p. 218.

20 Quoted in Sykes, *Church and State . . .* , p. 220. In enforcing the residence of the chapter of St David's, which sought a seventh supernumerary canon to undertake their residence, Bishop Charles Moss in 1767 wrote, 'for this chapter to elect, or ask the bishop to allow legislation for, a seventh canon for the good of the Church, must be countered by the point that it is in the good interests of the Church to safeguard its constitution and customs. . . . The bishop and dean and chapter have the power to change things for the good . . . but not to do so by subverting the old Church usages . . .'. W. Gibson, 'A Hanoverian Reform of the Chapter of St David's', *The National Library of Wales Journal*, 1988, vol. 25, no. 3, p. 287.

21 Jenkins (ed.), *op. cit.*, pp. 4–8.

22 Thomas Secker's second charge, quoted in Sykes, *Church and State . . .* , *op. cit.*, p. 251. I am grateful to Canon D. T. W. Price for this reference.

23 E. Gibson, *The Sacrament of the Lords Supper Explained: or the things to be known and done to make a worthy communicant . . .* , London, 1705, pp. 95–113.

24 S. L. Ollard and P. C. Walker (eds.), *Archbishop Herring's Visitation Returns, 1743*, Yorkshire Archaeological Society, vol. LXXVII, 1930, ii, p. 78.

25 Jenkins (ed.), *op. cit.*, p. 195.

26 *Ibid.*, p. 50.

27 Sykes, *William Wake, op. cit.*, vol. 1, p. 182.

28 *Charge Delivered to the Clergy at the Bishop's Personal Visitation of the Diocese of Winchester in the Year MDCCXXXVI*, J. Hoadly, (ed.), *The Works of Benjamin Hoadly DD*, London, 1773, vol. 3, p. 493.

29 A number of these were published in 1686 under the title *Letters of the Bishop of London to the clergy of his diocese*.

30 H. Compton, *The Bishop of London's Letter to his clergy . . . 'how they ought to behave themselves under a toleration'*, London, 1692, p. 3.

31 E. Carpenter, *Thomas Sherlock*, London, 1936; *idem, Thomas Tenison*, London, 1948; A. T. Hart, *William Lloyd 1627–1717*, London, 1952; Sykes, *William Wake, op. cit.*; *idem, Edmund Gibson*, Oxford, 1926; Bennett, *White Kennett, op. cit.*

32 C. J. Abbey, *The English Church and its Bishops 1700–1800*, London, 1887, vol. 1, p. 61.

33 J. H. Moorman, *The Curate of Souls 1660–1760*, London, 1958, p. 72. G. Burnet, *An Exposition of Church Catechism*, London, 1710, p. 1.

34 H. C. Foxcroft, *op. cit.*, pp. 329–30.

35 I. M. Green, *The Christians ABC*, Oxford, 1996, pp. 25, 120, 131, 208, 561.

36 R. D. Cornwall, 'The Rite of Confirmation in Anglican Thought during the Eighteenth Century', *Church History*, vol. 68, no. 2, June 1999.

37 Sykes, *William Wake*, vol. 1, p. 184.

38 *The English Theological Works of George Bull DD*, Oxford, 1844, p. 122.

39 *Ibid.*, pp. 391–2.

40 *Ibid.*, p. 123.

41 *Ibid.*, p. 392.

42 J. Hoadly (ed.), *The Works of Benjamin Hoadly DD*, London, 1773, vol. 3, pp. 477–8.

43 *Ibid.*, vol. 3, pp. 484–6.

44 *Ibid.*, vol. 3, pp. 490–3.

45 E. Gibson, *The Bishop of London's Third Pastoral Letter to the People of his Diocese . . .* , London, 1731.

46 R. Watson, *A Charge Delivered to the Clergy of the Diocese of Llandaff at the Visitation of Richard, Lord Bishop of Llandaff . . .* , London, 1791, p. 4.

47 G. Pretyman, *A Charge delivered to the Clergy of the Diocese of Lincoln . . . in June and July 1800*, London, 1800, pp. 8–10.

48 J. Butler, *A Charge to the Clergy of his diocese of Hereford . . . in the year 1792*, Hereford, 1792, pp. 5–14.

49 L. Bagot, *A Charge to the Clergy at the Primary Visitation of the Diocese of Norwich . . .* , Norwich, 1784, pp. 8–12.

50 B. Porteus, *A Letter to the Clergy of the Diocese of London . . .* , London, 1789, pp. 15–16; W. Cleaver, *A Charge delivered to the Clergy of the Diocese of Chester . . . 1799*, Oxford, 1799, pp. 12–13.

51 R. Hodgson, *The Works of the Rt Revd Beilby Porteus DD . . . With His Life*, London, 1811, vol. 1, pp. 173–4.

52 Abbey, *op. cit.*, vol. 1, p. 317.

53 B. Porteus, *A Charge delivered to the Clergy of the Diocese of London . . .* , London, 1793, p. 3; *idem*, *A Letter to the Clergy of the Diocese of Chester Concerning Sunday Schools*, London, 1786, pp. 21–2.

54 H. Majendie, *A Charge Delivered to the clergy of the Diocese of Chester in July and August 1804*, London, 1804, pp. 19–20.

55 J. Fisher, *A Charge delivered to the clergy of the Diocese of Exeter . . . 1804 and 1805*, Exeter, 1805, pp. 23–4. Conversely, Richard Watson held the view that poverty made people more virtuous and more happy. R. Watson, *A Charge delivered to the clergy of the Diocese of Llandaff in June 1809*, Bristol, 1809, p. 16.

56 S. Horsley, *A Charge to the Clergy of his Diocese, delivered by Bishop Horsley . . . in the year 1790*, Gloucester, 1790, pp. 11–13.

57 G. Pretyman, *A Charge delivered to the Clergy of the diocese of Lincoln . . . in May and June 1794*, London, 1794, p. 21. B. Porteus, *A Charge delivered to the clergy of the Diocese of London . . . MDCCXC*, London, 1790, p. 25.

58 43. Geo. III c. 84 and 44. Geo. III c. 2.

59 H. W. Majendie, *A Charge Delivered to the clergy of the Diocese of Chester in July and August 1804*, London, 1804, pp. 20–1.

60 S. Barrington, *A Charge delivered to the Clergy of the Diocese of Durham . . . MDCCXCVII*, Durham, 1797, pp. 23–4; J. Randolph, *A Charge delivered to the Clergy of the Diocese of London . . .* , *MDCCCX*, Oxford, 1810, pp. 25–7.

61 Watson *Charge . . . 1791*, *op. cit.*, p. 5.

62 J. Addy, *Sin and Society in the Seventeenth Century*, London, 1989.

63 13. Car, II, st 1, c. 12.

64 Addy dates the full impact of this at 1712 rather than 1694, *op. cit.*, p. 212.

65 Sykes, *William Wake, op. cit.*, vol. 1, pp. 199–200.

66 R. E. Rodes Jr, *Law and the Modernization of the Church of England: Charles II to the Welfare State*, Indiana, 1991, pp. 21 *et seq.* D. Lemmings, 'Marriage and the Law in the Eighteenth Century: Hardwicke's Marriage Act of 1753', *Historical Journal*, 1996, vol. 39, part 2, pp. 339–360. I owe this reference to Robert Ingram.

67 E. Gibson, *Codex Juris Anglicani*, London, 1713, vol. 1, p. xxxi.

68 W. B. Whitaker, *The Eighteenth Century English Sunday*, London, 1940, p. 115.

69 M. G. Smith, *Pastoral Discipline and the Church Courts: the Hexham Court, 1680–1730*, 1982, Borthwick Paper, no. 62, p. 2.

70 Besides Gibson's *Codex Juris Anglicani*, there was: J. Godolphin, *Repertorum Canonicum*, London, 1680; H. Consett, *The Practice of the Spiritual Courts*, London, 1700; J. Aycliffe, *Parergon Juris Canonici Anglicani*, London, 1726 and T. Oughton, *Ordo Judicorum*, London, 1728.

71 27. George III, c. 44. P. Hair (ed.), *Before the Bawdy Court*, London, 1972, p. 23.

72 Sykes, *Edmund Gibson, op. cit.*, p. 150.

73 Gibson, *Codex Juris Anglicani, op. cit.*, vol. 1, p. xxx.

74 Hampshire Records Office, Copy/605/37 and 68.

75 M. G. Smith, *Pastoral Discipline and the Church Courts . . . , op. cit.*, p. 14. However, some ecclesiastical lawyers maintained a thriving practice: W. Gibson, ' "Good Mr Chancellor", The Work of Dr John Audley, Chancellor of York 1710–1744', *Yale University Library Gazette*, 1998, vol. 73, nos. 1–2.

76 Gibson, *Codex Juris Anglicani, op. cit.*, vol. 1, p. xviii.

77 W. E. Tate, *The Parish Chest*, Cambridge, 1946, p. 148. J. Vaux bested Tate by finding a public penance as late as the 1880s. J. E. Vaux, *Church Folklore*, London, 1894, p. 178.

78 T. Wilson, *Parochialia*, Oxford, 1840; B. H. Kelly, 'Some Reflections on Church and State relations in the Time of Bishop Wilson', *Proceedings of the Isle of Man Natural History and Antiquarian Society*, 1963, n.s., vol. 6; A. Ashley, 'The Spiritual Courts of the Isle of Man especially in the seventeenth and eighteenth centuries', *English Historical Review*, 1957, vol. 72.

79 R. Trumbach, *Sex and the Gender Revolution, vol. 1: Heterosexuality and the Third Gender in Enlightenment London*, Chicago, 1998, p. 25.

80 W. Gibson, ' "A Happy Fertile Soil which bringeth forth Abundantly": The Diocese of Winchester, 1689–1800' in J. Gregory and J. Chamberlain (eds.), *The Church in its Local Identities, 1660–1800*, Woodbridge, 2001.

81 C. R. Chapman, *Sin, Sex and Probate*, Dursley, 1997, pp. 11–16.

82 Sykes, *William Wake, op. cit.*, vol. 1, p. 191.

83 M. Kinnear, 'The Correctional Court in the Diocese of Carlisle, 1704–1756', *Church History*, 1990, vol. 59.

84 Sykes, *William Wake, op. cit.*, p. 196.

85 Trumbach, *op. cit.*, p. 235. W. M. Jacob, *Lay People and Religion in the Early Eighteenth Century*, Cambridge, 1996, p. 143.

86 T. Hitchcock, *English Sexualities 1700–1800*, London, 1997, p. 97.

87 Hair, *op. cit.*, p. 243.

88 Trumbach, *op. cit.*, p. 25 *et seq.* Moreover, Trumbach ascribes the growth of unmarried couples in London – approximately a seventh of the total – to the survival of an ancient belief that the sacrament of marriage was one between man and wife, at which the priest was merely the witness. *Ibid.*, p. 267.

89 E. Gibson, *The Charge of Edmund, Lord Bishop of Lincoln at his Primary Visitation in the year 1717*, London, 1717, p. 16.

90 J. M. Albers, 'Seeds of Contention: Society, Politics and the Church of England in Lancashire 1689–1790', Yale University, PhD thesis, 1988, vol. 1, p. 222.

91 W. Jacob, 'Clergy and Society in Norfolk, 1707–1806', Exeter University, PhD thesis, 1982, p. 244.

92 Albers, *op. cit.*, p. 224.

93 F. C. Mather, *op. cit.*, p. 284. Though equally in Oxford and Hereford dioceses the numbers of the number of cases before the courts fell, see William Marshall, 'The Administration of the Diocese of Oxford and Hereford 1660–1760', Bristol University, PhD thesis, 1978, p. 78.

94 Albers, *op. cit.*, p. 227.

95 *Ibid.*, pp. 244–5.

96 *Ibid.*, p. 246.

97 *Ibid.*, p. 229.

98 T. Simpson Evans, *The Life of Robert Frampton, Bishop of Gloucester*, London, 1876, pp. 165–8. Commuted payments in lieu of penance increased in the eighteenth century: at Hereford one hundred and eight pounds was collected in eight years from commutations under Bishop Bisse, compared to three hundred and forty between 1722 and 1747, even though Bishop Gibson wrote that the practice had fallen into disuse. *Codex . . .* , *op. cit.*, vol. 2, p. 1092.

99 *Worcester Journal*, 18 December 1766.

100 J. Wickham Legg, *English Church Life from the Restoration to the Tractarian Movement*, London, 1914, p. 262.

101 H. D. W. Lees, *The Chronicles of a Suffolk Parish Church*, Lowestoft, 1949, pp. 270, 267.

102 *Ibid.*, p. 21.

103 J. A. Sharpe, ' "Such disagreement betwyx Neighbours": Litigation and Human Relations in Early Modern England', J. Bossy (ed.), *Disputes and Settlements: Law and Human Relations in the West*, Cambridge, 1983, pp. 178–81.

104 W. Jones, *Sermons: Practical, Doctrinal and Expository*, London, 1829, p. 389.

105 J. Talbot, *The Judicial Powers of the Church Asserted in a sermon at All Saints Pavement . . .* , York, 1707.

106 A. C. Wood, 'Nottingham Penances, 1590–1794', *Transactions of the Thoroton Society of Nottinghamshire*, 1944, vol. 48, pp. 53–4.

107 See for example, J. Wickham Legg, *op. cit.*; V. Staley (ed.), *Hierurgia Anglicana*, London, 1902–4, 3 vols.; W. E. Tate, *op. cit.*; T. F. Thistleton-Dyer, *Old English Social Life as told by Parish Registers*, London, 1898.

108 H. A. Lloyd-Jukes (ed.), *Bishop Secker's Visitation Returns, 1738*, 1957, Oxfordshire Record Society, vol. xxxviii, p. 63.

109 Smith, *Pastoral Discipline and the Church Courts . . .* , *op. cit.*, p. 6.

110 *Ibid.*, pp. 22, 26, 30, 32–4.

111 Addy, *op. cit.*, pp. 37–8, 89, 208.

112 Jacob, *op. cit.*, p. 144.

113 Albers, *op. cit.*, p. 241.

114 *The Newgate Calendar*, London, 1997, pp. 32, 87, 140 269, 242.

115 W. B. Whitaker, *op. cit.*, p. 64.

116 W. Gibson, 'An Eighteenth Century Paradox: The Career of the Decypherer-Bishop Edward Willes', *The British Journal for Eighteenth Century Studies*, 1989, vol. 12, part 1.

117 C. Wordsworth, *Social Life at the English Universities in the Eighteenth Century*, Cambridge, 1874, p. 14.

118 See Chapter Two.

119 E. Duffy, 'Pudding Time', P. Cunich *et al.* (eds.), *A History of Magdalene College, Cambridge, 1428–1988*, Cambridge, 1994, p. 163.

120 D. Greenwood, *William King, Tory and Jacobite*, Oxford, 1969, *passim.*

121 *An Account of the Proceedings of Jonathan, Bishop of Exeter, in his late Visitation of Exeter College . . .* , Oxford, 1690.

122 C. E. Mallett, *A History of the University of Oxford*, London, 1927, vol. 3, p. 77.

123 *Ibid.*, vol. 3, p. 110.

124 B.L. Add. Mss. 5, 852 f 119.

125 *The Life of The Revd Humphrey Prideaux DD*, London, 1748, p. 199.

126 Ward, *op. cit.*, p. 146.

127 S. L. Ollard, *The Six Students of St Edmund Hall, Expelled from Oxford in 1768*, London, 1911, *passim.*

128 Ward, *op. cit.*, pp. 242–4.

129 G. Horne, *A Letter to the Right Hon. The Lord North, Chancellor of the University of Oxford, Concerning the Subscription to the XXXIX Articles . . .* , Oxford, 1773.

130 Quoted in Wordsworth, *op. cit.*, p. 82.

131 Though Waterland also produced an academic study reading list that included the sermons of Hoadly as well as Atterbury and Sharp, and the work of Locke. C. Wordsworth, *Scholae Academicae: Some Account of Studies at English Universities in the Eighteenth Century*, Cambridge, 1877, pp. 332–4.

132 P. Nockles, 'Church Parties in the Pre-Tractarian Church of England, 1750–1833: the 'Orthodox' – some problems of definition and identity', Haydon, Walsh and Taylor, *op. cit.*, pp. 340–1.

133 G. F. Scholtz, 'Anglicanism in the Age of Johnson: The Doctrine of Conditional Salvation', *Eighteenth Century Studies*, 1988–9, vol. 22, no. 2; D. Green, 'How "Degraded" was Eighteenth Century Anglicanism?', *Eighteenth Century Studies*, 1990, vol. 24, no. 1; and *idem*, 'Latitudinarianism and Sensibility: The Genealogy of the "Man of Feeling" Reconsidered', *Modern Philology*, 1977, vol. 75.

5

THE CHURCH AND CULTURE

The culture of eighteenth-century English society was infused – indeed drenched – with Anglicanism. Its politics and parishes were part of the institutional structures that were bulwarks of English society; and the medium for the expression and transmission of Anglicanism outside the Church was the popular culture of eighteen century England. John Somerville has claimed that the religious cultural inheritance of eighteenth-century England was much reduced.[1] In addition, population growth affected the numbers of souls reached by the Church. London is a good example: in 1540 a London parish served an average of 500 souls; before the Fire of London it had risen to 3,000, but of course Wren was unable to rebuild all the churches lost. In 1708 he bemoaned the scale of his job in creating churches for a rising population.[2] Religious artistry was similarly impoverished in the seventeenth century; the Commonwealth had witnessed the ruination of much Church decoration and statuary, the abandonment of organs and Church music. It was not until the first decade of the eighteenth century that there was a renaissance of religious music, which included a revival of interest in organs. Renatus Harris, for example, attempted the ambitious goal of building the biggest organ in the country at Salisbury, where he created a vast four-manual instrument with thirty-nine ranks.[3]

In the most coherent study of eighteenth-century religious culture, Jeremy Gregory has recently argued that historians have tended to align enlightenment and secularity in eighteenth-century culture. But Gregory rejects the dichotomy of an emergent rationalist–enlightenment–Whig axis in competition with a Tory–revelatory–traditional movement. Instead Gregory sees rationalism and religion as complementary rather than competitive: thus men such as Newton, Boyle and Shipley were joined by numerous clergy as the powerhouse of the Royal Society.

Gregory also traces three critical interactions between the Church and culture. First, he demonstrates the dominant participation of the clergy in cultural life. Gregory lists such contributions as Thomas Burnet in cosmology, William Derham in science, Richard Bentley and Richard Hurd in classics, Stephen Hales in physiology, George Berkeley in philosophy, Gilbert White in natural history, Thomas Robert Malthus in economics, William Buckland in geology, William Gilpin in aesthetics, and a plethora of clergy in literature and poetry.[4] Secondly he shows how Anglicans employed new ideas and cultural forms to defend the Church, citing Thomas Hobbes, Thomas Sprat and John Wilkins as men who bridged philosophy, science and theology and paved the way for the development of natural theology as a synthesising phenomenon: 'the popularity of natural theology in the eighteenth century was crucial to the dissemination of the new science', he asserts.[5] As Boyle demonstrated, science and religion could be apologists for each other, and they acted as such in the works of William Paley. Certainly there is evidence that Anglican clergy were vital in the transmission of Voltaire's views in England; indeed eighty per cent of clerical libraries contained Voltaire's work.[6] Thirdly, Gregory argues that intellectuals like Edward Gibbon and John Wesley demonstrate that Christianity shaped the thinking of the enlightenment. Gregory's conclusion is that the eighteenth century can be counted as a century in which English culture was almost exclusively Christian:

> quite where the 'great divide' occurred between a Christian and a secular culture is a question for historians of the nineteenth and twentieth centuries. It hardly involves the historians of the eighteenth century.[7]

The issue of the secularisation of English culture is also addressed by John Sommerville who suggests that, as culture became more secular, English piety grew.[8] Certainly while the collective culture of the parish and town developed at the Reformation may have declined, individual piety and religious observance increased.

The cultural dominance of Anglicanism in the eighteenth century is particularly evident in the fine arts. By the early eighteenth century religious representation had returned to legitimacy and artists represented religion and the Church according to the religious and neo-classical ideas of the time. Thus Godfrey Kneller's *Triumph of Marlborough* (1706) shows the Duke directed by angels and crowned with a laurel wreath from Heaven. Similarly his *Queen Anne presenting the Plans of Blenheim to Military Merit* (1708) depicts an eagle crowning Marlborough and heavenly bodies sanctioning the rule of Anne. Elsewhere, artists portrayed religion in less elevated scenes. Hogarth's *Rake's Progress, Harlot's Progress* and *Marriage à la*

Mode portrayed the clergy in disreputable narratives produced for popular entertainment. Worse still, Hogarth's work portrayed some of the most shocking scenes of eighteenth-century life: *Gin Lane* and *The Four Stages of Cruelty* among them. But Hogarth's intention to shock operated from within the framework of Christian morality. The first print in the suite of *The Four Stages of Cruelty* shows a boy – wearing the badge of a charity school – impaling a dog in a direct reference to Callot's *Temptation to St Anthony*. It was a religious allusion and a cautionary tale that would not have been lost on the viewers of the print.

The Church was also at the centre of the movement of society towards the new cultural forms of sociability, politeness and civic humanism. Politeness was a self-conscious cultural artefact that aspired to moral rectitude and drew heavily on contemporary Christian values. The rejection of coarseness, vulgarity, swearing and profanity – the typical preoccupations of the Societies for the Reformation of Manners – was a major buttress of politeness. The attempt of the mayor of Lancaster in 1787 to ban the sale of alcohol on Sundays, was a move toward politeness which was inextricably linked to religious observance and the growth of sabbatarianism.[9] These developments, often evidenced by the sharper delineation of the private and public spheres, frequently used religion and the Church as a medium of polite and sociable values.[10] In the domestic sphere clergymen were some of the few outsiders admitted into the increasingly private world of the family. Paintings of the era typify the growth of politeness in intimate family scenes which include clergymen. Joseph Van Aken's *An English Family at Tea* (1720) shows a clergyman and a genteel family enjoying the domestic ceremony of tea, with all of accoutrements of the occasion, including silver teapot and lacquered tea caddie. Similarly, John Theodore Heins Snr's *A Musical Party at Melton Constable* (1734) depicts the sociability of provincial genteel society, including four clergy playing instruments; and Edward Haytley's *The Brockman Family and Friends at Beachborough Manor . . .* (1744) portrays a family scene in the grounds of a mansion, with a parson standing in the tableau. Arthur Devis's *Assheton Curzon, afterwards Viscount Curzon and Dr Mather, his tutor* (1754) is even richer in symbolic ideas of civic humanism, enlightenment and the mutual ties of patronage and condescension: Curzon, a youth, stands next to the older Mather, who dominates the picture, but both are intent upon the same goal, the education of a young man who would enter politics and make a significant contribution to his nation.

A powerful example of the way in which eighteenth-century ideas of civic humanism incorporated religion is the decoration of the London Foundling Hospital, established by Captain Thomas Coram. A promotional prospectus for the Hospital asserted:

> God forbid that in a Christian Nation, so enlightened with the
> bright beams of the Gospels as ours is, that the innocents should
> be punished for their parents' sin and be left to starve or exposed
> to violence for want of due care to preserve their lives.[11]

Within less than twenty years the Hospital was well-established and four
prominent artists were invited to contribute pictures for the General Court
Room. The paintings depicted biblical scenes of childhood and charity:
Francis Hayman's *Moses Saved from the Waters*; William Hogarth's *Moses
returned to Pharaoh's Daughter*, Joseph Highmore's *Angel with Agar and
Ishmael* and James Wills's *Little Children Brought unto Christ*. The theme
of the paintings was intended to draw the viewer from the familiar biblical
narratives towards a contemporary sense of charity and benevolence. On
public days the paintings were available to view and seemed to suggest the
divine sanction on such a worthy public enterprise. A similar venture was
Hogarth's twin works *The Good Samaritan* and *The Pool at Bethesda* on the
staircase at St Bartholomew's Hospital. The paintings dominate the staircase
and offered divine sanction on the physicians, patients and those pious
and munificent enough to fund the foundation. Comparatively socially
unattractive causes, such as the Magdalen Hospital, the Lock Hospital and
later the Lock Asylum, could attract the benefactions of the fashionable, as
they did after the Revd Martin Madan's appointment as chaplain in the
1750s.[12] Even a hardened cynic such as Henry Fielding felt such acts of
charity were

> characteristic of the nation at this time – I believe we may
> challenge the whole world to parallel the examples which we have
> of late given of this sensible, this noble, this Christian virtue.[13]

Charity, civic humanism, politeness and Anglicanism were connected in an
ideal of moderation and the social reconciliation of the affluent and disadvantaged.

The Church also benefited from advances in printing images, particularly
mezzotinting, which increased the output of printers six-fold. Prints of
churchmen became widely available, with bishops like Crewe, Compton,
Burnet and Hoadly depicted in a number of portraits which were copied
and offered for sale as engravings. The sumptuous episcopal portraits of
the Caroline Church were replaced by images which emphasised the
scholarship, meekness and humanity of the sitters. Tillotson, Herring,
Hoadly, Gibson, Waddington and Wake reach out of their portraits to the
viewer. Bishops were often depicted with scholars' square caps, books or
with buildings, rather than against the plain black backgrounds of their

predecessors' portraits. These were men located as firmly in this world as they sought to encourage others to look to the next. Only after 1780 did the episcopal portrait become one of grandeur and haughtiness.[14]

Clergy were also in the forefront of the development of travel and tourism in England. Thomas Gent's guides to Ripon, Hull and York focused particularly on the churches of the cities as places which travellers ought to visit. They were inspired by the common practice of visiting churches. Gent explained the origins of his book:

> Walking one evening with some friends towards Heslington, near York, and our discourse being of the Minster, &c. I happen'd to say 'twas a pity that when so many gentlemen and ladies came to view so far a fabrick, there should be wanting a little book, describing as much as possible the imitable beauties therof. . . .[15]

Similarly William Newton, vicar of Maidstone, wrote the *History and Antiquities of Maidstone* . . . to encourage visitors to the town to view its historical sites and the Revd John Letchiot's *Southampton Guide* (1768), listed not just the 'public buildings, charitable foundations, fairs, markets, play-house and assembly-room with the times of the coming in and going out of the stage-coaches . . .' but also the times of services in the churches of the city. The doyens of eighteenth-century travel guides were the Revd William Gilpin and his curate Richard Warner, who in the last two decades of the century wrote travel books on the Lake District, the West of England, the Wye Valley, the New Forest, the Scottish highlands and the northern counties of England.[16] These were enormously popular works, the guide to the Wye Valley running to five editions by 1800. Gilpin's preoccupation with the beauty of landscape and the religious inspiration it stimulated placed travel and recreation into a religious context. Travellers were reminded that in admiring the landscape they were appreciating divinely-inspired splendour.

The identification of the culture of the elite with the Church was a feature of the courts of James I and Charles I, though perhaps less so under Charles II and James II. However the relationship revived under William III, Anne and the Georges and the Church easily resumed its position at the heart of high culture. The epitome of royal cultural patronage of the Church were the coronations with the attendant music, sermons and ceremonial. Queen Anne's grant of a pension of £200 a year to Handel promoted the court as a centre for sacred music. Naturally, the leadership of the court quickly affected metropolitan society and culture. Handel's new musical form, the oratorio, was dominated by religious subjects: *Jeptha, Judas Maccabeus, Joshua, Solomon, Joseph and his Brethren,* and *The Messiah.* His competitors

William Defesh and Noccolo Porpora both realised that Old Testament figures were the subjects demanded by London audiences, and gave them such works as *Judith* and *David and Bethsheba*. The libretti for these works were often derived directly from the Bible, with the Revd James Miller in the forefront of librettists. They, and the contemporary plethora of Old Testament-derived sermons, drew on the metaphor of Britons as modern Hebrews, struggling free of the enslavement of popery, just as Israel had from Egypt. It was a frothy and potent idea that ran deep in the theology of Anglicans and Dissenters – for whom of course there was also a hint of liberation from penal laws – and even inspired the poetry of William Blake.[17]

Elite musical culture outside London often focused on great choral performances. In 1700 most major cities had music festivals located in the cathedrals. The foundation of the Three Choirs Festival in 1715 was undoubtedly due to the happy coincidence of the proximity of the cathedral choirs and the availability of Handel's work.[18] Occasionally choral impresarios, like John Marsh, emerged to provide regular choral festivals at Canterbury, Chichester and Salisbury. In each city the cathedrals provided performance spaces, organs, choirs and musicians. Musical performances also generated a demand for organs, even in provincial towns: Hull, Doncaster and King's Lynn purchased organs for over five hundred pounds each in 1711, 1738 and 1752 respectively.[19] The great organists and choirmasters of the eighteenth century, William Croft, William Boyce, John Stanley, Capel Bond, Charles Burney, Joseph Gibbs, Charles Avison, Thomas Chilcott and William Jackson were employed in cathedrals or in the great churches of London or the provincial cities. Some like William Herschel, accepted posts at the fashionable spas – in Herschel's case as composer and organist at the prestigious Octagon Chapel in Bath in 1766.[20] There were also more modest local musical festivals. Claver Morris founded a St Cecilia day festival at Wells and by the mid-eighteenth century there were St Cecilia day celebrations at Lichfield, Norwich, Oxford, Salisbury, and Winchester.[21] Elsewhere, churchmen encouraged music as Dean Cowper at Durham, repairing the organ and sponsoring musical concerts.[22] The St Cecilia Society was founded in 1694 at St Bride's Church, Fleet Street by Francis Atterbury, among others. Atterbury held that the Church should follow the example of David's psalms and regarded music as 'a help and advantage' in heightening piety and worship. Atterbury claimed that the 'awakening airs of Church Musick' had the potential to refresh the spirit during long services; but above all music could also support civic humanism of the era by enabling 'selfishness and narrowness of mind, all rancour and peevishness [to] vanish from the heart, where love of divine harmony dwells.'[23]

It was often the patronage of the laity that encouraged and promoted great musical ventures; they also financed events and comprised the audiences in great numbers. Lord Sandwich's patronage of the Concert of Antient Music, for example, was the impetus for the foundation of the annual Handel Festival in 1784, which was held in Westminster Abbey. These events were rich cultural phenomena. They promoted the professionalis-ation of music and gradually expanded the musical market wider into other classes. For the elite they were opportunities for condescension, patronage, conspicuousness and display. They helped to create a breadth in the culture of the elite and to establish for it an identity of politeness and civility. But in all these feature the medium was devotional music in a liturgical setting with the musicians and singers expressing sacred ideas.

As Jonathan Barry has shown, the musical revival was not just a metro-politan phenomenon. In Bristol Arthur Bedford, the vicar of Temple in 1733, was a convinced supporter of the revival in Church music. He was aware of the competing alternative denominations in the city which could attract his parishioners. Perhaps as a consequence, Bedford arranged regular concerts in his church and revived the use of counterpoint singing in services. There is also evidence that special musical occasions attracted Non-conformists to Anglican churches, such as the inaugural organ recital at St Peter's, Bristol. However, Bedford was aware of the potential dangers of music in churches. The low pay of many organists meant that they were encouraged to develop organ voluntaries which, Bedford felt, broke up services and were simply an attempt to display the organist's virtuosity often in an attempt to acquire private music pupils. He was also aware that the growth of other forms of music, particularly ballads and popular choruses, were diluting the dominance of English religious music in popular culture.[24] Elsewhere, particularly in Wessex, the hymns and sacred music of William Byrd music remained popular in the eighteenth century. Byrd had composed much music to be learnt by ear so that in country parishes – where those who could read music were rare – music could still be enjoyed in Church.

There was a deep division in the religious cultural heritage of eighteenth-century England. The bequest of the Puritans served to reject entertainment and cultural media, such as literature and the theatre, as sinful. Just as the seven deadly sins condemned gluttony and lust, so Puritans regarded other pleasures as inevitably aligned with sin. Theirs was a lapsarian view of mankind that accorded with Bernard Mandeville's view of man as irredeem-ably prone to sin and vice. It was predicated on an Old Testament notion of God sternly judging men and women on their labours, sobriety and devotion. It was also a notion that survived into the eighteenth century, fuelling the views of Law and John Wesley, who sought to deny people leisure time lest they should spend it in vice, preferring that they spend time in work. Similarly James Fordyce animadverted on the perils and dangers of women reading novels since they were repositories of sin and vice.[25]

It was on the stage that most Anglican opposition and ire was focused in the seventeenth and eighteenth centuries. In 1698 Jeremy Collier published *A Short View of the Immorality and Profaneness of the English Stage*, and in 1712 the SPCK asked him to compose an attack on the lewd songs and profane ballads of the stage. It was a venture that both the archbishop of Canterbury and Queen Anne endorsed. Arthur Bedford of Bristol, later chaplain to the prince of Wales, was another fierce opponent. His *Evil and Danger of Stage-plays*, cited two thousand examples of swearing, blasphemy, cursing, satires on the Bible, mocking virtue and encouraging vice.[26] Bedford claimed that 'the tenth part of what I have quoted, is sufficient to prove that our poets are the bane of religion, the promoters of vice, and the nuisance of the nation.'[27] William Law was the most strident opponent of the stage in the eighteenth century; his *Absolute Unlawfulness of the Stage Entertainment fully Demonstrated* (1726, and which ran to six editions by 1773) drew together the puritan–High Church arguments against the theatre. Law's debt to puritan ideas was self-conscious:

> if the worship of images did not cease to be sinful though it was intended for pious purposes, it must be great weakness to imagine that the entertainment of the stage cannot be any great sin because it is only used as a diversion. . . .[28]

For Law, attendance at the theatre assumed a disposition that was unChristian – indeed he quoted St John's injunction to 'abide by the spirit' as well as the Commandments as evidence of biblical circumscription of theatre. He claimed the theatre was an instrument of superstition, denouncing plays which depicted witches, ancient gods and fables. Law's was, moreover, an absolute position; he argued that a woman who took the sacrament regularly, who attended only modest plays, who did so with her aunt as chaperone and did not let the attendance at the theatre interfere with her regime of prayer, was nevertheless sinning if she attended the theatre. Law was a shrewd polemicist, even citing Tillotson's *Sermon on Corrupt Communication*, which had denounced lewd and immodest plays, as an argument against the stage.[29] However Law's arguments were not universally accepted. The theatre owner John Hippisley held that

> theatrical performances when conducted with decency and regularity, have always been esteemed the most rational amusements by the polite and thinking part of mankind.[30]

John Dennis's reply to Law *The Stage Defended from Scripture, Reason, Experience & the Common Sense of Mankind for two thousand years* was regarded as a complete vindication of the theatre, and even Law's biographer, John Overton, regarded his attack on the stage as an aberration which failed.[31]

In spite of Dennis's vindication of the stage, there remained disquiet within the Church over various forms of elite entertainment in the eighteenth century. Senior bishops repeatedly expressed concern at the immorality of the court entertainments, and especially of masquerades. In this the Church was a bulwark of politeness. Bishop Edmund Gibson joined the opposition to masquerades because of the drunkenness and lewdness that attended them, and in January 1723–4 preached a sermon before the Society for the Reformation of Manners denouncing masquerades.[32] Under George I, who revived the entertainment, Bishop Waddington of Chichester prompted Wake to 'appear at the head of the . . . bishops in so good a cause' as opposing royal masquerades. Accordingly a meeting of the bishops was called in 1724 at which a memorial to the King was drawn up on the subject. However, the memorial avoided the absolutist position that Law had taken:

> we are far from supposing that all who go to these assemblies have any wicked designs in it. We are rather persuaded that many who allow themselves this liberty do it out of curiosity to see what is done there . . . but fear at the same time that many who have gone innocently thither have very much lost ground in virtue there, and by seeing and hearing what they cannot but see and hear in such places and in such company may have had their passions raised. . . .[33]

The memorial was unsuccessful, indeed the parliamentary session of 1725–6 was opened by a masquerade so debauched as to scandalise even hardened masquerade-goers.[34] The concern at public entertainment continued. In 1728 Thomas Herring, a future archbishop of Canterbury, attacked John Gay's scandalous satire, the *Beggars' Opera*.[35] Horace Walpole complained on 22 January 1756 that

> we were to have had a masquerade tonight but the bishops who, you know, have always persisted in God's hating dominoes, have made an earthquake point of it and postponed it till after the fast.[36]

In 1766 Thomas Secker, the Archbishop of Canterbury, launched another attack on court masquerades.[37]

The bishops did not regard the masquerades as intrinsically objection-able, it was the drunkenness and promiscuity that they occasioned and the poor example they gave to the lower orders which the bishops found dangerous. Waddington, Wake, Gibson and Secker and the others saw their objections in the tradition of the reformation of manners, in staunching the flow of immoral and immodest behaviour, rather than in Puritan fundamentalism. Their efforts were formalised in the Proclamation Society and a plethora of other organisations which sought in the last years of the eighteenth century to promote sobriety and decorum on the sabbath. Nevertheless, as the diary of Anna Larpent shows, in the minds of many people of the eighteenth century there was no dilemma in attending both masquerades and charity sermons.[38] Nor was there a contradiction in the minds of the nobles who attended both court entertainments and divine services. Indeed William Dodd's *Prison Thoughts* (1777), recorded the piety of his aristocratic congregation of St George's Hanover Square, many of whom attended masquerades:

> When attentive sat
> Or at the Holy Altar humbly knelt
> Persuasive pleasing patterns – Athol's Duke
> The polish'd Hervey, Kingston the humane
> Aylesbury and Marchmont, Romney all rever'd
> With numbers more – by splendid titles less
> Than piety distinguished and pure zeal.[39]

Puritanism was not the only Anglican response to culture and entertainment. Some Anglicans believed that pleasure could be moral and good and that well-motivated pleasure was legitimate. This belief was derived from James I's *Declaration concerning Lawful Sports* (1618) which asserted that sports and recreations were legitimate and sanctioned Whitsun ales, morris-dancing and May games. Charles I's *Book of Sports* – which promoted the same notion – was commanded in 1633 to be read in churches. These royal statements were direct responses to Puritan censures of recreation. In the late seventeenth century this strand of thought was represented by John Tillotson, who preached that Jesus's example of doing good was one that men and women could follow with pleasure and joy.[40] Thomas Bayes followed Tillotson in arguing that 'the principal end of the divine providence and government is the happiness of his creatures'.[41] Similarly William Paley at the end of the eighteenth century argued that good works naturally engendered happiness.[42] The concept of the sanctity of pleasure reached its highest Anglican expression in the sermon of William Jones at Nayland in July 1787, at the inauguration of the parish organ. Music, argued Jones, was the work of God seen in the nature of mankind:

> for God hath undoubtedly made man to sing as well as speak. . . . But more than this, man is an instrument of God in his whole frame. Besides the powers of the voice in forming and of the ear in distinguishing musical sounds, there is a general sense, or sympathetic feeling, in the fibres and membranes in the body, which renders the whole frame susceptible to musical emotion.[43]

It was a view that was expressed by John Locke, who felt mankind possessed a right to happiness and even drew on the Commonwealth ideas of John Harrington who adopted utopian views of man's search for godly happiness.

The dichotomy in Anglican attitudes to pleasure and entertainment – and to culture more generally – remained throughout the eighteenth century. Bath, for example, attracted the Revd John Penrose, a moderate High Churchman, for the season in 1766. He wrote at length on the sermons and services in the Abbey and the frequent religious and charity festivals. He described a bourgeois society for whom devotion, philanthropy and charity were an important part of their cultural experience. But Charles Wesley described the city by coining the phrase 'Hell on Earth'. Wesley and Penrose's judgements reflected the traditions into which they had been born. Roy Porter, however, has suggested that for the most part eighteenth-century England built on the moderate ideas of Tillotson and Paley. The moral legitimacy of pleasure became the dominant ideology of eighteenth-century culture. In 1789 the Bishop of St David's preached at the annual festival of the Royal Humane Society, and paraded four hundred people saved by the society. In such settings, piety and philanthropy went hand in hand with public spectacle and entertainment.[44] Similarly, the work of Defoe, Swift, Steele, Addison and the Augustan writers built on the assumption that pleasure and culture could be put to work for religious as well as immoral ends.[45]

Equally, religion could be utilised for the benefit of pleasure. For London society the attractions of the Vauxhall and Ranleigh Gardens were opportunities for display and conversation. Yet here too there were concerns that misbehaviour might coarsen the gardens, and thereby deter the attendance of the growing affluent classes. As a result, the Vauxhall Gardens employed two clergymen 'who . . . are by their holy looks to keep decorum'.[46] The consequence was that the Vauxhall Gardens were able to attract attendees of a higher social strata, as one satire claimed

> Nor less diversions the strange group affords
> Where hungry parsons elbow o'ergrown lords.[47]

Music was also a feature of popular religious culture in the eighteenth century. Vic Gammon suggests that popular Church music remained largely unregulated into the nineteenth century.[48] In contrast, Donald Spaeth argues that the firm regulation of popular Church music came in Wiltshire in the eighteenth century. Up to 1730 members of Church choirs often chose their own hymns, anthems and psalms, organised their own musical instruments, separated themselves from the congregation and generally exercised the sort of autonomy that could lead to indiscipline. From 1730, however, archdeacons and bishops, like Thomas Sherlock, sought to impose greater order on choirs. They insisted that the choice of music must lie with the clergy, as did the direction of the choir. Rehearsals and performances without a parson present – which smacked of conventicle – were also censured, as was the choice of psalms which could be interpreted as political. Nevertheless music was extraordinarily popular: Parson Millard in 1718 recognised that his parishioners were extremely fond of Church music, one psalm recital by forty children attracted an audience of over two hundred men and women.[49]

The eighteenth century saw a huge growth in publishing, after a collapse during the Restoration.[50] The abandonment of State censorship after the Revolution enabled largely unfettered publication of religious and political tracts. Indeed so unregulated was publishing that the Revd Francis Clifton, a Jacobite parson, was able to operate a printing press from the confines of the Kings Bench Gaol.[51] The only recourse was to criminal trial, such as that imposed on the Non-juror Hilkiah Bedford for publishing *The Hereditary Right of the Crown of England Asserted* (1713). This relative freedom stimulated a huge growth in religious publishing. John Brewer has estimated that religious items were the single largest body of published work in the eighteenth century, making up 50,000 titles.[52] In Chester, of three printers in the early eighteenth century, two were exclusively printers of religious works.[53] Sampson Letsome's *Index to the Sermons Published since the Reformation* (1751), showed that 8,800 sermons had been published between 1660 and 1751, an average over ninety a year. From 1700 to 1790 in the region of two hundred and thirty religious books were published every year, and in the first eight years of the eighteenth century 1,152 religious books were published.[54] Moreover the dominance of religious books by Anglicans was evident, in 1700 around 2,500 Anglican sermons were in print compared with between three hundred and four hundred sermons by Dissenters.[55] It is clear that until the nineteenth century even Dissenters relied heavily on Anglican works such as those by Samuel Clarke, Thomas Balguy and Richard Cumberland.[56] Printers were dependent on the Church in a more direct way also. In 1716, when a form of prayer of thanksgiving was published, the cost of 15,000 copies to be circulated throughout the kingdom, 2,000 in Welsh and 14,000 books of prayers was nearly three hundred pounds.[57]

Much of this boom in religious publishing was generated by subscription to religious works. In 1701 thirty-four subscriptions were offered to the public, by 1711 this rose to eighty-nine and by 1721 to over two hundred subscription offers.[58] Throughout the century bishops and clergy were consistently among the most assiduous subscribers to religious works.[59] Undoubtedly book subscription, particularly to religious works, was a means of indicating religious and political affiliation. John Strype's *History of the Life and Acts of . . . Edmund Grindall* was commissioned and subscribed by Whigs in 1710 to counter the High-Church views advanced by Henry Sacheverell, in all thirty-four Whig MPs subscribed to it. Similarly religious works by Jeremy Collier, Thomas Hearne and George Smalridge consistently attracted Tory subscribers.[60] This role of religious books as a means of political as well as religious expression has not been lost on historians. Jan Albers claims that 'the Church's importance as a provider of political education and opinion in the first half of the century can scarcely be overestimated'.[61] Certainly the 40,000 purchasers of Sacheverell's sermon of 1710, and the many more readers of it, cannot have been blind to its political significance; nor can those who bought the works of Hoadly, Sherlock and the other popular writers have ignored their political reputations.

The clergy were also the most consistent book collectors in the eighteenth century. In the Cuckmere Valley in Sussex alone, Giles Moore, rector of Horsted Keynes, was a major book buyer and left a major theological library; Ezekial Clarke, rector of Waldron included his books in his will, as did John Tattershall and John Herring, successive vicars of Chiddingly; and in Heathfield parish the local bookseller, son of the vicar, left a library of over two hundred books to the parish incumbents in 1736.[62] The publication of religious tracts by the SPCK added to the boom in the printing of religious works; for the first time there was a national network of clergy and laity who bought and distributed religious books and tracts and were consciously seeking to stamp out the dual evils of illiteracy and irreligion. Many of the SPCK books were destined for parish libraries, on which successive episcopal visitations placed great emphasis. Significantly the SPCK also enabled the renaissance in religious books to reach beyond the metropolis. Circulating, parochial and subscription libraries enabled men and women in remote areas to read the works that had previously been the preserve of those closest to the cities.[63] In 1708 the King's Lynn corporation library consisted almost entirely of theological books.[64] By 1745 St Nicholas's Church in Newcastle had a parish library of 5,000 books, and even St George's Doncaster had a collection of four hundred works.[65]

In some towns the theological libraries were available to borrow, in Lichfield in the late eighteenth century about 3,000 books were on loan.[66] In this way religious works reached beyond the clergy to the laity. Individuals, like the diarist and shop-keeper Thomas Turner of East Hoathly, built up significant collections of sermons and religious works for regular reading. Indeed Turner read Tillotson's sermons to groups of family and friends five times, with as many as seven sermons read at each session.[67] For many clergy their sermons were among their most valuable possessions: in 1728 Giles Watkin, vicar of Chiddingly, left his nephew a gold ring and his forty sermons.[68]

There is considerable evidence of the buoyancy of the market in religious books and especially of Bibles and the liturgy: estimated sales of the Bible in England were 30,000 a year in the eighteenth century.[69] John Baskerville was prepared to borrow 2,000 pounds at an extortionate interest rate of five per cent to buy the rights to print a folio Bible in 1762. He knew that he would be ruined if the Bibles did not sell, but of course they did. Earlier in his career he had paid Cambridge University twenty pounds per thousand and twelve pounds ten shillings per thousand respectively for the right to print quarto and octavo editions of the Book of Common Prayer. He regarded the terms as 'shackles [that] greatly hurt me', but he turned the shackles into a profit by mass sales. By his death he left an estate worth 12,000 pounds.[70] Similarly Thomas Guy – the founder of Guy's Hospital – built his fortune on the profits of religious publishing in the first decade of the eighteenth century; and Thomas Osborne also made huge sums from the religious book trade.[71] The volume of sermons and religious works led the bookseller in Fielding's novel *Joseph Andrews* to say

> the trade is vastly stocked with them [sermons] that really, unless they come out with the name of Whitfield or Wesley, or some other such great man [such] as a bishop . . . I dont care to touch [them] . . . unless it was a sermon preached on the 30th January.

Indeed there were many booksellers who packed their trade cards with offers of sermons and religious works by popular authors.[72] The thirst of the public for sermons was so fierce that clergy were often hard pressed to keep up with demand; and so was the appetite of the clergy. Hence the Revd Dr John Trussler in 1771 produced one hundred and fifty sermons printed in imitation handwriting (described as 'caractères de civilité') for sale to his fellow clergy as preaching sermons at a shilling a piece. This ingenious labour-saving scheme was kept in print for twenty years, earning Trussler an annual income from royalties of one hundred and fifty pounds. One element of the marketing of Trussler's imitation manuscript sermons was that he would not sell the same sermon to two neighbouring clergy, to avoid parishioners hearing the same sermon in two different churches.[73] The similar pressure on Parson Joseph Price to meet the demands of his congregation led him to copy out sermons from Archdeacon Dodwell's works in 1772.[74]

Many of the books that eighteenth-century entrepreneurs produced were religious classics. Lewis Bayly's *The Practice of Piety* . . . was first published in 1612, but remained popular into the eighteenth century, reaching its fifty-eighth edition in 1734, with sales estimated at 100,000.[75] Part of the enduring popularity of the *Practice of Piety* was its role as a life-long guide to Christian devotion. Running to over a thousand pages in the first edition, it included prayers and meditations for all life's eventualities and circumstances and included instructions on making a will and what the last thoughts of a godly man should be. Another element in its popularity was that it avoided religious controversy and doctrinal divisions. The other standard religious work of the period was *The Whole Duty of Man*, probably written by Richard Allestree, and first published in 1658. By 1690 it had reached its twenty-fifth edition, and went through numerous further editions in the eighteenth century. It was frequently revised, so that a *New Whole Duty of Man* appeared and even attracted royal commendation in 1743. Edward Wickstead was licensed to enjoy the copyright of the *New Whole Duty of Man* for fourteen years because the work 'greatly tend[s] to the advancement of religion and the general good and benefit of mankind'. Wickstead's thirteenth edition included testimonials of the value of the book from Bishops Wilkins, Tillotson, Wilson and Gibson. Indeed Bishop Gibson's first and second pastoral letters commended the *Whole Duty of Man* to his clergy and laity alike. Like the *Practice of Piety*, the *Whole Duty of Man* took each reader through a cycle of self-examination and meditations which included such matters as the sin of sacrilege, the duty of parents, the care of a soul, and the preparation for worship. The scheme of the work focused first on the Christian's duty to God and then on a Christian's duty to his fellow men and women. In many extended editions there were prayers, concordances and biblical extracts for private use. By the mid eighteenth century it was probably the dominant religious work of the period. Samuel Johnson was forced to read it as a child and, characteristically, loathed it; but Charles Simeon was converted to Evangelicalism by reading it.[76] Lehmberg's view is that the *Whole Duty of Man* was so widespread in the seventeenth and eighteenth centuries that it was probably known to everyone in the country.[77] It was certainly an aspiration that every man, woman and child in the country would own a Bible, a Book of Common Prayer, a catechism and a copy of *Whole Duty of Man* and the

Practice of Piety.[78] As late as 1886 Michael Henchard in Hardy's *Mayor of Casterbridge* owned one.[79]

For some Anglicans the widespread access to the Bible in English was the fulfilment of the Reformation. Phillip Bearcroft in 1748 argued that 'it is by the especial blessings of heaven that ye have the free use of your Bibles, while the people of many other nations are deprived of it by the tyranny of the Church of Rome'. But Bearcroft could not forebear to draw a political point from the cultural possession of the Bible:

> May all British Protestants, but more especially and in particular may all the worthy members of our established Church, unite and oppose with ardour all the attempts of those crafty designing men who lie in wait to deceive and would take from us our Bibles, and together with them all that is truly valuable and worth living for here, I mean our happy constitution in Church and State.[80]

The King James, or Authorised, Version of the Bible was a focus of Protestant unity. It was regarded by Anglicans and Dissenters alike as the 'common version'. This national version of the Bible stood in stark contrast to the alien Catholic Douai Bible. In fact Bible revision, a long-held desire of many Anglicans and Dissenters, was shelved by Archbishop Secker to prevent divisions and disagreement that the King James Bible had largely prevented.[81] Besides the Bible and liturgy, there were hugely popular authors whose sermons attracted mass readership. Bishop Joseph Hall's works reached a twenty-fourth edition in 1799; Edward Stillingfleet's works were also enduringly popular and John Tillotson's sermons ran through re-printings too numerous to be counted. Hall's popularity is particularly significant since he was best known for his admonition 'to walk ever in the beaten roads of the Church' and to disavow Dissent.[82] These writers were held up as models for the clergy, and described by Bishop Richard Smallbrooke in his charge to his clergy in 1726:

> the best pattern that can be placed before us for contemplating a preacher and which indeed includes all the precepts of that art is that of the incomparable Archbishop Tillotson. . . .[83]

In Wales where poverty often constrained levels of literacy and publishing, diocesan libraries for clergy were founded in Bangor, Carmarthen, Cowbridge and St Asaph between 1705 and 1711.[84] Wales became an important centre of interest in religious books in the eighteenth century, largely because the poverty of the people and the paucity of presses in Wales was overcome by publishing and fund-raising in London. In 1689–90 over

10,000 Bibles were distributed free in Wales, and paid for by funds raised in London. By the early years of the eighteenth century the demand for religious books in Wales was enormous. In 1716 when Phillip Phillips announced a subscription for a new edition of the Bible in Welsh, he received 1,200 subscribers within a few days. The final printing produced 10,000 volumes, of which 1,000 were distributed free of charge. Another edition was produced in 1727, each volume costing four shillings. In all, between 1660 and 1730, about 40,000 Bibles were bought or sent to Wales.

The Bible and the Book of Common Prayer were not the only religious works sought after in Wales. In the first third of the eighteenth century a torrent of Welsh devotional literature poured across Wales; between 1700 and 1730 the number of Welsh books printed in the principality rose from seventy six to one hundred and eighty. Some of these, such as John Lewis's *Church Catechism Explained*, were works popular in England which were translated into Welsh – Lewis's work was published first in England in 1700 and translated in 1713. The subscription lists for religious works indicate that they were in demand by a wide cross-section of Welsh society, including yeoman farmers. Moreover Anglicanism dominated this religious literary renaissance in Wales; in 1730 seventy per cent of religious works were those of Anglicans rather than Dissenters.[85]

Religious publishing was not restricted to religious tracts and sermons. *The Guardian* and *The Spectator*, the foremost journals available in coffee houses and clubs, included religious articles and debates. Popular literature also enjoyed religious themes: Hannah More, Thomas Merton, Henry Fielding and others produced a mass of sentimental literature in which religion played a central role. One historian has recently suggested that Samuel Richardson's novels are in many ways Christian parables.[86] The impact of such literature on the lives of people was often subtle and intangible; Samuel Johnson asserted in *The Adventurer* 'he that entertains himself with moral and religious treatises will imperceptibly advance in goodness'.[87]

Churchmen were also assiduous collectors of manuscripts and works of history and classical scholarship. The contribution of eighteenth-century clergymen to the creation of a great national collection can be seen in the diary of Humphrey Wanley, librarian and agent for Lord Oxford. Wanley assiduously cherry-picked historical manuscripts from the libraries of a huge number of clergy; his previous station as secretary of the SPCK meant he enjoyed a large number of clerical connections. Occasionally, as with Francis Astrey, Canon of St Paul's, Wanley was able to solicit a manuscript as a gift for Lord Oxford's library. Wanley was also not above taking advantage of clerical desperation, in 1716 he bought Thomas Baker's manuscripts just before he was expelled from his fellowship at St John's College, Cambridge for Non-jury.[88] Frequently Wanley obtained books and manuscripts from the legatees of clergymen, as for example when he bought Archdeacon John Batteley of Canterbury's collection from his nephew and Archdeacon Robert Burscough of Barnstaple's collection from his widow.[89] Occasionally, Wanley used agents at book auctions, as when he bought the Revd Ralph Bridge's books. Clergy were also allies: Thomas Frank, Archdeacon of Bedford, acted as intermediary in 1720 in obtaining the Newnham Cartulary from Bedford Library for Wanley. A number of antiquaries, such as Browne Willis, donated manuscripts to the library in exchange for free access to it for research. By 1753 Harley's library, so carefully assembled from the best clerical collections in the country was bought for the nation for 10,000 pounds to be the core of the British Museum library.[90] But the importance of the religious republic of letters in the eighteenth century was not just in the great national collections, though they show a significant element in elite values; its importance lay in the fact that Anglican culture reached deep into society and touched the lives of nearly all men and women of all conditions.

When the bookseller in Fielding's novel *Joseph Andrews* referred to the commercial popularity of the 30 January sermons commemorating the martyrdom of Charles I, he was touching on a feature of the religious calendar that dominated eighteenth-century life as much as it had done in the preceding centuries.[91] The religious calendar located Britain and her history in the triumph of Anglicanism. It permeated both the poor and elite in sermons and festivals, such as the celebration of 29 May as Royal Oak Day, which the Revd John Penrose witnessed in Bath in 1766.[92] Such anniversaries acted as a bridge between elite and popular folk cultures, drawing together rich and poor in a shared affection for the Church and the Anglican establishment. Donald Spaeth has shown that in consistory depositions in Salisbury diocese in the early eighteenth century there is frequent use of holy days as a popular calendar to refer to seasons and days; saints days such as St James's and St Katherine's were used as reference points.[93] The calendar of the Church: Christmas, Candlemas, Lent, Easter, Whitsun, Rogationtide, Michaelmas, All Hallows, and individual saints' days were occasions for popular customs rich in historical associations. The calendar of the State was equally rich in religious symbolism: 30 January anniversary of the martyrdom of Charles I; 29 May Charles II's birthday; 5 November the dual anniversary of the gunpowder plot and the landing of William III in England and the torrent of other birthdays and anniversaries were all occasions of public celebration. At St Michael's, Southampton in 1707 there were seven national celebrations at which bells were rung. Next door in the parish of St Lawrence, Southampton, the celebration of the release of the seven bishops from the Tower in 1688 was three times as long as the usual ringing.[94] Parishes also enjoyed their own feasts: plough day; harvest home; spring marling (manuring); May day; well dressing; Church wakes (which often celebrated the saint's day to which the Church was dedicated); St Cecilia's day (for musical celebrations) and rushbearing. Sometimes parishes made arrangements to move popular festivals to permit Sunday observance, as in 1738 when a writer in the *Gentleman's Magazine* recorded:

> I am now in the country at that season in which parish feasts abound. I hear of one every Sunday kept in some village or other of the neighbourhood and see great numbers of both sexes in their holiday clothes constantly flooding thither. . . . These feasts on Sundays are still observed as times of entertainment and pleasure; but to avoid unseemly noise and disturbance upon a day of holiness the sports and diversions are now in many villages prudently deferred till the Monday after.[95]

These were popular events which touched the lives of most of the population. It was the ability of the Church to attract mass attendance at national and local festivals that wedded religion so closely to popular culture. Popular religious festivals were also often marked by features that provided a sense of theatre and spectacle. As Gerald Newman suggests, 'mustering the people' in folk festivals was an important expression of national identity:

> the crowd becomes a congregation celebrating itself in a secular liturgy, democratically participating in the newly-articulated myths and symbols of the whole community.[96]

In Wales the Christmas 'plygain' (or cockcrow) service attracted most parishioners because of the excitement of seeing the dawn of Christmas day; similarly Henry Bourne of Newcastle wrote of the popularity of getting up early on Easter day to see the sunrise, and processional perambulations were mass expressions of the territorial integrity of each parish.[97]

Expressions of popular adherence to the Church were often motivated by enlightened self-interest. Lancashire churches were sometimes used by market sellers, as at St George's Liverpool, and for publishing notices of the sale of goods and land, as at Westhoughton in 1743.[98] There was, moreover, much charitable benefit for the poor to be obtained from the Church. At festivals Church 'dole' for the poor was often distributed after services. At Halstead in Kent, the twenty acres of 'bread and cheese lands' left to the parish yielded six hundred loaves for the parishioners who attended Easter day services.[99] It was usual for alms for the poor to be only available to those attending services of the Church. More importantly, Church celebrations permitted parishioners some leisure time and opportunities for recreation, such as the drinking of Church ales at Whitsun.[100] The 'rites of passage' of baptism, marriage and funerals were also the occasion of large-scale family and community expressions of popular piety. However, there were some paradoxes in English popular attitudes to religious observance. Evidence from Wiltshire suggests that folk superstition tended to inhibit parishioners from communicating. Men and women felt that they had to be morally spotless before they could receive Communion and since such a state of moral perfection was unattainable, some people avoided receiving Communion rather than risk damnation for doing so while in a state of sin. Sometimes parishioners would not communicate if they were engaged in law suits or disputes. This created the paradox that an elevated respect for the Eucharist led men and women to neglect its observance.[101] As late as 1783 the parson at Winterborne Monkton responded to the episcopal visitation enquiries that

> the number of communicants is . . . few . . . [some] are deterred from communicating under a notion that they thereby bind themselves to lead a better and more Christian life than they are otherwise obliged to do, under a heavier and more severe punishment hereafter.[102]

Indeed there seems to have been a trend in popular interpretations of Anglicanism to elevate and tighten the rituals and regulations of Christianity; the Revd Richard Wavell of Winchester was even asked by a parishioner in 1753 whether it was permitted to eat meat on Ash Wednesday.[103]

William Jacob has suggested that the division of superstition from orthodox religion was an artifice created by modern folklorists as they reclaimed examples of popular traditions. In the eighteenth century there was not always such an easy separation: astrology and superstition were difficult to separate from popular religion and were often regarded as consistent with it. Jacob argues that up to the early eighteenth century astrology existed comfortably alongside Christianity for the elite as much as for the poor; certainly there were astrologers at most of the Stuart courts. But in the early years of the eighteenth century, Jacob also suggests that growing rational-scientific learning drove astrology out of fashion with the educated classes. But this phenomenon took some time to spread throughout society. Hence William Salmon and other astrologers remained hugely popular in the eighteenth century and their almanacs were stocked by booksellers alongside Bibles. In fairs and markets fortune tellers were frequently to be found, and prophecies retained a hold on the popular imagination: Mother Shipton's prophecies of 1641 remained widely-known in the eighteenth century, and Robert Nixon's *Cheshire Prophecies* (1714) was re-printed twenty-one times by 1745.[104] Nevertheless there were emerging ideas of superstition. In 1718 the Commissioners for Forfeited Estates evicted tenants from the manor of Eccleston in Lancashire because the lands were being put to superstitious uses.[105]

Witchcraft was also a common feature of popular superstition, Jacob recounts cases in 1709, 1712, 1736 and 1751.[106] Witchcraft counted some educated men like Ralph Thoresby and John Wesley among those who believed in it. As with astrology, witchcraft was abandoned as implausible by the educated classes in the early eighteenth century. The last sentence of execution for witchcraft took place in England in 1712, when a Hertfordshire woman was condemned, though pardoned by Queen Anne through the good offices of the presiding judge. Three years previously a woman in Dumfries had been condemned for witchcraft and had been sentenced to have a brand put on her cheek, and in 1697 a Scottish woman was burnt to death in a tar barrel for witchcraft. These brought to an end two hundred years of witchcraft trials in England and Scotland that had seen the executions of about 30,000 people.[107] In 1736 witchcraft was abolished as a crime, but witches were still brought to trial for nuisance and complaints of breach of the peace, and there remained occasional direct action against them by local people. In 1759 the *Gentleman's Magazine* recounted that an Aylesbury woman was accused of bewitching a spinning wheel and was weighed against the Bible in the local Church and acquitted.[108] Moreover, witches open to the actions of the mob were occasionally killed. In 1751 an old woman, Ruth Osborne, was charged with bewitching calves whose owners had refused to give her some buttermilk. Osborne and her husband were surrounded by a mob and Ruth was drowned. The ringleader of the mob was subsequently tried and hanged for murder. Fear of witches persisted until late in the eighteenth century. In 1773 the *Reading Mercury and Oxford Gazette* noted that 'the ridiculous notion of witches and witch-craft still prevails amongst the lower sort of people' and gave an account of a woman in Seend, Wiltshire who was attacked by a mob and accused of witchcraft for apparently causing fevers. In 1761 *Lloyd's Evening Post* also recorded a witch in Wilton, Wiltshire, defended from mob action by the swift actions of a magistrate. As late as 1800 a celebrated case of witchcraft in Bristol attracted accounts of familiars, spirits, the bewitching of children and animals.[109] As Jeremy Black has indicated,

> popular religious belief, however removed from the teachings of the churches, did not amount to an alternative religion. Pagan

practices were not the same as paganism. Instead such beliefs and practices co-existed or were intertwined with Christian counterparts with little sense of incompatibility, especially among ordinary folk in rural areas.[110]

The widespread conviction that evil could be so immediately embodied is evidence of the faith of many people in a supernatural world in which good and evil fought for the souls and lives of its inhabitants. The same applies to the plethora of superstitions and folk traditions which existed alongside Christianity in the eighteenth century and were inextricably enmeshed with it. Men and women did not see any distinction between the divine intervention in the world preached by the parson in the pulpit on Sunday, and evidenced by the salvation of the country from Catholicism, and the everyday manifestations of soured milk, ruined crops, prophecies and magic. All were part of the same revelatory faith and the same system of beliefs. It is not surprising therefore that many superstitions grew up around Christian worship, and apparently with the collusion of the clergy. In Wales it was common for women to take candles to their parish church on All Hallows Eve and light them in the presence of the sexton, and judge from the brightness of the flame whether the coming year would be good or bad. The vicar of Winchcombe, Gloucestershire provided turf from the churchyard to be used as a cure for dropsy, and in Charlcombe the church paten with salt on it was used to place on the breast of a dying man to make his passing easier.[111] In 1724 Mr Lewis, vicar of Margate, reported to Archbishop Wake that in some parts of Kent confirmation was superstitiously regarded as the bishop's blessing rather than a sacrament and that it was common for people to receive confirmation on every occasion on which a bishop visited the parish for the purpose.[112] Eighteenth-century Anglicanism existed at a transitional moment between seventeenth-century Puritanism and nineteenth-century Tractarianism, both of which placed inordinate emphasis on attendance at church, sobriety, moral rectitude, voluntary religious observances, and a self-conscious respectability. Yet these were social and ideological constructs rather than hard indicators of faith or religious conviction. The fact that the poor absented themselves from church to work, or that they retained folk superstitions or had a powerful sense of the immediacy of supernatural religion is an alternative rather than a lesser or conflicting construct of piety and conviction.

The Church's contribution to and the patronage of culture was also evident in church building and repair. The Newbury churchwardens' accounts list the employment of stonemasons, plumbers, carpenters, glaziers, paviours, blacksmiths, gilders, painters, plasterers and roofers.[113]

The eighteenth-century Church has erroneously become a by-word for plainness and absence of decoration. In fact, the account of the work of William Wace of London for Bletcheley Church, for which Browne Willis paid, suggests otherwise. Wace's work included

> painting the chancel, painting and gilding the glory and 37 cherubs' heads, the 12 apostles as big as life, 17 panels done with ornament, 84 foot of cornish, three members inriched; 56 ft 4 inch astical inriched; 26 of 5 inch hollow round the window inriched, gilding all the mouldings round the 39 panels, painting the columns, five large curtains and painting all the wall three times in oyle. . . .[114]

Similarly, when Christ Church, Bristol was rebuilt in 1786 William Paty was employed to build 'an unrivalled example of English rococo': the altar was painted blue and white, ornamental panels of the decalogue, the Creed and the Lord's Prayer were installed and the nave decorated with columns and plasterwork. The altar alone cost one hundred and five pounds, a table twenty-five, iron railings thirty-one and silver candlesticks ninety pounds respectively.[115] Nor was such generous patronage rare. Some benefactors were regular providers for their church, at St Andrew, Undershaft it was recorded that

> Mr Henry Tombs, 1725, a worthy inhabitant did, at his own cost and charge, guild the organ 1725; gave the centre piece of painting over the altar, 1726; painted the pillars and arches in oyle, with the figures of the apostles and scripture pieces under them; besides having given formerly the Book of Martyrs and been a liberal subscriber to the building of the organ and the altar pieces.

Often the patron was also the incumbent. At Foxley, Wiltshire there is an inscription:

> This Chancel was
> pav'd by John Stump
> Rector here June
> the 29th 1708. Never
> done before.

Other patrons made generous gifts: in 1753 at St Bartholomew, Birmingham it was recorded that at the annual meeting of the Bean Club at the Swan, a proposal being made for beginning a subscription to erect an altarpiece in the new chapel, Lord Fielding generously gave the whole sum, being £120. . . .[116]

Municipal corporations were frequent donors for church buildings in the eighteenth century: Leeds Corporation members voted five hundred and eighty pounds towards a new church; in Bristol in 1732 the Common Council gave one hundred pounds for St Stephen's Church; Beverly Minster was granted 3,720 pounds from a corporation charity between 1726 and 1745, Lincoln Corporation – which met at St Peter at Arches – rebuilt it at its sole charge in 1724 and four years later gave a peal of bells and an altarpiece; and in King's Lynn the corporation led the benefactors to the rebuilding of the nave in 1741.[117]

Altarpieces were increasingly popular in the eighteenth century and indicate both a reaction to the destruction of the seventeenth century and a growing sense of the Church as a patron of the visual arts. Altarpieces were examples of public art, and often attracted visitors to admire them. But there were dangers in such proliferation of artistry. In 1725 Bishop Edmund Gibson of London had to order the altarpiece at St Clement Dane to be removed when it was realised that the portrait of St Cecilia was a representation of the Pretender's wife and the angels the rest of her family.[118] Eleven years earlier Bishop John Robinson of London had ordered an altarpiece removed from Whitechapel Church. The painting had been commissioned by the rector, the Tory Dr Welton, and depicted the Last Supper, but Judas was portrayed as the Whig White Kennett, even to the extent of including the black patch Kennett wore on his forehead to cover the effects of an accident with a pistol.[119]

Motives for building and restoring churches were varied. Browne Willis, who rebuilt a large number of churches near his home in Bletcheley, gave two explanations. In restoring Bletcheley Church itself he was moved by the fact that it was the resting place of his parents:

> Considering this therefore and withal observing how incongruous it would be for him to cover the remains of his parents with marble statues and fine embellishments, whilst the other parts of God's house, in which they lay, wanted both a requisite decency and convenience for his worship, he determined in the first place to provide for God's honour and to do justice to the memory of his earthly parents. . . . And thus . . . with a free will and devout heart he thus repaired the Church and the chancel.

Equally unselfish motives lay behind Willis's rebuilding of Wappenham Church, Northamptonshire, but were joined with a sense of those eighteenth-century virtues of politeness and sociability:

> religion teaches civility and good manners toward man, as well as piety and devotion toward God and I hope the erecting of this chapel among them may in good time have this visible effect upon the inhabitants, as in both respects to reform them.[120]

The development of a communal religious sense, lay behind some municipal restorations. As William Jacob has shown, in King's Lynn, the rebuilding of the church was because

> the form of religion was central to the life of the borough. In every borough the mayor and common council attended the Church in State with swords and maces on Sundays and the holy days of the Church and State. The parish Church rather than the town hall was the arena for the enacting of rituals of the borough: it was the only covered space large enough for representatives of the whole population to meet to worship God. . . . The common council had specified the nature of the worship, daily morning and evening prayer to be accompanied on Sundays and holy days by a sermon and on the first Sunday in the month to include a celebration of the holy Communion.[121]

There were sometimes less edifying motives for the particular form of building. The Octagon Chapel in Bath was paid for by the sale of season tickets; the chapel was designed to enable the fashionably elite congregation to gain the maximum exposure. In some subscriptions for churches there was more than a small element of self-advertisement: at Tunbridge Wells the Chapel of King Charles the martyr was paid for by the subscriptions of over 2,000 subscribers whose names were commemorated in two ostentatious frames in the building.[122]

The public nature of churches in the eighteenth century was one of the ways in which they contributed to the popular culture of the age.[123] The importance of the public nature of worship in the eighteenth century was reflected in the urging of bishops to ensure that the congregations could hear what was said. William Fleetwood of St Asaph in 1710 ordered his clergy to remember that

> the minister, in the public service, is, as it were, the mouth of the congregation. His voice is to reach the ears and to direct the hearts

of all his audience to his proper object . . . and I venture to affirm that much of their devotion will depend upon the way and manner of his uttering forth his prayers and praises. . . .[124]

The public nature of worship was also reflected in the sermons which celebrated great national events. Sermons were preached across the country during the Seven Years War, the American War of Independence, during epidemics, after the earthquake of 1755 and on royal births and deaths.[125] Churches became public spaces, and their form changed to accommodate this new status. In 1681 William Beveridge had supported the installation of a chancel screen at the new Wren Church of St Peter's Cornhill on the grounds that it represented continuity of practice with the past and avoided novelty in worship. But such ideas were outmoded. When Avington Church in Hampshire was built the focus was on making an 'auditory' church, one in which the congregation's participation was reinforced by the acoustics and the arrangement of the furniture.[126] Similar auditory churches were built at All Saints, Derby by James Gibbs, and All Saints, Newcastle, which was circular in design. As frequent Communions grew, with greater numbers of communicants, altars needed to be larger and with more space to accommodate the people at the rails. Similarly the greater regulation of marriage required larger sanctuaries. Evidence of the need for more space for baptism parties comes from All Saints, Newcastle, built in 1789 where a separate room was built for baptisms. In 1755 the north transept of St Mary Redcliffe, Bristol was renovated and turned over exclusively to baptisms, with a font costing £119.[127]

Churches themselves also contributed to the public space in towns. New churches were often the centrepiece of the English urban renaissance. St Mary's, Warwick, St Nicholas's, Whitehaven, St Anne's, Manchester, St Phillip's, Birmingham and St George's, Hanover Square in London all formed backdrops to promenades and vistas of the new urban areas in which they were located. For John Downes, preaching before the Society of Cutlers in Sheffield in 1743, these developments were symbols of progress:

under the happier auspices and protection of society we may behold towns and cities . . . rising up out of the barren wastes and unpeopled deserts: Arts and Sciences out of ignorance and error, light out of darkness, harmony out of discord; and order out of confusion . . . such are the blessings and advantages arising from society. . . .[128]

Visiting churches and cathedrals became a genteel pastime for the leisured classes, and written accounts of churches and cathedrals were part of the cultural exchange of men and women with sufficient wealth and leisure to travel and appreciate architecture.[129]

The volume of church building and repair has been generally under-estimated by historians. Basil Clarke found over four hundred examples of building, significant renovations or major benefactions in the eighteenth century, and over the century there were at least one hundred and fifteen Acts of Parliament for the rebuilding of parish churches.[130] As Peter Borsay noted,

> the number of towns which acquired fine new churches in the first sixty years of the eighteenth century is quite remarkable given the preceding dearth of activity.[131]

Classical and Palladian architecture was reconciled to Christianity and adopted a moral dimension in beauty and function which allowed it to be widely adopted for religious buildings.

The Church's relationship with a variety of trades and crafts was symbiotic. As Jonathan Barry has pointed out, in Bristol a wide range of guilds, charities, hospitals, Freemasonic lodges and other organisations held annual festivals, usually involving a service in a church and the invitation to a clergyman to be their chosen preacher, with the expectation that there would be a market for the published sermon.[132] In Bolton, the Society of Weavers in 1755 asked the curate to conduct an annual service, and paid him ten shillings and sixpence for the sermon. Subsequent clergy who celebrated the work of the Society included the Low-Church Whig Edward Whitehead, vicar of Bolton, and his High-Church successor John Clayton, both of whom were sympathetic to the charitable purposes of the Society.[133] Equally the Church as a consumer fuelled demand for certain goods. The services of the Church created a market for ceremonial items (including printed orders of service, funeral directions and monumental masonry), furniture (altarpieces, railings, carvings, pews, candelabra, lecterns, scriptural texts) and even clothing (wedding and funeral rings, gloves, scarves and headgear). When Hugh Poole, incumbent of Babbington, died in 1738 his funeral accounts included payments for a coach and hearse, coffin plate and covering cloth, a crepe suit, fifty pairs of gloves for mourners, and mourning hatbands.[134] For some artists and churches this could represent a significant investment: Hogarth's altarpiece for St Mary Redcliffe, Bristol depicting the high priest's servants sealing the tomb, the women at the tomb and the Ascension, cost an astonishing £525. Edward Colston, the Bristol Tory philanthropist, promised financial help to any local church seeking to repair or decorate its altars, organs, galleries and furniture.[135] Barry regards this cultural patronage as an instrument which could promote and support the religious identity of Anglicanism. However, Dissent was also a major factor in the development of English religious culture in the eighteenth century. In music, publishing, visual arts and most other cultural media, Nonconformists were growing in significance as consumers and suppliers. Therefore cultural patronage had the potential to intensify divisions between denominations. Certainly Anglican popular culture included satirical attacks on those who stood outside the mainstream of the Church. Methodists were especially subject to such attacks.

In contrast, Jeremy Gregory suggests that the notion of the English urban renaissance advanced by Peter Borsay implies that culture operated beyond denomination and was a healing and unifying force – and therefore it was not by chance that the English urban cultural renaissance coincided with the decline of factional religious and political strife and division:[136]

> The new culture's antipathy to ideological and religious bigotry, its emphasis on aesthetic rather than overtly political values, and its celebration of polite and gregarious behaviour provided a healing current to mend the self-inflicted injuries of the traditional elite. . . .

Certainly this is true of members of the new middle classes, who took advantage of the civilising influences of the new urban environments and leisure activities. But Borsay also emphasises that an element in the urban renaissance was cultural differentiation between classes and activities: 'though the urban renaissance promoted greater cohesion among the upper echelons of the nation, within society as a whole it was undoubtedly a divisive force'.[137]

The urban renaissance created different spheres for the middle and working classes to enjoy. But the Church remained one of the few cultural forums in which rich and poor could meet on the same terms, this was the key to the healing power of English religious culture, which drew together the elite, professional and pauper classes for worship. What Thomas Naish said in his sermon to the Society of Musick Lovers in 1700 of music might be applied to religious culture in general:

> now, as the true pleasures of life consists in the due and regular obedience of our passions, so musick serves to bring them into harmony and order. . . . It abateth spleen and hatred, and removes melancholy and despair, and makes man easie within himself.[138]

The principal products of eighteenth-century religious culture were men and women who were polite, civil and at ease with themselves and others.

Books, sermons, painting, music, church building and decorations, and urban renewal all created shared experiences which bound society together. Religious culture served as a series of social transactions that developed into a patina of mutual regard and trust. It enabled rich and poor to share the same values and assumptions, particularly the refining ones of politeness, aestheticism, and social humanism.

Notes

1 C. J. Somerville, 'The Destruction of Religious Culture in Pre-Industrial England', *Journal of Religious History*, 1988, vol. 15, no. 1. W. K. Jordan has claimed that the seventeenth century witnessed the decay of hundreds of parish churches: 306 churches were lost between 1480 and 1660. W. K. Jordan, *Philanthropy in England 1480–1660 . . .*, London, 1955.

2 See Appendix two in B. F. L. Clarke, *The Building of the Eighteenth Century Church*, London, 1963.

3 S. E. Lehmberg, *Cathedrals Under Siege 1600–1700*, Philadelphia, 1996, p. 180. The same might be said of bell-ringing. At Lowestoft, for example, there was expenditure on the recasting of bells on three occasions, in 1709, 1711 and 1729. H. D. W. Lees, *The Chronicles of a Suffolk Parish Church*, Lowestoft, 1949, p. 31.

4 J. Gregory, 'Christianity and Culture: Religion, the Arts and the Sciences in England 1660–1800', J. Black (ed.), *Culture and Society in Britain 1660–1800*, Manchester, 1997, p. 109.

5 *Ibid.*, p. 113.

6 R. S. Crane, 'The Diffusion of Voltaire's Writings in England 1750–1800', *Modern Philology*, 1923, vol. 20, pp. 261–74.

7 *Ibid.*, p. 117.

8 J. Sommerville, *The Secularisation of Early Modern England: From Religious Culture to Religious Faith*, Oxford, 1992, *passim*.

9 J. Black, *An Illustrated History of Eighteenth Century Britain*, Manchester, 1996, p. 156.

10 See for example W. Gibson, *A Social History of the Domestic Chaplain, 1540–1830*, London, 1996, *passim*.

11 *A Memorial Concerning the Erection in the City of London or the Suburbs of an Orphanotrophy or Hospital for the Reception of Poor Cast Off Children or Foundlings*, London, 1728, p. 31.

12 R. Trumbach, *Sex and the Gender Revolution, vol. 1: Heterosexuality and the Third Gender in Enlightenment London*, Chicago, 1998, pp. 189–90.

13 *The Covent-Garden Journal*, 2 June 1752, vol. 44.

14 J. Ingamells, *The English Episcopal Portrait 1550–1835*, London, 1981, pp. 1–45.

15 T. Gent, *Ancient and Modern History of the Famous City of York; and in a particular manner of its Cathedral, commonly call'd York Minster*, York, 1730, p. 1; his volumes on Ripon and Hull were published in 1733 and 1735 respectively.

16 W. Gilpin, *Observations relative chiefly to Picturesque Beauty . . . particularly the Mountains and Lakes of Cumberland and Westmorland*, London 1786;

Observations on the River Wye . . . , London 1782; *Observations on ti* *Part of England* . . . , London, 1798; *Remarks on Forest Scenery* . . . , 1808; *Observations relative chiefly to Picturesque Beauty in the year particularly in the Highlands of Scotland* . . . , London, 1776; R. Warner *A Tour Through the Northern Counties of England* . . . , London, 1802; *Walks Through Wales* . . . , London, 1798. There are many examples of dissenting ministers writing similar works.

17 Colley, *op. cit.*, p. 31.

18 Handel's librettist, Charles Jennens, was a Non-juror.

19 W. M. Jacob, 'Church and Borough: King's Lynn 1700–1750', W. M. Jacob and N. Yates (eds.), *Crown and Mitre*, Woodbridge, 1993, p. 72.

20 P. Borsay, *English Urban Renaissance: Culture and Society in the Provincial Town 1660–1770*, Oxford, 1991, p. 125.

21 *Ibid.*, pp. 332–5.

22 E. Hughes (ed.), *The Letters of Spencer Cowper, Dean of Durham 1746–1774*, Surtees Society, 1956, vol. 165, p. viii.

23 T. Moore (ed.), *Sermons on several occasions by the Right Revd Father in God Francis Atterbury DD, late Lord Bishop of Rochester and Dean of Westminster*, London, 1734, vol. 2, pp. 235–50.

24 J. Barry, 'Cultural Patronage and the Anglican Crisis: Bristol 1689–1775', J. Walsh, C. Haydon and S. Taylor (eds.), *The Church of England c.1689–1833*, Cambridge, 1994, pp. 203–6.

25 J. Fordyce, *Sermons to Young Women*, London, 1766.

26 Subtitled: '*Shewing their natural tendency to destroy religion and introduce a general corruption of manners, in almost two thousand instances, taken from the plays of the last two years, against all the methods lately used for their reformation*, Bristol, 1707.

27 A. Bedford, *Evil and Danger of Stage-plays* . . . , Bristol, 1724, p. 13.

28 W. Law, *The Absolute Unlawfulness of the Stage Entertainment fully demonstrated*, London, 1726, p. 1.

29 *Ibid.*, pp. 5, 17, 28, 34.

30 Borsay, *op. cit.*, p. 260.

31 Quoted in A. Whyte, *Characters and Characteristics of William Law* . . . , London, 1893, p. xxiii.

32 E. Gibson, *A Sermon Preached before the Society for the Reformation of Manners 6 January 1723*, London, 1724, p. 8.

33 A. W. Rowden, *The Primates of the Four Georges*, London, 1917, p. 107.

34 N. Sykes, *Edmund Gibson*, Oxford, 1926, p. 191.

35 J. Black, *An Illustrated History of Eighteenth Century Britain, op. cit.*, p. 149.

36 Rowden, *op. cit.*, p. 223.

37 *Ibid.*, p. 287.

38 J. Brewer, *The Pleasures of the Imagination*, London, 1997, p. 71.

39 Turner, *op. cit.*, p. 84.

40 Sermon No. 18 in *The Works of the Most Revd Dr John Tillotson, Late Lord Archbishop of Canterbury*, London, 1720, p. 172.

41 T. Bayes, *Divine Benevolence, or an attempt to prove that the principal end of divine providence and government is the happiness of his creatures, being an answer to a pamphlet entitled 'Divine Rectitude'*, London, 1728–31, five vols.

42 W. Paley, *The Principles of Moral and Political Philosophy*, London, 1785, p. 56.

43 W. Jones, *Sermons: Practical, Doctrinal and Expository*, London, 1829, p. 570.

44 C. D. Williams, 'The Luxury of Doing Good', R. Porter and M. M. Roberts (eds.), *Pleasure in the Eighteenth Century*, London, 1996, p. 99.
45 *Ibid.*, pp. 4–20.
46 H. MacSturdy (pseud.), *A Trip to the Vaux-Hall or a General Satire on the Times*, London, 1737.
47 *Vaux Hall*, print of the English School, London, 1741.
48 V. Gammon, ' "Babylonian Performances": The Rise and Suppression of Popular Church Music, 1660–1870', E. Yeo and S. Yeo (eds.), *Popular Culture and Class Conflict, 1590–1914: Explorations in the History of Labour and Leisure*, Sussex, 1981.
49 D. A. Spaeth, 'Parsons and Parishioners: Lay-Clerical Conflict and Popular Piety in Wiltshire Villages', Brown University, PhD thesis, 1985, pp. 144–79.
50 J. Somerville claims that there was 'a shrinking of confidence and a narrowing of interest' in religious writing during the Restoration: C. J. Somerville, *Popular Religion in Restoration England*, Gainsville FL, 1977; and *idem*, 'Religious Typologies and Popular Religion in Restoration England', *Church History*, 1976, vol. 45, pp. 1–10.
51 Brewer, *op. cit.*, p. 131.
52 *Ibid.*, p. 170.
53 Borsay, *op. cit.*, p. 128.
54 T. R. Preston, 'Biblical Criticism, Literature and the Eighteenth Century Reader', I. Rivers (ed.), *Books and their Readers in Eighteenth-Century England*, London, 1982, pp. 98–9.
55 F. Deconinck-Brossard, 'Eighteenth Century Sermons and the Age' W. M. Jacob and N. Yates (eds.), *op. cit.*, pp. 108–9. By 1760 the figures were 1,800 Anglican and 900 Dissenter sermons.
56 I. Rivers, 'Dissenting and Methodist Books of Practical Divinity', I. Rivers (ed.), *op. cit.*, p. 136.
57 Harry Ransom Humanities Research Center, University of Texas, Austin, Ms. Phillips, T, Misc. I, B.
58 P. J. Wallis, 'Book Subscription Lists', *The Library*, 1974, vol. XXIX, p. 273.
59 G. H. Jenkins, *Literature, Religion and Society in Wales 1660–1730*, Cardiff, 1978, pp. 258–9.
60 W. Speck, 'Politicians, Peers and Publication by Subscription, 1700–1752', I. Rivers (ed.), *op. cit.*, pp. 53–4.
61 J. M. Albers, 'Seeds of Contention: Society, Politics and the Church of England in Lancashire 1689–1790', Yale University, PhD thesis, 1988, vol. 2, p. 308.
62 A. E. Doff, 'Social Conditions in the Cuckmere Valley 1660–1780: the influence of Church and Dissent', Open University, PhD thesis, 1986, pp. 101–2.
63 M. Clement, *Correspondence and Minutes of the SPCK Relating to Wales, 1699–1740*, Cardiff, 1952. W. K. Lowther Clarke, *Eighteenth Century Piety*, London, 1945.
64 W. M. Jacob, 'Church and Borough: King's Lynn 1700–1750', W. M. Jacob and N. Yates (eds.), *op. cit.*, p. 68.
65 Brewer, *op. cit.*, p. 183. The vicar of Newcastle, John Brown DD was a stern opponent of Bernard de Mandeville, contesting his view that there was no such things as altruism and denying the rule of selfishness.
66 Borsay, *op. cit.*, p. 132.
67 D. K. Worcester, *The Life and Times of Thomas Turner of East Hoathly*, New Haven, 1948, p. 60.

68 Doff, *op. cit.*, p. 109.

69 Jenkins, *op. cit.*, p. 63.

70 C. Clair (ed.), *John Nichols's Literary Anecdotes*, Carbondale Ill, 1967, pp. 35–6.

71 *Ibid.*, pp. 164, 264.

72 30 January being the anniversary of the martyrdom of Charles I and a regular celebration of militant Anglicanism. H. Fielding, *Joseph Andrews*, Book 1, Chapter 17. Brewer, *op. cit.*, p. 474.

73 Turner, *op. cit.*, pp. 167–9.

74 G. M. Ditchfield and B. Keith-Lucas (eds.), *A Kentish Parson*, Canterbury, 1991, p. 169. I owe this reference to G. M. Ditchfield.

75 J. C. Baily, 'Bishop Lewis Bayly and His *Practice of Piety*', *Manchester Quarterly*, 1883, vol. 2, pp. 204–16.

76 C. J. Stranks, *Anglican Devotions*, London, 1961, pp. 125, 143. P. Elmer, 'Richard Allestree and *The Whole Duty of Man*', *The Library* 1951, fifth series, vol. 6, pp. 19–27.

77 Lehmberg, *op. cit.*, p. 115.

78 Jenkins, *op. cit.*, p. 48.

79 I owe this to G. M. Ditchfield.

80 P. Bearcroft, *The Wise and Useful Institution of our Charity Schools, A Sermon Preached in the parish Church of Christ Church, London . . . April 28th 1748*, London, 1748, pp. 16–17.

81 N. W. Hitchen, 'The Politics of English Bible Translation in Georgian England', *Transactions of the Royal Historical Society*, 1999, sixth series, vol. IX, pp. 69–92.

82 C. Oldacre, *The Last of the Old Squires*, London, 1854, p. 72.

83 R. Smallbrook, *A Charge to the clergy of the Diocese of St Davids*, Carmarthen, 1726, p. 24. The endurance of an author's reputation may be gauged by the popularity of Simon Patrick's poem *Upon the Morning we are to receive Holy Communion* (1717), twelve years after he died. Lehmberg, *op. cit.*, pp. 116–29.

84 Jenkins, *op. cit.*, p. 252.

85 *Ibid.*, pp. 35, 60, 61–2, 81, 121, 195.

86 J. Black, *An Illustrated History of Eighteenth Century Britain*, *op. cit.*, p. 150.

87 Brewer, *op. cit.*, p. 167.

88 C. E. Wright and R. C. Wright (eds.), *The Diary of Humphrey Wanley 1715–1726*, London, Bibliographical Society, 1966, p. 440. Baker was able to retain possession of some of his manuscripts, but they went to the Harleian Library on his death.

89 Wanley paid forty pounds for Burscough's collection, *ibid.*, pp. 2–11.

90 *Ibid.*, pp. 439–66.

91 See D. Cressy, *Bonfires and Bells: National Memory and the Protestant Calendar in Elizabethan and Stuart England*, London, 1989.

92 See W. Gibson, *Religion and Society in England and Wales 1689–1800*, London, 1998.

93 Spaeth, *op. cit.*, p. 91.

94 Southampton City Archives, PR7/5/1, f. 53; PR4/2/1, f. 233.

95 *Gentleman's Magazine*, 1738, pp. 465, 523.

96 G. Newman, *The Rise of English Nationalism, A Cultural History 1740–1830*, London, 1997, p. 166.

97 J. Wickham Legg, *English Church Life from the Restoration to the Tractarian Movement*, London, 1914, pp. 207, 228.

98 Albers, *op. cit.*, vol. 1, p. 192.

99 J. E. Vaux, *Church Folklore*, London, 1894, p. 242.

100 *Ibid.*, p. 2.

101 Spaeth, *op. cit.*, pp. 62–72. Interestingly there is some evidence that wealthier people were more likely to communicate than the poor. *Ibid.*, p. 295.

102 M. Ransome (ed.), *Wiltshire Returns to the Bishop's Visitation Queries, 1783*, Wiltshire Record Society, vol. XXVII, 1972, p. 238.

103 Hampshire Record Office, Copy/605/75.

104 W. M. Jacob, *Lay People and Religion in the Early Eighteenth Century*, Cambridge, 1996, pp. 113–14.

105 Harry Ransom Humanities Research Center, University of Texas, Austin, Ms. Phillips, T., Misc. I. B.

106 Jacob, *op. cit.*, p. 117.

107 A majority of these were in Scotland.

108 Vaux, *op. cit.*

109 H. Durbin, *A Narrative of some extraordinary things . . . supposed to be the effect of Witchcraft . . .*, Bristol, 1800.

110 J. Black, *An Illustrated History of Eighteenth Century Britain, op. cit.*, pp. 12–13.

111 Vaux, *op. cit., passim.*

112 N. Sykes, *William Wake*, Cambridge, 1957, vol. I, p. 221.

113 B. F. L. Clarke, *The Building of the Eighteenth Century Church*, London, 1963, p. 10.

114 *Ibid.*, p. 170.

115 G. W. O. Addleshaw and F. Etchells, *The Architectural Setting of Anglican Worship*, London, 1958, pp. 172–3.

116 Clarke, *op. cit.*, pp. 69, 83.

117 W. M. Jacob, 'Church and Borough: King's Lynn 1700–1750', W. M. Jacob and N. Yates (eds.), *op. cit.*, pp. 72–3.

118 Clarke, *op. cit.*, p. 163.

119 G. V. Bennett, *White Kennett, 1660–1728*, London, 1957, pp. 127–30. There were also some responses to religious imagery which recalled the anti-Catholic hatred of the late seventeenth century. In 1773 for example, Bishop Richard Terrick of London blocked the dean of St Paul's attempt to commission a series of religious paintings for the interior of St Paul's Cathedral. J. Black, *An Illustrated History of Eighteenth Century Britain, op. cit.*, p. 149.

120 J. G. Jenkins, *The Dragon of Whaddon, The Life of Browne Willis*, High Wycombe, 1953, pp. 57, 68.

121 W. M. Jacob, 'Church and Borough: King's Lynn 1700–1750', W. M. Jacob and N. Yates (eds.), *op. cit.*, p. 76.

122 Borsay, *op. cit.*, pp. 273, 251.

123 D. Eastwood, *Government and the Community in the English Provinces, 1700–1870*, London, 1997, p. 26.

124 Addleshaw and Etchells, *op. cit.*, p. 74.

125 Eastwood, *op. cit.*, p. 27.

126 Avington Church was built by Margaret, Marchioness of Carnavon, described – intended as a compliment – as 'religious without enthusiasm, generous without profusion'.

127 Addleshaw and Etchells, *op. cit.*, pp. 50, 59, 68.

128 J. Downes, *A Sermon Preached in the Old Chapel in Sheffield . . . 26 August 1742 before the Society of Cutlers*, London, 1743, pp. 14–15.

129 N. Aston, 'From a Deanery Window: An Eighteenth Century View of Lincoln Cathedral', *Archives*, 1998, vol. xxiii, no. 98.

130 Clarke, *op. cit.*, pp. 50, 216, Appendix two.

131 Borsay, *op. cit.*, p. 111.

132 J. Barry, 'Cultural Patronage and the Anglican Crisis: Bristol 1689–1775', J. Walsh, C. Haydon and S. Taylor (eds.), *op. cit.*, pp. 195–202.

133 Albers, *op. cit.*, I, pp. 192–5.

134 R. J. Pope, 'The Eighteenth Century Church in the Wirral', University of Wales, Lampeter, MA thesis, 1971, p. 69.

135 J. Barry, 'Cultural Patronage and the Anglican Crisis: Bristol 1689–1775', J. Walsh, C. Haydon and S. Taylor (eds.), *op. cit.*, pp. 195–202.

136 The dichotomy between Barry and Borsay is advanced in J. Gregory 'Christianity and Culture: Religion, the Arts and the Sciences in England 1660–1800', *op. cit.*, p. 108.

137 Borsay, *op. cit.*, pp. 318–19.

138 T. Naish, *A Sermon Preached at Sarum Cathedral before the Society of Musick Lovers 22 November 1700*, London, 1701, pp. 12–13.

6

THE UNITY OF PROTESTANTS

The instinct for unity between Protestants was not eroded by the defeat of Comprehension or the passage of the Toleration Act. Nor did the development of the sense of an 'elect nation' rooted in Anglicanism diminish the Church's sense of Protestant universalism. Hoadly's sermon of 1703 on the anniversary of the martyrdom of Charles I concluded with a call for

> Christian moderation [which] will dispose men not to be too hard upon their brethren of different parties or different denominations . . . [it] will dispose us to yield up things of little importance and small concern for the sake a greater union . . . is it not Christian disposition sometimes to yield even to the unreasonable humours of others . . . to promote the agreement of Christians?[1]

In 1717 Hoadly's Bangorian sermon was calculated to establish the intellectual and theological basis of the Church's Comprehension of Dissent. But for those pragmatic Church leaders who recognised the political difficulty attendant upon Comprehension at home, union with Protestant churches abroad was nevertheless attractive. Well before the Glorious Revolution there was a marked Anglican interest in dialogue with foreign Protestants. James I encouraged schemes of union, and there was a suggestion of the union of the Church of England with that of Mecklenburg in 1663.[2] Significantly, High Churchmen, such as Cosin, Ussher, Sharp and Granville, approved of intercommunion with certain foreign Protestants. Moreover, William Sherlock's *Discourse Concerning the Nature, Unity and Communion of the Catholic Church* emphasised the importance of the union of all European Protestants as a means of containing Rome. At home re-union between Nonconformity and Anglicanism also had strong advocates. Archbishop Robert Leighton of Glasgow sought the Comprehension of Episcopalians and Presbyterians in 1670.[3] As so often, the interest in unity cut across party lines. Avis concluded that, in an examination of the Church's relations with foreign Protestants, 'it is impossible to play off High Churchmen against Latitudinarians or to try to trace a party line'.[4]

Support for Comprehension in the early modern Church was encouraged by William Chillingworth, a former Catholic and godson of Laud. Chillingworth's *The Religion of Protestants, A Safe Way to Salvation* (1637), sought to lay aside ceremonial and dogma, in favour of a unity based solely on the Bible. Chillingworth even abandoned Anglican tenets:

> by the religion of Protestants, I do not understand the doctrines of Luther, or Calvin . . . ; nor the confession of Augusta or Geneva . . . , nor the Articles of the Church of England, no, nor the Harmony of Protestant Confessions; but that wherein they all agree, and which they all subscribe with a greater harmony, as a perfect rule of their faith and actions – that is the Bible. The Bible, I say, the Bible only is the religion of Protestants. . . .[5]

Chillingworth's work was enormously popular and influential in developing the principle of *sola scriptura* and reached seven editions by 1704. Among those who drew on Chillingworth was Edward Stillingfleet, the author of *Irenicum: A Weapon-Salve for the Church Wounds, or the divine right of particular forms of Church-government discussed . . . whereby a foundation is laid for the Churches Peace* (1659). But Stillingfleet, unlike Chillingworth, felt that doctrine could not be ignored in discussing unity. Long before Hoadly, Stillingfleet argued that the exact form of Church government was not laid down by the laws of God; however, Stillingfleet also concluded that for the peace and order of society Dissenters should conform to episcopacy and the Church of England. Later, in *The Mischief of Separation* (1680) and *The Unreasonableness of Separateness* (1681), Stillingfleet justified Anglican separation from Rome on doctrinal grounds, but also argued that no doctrine separated Anglicans and Dissenters, and therefore Dissenters ought to be comprehended into the Church. Above all, Stillingfleet held that conscience alone could not determine separation from the Church:

> if the bare dissatisfaction of men's conscience do justify the lawfulness of separation, and breaking an established rule, it were to little purpose to make any rule at all.[6]

Stillingfleet asserted the importance of the union of all Protestants. Like Chillingworth, his thought was profoundly influential in the eighteenth century: Stillingfleet's collected works were published posthumously in

1710, and Berkeley, Butler, Paley, Watson, and Coleridge all acknowledged a debt to him. Stillingfleet's work subtly evolved among his followers, such as Gilbert Burnet, who became a supporter of the doctrine of *adiaphora*, the practice of seeking doctrines in common with Dissenters rather than those which separated.[7]

Thomas Tenison was foremost among the followers of Stillingfleet who advocated dialogue with foreign Protestants. In 1686 he translated Claude's *Account of the Persecution and Oppression of the Protestants in France . . .* and from that point on he showed a marked sympathy for the French Protestants. The revocation of the Edict of Nantes in 1685 caused many Huguenots to flee France and most looked to England for safety. Both Church and State in England were keen to help the refugees from their Catholic enemy. In 1709 a law naturalised French Protestants, and over a score of French clergy were quickly absorbed into the Church, many to cathedral dignities.[8] In the same year about 14,000 Lutherans from the Rhineland Palatinate sought refuge in England from persecution. Tenison's *Letter to the Clergy of the Province of Canterbury*, published soon after these two waves of Protestant arrivals, placed his support for the refugees in an historical context:

> The Church of England hath been a shelter to other neighbouring churches when a storm hath driven upon them. It was such in former times, it hath been so of late. . . .

Tenison was also a generous supporter of the coffers of German, French, Dutch and Swiss Protestant refugees, as were William III and Queen Anne.[9] The Royal Bounty of William III granted a fund of 15,000 pounds a year to the French refugees, administered by the archbishop of Canterbury, the bishop of London and the lord mayor of London. Yet even this money was gradually applied in favour of union, with Secker in 1759 concluding that it was not appropriate to allow the funds to go to those French congregations that chose not to conform to the Church of England.[10] The moral and financial support afforded to foreign Protestants was such that by the mid eighteenth century the Church of England was regarded as 'the bulwark of Protestantism' in Europe.[11] To parishes up and down England church briefs were issued to raise funds to support continental Protestants. In Winchester diocese in the eighteenth century congregations were extraordinarily generous. French, Dutch and German Protestants received monies from church briefs and at Odiham in 1716 the congregation raised an astonishing three pounds and thirteen shillings for 'the Reformed Episcopal Churches in Great Poland and Polish Prussia', the largest response to a church brief in Winchester in the century.[12]

The contact with refugees, together with the aggression of Catholic France, created a sense of unity among Protestants. In 1699 this sense of unity prompted Jablonski, chaplain to the King of Prussia, to suggest a union between the Church of England and German Protestants. The proposal progressed as far as the discussion of common articles of faith, but foundered on the concern that any union would disturb the fragile unity of the Church of England. As Gilbert Burnet told Tenison in 1702 at the height of the Convocation controversy, 'God knows we are not at present united enough among ourselves to have much credit abroad'.[13] A similar quandary confronted Dissenters who were equally attracted to European Comprehension, but who feared that Jablonski's proposal would import episcopacy from England to the Lutheran and Calvinist churches. It is clear from Tenison's correspondence with Jablonski and others that in the circumstances of the first decade of the eighteenth century, many European Protestants viewed the Church of England as the principal reformed Church, from which leadership on the issue of unity was expected. This was a responsibility that Tenison was reluctant to accept. In 1704 he failed to reply to a letter from the German Calvinist bishop, Ursinus, which sought a dialogue with the Church of England, and for some years the realistic prospects of union were in abeyance.[14]

Tenison's successor, William Wake, was even more strongly committed to dialogue with European churches. Wake viewed the Nine Years War as a pan-Protestant struggle against a universalist Catholic tyrant, Louis XIV, in which England needed to ally herself closely with European churches. Wake's emphasis on scripture gave him a kinship with other Protestant churches. His *Exposition of the doctrine of the Church of England* (1686) indicated his belief that

> the Holy Scripture and whatsoever they teach or command, we receive and submit to as the word of God. We embrace all the ancient creeds and in them all that faith which religious emperors, by their advice, decreed should be sufficient to intitle them to the common name of Catholic.[15]

His commitment to union stemmed from his time in France as a young clergyman. In Paris he had met French, Dutch, Danish, and German clergy who had strongly impressed him. As he wrote in 1719,

> the consideration of the learning, good lives and friendly conver-sation of all these, moved me very seriously to consider the differences of our several sentiments in matters of religion; and made me almost ready with Descartes, to suspect, or rather

suspend my judgement of all my principles, and with the utmost impartiality [I] began to examine anew what were the grounds upon which I received them, and how far I ought to continue in them. . . . It was no difficult matter upon this foundation, as I went on, to come at last to this opinion; that the peace of Christendom can no way be restored but by separating the *fundamental articles* of our religion (in which almost all churches do agree) from others, which in their several matters though not strictly funda-mental, may yet be of more or less moment to us in the way of our salvation; and if possible to dispose men to think that the first being absolutely provided for . . . communion ought not to be broken for the rest, but a prudent liberty be granted to Christians to enjoy their own opinions without censuring or condemning any that differ from them.[16]

Though difficult to achieve at home, Wake seemed anxious to pursue Hoadly's prescription of unity abroad. It was a strategy that others embraced: Lancelot Blackburne in 1716 advised foreign Protestants to adopt articles of faith similar to those of the Church of England, couched in 'such general terms as all Protestants may well agree in'.[17] Sometimes such views caused problems for their supporters: the High-Churchman John Sharp, an advocate of intercommunion, sought to prevent widespread publication of his views because he knew that they implicitly condoned communion with nonconformist Protestants at home.[18]

Wake's instinct for ecumenism was restrained somewhat by the wars with France. But in 1716 the recall of the liberal Cardinal De Noailles to Paris and a growth in the French Church of separatist feelings to Rome, following the suppression of Jansenism, led Dr Louis Du Pin of the Sorbonne to enter into correspondence with Wake. It was a correspondence pregnant with ecclesiastical and political possibilities, particularly after England signed the Quadruple Alliance with France in 1718. A union with the Gallican Church would be more acceptable to the High Churchmen in England than such an arrangement with the largely non-Episcopalian German churches. It was also attractive to Low Churchmen. Years before, Gilbert Burnet had claimed of the Gallican Church

some of their bishops have set their clergy great examples; and in a disposition of reforming men's lives and restoring the govern-ment of the Church according to the primitive rules, hath been such that even those who are better reformed, both as to their doctrine and worship, must yet acknowledge that there are many things among them highly suitable.[19]

Moreover the detachment of the Gallican Church from Rome would be politically welcome in England. The correspondence between Du Pin and Wake was warm and cordial, but De Noailles was less enthusiastic. At the centre of the discussions lay Wake's insistence that the Gallicans break with Rome. Ironically, almost simultaneously with Hoadly's Bangorian sermon which repudiated a divinely-sanctioned form of Church government, Wake wrote to France,

> if Christ committed to him [the Pope] any power over other bishops, let the proof be produced, let the claim be demolished and we do not refuse to yield to it.[20]

In spite of a fruitful exchange of letters with Du Pin, the weight of French policy swung against De Noailles and the union, probably never politically realistic, was ruled out in 1719. Du Pin's death in the following year ended the correspondence with the most active supporter of union, though from 1722 Wake enjoyed a friendly relationship with Pierre Le Courayer. In spite of the failure of the union with the Gallicans, relations between Anglicans and French Protestants remained good. The perpetual lease on the under-croft of Canterbury cathedral remained in the hands of French Protestants, and gradually many of the refugee French Protestant communities conformed to the Church of England. The flagship communities that worshipped at the Savoy Chapel and at the Church of St Julian in Southampton both accepted the Prayerbook and Anglican episcopal authority by 1720. By 1750 nineteen out of thirty such communities had effectively been absorbed by the Church,[21] and Thomas Secker felt French Protestants sufficiently orthodox to confirm their right to meet in the deanery of St Paul's.[22] The English also expressed strong feelings at occasional oppression of their French brethren. In 1762 Archbishop Secker and ten bishops were among the one hundred and thirty-seven subscribers to Voltaire's campaign to defend Jean Calas, a Protestant pastor who had been prosecuted, tortured and killed by French authorities on trumped-up charges of murdering his son.[23]

In parallel with his correspondence with the French, Wake renewed Tenison's contact with other European Protestants. In April 1716 he told Le Clerc he wished episcopacy could be restored in continental Protestantism, but assured him

> far be it from me to be so iron-hearted that because of a defect of this kind (if I may be allowed to call it without offence) I should hold that any of them ought to be cut off from our communion . . . or that . . . I should declare them to have no true and valid sacraments and therefore to be scarcely Christian.[24]

Once again, a few months before Hoadly's assertion that Christ had laid down no absolute form of Church government, Wake appeared prepared to grant some latitude on the issue of episcopacy. Wake's encouragement to the continental Protestants was friendly, and he sustained correspondence with a wide range of churches, from the *Unitas Fratrum* of the episcopal Moravian Church, and the Lutheran and Calvinist German churches to the Lithuanian and Swiss churches. The most powerful encouragement was the succession of the Lutheran George I, which demonstrated that those of that Church could easily enter communion with the Church of England. High Churchmen were deployed to advance this view: William Dawes's *King George's Religion* (1714) reassured Anglicans that Lutherans were essentially episcopalian (he cited the prince-bishopric of Osnabruck) and close to Anglicanism in liturgy.

The correspondence with the reformed churches foundered, in part, on their own divisions, principally over Calvinism. The issue of Calvinism was a debate that had not divided the Church of England, as Wake observed in 1719:

> in our universities and in our churches rarely, if indeed ever, are these topics treated, except in so far as it should be thought necessary for the practice of the Christian life. If any person discussed them in writing, they have done so without any disturbance of public quiet, and in most cases without any breach of private charity.[25]

The correspondence with reformed churches threw up the paradox of Wake's position. As Norman Sykes noted of Wake's contact with the Geneva Protestants in 1719,

> on the one hand . . . [he] stated unequivocally his own belief in the wisdom of allowing a wide latitude of opinion on matters not fundamental to salvation; but on the other it bore the implicit admission that only the strong arm of the civil magistrate had been able to impose peace by silence on the theologians of the Church of England.[26]

George I's letter to the Swiss Protestants in 1722 came close to securing a union, but the tender consciences of some Swiss on the notion of subscription to a doctrinal formula led the matter to lapse in 1723. Wake's negotiation with the German churches and Daniel Jablonski were framed by the improving relations between Hanover and Prussia. The Treaty of Charlottenburg of 1723 between Britain and Prussia thawed relations just as Wake was eclipsed by Edmund Gibson as the government's ecclesiastical adviser. Wake certainly held the view that theology alone had not broken the chance of a union with the German Lutheran Church. He told Abbot Lokkum in 1726 that

> our Church of England differs in only a very few articles from your tenets; only a little in the question of the Eucharist, and in other matters I do not know if we differ even a little from you.[27]

The sympathy for German Protestants remained strong in England, and in 1760 the Revd Richard Wavell expressed the fear that any abandonment of the war in Europe would endanger German Protestantism and risk its destruction.[28]

The only fruitful outcome of negotiations with European churches was the legal recognition accorded by Parliament to the Moravian Church in 1749. The Moravian Church had been founded by the Hussites in the fifteenth century, and after suppression in the seventeenth century they established a colony in Herrnhut, the home of the Pietist Count Zinzendorf, in 1722. The Moravians' connections with England were partly ecumenical, encouraged by the activities of the SPCK, and partly scholarly. The Moravians sought an ecumenical relationship with the Church of England and access to British colonies for evangelism. The Moravian influence was effected through the societies like that in Fetter Lane, established in 1738. The Fetter Lane society was a group of Anglicans who sought an old-style society for religious observance, but framed it according to Moravian rules. It was this group that Wesley joined, though he left it after his conversion due to theological differences. In spite of the split with Wesley, and a fluctuating relationship with Methodism generally, the Moravians established a permanent base in England, with congregations in Yorkshire, Bedford, Derbyshire, Cheshire, Wiltshire and Herefordshire, often building on existing religious societies. By 1753 they had a thousand members and attracted a wide range of admirers, including Grimshaw of Haworth, Bishops Thomas, Potter and Sherlock and Dissenters such as Phillip Doddridge. Moravianism's celebration of all aspects of life, its enjoyment of music, entertainment, sex and recreation as gifts from God – in stark contrast to the Methodists – also made it attractive to the masses.

The Anglican hierarchy recognised the Moravians as 'an old Lutheran' episcopal Church. The Moravians in Bristol were welcomed in August 1756 by Prebendary Walter Chapman and four other clergy, who listened to an account of the Moravians' history and greeted them warmly.[29] Bishop Thomas Wilson of Sodor and Man even accepted a role in the ecumenical *tropus* system. The majority of Anglican bishops did not see Moravianism as a threat, Potter, Herring, Wilson and Thomas saw the Moravians as fellow-labourers in promoting piety and defending the State in 1745–6.[30] Gibson's death in 1748 removed the block to recognition of the Moravians by the Moravian Act of 1749. The Act accepted the Moravians as 'an ancient Protestant Episcopal church' and granted them privileges in the American colonies. The passage of the Act was also an occasion on which the bench of bishops united to promote a piece of legislation. The Moravian Church was made respectable; but within a few years this had been lost. In 1753 Henry Riminus translated Moravian material which revealed the Church's rite for blessing genitals. With mounting debts, the revelations sent erstwhile supporters scurrying for cover. Archbishop Herring turned against the Moravians and when Count Zinzendorf left England in 1755 the Church's role in England was diminished, though its schools and congregations survived.[31]

The Church of England also explored communion with the Greek Orthodox Church. Bishop Henry Compton of London provided a sanctuary for refugee Greek priests and favoured the establishment of a Greek Church in London. There were also plans in the 1690s to convert Gloucester Hall, at Oxford, into a seminary for Greek priests. Early in the eighteenth century Edward Stephens proposed a full 'restitution of catholick communion between the Greek churches and the Church of England'. It was a strong sympathy for the Greek Church that lay behind the concern of some bishops over the use of the Athanasian creed, which seemed to condemn the Greeks. The visit of the Archbishop of Philippopolis to England in 1701 spurred interest in Orthodoxy, and six years later the Archbishop of Gotchan's visit to buy a printing press elicited strong financial support from the political and religious establishment. This initial fascination with the East cooled, though cordial relations were maintained. In 1725 William Wake warned the patriarch of Jerusalem that the Non-jurors, who had sought communion with the eastern patriarchates, were separatists from the Church of England. Ten years later the SPCK supplied hundreds of Greek Bibles, psalters and other works to the consul in Aleppo for the patriarch of Alexandria. Undoubtedly the Anglican interest in the Greek Church lay in the conviction that Greek Christianity was an ancient form of the faith. The breach between the Greek and Roman churches, and the refusal of the Greeks to accept the claims of the papacy also suggested a strong bond between the two.[32]

Though the Church of England's contact with foreign churches bore only modest fruit, its importance should not be overlooked. The process of dialogue with foreign churches clarified for leaders of the Church those features of Anglicanism that were at the heart of their faith. For a few, like the Tory High-Churchman George Smalridge, episcopacy was a *sine qua non.* But in many of his dialogues William Wake was prepared to overlook the issue of episcopacy, as when he permitted Anglicans intercommunion with Zurich Protestants,[33] though he asserted that in talks with foreign churches 'we should still be importunate with them to receive episcopacy'.[34] Nevertheless, even the High-Church Lower House of Convocation supported the process of closer relations, albeit on their own terms: in 1710 expressing gratification that 'the present endeavours of several reformed churches to accommodate themselves to our liturgy and constitution'.[35] But the most significant feature of the correspondence with foreign churches was that Tenison, Wake and others proved willing to compromise on matters of ecclesiology, doctrine and worship in a way that, for political reasons, they had not been able to at home. Their desire for the unity of the Church of England and for peace in the political sphere was a greater imperative, which led them to insist on a position in England which they did not seek in their correspondence with foreign churches. John Hough, later bishop of Worcester, noted the paradoxical imperatives when in 1707 he told Arthur Charlett,

> to speak my mind freely, I think one cannot well treat the Reformed abroad with too much tenderness, or the Dissenters at home with too much plainness.[36]

In spite of the abortive nature of dialogue with European churches, the influence of the Anglican Church abroad was powerful: Lewis Bayly's *Practice of Piety* was hugely popular, running into over forty-five foreign language editions during the century; and works by divines like Tillotson and Burnet influenced foreign Protestantism almost to the embarrassment of bishops such as Thomas Sprat.[37]

The issues that appeared to divide the Church from its foreign counterparts were in considerable degree 'negotiable'. The Anglican and European Protestant divines saw their churches as doctrinally compatible, and therefore their concerns were largely matters of form. The same is substantially true of the Church and Dissent in the eighteenth century, though their relationship was framed by political circumstances and by the Test and Toleration Acts. In fact, the accord between the Church of England and Dissent in the eighteenth century was far greater than allowed by historians, who have tended to view the Church's relationships with other denominations as those of fierce competitors.[38] Admittedly Dissenters and Anglicans were divided by the Test Act and by its political consequences. But these divisions should not lead historians to ignore the strong sense of accord between the Church and those who did not conform to her liturgy.

Jan Albers has shown that in civic improvements, educational advances and campaigns against slavery there was as much that united Dissenters and Anglicans as there had been to divide them.[39] In these voluntary activities, as in their co-operation in the activities of the SPCK, the Societies for the Reformation of Manners, the Proclamation Society and various sabbatarian societies, Anglicans and Dissenters were content to share common goals derived from their mutual Protestant heritage.

Churchmen, like Gilbert Burnet, were also explicit in their desire to promote the Comprehension of Dissent. For Burnet, while the Toleration Act was a generous measure, it contained the danger of inhibiting the instinct for unity. In his advice to clergy in *Discourse of the Pastoral Care*, Burnet wrote

> nor are we to think that Toleration, under which the law has settled the Dissenters, does either absolve them from the obligations that they lay under before, by the laws of God and the Gospel, to maintain the unity of the Church . . . , or us from using our endeavours to bring them to it.[40]

His advice to clergy was to try to promote a mood of unity between Anglicans and Dissenters:

> there is too visible a coldness among us, in that which requires our greatest heat and zeal; there is a great deal of flaming heat about matters, in which more gentleness and a mild temper would both look better, and more effectually compass that which is designed by it; I mean the bringing the Dissenters into our communion. . . . To study the grounds of their separation thoroughly to answer them calmly and solidly, to treat their persons with all gentleness, expressing no uneasiness at the liberty granted them by law, is a method that will never fail of succeeding to a great degree. . . .[41]

But Burnet also made clear that his fierce support for the cause of unity was motivated by fear of the consequences. Disunity, argued Burnet was

> rending the body of Christ . . . disturbing the order of the world and the peace of mankind, thereby drawing on that train of ill consequences that must and do follow upon such a disjointing [of] the society of Christians; by which they become alienated one from another, and in sequel grow to hate and devour each other, and by which they are in danger of being consumed one of another. . . . Thus I wish the terms of communion were made larger and easier. . . .'[42]

The Latitudinarian agenda was clearly focused on unity; even those Latitudinarians whose reputations have been for the creation of disharmony were also motivated to promote the unity of the Church and Dissent. Hoadly's *Letter to a Clergyman concerning the Votes of the Bishops against Occasional Conformity* (1703) defended the Whig bishops who had voted against the Occasional Conformity Bill in the House of Lords.[43] Bishop Burnet's experience of occasional conformity was a personal one, having been an occasional conformist with the Protestant churches of Geneva and Holland. In the debate on the Occasional Conformity Bill he said in the House of Lords,

> if the designs of some of the promoters of this Bill should be brought about, and I driven beyond sea[s] . . . [I] would communicate with foreign churches, but would likewise gather all of this Church about me and still continue to worship God according to the liturgy to my life's end. So I think occasional conformity with a less perfect Church may well consist with the continuing to worship God in a more perfect one.[44]

Hoadly's *Letter* directly addressed the political circumstances: he indicated his loathing for the divisions within Protestantism at home, and saw them as especially inauspicious while Britain was at war with Catholic France, in which endeavour the Dissenters were natural allies of the Anglicans. He expressed his admiration for the bishops of William III's reign for seeking Comprehension of Dissenters within the Church. But the core of Hoadly's argument was that proscription of occasional conformity was not in the best interests of the Church. The practice of occasional conformity worked toward the ideal of a union of Christians by abating 'men's prejudices towards those small matters, the constant use of which is disliked, and to reconcile them still more to constant Communion.'[45] Hoadly also challenged one of the tenets of Tory High Churchmen: that the Church's position had been eroded since the passage of the Toleration Act. To the Tories, the Act was a severe erosion of the rights of the Church, but to Hoadly Toleration and occasional conformity benefited the Church, by keeping within a reasonable distance those moderate Dissenters who might gradually become amenable to return to the Church. To outlaw occasional conformity therefore would inflame division and help to divide Christian opinion. To do this so early in the new reign, when the succession issues had been – at least in the short term – settled would be destructive of peace and tranquillity.

Reunion with Dissent for Hoadly was a greater good than the Tory fear that occasional conformity threatened the Church's integrity and dominance. Hoadly also feared that the Occasional Conformity Bill would encourage the Roman Catholics, by driving a wedge between the Protestants – it was to be the first of a number of views that Hoadly held with one eye on events on the continent.[46] In the 1715 reprint of the *Letter* he emphasised that his motives in publishing it were 'removing the chief objections of our Dissenting brethren against conformity. . . .'[47] At the same time as Hoadly sought to encourage the clergy to regard the votes of the bishops against the Occasional Conformity Bill as the actions of moderate churchmen, he exhorted Dissenters to maintain the unity of Protestantism by entering into full communion with the Church of England. He did this in his *Reasonableness of Conformity to the Church of England Represented to the Dissenting Ministers* (1703). Hoadly's goal was complex. He did not seek to encourage rigid conformity to the Church, rather he wanted to promote a *general* agreement within Dissent to the teachings of the Church of England. His argument was that small imperfections did not justify separation from the Church. Hoadly also attacked the political nature of occasional conformity:

> it is manifest that there is hardly any occasional communicant who ever comes near the Church but precisely at that time when the whole parish knows he must come to qualify himself for some office.

However Hoadly's view was that this 'scandal' arose from the punitive Test Act that required evidence of Anglican communication by office-holders, and that it was as scandalous when ill-living Anglicans communicated simply to obtain a qualification.[48] This came close to the views of Baxter and Calamy that Dissenters' communication with the Church of England had been a practice for decades 'to show their charity to the Church' and had been done even before the law required them to communicate for purposes of qualification.[49] Hoadly's *Reasonableness* went closer to the Dissenting position. On episcopal ordination, he admitted that

> those of you who were ordained by Presbyters without bishops because episcopal ordination could not be had . . . had a real ordination; and your authority . . . lasted so long as the necessity lasted; and consequently all your acts were valid . . . this necessity making [them] so as effectively as if you had had regular ordination.

But Hoadly held that since the disturbances of the seventeenth century were at an end, there was no reason why Presbyterians in particular should not conform by taking episcopal ordination. Hoadly held this view, however, not for the High-Church reason that apostolic succession was a vital tenet of Anglican doctrine, (indeed he asserted 'I think not our uninterrupted line of succession of regularly ordained bishops necessary') but because the imposition of episcopal ordination was 'so little burdensome' and that episcopal ordination 'may honourably constantly [be] complied with for the sake of [the] Public Good'. In short, episcopal ordination would maintain the peace, and peace was a greater good than the issue of taking episcopal orders.[50]

Hoadly took a similar view to the Dissenters' scruples concerning the subscription to the Thirty-Nine Articles and the use of the *Book of Common Prayer*. He argued that the requirement for their assent was not 'rigid and unreasonable' because most Dissenting ministers would be quite happy to agree that the *Book of Common Prayer* was suitable for use. If they chose to use material from outside it, they could do so without impugning their oaths.[51] This minimalist approach to the liturgy of the Church was an idea that Dissenting ministers viewed with scepticism, and was unrepresentative of most Anglicans' attitudes. The dependence of the argument on the conscience of the individual minister and the prerogative of private judgement was the first sign that Hoadly had concerns about the authority of the Church. But in the final analysis, Hoadly recognised that this was the weakness of his argument:

> if there be persons who will be persuaded by no arguments that a compliance with these terms is . . . lawful, I confess it is my opinion that, whilst they are thus persuaded, it is as much their duty to separate from us, as it is our duty to separate from the Church of Rome. . . .[52]

If private judgement was a valid ground for scruples, then Hoadly could not deny the Dissenters the right to separateness. Norman Sykes called this 'the enthronement of private judgement as the final arbiter in matters of faith'.[53]

The Latitudinarian strategy was clearly successful; Thomas Secker, Joseph Butler, Isaac Maddox and John Potter were brought from Dissent to the Church, in Secker's case through reading and agreeing with Samuel Clarke on the Trinity and William Whiston's *Primitive Christianity*.[54] Similarly, Peter King, lord chancellor under Walpole, was born a Presbyterian but found that his study of early Christian history led him to Anglicanism and to a belief in the providential intervention in the events of 1688.[55] Moreover the Latitudinarian case for Comprehension stimulated a concerted attempt to win Dissenters for the Church in the form of the publication of

A Collection of Cases, and Other Discourses, lately written to recover Dissenters to the Communion of the Church of England, by some divines of the City of London. The book, first published in 1685 and re-printed in 1698, ran to well over a thousand pages and contained twenty-four sermons, tracts and discourses, brought together in three volumes. The *Collection of Cases . . .* represented the most coherent and developed statement of the desire of the Church for the Comprehension of Dissent in English history. The authors of the *Collections of Cases . . .* were the leading divines of the Church, crossing all theological and political views: William Sherlock, Nicholas Clagget, John Tillotson, Simon Patrick, Thomas Tenison, William King, John Sharp, and George Hooper. In spite of its size, the work was enormously popular and reached a third edition by 1718.

High Churchmen also conceded that Dissent was intimately connected to the Church and that dissenters could legitimately enjoy an 'occasional' relationship with the Church. William Sherlock in 1683 commented:

> we conclude that those who communicate occasionally with the Church of England, do thereby declare that they believe there is nothing sinful in our Communion, and we thank them for this good opinion.[56]

But the apogee of the High Church case for unity with Dissent came in Edmund Gibson's *Sermon of the Growth and Mischief of Popery . . .* preached at the Kingston Assizes in 1706. In comparing Popery and Dissent, Gibson concluded that the latter was 'of a less dangerous nature', because Dissenters owed no foreign allegiance, and Gibson claimed that a letter from country Dissenters to those in the city had expressed strong support for the Queen and the Protestant Succession. More significantly, Gibson argued that Dissent was less dangerous because 'in doctrinal parts of religion they are at a less distance from us, and so are brought over with greater ease to the Established Church'. For Gibson, charity and a kindly relationship with Dissent was a means of Comprehension by stealth. Gibson noted with some satisfaction that an 'abundance have been brought over by gentle and courteous usage and their numbers undoubtedly decrease by the Toleration'; gentle methods 'appear much more effectual than severe ones'. In a proto-Hoadleian observation, and one that bore fruit in 1829, Gibson concluded 'there ought to be no persecution purely for the sake of religion'.[57]

Dissenters themselves were no strangers to communion with the Church. The staunch Dissenter Ralph Thoresby attended Anglican services when he travelled and was unable to attend a meeting house.[58] Such a position had a long and respectable history within the Church: in 1611 Henry Jacob advocated 'occasional participation' and Richard Baxter and Edmund

Calamy periodically communicated in the Church of England, which they regarded as an act of unity.[59] Equally, Bishop Samuel Peploe of Chester, a convinced Whig and Low Churchman who was also vehemently anti-Catholic, pithily told his clergy at his first visitation

> it is a great pity that the unhappy divisions among Protestants should be us'd to destroy Protestantism itself. Thus you'd be grateful to the common enemies, but not to the friends, of the Reformation.[60]

The clergy took such exhortations seriously. In Dorchester the staunch Dissenter Daniel Defoe found

> the Church of England clergyman and the Dissenting minister or preacher drinking tea together, and conversing with civility and good neighbourhood, like Catholic Christians and men of a Catholic and extensive charity.[61]

Although for much of the eighteenth century occasional conformity took on a specific flavour, as an attempt to avoid the consequences of the Test Act, nevertheless it was extraordinarily common. The records of visitations throughout the century confirm that Dissenters regularly attended the services of the Church of England, and not simply for reasons of qualification under the Test Act.[62] Even when simply seeking legal qualification Dissenters sometimes found their relations with the Church were good. In 1783 the incumbent of Wootton Bassett told his bishop that Dissenters conformed 'to qualify for their respective offices in the corporation' but that the mayor and three or four others were exceptions in that they 'were not ashamed to be seen at church'. Whilst occasional, or regular, attendance at the services of the Church were most common, there were some other practices that Dissenters adopted which had no effect on their qualification for public office. One of these was that their children should be raised in the Church. For example, at Steyning in Sussex in 1724, Elvethan in Hampshire in 1725 and Swincombe in Oxfordshire in 1738 parsons reported that children of Dissenters routinely attended the Church services. At Shiplake the vicar, Joseph Cane, informed Secker that

> there are four puny farmers, Presbyterians; but no meeting house in this parish. And I do with pleasure observe that their wives, children and servants do not follow, nor be led by them; in as much as they do and have for some years past frequented the Church more than ever they were known to have done before.[63]

This was also a feature in Defoe's *The Family Instructor* which depicted an Anglican who married a Dissenter, the Dissenting wife worshipped at the meeting house, but did not object in the evening to hearing household prayers, read by her Anglican husband.[64]

In some parishes the Dissenters habitually sought christening from the Church. In 1708 alone, John Tanner, vicar of St Margaret's Lowestoft, baptised the children of three Dissenting families.[65] In 1764 Thomas Colby, vicar of Birstall, Yorkshire, told Archbishop Drummond that of the Presbyterians, Methodists, Moravians and Anabaptists and Sandimonians in his parish 'most of them bring their children to be christened at the Church.'[66] The willingness of Dissenters to send their children to Anglican schools had long been established, especially before the Revolution when there was a fear among both Anglicans and Dissenters of Jesuit schools. Similarly later in the century Sunday schools, like that at Bingley visited by Wesley in 1784, was a joint venture between Methodists, Dissenters and Anglicans.[67] Circulating schools in Wales, and elsewhere, were strong in insisting on teaching the Church's catechism to their pupils.[68]

In some areas, bishops were sensitive to the views of Dissenters regarding the consecration of churches, to encourage them to attend. In 1715 Bishop William Nicolson of Carlisle wrote,

> I have consecrated or restored nearly forty churches, and some in a crowd of Dissenters; and yet so managed the matter that they seemed v. well satisfied with what was done; and in truth great care ought to be taken to make the form [of consecration] unexceptionable.[69]

Similarly Bishop Richard Cumberland allowed local congregations considerable latitude in the type of churchmanship of their incumbent, with the deliberate intention of eroding separatist feeling within the Church and Dissent.[70] The evidence of the kindliness of men of differing religious principles existed elsewhere at the end of the eighteenth century. During the Napoleonic Wars with France, it was decided to present the Manchester Yeomanry with their colours in Church. However the colonel and many of the Yeomanry were Presbyterians and the day fixed for the presentation of the colours was St Matthew's day, on which by tradition the Athanasian creed was read at the Collegiate Church in Manchester. It was left to Mr Hill, the curate of St Ann's, Manchester, who had been chosen to lead the service, to risk the wrath of the High-Church chapter of Manchester in omitting the creed, rather than offend the Yeomanry. His decision carried both a penalty and benefit. Soon after, a chaplaincy at the collegiate Church was vacant and the chapter refused to elect Hill; but when it was widely known why Hill had been refused the post he was chosen as incumbent of the newly-built St Peter's Church, Manchester.[71]

In some places Dissenters even accepted the discipline of the Church, as in 1758 at Mertsham in Surrey when a Presbyterian in the parish was admonished for not attending Church and promised to do so in future. In 1788 at Weyhill the Dissenters chose to attend the Church services, 'but not the sacrament'. Similarly at Cheam in 1758 the parson reported that

> there are none but a few Presbyterians and they usually come to Church, except upon their sacrament days. It seems it is not sinful to come to Church, but they do not communicate with us in the sacrament of the Lord's Supper.

At Witney in 1738 the rector, Robert Friend, reported that Dissenters attended Church 'especially at sermon time' and the incumbent of St Vedast, Foster Lane, told Secker that Dissenters 'often come to Church, all subscribe to Morning Prayers and treat the minister with respect'. In the *Gentleman's Magazine* (October 1736) the obituary of Thomas Wright, a leading London Dissenter read

> though an independent, and a member of Mr Howe's congregation, he was a strict monthly communicant of the Church of England.[72]

Similarly in some places Dissenters were willing payers of tithes: John Birkett, vicar of Milton, Hampshire in 1722 noted in his account book those tithe payers who were Anabaptists, Presbyterians and 'non communicants' all of whom were as regular in their payments as Anglicans.[73]

Occasional conformity sometimes worked in unexpected directions: in 1788 the rector of Whippingham, Isle of Wight, reported at the bishop's visitation that some of the Anglicans in his large parish attended the services of a Presbyterian chapel, which was more convenient to them. Archbishop Secker discovered that in Canterbury diocese there were eight clergy who, like himself, had been brought up as Dissenters.[74] His reaction was one of moderation:

> with the Dissenters his grace was sincerely desirous of cultivating a good understanding. Though firmly attached to the Church of England, and ready on all proper occasions to defend its discipline and doctrines with becoming spirit; yet it never inspired him with any desire to oppress or aggrieve those of a different way of

thinking, or to depart from the principles of religious liberty, by which he constantly regulated his own conduct, and wished that all others would regulate theirs.'[75]

In some places, clergy resented the kindliness displayed by the Church to Dissent. In 1721 Parson Benjamin Robertshaw of Amersham noted:

> I was so unfortunate as to fall under the displeasure of my diocesan, Bishop Gibson, ... the occasion was my refusing to bury a Presbyterian's child, sprinkled in their unauthorised way, in my parish at Penn. Upon my absolute refusal the parents ... carried it to Wycombe where it was buried by one who I suppose would have given Christian burial even to Pontius Pilate himself. . . .[76]

Elsewhere Anglican clergy assisted their Dissenting fellows: Henry Venn was supportive of the establishment of a Dissenting chapel in the parish, even subscribing to the building in 1771. A year later he wrote to the preacher at the new chapel,

> God's name be praised that your chapel is in such a flourishing condition. It has my daily prayers.[77]

Such co-operation between the Church and Dissent also promoted good relations between individuals. At Lacock in 1783 the vicar reported that the one Dissenter was 'a quiet man and a good neighbour' and at Britwell Salham in Oxfordshire in 1738 the sole Presbyterian was 'very well affected to the Church'.[78]

The most telling observations, like those of Edmund Gibson, indicated that Anglicanism and Trinitarian Dissent self-consciously shared common doctrines. At Tintern in 1763 the rector, John Williams, reported that the Dissenters in his parish were 'all professing the doctrine of the Church of England'. This was the heart of the matter. In most matters of doctrine the Dissenters differed little from Anglicans; their distinctions lay in matters of Church government and form of worship. As a result it was not surprising that Dissenting academies widely used Anglican works in their teaching, confirming it was form rather than doctrine which divided the two. As noted in Chapter Five, the King James Version of the Bible was the 'common' version of Church and Dissent. Equally the works of Dissenting divines were widely used in the Church: for example, Doddridge's *Family Expositor* was a common Anglican devotional work and commended by Bishop Shute Barrington.[79] A strong Trinitarian Dissenter, such as Henry Grove, tutor at the Taunton Dissenting Academy, who had carefully avoided any stain of Unitarianism at the Salter Hall meeting, found that his work was read and subscribed to by Bishops Hoadly, Secker and Hutton, and Bishop Gibson included an essay by Grove in his 1731 edition of Addison's *Evidences of the Christian Religion.*[80] Henry Venn's *The Complete Duty of Man* – which he intended to replace *The Whole Duty of Man* – illustrates the doctrinal closeness of Anglicans and Dissenters. Venn, incumbent of Huddersfield, ignored issues of form, concentrating instead on breathing warmth and vitality into the biblical articles of faith. Ironically the emphasis of *The Complete Duty of Man* on moral renewal (for which the Methodists could read 'conversion') seemed to erode the earlier emphasis on natural religion, which had previously been a bridge between Anglicanism and Dissent. Perhaps some of this was written to attract followers and should not be taken at face value.[81] However, Anglicanism and most of Dissent also shared the defence of Trinitarianism. Indeed one of the features that re-assured Anglicans regarding Dissent was the marginalisation of Arianism at the Salters Hall meeting in 1719, though, of course, in other respects the meeting promoted the spread of heterodoxy. As Daniel Waterland, the monitor of Trinitarianism, commented in 1721,

> I am glad to find them now owning that their former differences with the Church are no more to be compared with their present dispute against the Arians, than a gnat to a camel.[82]

Even where relations with Dissent were strained there was a recognition that its members sought a relationship with the Church founded on shared customs. Thus for example, in the first decade of the eighteenth century, William Nicolson, Bishop of Carlisle, found that Dissenters resisted paying for Church repairs but still sought to be buried within the walls of the structure.[83] The relationship between the Church and Dissent was also overlain by the complexity of the class structure. At the end of the seventeenth century the Dissenters of Forest Green, Gloucestershire, who were largely tradesmen, leased land for a chapel from sympathetic Puritan landowners who tended to conform to the Church of England. While the chapel was being built the Dissenters continued to attend the services of the Church of England. The affluent patrons of the Dissenting chapel got the best of both worlds: they conformed to the Church, but generously supported the new congregation. Similarly, nearby Shortwood Baptist Chapel, which separated from the Forest Green congregation in 1707, was sustained by the Anglican Samuel Sevil of Bisley.[84]

Significantly Jan Albers found that in Lancashire, when Dissenting numbers fell below what was sustainable, it was common for them to be re-absorbed into the Church, a feature that the Revd Joseph Greene also noted in Stratford on Avon.[85] In Liverpool in the 1770s one Presbyterian congregation was absorbed into the Church, and two other Presbyterian chapels were bought and converted to Anglican churches.[86] Indeed one of the reasons for the decline of old Dissent was that it lacked sufficient adherents as well as differences to sustain separation from the Church. In comparison, Quakers, who consciously and conspicuously separated themselves from the Church, were able to survive more easily.

The warmth and strong relations at a parish level were also reflected in the Anglican hierarchy, particularly when the possibility of the Comprehension of Dissent in England was periodically revived. Bishop Hough of Worcester was a keen advocate of greater Toleration and greater Comprehension of Dissent, and urged these policies on Bishop Gibson. Writing to Gibson of the Toleration Act in June 1735, Hough asked

> was such a liberty indulged with a design of keeping them [Dissenters] in a state of separation? Was it not struggled for chiefly as a means of calming their spirits, that had been exasperated by ill usage; and bringing them impartially to consider . . . how dangerous their continuance in schism was to all reformed churches . . . and how much it was to their interest as well as to ours to compromise and adjust matters amicably.

Norman Sykes agreed that these views 'represented a strong body of opinion within the Church'. Gibson's own inclinations were not those that might be expected of a High-Church canonist. He was a friend of Isaac Watts and in 1735 received from Watts a copy of *The Redeemer and Sacrificer*. It stimulated Gibson to record 'the seeing so shameful a departure from true Christianity . . . had long been a sensible concern and grief to him'.[87]

It was against this background that a *rapprochement* occurred between Anglicanism and Dissent in the 1740s. The bridge to the Dissenters was Samuel Chandler, whose work on miracles, in answer to Collins and the deists, had attracted Wake's approval. Chandler enjoyed the advantage of having been educated with two English bishops, Secker and Butler; he was also a divine of great piety, of whom Herring wrote that he wished 'with all my soul that the Church of England had him; for his spirit and learning are certainly of the first class'.[88] Curiously, the talks arose from Chandler mildly contradicting Bishop Thomas Gooch of Norwich who claimed that the 1745 rebels were Dissenters.[89] Gooch harboured no rancour however and introduced Chandler to his relative Thomas Sherlock, to whom it became obvious that little divided the Church from such Dissenters. On matters of doctrine Sherlock and Chandler agreed on the superfluity of the Athanasian creed and on the difficult question of re-ordination of Presbyterians. Chandler signalled his willingness to accept a measure of episcopal 'commendation' to accompany their existing Presbyterian orders. The talks went so well that Chandler was invited to meet Archbishop Thomas Herring at Lambeth in 1747. Herring embraced Comprehension as 'a very good thing' and warmly agreed to the suggestion that the Thirty-Nine Articles be re-written in words from the scriptures.[90] Herring and Chandler also agreed to the occasional exchange of pulpits by Dissenters and Anglicans. The warm discussions begun so well fell apart in the face of Herring's timorousness,[91] and of some Dissenters who cried 'we won't be comprehended, we won't be comprehended'.[92] In reality, by 1747, most Anglicans regarded Dissent as a declining denomination and perhaps therefore not worth the risk of disputes that might be occasioned within the Church by Comprehension. Some believed, as Gibson claimed, that latitude to Dissent would be their undoing. Mosheim wrote in 1740,

> those that are best acquainted with the State of the English nation tell us that the Dissenting interest declines from day to day and that the cause of nonconformity owes this gradual decay in great measure to the lenity and moderation that are practised by the rulers of the established Church.[93]

It was a view that rector of St Andrew's Canterbury shared, claiming that the decline of Dissent was due to the 'moderation with which they have been treated'.[94]

In the Anglican hierarchy there was also evidence of strong support for those clergy who operated in the margins between the Church and Dissent. In Bath and Wells diocese, for example, the second half of the eighteenth century witnessed a heterodox evangelical revival supported by Edward Willes and Charles Moss, bishops from 1743 to 1802. The Bishops tolerated heterodox clergy like Robert Jarrett and Thomas Carr of Wellington who collaborated with Dissenters in the Church Missionary Society and Thomas Cowan and George Baring who established proprietary chapels. Willes and Moss offered ordination to those evangelicals who could not obtain orders elsewhere, especially from the fiercely orthodox Lavington of neighbouring Exeter diocese. In 1773 Willes even ordained Rowland Hill to the diaconate, though Hill's heterodoxy was so extreme that he could not obtain priests orders from any bishop, and remained a deacon all his life. Among the other heterodox clergy ordained and preferred within the diocese were Augustus Toplady, James Rouquest, Richard Whalley and John Richards. In effect, Bath and Wells became a diocese in which the boundaries between the Church and Dissent became blurred.[95] The evidence of the attempt of Sherlock, Gooch, Herring and Chandler in 1747, and of the moderation of Bishops Willes and Moss suggests a strong degree of episcopal support for Comprehension. The establishment seemed to have been well inclined toward Dissent. By the close of the eighteenth century one writer concluded

> it is true that the statute-book still continues to be blackened by the existence of penal laws established against sectaries; but it is equally true that the hearts of most men . . . revolt at the idea of putting them in force.[96]

The Church's emphasis on unity and accord also influenced its relationship with Methodism. Though Methodism remained a society within the Church for most of the century, the majority of Methodists gradually came to worship separately from the Church during the century, though some, like Hannah More was determined to be both a Methodist and Anglican to the end.[97] Nevertheless, even when they worshipped separately, occasional conformity operated as strongly in the Church's relations with Methodism as it did with Dissent. James Sykes, vicar of Bradford, reported to Archbishop Drummond in 1764 that the Methodists 'meet before and after the service of the Church and usually attend at church'. The vicar of nearby Calverley told Drummond that the Methodists sought baptism from him, and in the parish of Cantley Methodists came in lent to be catechised in the Church.[98] In Caunton, Nottinghamshire the curate wrote of the Methodists

> some of them are our most regular communicants. There is one old man of eighty-four who regularly communicates on Sunday at 8.30, goes to the meeting house, which is close by, at 9.30. . . . He used to come to matins and preaching at 11, but now he cannot manage it.[99]

In Anglesey Methodists came 'regularly and zealously' to Church.[100] In some places the Methodists, though they worshipped separately, denied that they were Dissenters from the Church. In Fylingdales, Yorkshire, the incumbent told Drummond that there were only two Dissenters in his parish 'unless the Methodists are so, which they absolutely deny'. Similarly in Gisburn 'the Methodists do not call themselves Dissenters'. In Hampshire at the 1788 visitation of the bishop of Winchester, the vicar of Portsea reported that the Methodists held services, which conformed to the Church's liturgy and the minister 'calls himself a true Church of England man'. Portsea remained a parish in which contact between the Church and Dissent was a strong feature. In 1796 Mr Howells of St John's Portsea permitted Thomas Haweis to preach in his pulpit, though Haweis was censured for his co-operation with Dissent.[101]

The connection between the established Church and Methodism was strongest in Wales, where, as Roger Brown asserts,

> many [Methodist] clergymen remained within it [the Church], holding both their own parochial appointment and also exercising a ministry among the Methodists, some of whom resorted to the churches for the communion Sunday.

Indeed the strength of this shared pastoral role of Welsh Anglicans and Methodists survived the breach of first English and then Welsh Methodists from the Church of England; some Anglican clergymen were only faced with an ultimatum to choose between them in 1818.[102] As with Dissenters, some Anglicans, such as those at Sutton Benger in 1783, found that Methodists were 'well-meaning people'.[103] On occasion, before their schism, some parsons of the Church of England were also Methodists. When Parson William Grimshaw of Haworth, a leading Yorkshire Methodist, was presented to Archbishop Hutton in 1748, Hutton responded 'we cannot find fault with Mr Grimshaw as he is instrumental in bringing such numbers to the Lords Table'.[104] In 1744 the Exeter Visitation revealed that at Kilkhampton

> there are sixteen persons, Dissenters, who call themselves Methodists; they have no licensed meeting house but assemble at the house of William Simmons, officer of Excise; and their teacher is Mr George Thompson, vicar of St Gennis.[105]

At Shoreham, Archbishop Secker discovered that the vicar, Vincent Perronet, encouraged Methodism, whose adherents attended meetings led by his daughter Damaris, who offered hospitality to itinerant preachers. Perronet's son, Edward, was also a Methodist who leased his meeting house in Harbledown from Secker himself.[106] Elsewhere Anglican clergy displayed a fascination with Methodism: in November 1777, John Ford, curate of Andover, visited London and made a point of hearing a sermon by William Romaine, 'the famous Methodist of St Dunstan'.[107]

The interchange between Methodist and Anglican clergy continued late into the eighteenth century, in 1775 the Methodist Erasmus Middleton was appointed lecturer at St Leonard's, Eastcheap.[108] The relations between the Church and Methodism was accurately summed up by Charles Wesley, writing to his brother in 1785:

I do not understand what obedience to bishops you dread. They have left us alone, and left us to act just as we pleased for these fifty years. At present some of them are quite friendly toward us, particularly towards you.[109]

Even clergy who were hostile to Methodism saw the advantage of quieting opposition to it. In April 1763 Parson Wavell of Winchester wrote

we have had some little noise here about the Methodists, our people, the mob I mean, have foolishly disturbed them. I wish they may not make them increase. Let such fellows alone (as I heard a great man say of a great Hebrew Oxford Doctor) and they will return to the dunghill from whence they were taken.[110]

For the most part, the Anglican interaction with Methodism at the end of the eighteenth century is typified by the ambivalence of Parson William Holland of Over Stowey in Somersetshire and his Methodist parishioners. In 1799 he gave the Methodists a sharp reminder of their duty to the Church, and preached against 'trimming' in a sermon that offended them, and had the adverse effect in making them stay away from Church. A few months later, Holland, in another sermon, 'gave the followers of Methodism, who run about with itching ears, a good dressing'. However, in 1809, Holland accepted a Methodist as a godparent at a baptism in the parish, and six years later welcomed back to the Church the Rich family, who fluctuated between Methodism and Anglicanism.[111]

Though it was a society within Anglicanism, and committed to remain such by Wesley for most of the century, Methodism aroused strong reactions in the Church. These were the responses of an institution in which change was regarded with some suspicion. But the strength of the hostility had its taproot in the fear that Methodism was likely to cause a schism in the Church and State on the scale of the seventeenth century. As the pseudonymous Peter Paragraph versed in his poem *The Methodist and the Mimick* (1767):

> Cromwell like you did first pretend
> Religion was his only end
> But soon that mask away did fling
> Pulled down the Church and kill'd the King.

Equally significant in the vehemence with which Methodists were denounced was the means adopted by the Methodists. In *A Spiritual Quixote* Richard Graves's Parson Greville feared that Methodist preachers would make parishioners prey to any uneducated and unscrupulous preachers and lead them to schism. William Dodd in 1761 wrote in similar vein:

> I cannot for my own part conceive what sophistry of argument can be sufficient to disprove their separation, who have broken loose from all obedience to their ordinary; entirely leaped over all parochial unity and communion; . . . who preach in all places without reserve; and . . . who employ and send forth laymen of the most unlettered sort, to preach the gospel, without any authority or commission from God or man.[112]

This was also the complaint of the most senior churchman to assault Methodism in its early years, Edmund Gibson:

> This new sect of Methodists have broken through all those provisions and restraints; neither regarding the penalties of the laws which stand in full force against them nor embracing the protection which the Act of Toleration might give them. And, not content with that, they have had the boldness to preach in the fields and other open places, and by public advertisements to invite the rabble to be their hearers; notwithstanding an express declaration in a statute (Car. II, c. I).[113]

The theme which ran throughout these attacks on Methodism was not its doctrines, though there was a horror of any similarity with Catholicism, but the concern that Methodism was separating itself from the Church. Schism was regarded as a sinful transgression of religious unity and accord, it was a long-standing horror of churchmen, and undoubtedly influenced the squirearchy against Dissent, who 'spoke most severely of Separatists and Dissenters.'[114] In Gilbert Burnet's *Four Discourses* (1693) he had argued in favour of the duty of communion and that any abandonment of the national Church was a sin.[115] Similarly in 1710, during the divisions over Sacheverell, Michael Stanhope preached that 'schism is a damnable sin . . . from diversity of opinion and external rites resulteth dislike; thence enmity, thence opposition, thence schism. . . .'[116] This was the slippery slope down which Methodism appeared to slide. Thomas Haweis, himself an Anglican supporter of Lady Huntingdon's Connection, wrote in 1766:

> Among the deadliest evils that have befallen the Church of God we may justly reckon the divisions, disputes and animosities which have from time to time so grievously rent it, disfiguring its beauty,

destroyed its peace. O that we had passed at last the waters of strife and begun to taste the blessedness of loving one another out of a pure heart fervently.[117]

It was this view that influenced the clergy and the Commons in their rejection of the Feathers Tavern Petition in 1772. For while the proposers of the petition, such as Francis Blackburne, sought to relax the ties that bound clergy to the Thirty-Nine Articles, the initiatives occurred at a time when Methodism had made churchmen suspicious of schism and determined to defend orthodoxy.

William Pine, a Bristol Methodist, considering the value of an address to the King in 1794, rejected the idea principally on the ground that schism had affected the view that the establishment would take of Methodism:

> The Methodists are become a body of Dissenters, though they are ashamed openly to avow it. For the charge brought against them is not so much for their disloyalty in general as for their departure from the established Church. . . .[118]

Yet, as this chapter has suggested, the boundaries between the Church and Dissent were not well-defined. Worshippers sometimes found themselves inhabiting a no-man's land, as did the congregation reported by John Ballard, vicar of Portsea in 1788. It was, he wrote,

> a meeting of no certain sect, David Orange, teacher; first in Lady Huntingdon's Connection, then Mr Westley's [sic], next an independent, then an Anabaptist, now approaching the Church of England.[119]

For some Anglicans these boundaries could be extended further. Bishop Gilbert Burnet of Salisbury did not confine his eirenicism to foreign Protestants and English Dissenters. His son wrote of him,

> no principle was more clear rooted in him than that of Toleration; it was not confined to any sect or nation; it was as universal as Christianity itself: he [even] exerted it in favour of a Non-juring meeting house in Salisbury . . . this spirit of moderation . . . extended to the Dissenters . . . by Christian methods of charity and persuasion . . . he was so successful that many Dissenting families in his diocese were by him brought over to the Communion of our Church. . . .[120]

The instinct for unity in the Church was powerful in the eighteenth century. Just as the Comprehension of difference was easier to contemplate in dialogues with foreign churches, so united effort was a more realistic goal in missionary work abroad. Thomas Haweis's work for missions abroad was founded on that hope that the differing denominations would

> agree to differ with candour and Christian charity, but in the great point unite . . . to make the name of God our saviour better known and his Authority over conscience more respected.[121]

In 1797 when the London Missionary Society was founded, its regulations laid down the Hoadleian principle that

> as the union of God's people of various denominations in carrying on this great work is a most desirable object, so, to prevent if possible any cause of further dissension, it is declared to be a fundamental principle of the Missionary Society, that our design is not to send Presbyterianism, independency, Episcopacy or any other form of Church order and government . . . but the glorious Gospel.

Two years later Haweis wrote to Sir Joseph Banks:

> we desire to be neither exclusively Churchmen nor Dissenters; we contain a considerable number of both. . . . It is the inviolable rule with us . . . that no exclusive mould of worship shall be presented to our missionary brethren, but every man left to his own private judgement, acknowledging only the *doctrinal* articles of the Church of England, as containing the substance of our religious sentiments.[122]

The eighteenth-century Church, though unsuccessful in many of its aspirations toward fellow Protestants, was infused with the sense that it was part of a wider community of Christians. Ecumenism abroad and eirenicism at home pulled in different directions, the former toward latitude the latter toward orthodoxy. Nevertheless, while on the national stage the Church's commitment to orthodoxy was strengthening, local accommodations between Anglicanism and Dissent were a significant experience of eighteenth-century religion. The aspiration of Bishop Henry Compton that the Toleration Act would frame the behaviour of the clergy toward Dissent was in a large measure fulfilled in those many parishes in which Anglicans and Dissenters regarded themselves as fellow-labourers. The lost opportunities of Tenison and the Lutherans and Herring and the Dissenters may reflect lack of courage or imagination, or they may betoken the importance of the avoidance of religious disturbance. However, just as Sacheverell and Atterbury stimulated incidents of disturbance in Church and State, there were moments of religious intolerance between Anglicans and their fellow Protestants. But such moments should not detract from the spirit of concord that generally marked the relationship between the Church and Dissenters. Indeed the relative decline in the support for the Church, and the rise of that for nonconformity during industrialisation may in part be due to the amity between the two. A more aggressive Church, hostile to its fellow labourers, might have held more ground against Nonconformity but would have done so at the expense of its most prized tenets, charity to all Protestants and preservation of the public peace.

Notes

1 B. Hoadly, 'Sermon at St Swithin's Church 30 Jan 1702–3 On Christian Moderation . . .', B. Hoadly, *Sixteen Sermons by Benjamin Bishop of Winchester*, London, 1754.

2 W. B. Patterson, *James VI and I and the Reunion of Christendom*, Cambridge, 1997, *passim*; W. R. Ward, 'The Eighteenth Century Church, A European View', J. Walsh, C. Haydon and S. Taylor (eds.), *The Church of England c.1689–1833*, Cambridge, 1993, pp. 294–5.

3 T. E. S. Clarke and H. C. Foxcroft, *A Life of Gilbert Burnet . . . with an Introduction by C. H. Firth*, Cambridge, 1907, p. 89.

4 P. Avis, *Anglicanism and the Christian Church*, Edinburgh, 1989, p. 38. I owe this reference to Robert Ingram.

5 *The Works of William Chillingworth M.A.*, London, 1762, vol. 1, p. 95.

6 *Ibid.*, vol. 1, p. 282.

7 M. Grieg, 'The Reasonableness of Christianity? Gilbert Burnet and the Trinitarian Controversy of the 1690s', *Journal of Ecclesiastical History*, vol. 44, no. 4, 1993.

8 S. Baring-Gould, *The Church Revival*, London, 1914, pp. 42–3.

9 E. Carpenter, *Thomas Tenison*, London, 1948, pp. 324–32. Clergy were also generous in helping itinerant foreign Protestants, the Revd John Crakanthorp of Fowlmere gave to French Protestants and on one occasion to an Italian apostate from catholicism. P. Brassley, A. Lambert and P. Saunders (eds.), *The Accounts of the Revd John Crakanthorp of Fowlmere 1682–1710*, Cambridgeshire Records Society, 1988, vol. 8, *passim*.

10 I owe this information to Robert Ingram of the University of Virginia. His detailed study of Secker promises to reveal the thinking behind Secker's treatment of the Huguenots.

11 J. E. Pinnington, 'Anglican Openness to Foreign Protestant Churches in the Eighteenth Century', *Anglican Theological Review*, 1969, vol. 51, p. 136. I owe this reference to Robert Ingram.

12 Hampshire Records Office, 47M81/PW1.

13 Carpenter, *op. cit.*, p. 339.

14 *Ibid.*, p. 342.

15 W. Wake, *An Exposition of the Doctrine of the Church of England*, London, 1686, p. 82.

16 N. Sykes, *William Wake*, Cambridge, 1957, vol. 1, pp. 252–3.

17 N. Sykes, '"The Buccaneer Bishop": Lancelot Blackburne 1658–1743', *Church Quarterly Review*, April–June 1940, p. 88.

18 N. Sykes, *Old Priest and New Presbyter*, Cambridge, 1956, pp. 151–2; A. L. Peck, *Anglicanism and Episcopacy*, London, 1958, p. 47.

19 G. Burnet, *A Letter to the Late Assembly of Clergy of France . . .* , London, 1683, quoted in N. Sykes, *From Sheldon to Secker*, Cambridge, 1959, p. 116.

20 Sykes, *Wake, op. cit.*, I, p. 217.

21 Pinnington, *op. cit.*, pp. 141–2.

22 J. S. Macauley and R. Greaves, *The Autobiography of Thomas Secker, Archbishop of Canterbury*, Lawrence, Kansas, 1989, p. 30. John Whitfield raised £400 for Prussian Protestants in 1760.

23 G. Newman, *The Rise of English Nationalism, A Cultural History 1740–1830*, London, 1997, p. 8.

24 Sykes, *Wake, op. cit.*, II, p. 4.

25 *Ibid.*, II, p. 39.

26 *Ibid.*, II, p. 42.

27 *Ibid.*, II, p. 86.

28 Hampshire Record Office, Copy/605/94.

29 A. S. Wood, *The Inextinguishable Blaze*, London, 1960, p. 77. M. Dresser (ed.), 'The Moravians in Bristol', J. Barry and K. Morgan (eds.), *Reformation and Revival in Eighteenth Century Bristol*, 1994, Bristol Record Society, vol. XLV, p. 116.

30 Though Bishops Gibson and Lavington were hostile to it.

31 C. Podmore, *The Moravian Church In England, 1728–1760*, Oxford, 1998, *passim*.

32 J. Wickham Legg, *English Church Life from the Restoration to the Tractarian Movement*, London, 1914, pp. 393–402.

33 Avis, *op. cit.*, p. 135.

34 Quoted in N. Sykes, *From Sheldon to Secker, op. cit.*, p. 137.

35 *Ibid.*, p. 139.

36 J. Wilmot, *The Life of the Revd John Hough DD, Bishop of Oxford, Lichfield and Coventry and Worcester*, London, 1812, p. 148.

37 W. R. Ward, 'The Eighteenth Century Church: A European View', *op. cit.*, pp. 289–90.

38 Jan Albers ably shows this concentration on division J. M. Albers, 'The Seeds of Contention: Society, Politics and the Church of England in Lancashire 1689–1790', Yale University, PhD thesis, 1988, vol. 2, pp. 356–8. See also J. Walsh, C. Haydon and S. Taylor (eds.), *op. cit.*, p. 16.

39 Albers, *op. cit.*, vol. 2, p. 472.

40 R. Cornwall (ed.), *Bishop Burnet's Discourse of the Pastoral Care*, Lewiston, 1997, pp. 182–3.

41 Burnet's *Preface to the third edition* in R. Cornwall (ed.), *op. cit.*, pp. 55–6.

42 G. Burnet, *History of My Own Time*, London, 1838, p. 905.

43 A. Barrow, *The Flesh is Weak*, London, 1981, p. 82. The Non-juror Thomas Hearne noted in his diary that Bishop Burnet of Salisbury – who had claimed in the debate that 'I have long looked on liberty of conscience as one of the

rights of human nature' – was accused in 1705 of having received a bribe of 5000 pounds to vote against the Bill. P. Bliss, *Reliquiae Hearnianiae*, London, 1869, vol. I, pp. 38–9.

44 Quoted in Sykes, *Old Priest and New Presbyter*, *op. cit.*, p. 143.

45 J. Hoadly (ed.), *The Works of Benjamin Hoadly DD*, London, 1773, vol. I, p. 28.

46 J. T. Rutt (ed.), *An Historical Account of my Own Life by Edmund Calamy . . .* , London, 1830, vol. 2, p. 5.

47 Hoadly, *Works*, *op. cit.*, vol. I, p. xiii, the 'engagement' is a reference to *The Reasonableness of Conformity*. . . .

48 C. J. Abbey and J. H. Overton, *The English Church in the Eighteenth Century*, London, 1887, pp. 184–5.

49 J. T. Rutt (ed.), *op. cit.*, vol. II, pp. 282–7.

50 Hoadly later developed this argument in *A Brief Defense of Episcopal Ordination* in J. Hoadly, *op. cit.*, vol. I, p. 395.

51 *Ibid.*, vol. I, p. 199.

52 *Ibid.*, vol. I, p. 282.

53 N. Sykes, 'Benjamin Hoadly', J. F. C. Hearnshaw (ed.), *Social and Political Ideas of Some English Thinkers of the Augustan Age*, London, 1928, pp. 125–6.

54 Macaulay and Greaves (eds.), *op. cit.*, pp. 4–5.

55 P. King, *The History of the Apostles Creed: With Critical Observations on its Several Articles*, London, 1702. In spite of his Anglicanism, King concluded that the earliest creeds varied from Church to Church, and it was not standardised until the fourth century.

56 W. Sherlock, *A Resolution of Some Cases of Conscience Which Respect Church Communion . . .* , London, 1683, p. 50.

57 E. Gibson, *A Sermon of the Growth and Mischief of Popery Preached at the Assizes held at Kingston in Surrey, Sept 5, 1706*, London, 1706, pp. 14–15.

58 W. B. Whitaker, *The Eighteenth Century English Sunday*, London, 1940, p. 17.

59 R. Cornwall, *Visible and Apostolic: The Constitution of the Church in High Church Anglican and Non-Juror Thought*, Newark, 1993, p. 36.

60 S. Peploe, *A Charge by the Rt Revd Samuel, Lord Bishop of Chester to the Clergy of his Diocese in his Primary Visitation begun at Chester June the 19th 1728*, London, 1728, pp. 10–11.

61 D. Defoe, *A Tour Through the Whole Island of Great Britain*, London 1724, p. 526.

62 W. K. Ford (ed.), *Chichester Diocesan Surveys 1686 and 1724*, 1994, Sussex Record Society, vol. 78, pp. 88, 188, 191. W. R. Ward (ed.), *Parson and Parish in Eighteenth Century Hampshire: Replies to Bishops' Visitations*, 1995, Hampshire Records Series, vol. 13, pp. 8, 39, 51, 205, 231, 303, 314, 315, 331, 332, 333. *Idem* (ed.), *Parson and Parish in Eighteenth Century Surrey: Replies to Bishops' Visitations*, 1994, Surrey Records Society, vol. XXXIV, pp. 158, 159, 160, 164. H. A. Lloyd-Jukes (ed.), *Bishop Secker's Visitation Returns, 1738*, 1957, Oxfordshire Record Society, vol. xxxviii, pp. 25, 55, 76, 82, 132, 146, 157, 174, 180. J. R. Guy, *The Diocese of Llandaff in 1763*, 1991, South Wales Record Society, pp. 28, 51, 54, 71, 74, 126, 153. C. Annesley and P. Hoskin (eds.), *Archbishop Drummond's Visitation Returns, 1764*, vol. 1, Yorkshire, A–G, 1997, Borthwick Texts and Calendars, vol. 21, pp. 1, 5, 18, 25, 33, 48, 54, 60, 64, 74, 76, 101, 103, 118, 177, 183. M. Ransome (ed.), *Wiltshire Returns to the Bishop's Visitation Queries, 1783*, 1972, Wiltshire

Record Society, vol. XXVII, pp. 19,20, 36, 82, 86, 91, 108, 124, 134, 153, 197, 208, 220, 235, 240, 244.

63 H. A. Lloyd-Jukes (ed.), *op. cit.*, pp. 25, 55, 76, 82, 132, 146, 157, 174, 180.

64 D. Defoe, *The Family Instructor*, London, 1722, *passim.*

65 H. D. W. Lees, *The Chronicles of a Suffolk Parish Church*, Lowestoft, 1949, p. 182.

66 C. Annesley and P. Hoskin (eds.), *op. cit.*, pp. 1, 5, 18, 25, 33, 48, 54, 60, 64, 74, 76, 101, 103, 118, 177, 183.

67 M. G. Jones, *The Charity School Movement*, London, 1964, pp. 111, 148.

68 G. N. Evans, *Religion and Politics in Mid-Eighteenth Century Anglesey*, Cardiff, 1953, p. 108. G. Morgan *Circulating Schools in Cardiganshire 1738–1777*, Occasional Papers in Ceredigion History, no. 1, *passim.*

69 V. Staley (ed.), *Hierurgia Anglicana*, London, 1902–4, vol. 3, p. 191.

70 W. C. Watson, 'The Late Stuart Reformation: Church and State in the First Age of Party', University of California, Riverside, PhD thesis, 1995, p. 69.

71 F. Renaud (ed.), *The Fellows of the Collegiate Church of Manchester*, 1891, Chetham Society, Part 2, pp. 170–1.

72 W. R. Ward (ed.), *Parson and Parish in Eighteenth Century Surrey: Replies to Bishops' Visitations* Surrey Records Society, *op. cit.*, pp. 158, 159, 160, 164. J. Gregory (ed.), *The Speculum of Archbishop Thomas Secker*, 1996, Church of England Record Society, vol. 2, pp. xxviii–xxix. *Gentleman's Magazine*, quoted in J. E. Vaux, *Church Folklore*, London, 1894, p. 70.

73 Hampshire Record Office 31M67 P19.

74 J. Gregory (ed.), *op. cit.*, pp. xxviii–xxix.

75 B. Porteus, *A Review of the Life and Character of Archbishop Secker*, New York, 1773, p. xlii.

76 Quoted in J. Black, *An Illustrated History of Eighteenth Century Britain*, Manchester, 1996, p. 106.

77 J. Venn, *Annals of a Clerical Family*, London, 1904, pp. 95–6. Later, when the incumbents of the chapel and the Church had fallen out Venn regretted his decision. His advice to parishioners who wanted to set up a Methodist or Dissenting chapel was 'Stick to the Church: by all means stick to the Church, and pray for the conversion of your minister; and if you cant approve of his preaching, remember you have the Gospel in the prayers'. Venn's colleagues also detested his decision to subscribe to the conventicle. John Berridge admitted 'God sends gospel ministers into the Church, to call the people out of it. What has happened to Venn's Yorkshire flock will happen to Yelling's flock and to mine. . . .' quoted in S. Baring-Gould, *The Church Revival*, London, 1914, p. 93.

78 H. A. Lloyd-Jukes (ed.), *op. cit.*, p. 25.

79 T. R. Preston, 'Biblical Criticism, Literature and the Eighteenth Century Reader', I. Rivers (ed.), *Books and their Readers in Eighteenth-Century England*, London, 1982, p. 106.

80 *DNB.*

81 I am grateful to G. M. Ditchfield for this point.

82 R. T. Holtby, *Daniel Waterland 1683–1740. A Study in eighteenth century Orthodoxy*, Carlisle, 1966, p. 37.

83 F. G. James, *North Country Bishop*, New Haven, 1956, p. 106.

84 A. Urdank, *Religion and Society in a Cotswold Vale, Nailsworth 1780–1865*, Los Angeles, 1990, pp. 87, 92.

85 Albers, *op. cit.*, vol. 2, pp. 471 *et seq.* L. Fox, *The Correspondence of the Revd Joseph Greene 1712–1790*, London, HMC, 1965, p. 157. Later in the century Bishop William Cleaver of Chester was to argue that people turned to Dissent when the churches were full; in itself an indication of the doctrinal proximity to Anglicanism.

86 Albers, *op. cit.*, vol. 2, p. 371.

87 N. Sykes, *Edmund Gibson*, Oxford, 1926, pp. 286–90.

88 Quoted in A. W. Rowden, *The Primates of the Four Georges*, London, 1916, p. 208.

89 In fact Chandler had attacked Catholicism violently in *Great Britain's Address to the Pretender . . .* , London, 1745. I owe this to G. M. Ditchfield.

90 A suggestion first made at the Convention of 1689.

91 N. Sykes, *From Sheldon to Secker, op. cit.*, p. 89.

92 W. Gibson, *Religion and Society in England and Wales 1689–1800*, London, 1998, pp. 118–22.

93 Mosheim, *Ecclesiastical History* quoted in C. J. Abbey and J. H. Overton, *op. cit.*, p. 177.

94 J. Gregory (ed.), *op. cit.*, p. xxviii.

95 W. Gibson, 'Somerset Evangelical Clergy', *Somerset Archaeology and Natural History*, 1986, vol. 130, pp. 135–9.

96 *A Consistent Protestant . . . 1790* quoted in R. J. Pope, 'The Eighteenth Century Church in the Wirral', University of Wales, Lampeter, MA thesis, 1971.

97 As late as 1821 the Methodists of Bridgerule, Devon, attended services at the Church. A. Warne, *Church and Society in Eighteenth Century Devon*, Newton Abbot, 1969, p. 109. For Hannah More see W. B. Whitaker, *op. cit.*, 175.

98 C. Annesley and P. Hoskin (eds.), *op. cit.*, pp. 1, 5, 18, 25, 33, 48, 54, 60, 64, 74, 76, 101, 103, 118, 177, 183.

99 Vaux, *op. cit.*, p. 70.

100 Evans, *op. cit.*, p. 107.

101 A. S Wood, *Thomas Haweis 1734–1820*, London, 1957, p. 210.

102 R. L. Brown, *Llandaff Figures and Places*, Gwasg Eglwys Trallwng, 1998, pp. 7, 55–6.

103 W. R. Ward (ed.), *Parson and Parish in Eighteenth Century Hampshire: Replies to Bishops' Visitations, op. cit.*, pp. 8, 39, 51, 205, 231, 303, 314, 315, 331, 332, 333. C. Annesley and P. Hoskin (eds.), *op. cit.*, pp. 1, 5, 18, 25, 33, 48, 54, 60, 64, 74, 76, 101, 103, 118, 177, 183. Ransome (ed.), *op. cit.*, pp. 19, 20, 36, 82, 86, 91, 108, 124, 134, 153, 197, 208, 220, 235, 240, 244.

104 Quoted in A. Armstrong, *The Church of England the Methodists and Society 1700–1850*, London, 1973, p. 110.

105 Quoted in G. C. B. Davies, *The Early Cornish Evangelicals 1735–1760*, London, 1951, p. 25.

106 J. Gregory (ed.), *op. cit.*, p. xxix *et seq.*

107 Hampshire Record Office, 29M65/2.

108 J. Gregory (ed.), *op. cit.*, p. xxiv.

109 Quoted in A. Armstrong, *op. cit.*, p. 108.

110 Hampshire Records Office, Copy/605/108.

111 J. Ayres (ed.), *Paupers and Pig Killers, the Diary of William Holland, A Somerset Parson 1799–1818*, Gloucester, 1984, pp. 15–16, 31, 186, 264–5.

112 A. M. Lyles, *Methodism Mocked*, London, 1960, pp. 28, 63.

113 E. Gibson *Observations upon the Conduct and Behaviour of a certain Sect usually distinguished by the name of Methodists*, London 1744, p. 13.

114 Robert South was another stern critic of dissenters on these grounds, see C. Oldacre, *The Last of the Old Squires*, London, 1854, p. 78–9.

115 T. E. S. Clarke and H. C. Foxcroft, *A Life of Gilbert Burnet . . . with an Introduction by C. H. Firth*, Cambridge, 1907, p. 323.

116 M. Stanhope, *'The Sinfulness of Separation' from the Establish'd Church of England in a Sermon Preached in the Parish Church of St Clement Danes . . .*, London, 1710.

117 T. Haweis, *The Evangelical Expositor; or a Commentary on the Holy Bible . . .*, London, 1765–6, vol. II, p. 263.

118 K. Morgan (ed.), 'Letters from William Pine to Joseph Benson 1794–1796', J. Barry and K. Morgan (eds.), *Reformation and Revival in Eighteenth Century Bristol*, 1994, Bristol Record Society, vol. XLV, p. 164.

119 W. R. Ward (ed.), *Parson and Parish in Eighteenth Century Hampshire: Replies to Bishops' Visitations*, op. cit., p. 314.

120 G. Burnet, *Bishop Burnet's History of My Own Time*, London, 1838, pp. ix–x.

121 T. Haweis, *A Word in Season . . .*, London, 1795, p. 9.

122 Quoted in A. S. Wood, *Thomas Haweis 1734–1820*, op. cit., pp. 208, 233–4 (my italics).

7

THE CHURCH AND
NATIONAL IDENTITY

National identity as a religious concept in eighteenth-century society has been the subject of considerable historical debate. Linda Colley has argued that Protestantism was one of the critical ingredients in the development of a sense of national identity and consciousness and a vital constituent in the creation of the idea of Britain. It was Protestantism that enabled Scotland and England, which shared the use of the King James Bible, to unite against a Catholic threat. And it was integral to the idea of Britishness that the nation had, in the words of *Rule Britannia*, arisen from the seas 'at heaven's command'.[1] Colley identified Protestantism as a progressive force in the development of national identity, in contrast to Jonathan Clark's emphasis on the continuity of seventeenth-century religious values in the identity of eighteenth-century Britain. The specific ways in which Anglicanism contributed to Britishness is a synthesis of these views: the survival of the idea of the State and government as a religious construct, the role of the Church in the emergence of a common national experience, and the definition of values of moderation and restraint which became identified as essentially British.

The debates considered in Chapters Two and Three were essentially about the nature of the religious foundations of the government of Britain. Irrespective of whether the nation had the God-given right to resist James II, or a biblical duty to obey him without resistance, both interpretations sought to settle government on firm religious foundations, derived from interpretations of the Bible and ecclesiastical tradition. Indeed this had been the unanimous view of the Convention Parliament of 1689 when it decreed that government by 'a popish prince is inconsistent with the safety and welfare of this Protestant kingdom.' Non-jurors left the Church rather than recognise a ruler who transgressed their oaths to James; but for those who swore oaths to William and Mary the defence of Protestant government superseded all other calls on their allegiance. In short, the core of the debates of 1689, of the Convocation Controversy, of the Sacheverell Trial, of the

Bangorian crisis, even of the Gibson–Walpole alliance and the debates on the validity of the Toleration and Test Acts, was not *whether* but *how* government derived its authority from God. High and Low Churchmen shared a sense of the particular divine sanction accorded to the English government, and differed only on its origins. This was an element in the Glorious revolution that had been consciously developed by Gilbert Burnet and the architects of William's victory. Tony Claydon suggests that 'Burnet and his circle advanced a 'Hebraic' view of their nation which described it as a body united by its peculiar relationship with God.'[2] Moreover, the Nine Years War was presented to the nation as a Protestant international crusade with Britain at its head, and for similar reasons Charles II, James II and Queen Anne chose St George's day as the date of their coronations.

A key element in this religiously-founded view of government and nationhood was anti-Catholicism. Jeremy Black has asserted that anti-Catholicism was 'arguably the prime ideological commitment of most of the population.'[3] Hatred of Popery pervaded society, and its identification with Jacobitism was complete, at least in the minds of the majority of the population. No other fear could justify the ruling of the Privy Council on 5 September 1745 that all Catholics should swear the oath of allegiance to George II. In Winchester this necessitated the attendance of the Hon. Henry Arndell, Lady Margaret Jarnagan, Lady Mary Wells, Thomas Fitzherbert, and other notable citizens at the Guildhall to swear the oaths while fowling pieces and pikes were stripped from their homes.[4] Popular works, such as Bunyan's *Pilgrim's Progress* and the SPCK's *Protestant Catechism* (1766) were vehement in their anti-Catholicism, and dogmatic writers like Arthur Ashley Sykes and John White argued that Catholicism represented a danger to Church and State.[5] Catholicism seemed to be an immediate threat, from the Revolution to the end of the century.[6] Even occasional outbursts, such as that in June 1720 by a 'tall, lusty' man outside a Winchester public house, for the health of 'King James the Third' were deemed serious enough to report to the magistrate.[7] Colin Haydon suggests that anti-Catholicism was connected with fear of foreign invasion, with the result that anti-Catholic unrest coincided with periods of military ventures abroad and of foreign threats.[8] Undoubtedly the hatred of Catholics was a variegated phenomenon, geographically uneven and prone to fluctuations. It was also connected to popular folklore such as the burning of papal effigies and annual celebrations on 5 November. But the significance of anti-Catholicism was that it exerted a constant force on eighteenth-century society by identifying the monarchy, State and government exclusively with Protestantism. Anti-Catholicism could also bring Anglicans and Dissenters together, as when the Dissenter Samuel Chandler joined Anglican clergy in opposing the rising of 1745 in *Great Britain's Memorial Against the Pretender and Popery*. While Jeremy Black has argued that Linda Colley understates the divisions between Anglicanism and nonconformity, and Jonathan Clark and Brian Young have emphasised the divisions in the Church, anti-Catholicism provided a focus for unity and one which did not require any doctrinal conformity by its supporters.[9] In *The Fears and Sentiments of all True Britons with Respect to National Credit, Interest and Religion*, Hoadly asserted what most other Anglicans and Protestants held to be true, that the defeat of Catholicism was a pre-condition for security, when he asked rhetorically:

> will faith and piety and universal virtue increase together with the hopes of France, and of the Pretender? Or will the Protestant reformed Church of England then at length be secure from dangers when the popish interest shall be most formidable?[10]

The religious foundations of the State were not limited to anti-Catholicism. Latitudinarians sought to construct an explicit synthesis of the Hanoverian State and Anglicanism. In 1710, with the succession of the house of Hanover in sight, Latitudinarian ideology joined that of the High Churchmen in arguing that there was a direct, causal link between divine sanction and political events. Benjamin Hoadly's writings for the *London Gazette* and other newspapers during the general election campaign of 1710 and in the 1720s explicitly addressed issues of nationhood and the religious constitution of the government. His articles and pamphlets in 1710 were set against the backdrop of resurgent Toryism and Jacobite threats from France at a time when Queen Anne was growing old. The focus of Hoadly's *The Genuine Tory Address* and of *The Voice of the Addressers* was to align absolutism and arbitrary power with popery, extremism and the French. Hoadly's view was that the Tory High Churchmen were seeking to make 'the whole nation uneasy at the Revolution, and [are] desirous to return back to the old excluded line'.[11] In contrast, Hoadly's defence of the Whigs was founded on the premise that 'you are churchmen as you are Englishmen' and that the Church of England 'is a Protestant Church, to be supported only by a Protestant government.'[12] In effect, Hoadly was calling on a more potent, purer loyalty than dynastic monarchism, and one with proven potency in the events of 1688–9: loyalty to the Church. But the alignment of Anglicanism and the Revolution of 1689 was not presented by Hoadly as only of partisan advantage. It went beyond divisions between Whig and Tory, and addressed issues of national self-image and aspiration: 'in vain do we boast of British Liberty, and British Glory if we can be content to part with the blessings of laws and parliament'.[13]

Hoadly's argument was that the Revolution of 1689 installed a dual establishment of political freedoms from arbitrary and absolute power, with an ecclesiastical framework equipped to defend Anglicanism and encourage Toleration. He also argued, like Jonathan Trelawny, that in 1689, during the immediacy of the Revolution, there had been a measure of agreement on this, and that though the Tories had been content to accept this establishment, their support had later evaporated:

> did not all, even the highest of churchmen, then [in 1689] perceive that the interest of all Protestants in this nation, was the thing to be regarded, that Toleration and uniting with one another were the only methods against so terrible enemies as popery and slavery? Had any one at that time stood up and told you that this was treachery to the Church . . . and that temper and moderation were only lukewarmness and falsehood to the Church; I am persuaded he would have been looked upon and used as a common enemy. And this is the case now.[14]

For Hoadly, the Jacobite threat from France threw into stark relief the fact that Anglicanism and nationhood had a common heritage and a shared interest in defending the regime against its enemies. It was this shared interest that, for Hoadly, eroded the divisions between Anglicans and Dissenters. In 1710, he wrote to electors about the French sponsorship of Jacobitism:

> is not that the one common interest of Protestants and Britains; of Protestants considered as all equally threatened by our professed enemies; and of Britains considered as a people governed by laws and now threatened by . . . absolute power and arbitrary government? Here is a Church happily established. Here are other Protestant congregations tolerated. . . . We are now in open war with a monarch, who threatens all our churches and all our liberties.[15]

Hoadly's arguments fell on deaf ears in 1710. But it was no coincidence that his election pamphlets of 1710 were re-printed in 1718 and 1773. In fact Hoadly's analysis of the intimate connections of nationhood to the Church and to religious freedom was to become the dominant political ideology of the eighteenth century, and was to be at the forefront of the definition of national identity.

In 1727 Hoadly returned to political pamphleteering in seeking to defend the conduct of foreign policy under Robert Walpole. Again, he expounded a view that rested national identity, aspirations and overseas interests on the foundations of religious liberties:

> where can that Church, or where can the Protestant religion, hope ... for countenance [or] for sufferance, when the whole Protestant power in Europe, in its present condition is little better than a creature with pain and difficulty, struggling for life.

For Hoadly the response of Protestantism and liberty to the threats of popery and autocracy was expressed through the contest for naval power, in trade conflicts and the acquisition of overseas territory.[16] These facets of national interest were inextricably linked:

> the many and complicated evils of [the] alliance between the Emperor and Spain; [were] the just apprehensions and well-grounded fears which the court of Great Britain could not but entertain ... about the nature and tendency of it with regard to the present establishment of the crown of Great Britain; to our possessions; to our commerce; our religion; our liberties, and to those of all Europe.[17]

This view of religion and government united in foreign policy was one around which High and Low Churchmen alike could draw together. In 1702 the High-Church Bishop Trelawny of Exeter had preached before the Queen and parliament on the successes of Marlborough's English forces abroad. His sermon was predicated on the view that religious and political acts were one, as a result 'all sin is a sort of treason and the malignity of it is not shut up in our selves, or only taints our blood, but diffuses itself with a contagious influence on our prince and our country'.[18] For Trelawny moral reform underpinned the religious sanction of the State, and established a nexus of patriotism and faith which was the matrix of national pride and identity: God would

> bless our Queen with good councils in parliament ... with due and happy execution of them by those she employs, with the hearts of her subjects, like her own entirely English. ... Such an example as this must needs stir up in every Englishman's breast such a generous zeal as will occasion an universal goodness.[19]

Equally, the High-Church Thomas Sherlock, preaching on the anniversary of the accession of Queen Anne in 1714, claimed that the Queen's commitment to Anglicanism was the taproot of Britain's success at home and abroad. Anglicanism had made Britain 'happy at home, under the influence of a mild government, [Britannia] has not been less glorious abroad . . .'.[20]

The union of Church and State was reflected in all sorts of images and media, but few were more potent than the response to the 1745 Rebellion. An engraving that graced the head of the broadsheet edition of Archbishop Thomas Herring's speech at York Castle in September 1745 in favour of an association for the defence of the North exemplified the union. Herring's portrait was placed in a medallion, surrounded by martial symbols, cannons, drums, smoke and pikes. From the smoke of battle emerged the symbols of virtue, the prayerbook and the flag of the see of York, raised above the symbols of evil, a popish mitre and a cudgel. It was a supreme moment for the Church: Herring 'awakened the nation from its lethargy' a service, claimed his biographer, that 'will always be remembered to his honour by every sincere Protestant'. The speech was rushed into print in York, and subsequently reprinted in London and in Ireland. The message contained in the masthead was clear: here was a primate whose martial valour had rallied the North against the Jacobites and had saved both the political and religious establishment. In the year following the rebellion, Thomas Hayter addressed the providential salvation of the regime. He considered the circumstances of the Rebellion: 'our armies were abroad, fighting in the cause of liberty, when the last day of British liberty seemed nigh.' Yet the rebels were 'withheld from entering England, til England was provided with armies to defend itself against them'. Hayter could not forbear from comparing the return of British troops from the continent with 'those providential gales which at the nicest and most decisive juncture favoured the success of the [Glorious] Revolution'. Yet another blessing was the unity with which the nation responded to the rebellion: 'how did all these eager discontents and keen divisions, instead of breaking out into open acts of hostility, immediately subside into mutual concord! How instantly did a warm zeal for our religious and civil liberties revive!' Moreover the lesson of the rebellion was clear:

> Union amongst ourselves must be allowed, at such a juncture, to be absolutely necessary; and to render it perfect, it should be the union of the whole society in centering in him who is the head of it: who hath been (what all good princes are) in the Hands of providence, an instrument of dispensing blessings to us and to our country. It should be a union of fellow subjects and Protestants, bound together by the common natural ties of loyalty and religion.'[21]

Few episodes could have argued more strongly in the minds of the people of the identification of the Church with the State, and that their membership of the Church was an aspect of nationhood.[22]

The coincidence of national identity and religious zeal was powerfully advanced throughout the eighteenth century, but particularly so during the Napoleonic War. In 1801 Parson William Holland of Overstowey regarded war with France as 'the cause of virtue and religion' and the stand against Napoleon gave Britain 'a superiority among the nations.' Five years later, Holland indicated a sense of religious destiny:

> by no power is he [Napoleon] to fall but by British alone, for hitherto no other nation has been able to struggle against this Anti-Christ.

To Holland, Trafalgar, like Marlborough's victories, recalled the Hebraic inheritance of 1689, which had made her,

> the favoured nation which is destined not only to withstand, but even to annihilate his power and to convey the pure precepts of Christianity to future ages.[23]

It was a view that appeared to be confirmed by imperial acquisition. Kathleen Wilson holds that Captain Cook was the archetype of a Protestant Englishman, epitomised on stage, in newspapers and art as a Church hero who embodied Britain's elect status and imperial destiny.[24]

Parson William Jones of Broxborne in 1804 also made a claim to a unique and sacred mission, this time in an explicit link between the economic weapons of war and the sanction of religion. Citing the Mosaic law in *Deuteronomy*, Jones asserted:

> if lending be a test of the blessedness of a people, we must be a right blessed and flourishing people indeed; for in one form or another, either loans, subsidies, etc., almost every nation in Europe has done us the favour of borrowing of us! Good Johnny Bull is too generous and too credulous. However, grant that his constitution may be always sound and his finances never fail![25]

Samuel Horsley went further by identifying Britain's enemies as the nexus of evil. In his millenarian sermon to the clergy of the diocese of Rochester in 1800 he claimed:

in this odious French Republic, aping the manners, grasping the dominion, speaking to friends and enemies the high vaunting language of antient Rome, we seem to behold the dreadful Apocalyptic Beast, which at the time of the desolation of the pagan whore [was] exhibited in vision to St John.[26]

In such circumstances, nationhood and the power it exerted over men and women was consciously exploited by clergy when exhorting men to fight for their country. At the end of the eighteenth century the *Navy Chronicle* published 'The Present Management and Discipline of the Navy' in which the writer suggested that naval chaplains should draw upon the image of the nation in this way.[27]

Gerald Newman is among writers who have argued that national identity in the eighteenth century was dominated by Francophobic views played in the demonising of France.[28] Whether anti-French feeling caused anti-Catholicism or vice versa, the rejection of Jacobitism and Catholicism undoubtedly played an important role in this xenophobic definition of national identity. It renewed the Reformation in England and the world view that went with it. The Church of England repudiated the universal claims of Catholicism to a monopoly on salvation; as a result Anglicanism sought to advance her own claims to a unique and separate path to redemption. Equally, those who felt Dissent was a greater threat than Catholicism, often Tories, had similar xenophobic feelings towards the Dutch and Hanoverians.[29] Such views fuelled a belief in a unique national identity. It was a belief that emerged clearly in the Revd John Brown's *Estimate of the Manners and Principles of the Times*:

the genius of our country, above all others, is particularly distinguished from that of its neighbour nations.[30]

Anglicanism and Britishness were aligned forces therefore: emphasising the unique national and international spiritual and political role of Britons. In continental warfare, or naval actions, Britons were as much engaged in the sacred work of Anglicanism as when they knelt in prayer.

The second contribution of Anglicanism to national identity was its role in developing a truly shared national experience. There were no other institutions that could claim to have geographical coverage of England in the way that the Church's ten thousand parishes covered every acre. But the distinctive experience of eighteenth-century Anglicanism lay also in the growth of a common, comparatively homogeneous experience that can be recognised as genuinely national, and even one which contained the emergent idea of empire as part of a shared experience. Scott Mandelbrote has identified the Bible as a unifying factor in eighteenth-century Britain. By the end of the seventeenth century the Bible was available in Welsh and both Scottish and Irish Gaelic. Whilst, therefore, it emphasised British cultural identities beyond England, it was the one book that was known to all the subjects of William III and his successors.[31] This also applied beyond Britain, C. J. Stranks has noted the 'national' character of the *Book of Common Prayer*:

> the ordinary Englishman was familiar with the Prayerbook at home as well as in Church. It was part of his way of life which he took with him when he left his own country. Wherever English colonists and particularly English ships went, the Prayerbook went also. Without it many a Sunday spent far from civilisation would have passed without prayer and many a lonely grave would have been unhallowed if the Prayerbook had not provided such a service as a layman might read.[32]

The uniformity established by the prayerbook amazed Carl Moritz, when he visited England in 1782. Sitting with his host at breakfast one Sunday, leafing through the Prayerbook 'my attention was taken by the fact that every word was set down for the priest for his conformity'. Not only Carl Moritz, but Cesar De Saussure and Francois de la Rochfoucauld also regarded Anglicanism as a single national phenomenon. Viewing it from the broader perspective of European religion, they did not identify or describe great variation or differences between practices; they regarded Anglicanism as part of a homogeneous national experience.[33] Arguably the eighteenth century was a period in which many local practices and superstitions gave way to a centralising, rationalist urge in the Church. This was the fulfilment of a principal motivation of the Reformation: to create a unified and uniform Protestant community.

As is clear from Chapter Five, the liturgy of the Church and associated works were the largest body of writing with which most Englishmen and women would have been familiar, in particular sermons were becoming part of the shared experience of nationhood. The popularity of the works of Tillotson and others, and the fashion for reading sermons at home and as a centre-piece of Church services, meant that many thousands of parishioners shared the experience of hearing the words of the leading preachers. *The Preachers Assistant* (1753), listed over 14,000 published sermons in the ninety years since the Restoration, over ninety per cent of which were Anglican. These cheap and widely available sermons formed a vast body of theology on which the eighteenth-century clergy drew.[34] Moreover, with the encouragement of bishops, the opportunities for extempore sermons and prayers, which inevitably diverged from the uniformity of religious experience, were in decline. In his visitation charge of 1696, Bishop Edward Stillingfleet of Worcester denounced extempore prayer and sermons as promoting,

> a loose and careless way of talking in the pulpit, which will neither profit you, nor those that hear you. He that once gets an ill habit of speaking extempore will be tempted to continue it by the easiness of it to himself and the plausibleness of it to less judicious people. . . .[35]

John Bowtell, a fellow of St John's College, Cambridge, also advocated

> a strict conformity to those excellent rules by which the Church of England directs her clergy in the use of the liturgy; and to show more particularly how many obligations we lie under to bring no other prayers into the public worship.[36]

Similarly, William Wake argued

> to pray to God by a set form, is so far from being a thing either in itself unlawful, or injurious to the Holy Spirit, that we see our saviour himself has here given us an example for it, as under the Law God was pleased in several cases to direct the very words in which he would be addressed. . . .[37]

Francis Atterbury regarded the 'pre-meditated' liturgy of the Church of England as a great advantage. Extempore prayer might sometimes have the advantage of impact, but Atterbury held that this was simply a matter of surprise and curiosity rather than genuine piety. Atterbury also held that a worshipper could not commit himself to a prayer without knowing its content and end:

> whereas he who offers up his requests to God in a known and stated form has no avocations of this kind to struggle with; and can therefore apply himself directly and vigorously to his holy tasks and ask in faith, doubting nothing. . . . This I say is a peculiar advantage which attends the use of pre-composed prayers.[38]

The concern over extempore prayer was intimately connected to the idea of unity and uniformity. Thomas Bennet, who hated schism and disunity and denounced it in a series of books, saw extempore prayer as a feature of separation.[39] Bennet produced a number of books of prayers derived from the Bible which he felt could be used by all churches.[40] Bennet himself was a dazzling preacher, twice appointed to parish livings as a result of the popularity of his preaching, but he abhorred the temptation gradually to diverge from the Church that extempore prayer offered.[41] Bennet also connected uniformity with orthodoxy in the same way that Anglicans tended to align enthusiasm with heterodoxy. His determination to defend the doctrinal integrity of the Church was expounded in *An Essay on the XXXIX Articles* . . . (1715) and in his defence of the Trinity from Samuel Clarke *A Discourse on the ever-blessed Trinity in Unity* . . . (1718). The laity also disliked extempore prayer and preaching, with squires denouncing its ostentation and repetition.[42]

Like the insistence on the use of the liturgy, the practice of reading sermons, and of composing them using the examples of published collections, resulted in an increasingly homogeneous national experience in worship. This was a powerful movement toward uniformity of religious experience. The developing shape of Anglicanism, with more frequent communion celebrations and more widespread achievement of 'double duty', added a commonality to the religious experience of the English parishioners in the eighteenth century.[43] Morning and evening prayer, the eucharist, hymns and the catechism became familiar elements in the collective inner landscape of eighteenth-century society. Few, if any, who lived in eighteenth-century England were beyond their reach. Across the country decalogue boards were erected in the eighteenth century with the same fervour with which they were abandoned in the nineteenth.[44] The reason why so many parishes in the eighteenth century repaired or installed peals of bells was to advertise themselves in an age of tolerance, but in doing so they drew attention to the national experience available only from Anglicanism. For Cecil Oldacre bells were 'the gentlest notes of invitation and persuasion.'[45]

The clergy also provided an emerging national standard of pastoral care. Ordinands were increasingly guided to a number of seminal works in their training: Burnet's *Discourse of the Pastoral Care*; Henry Owen's *Directions for Young Students of Divinity*; George Bull's *Companion for Candidates of Holy Orders* and ordination sermons by celebrated divines like Tillotson and Secker. These works, together with a significant growth of university graduates entering the Church, gave eighteenth-century Anglican clergy a more uniform education and training and a more widely shared expectation of professional standards than had been achieved hitherto. Uniformity of clerical performance was also underscored by the growing similarity of visitation enquiries. Episcopal expectations of the clergy converged during the eighteenth century on the visitation enquiries of Bishops Wake and Gibson and were more consistently maintained.[46] The translations of eighteenth-century bishops also facilitated the spread of good practice in the visitation of dioceses. Thomas Secker, for example, moved from Bristol to Oxford to Canterbury, and in each diocese established a managerial approach to codifying records of the parishes and incumbents in his charge, and brought the same systematic approach to visitations.[47]

The uniformity of religious experience was also consciously fostered by the Church. Within the new professional corps of clergy, the widespread awareness of the activities of other clergy, evident in their correspondence, was a strong feature of eighteenth-century Anglicanism. In 1745, Prebendary Edmund Pyle asked Parson Kerrich, 'do you preach against popery as is now the way everywhere?'[48] The correspondence of Parsons Wavell and Woolls, both Hampshire incumbents, also shows how the weight of clerical connections tended toward homogeneity. Wavell and Woolls shared books, ideas and sermons. Probably hundreds of sermons, composed by them and other clergymen of the area, as well as published collections of sermons, were heard by their congregations in Winchester, Fareham and the other parishes in which they performed duties on a regular or occasional basis. In 1778 Wavell asked Woolls

> if you have any sermon against any particular doctrine of the Church of Rome, or against popery in general it would now be v. seasonable, I design to sound popery in the people's ears til they shall be sick of its very name.[49]

Such sermons were likely to be so widely heard that Wavell joked that he might have to excommunicate one particular member of his congregation who he feared knew that he exchanged sermons with other clergy, and might have heard some of them before.[50] Such professional connections existed in clerical clubs and societies up and down the land and were promoted by social gatherings such as visitation dinners.

The SPCK formalised both networks of clergy and access to devotional works. Indeed the SPCK's role was self-consciously an attempt to develop a national clerical connection. At the Society's first meeting on 2 November 1699 the committee

> resolved that this society will establish a correspondence with one or more of the clergy in each county, and with one clergyman in each great town and city of England in order to erect societies of the same nature with this throughout the kingdom.[51]

In the flood of tracts, sermons and devotional works the SPCK gradually exerted a subtle gravity on the Church and the experience of its parishioners toward greater uniformity. Occasionally the SPCK provided national circulation of works that otherwise would not have achieved widespread publication in England, such as the archbishop of Tuam's primary visitation charge of 1742, which advanced a model of clerical professionalism.[52] Moreover the authorisation by the Admiralty for the SPCK to circulate the Bible, Book of Common Prayer and devotional works on board Royal Navy ships gave them a further claim to national coverage.[53] The SPCK's interest in the establishment of parochial workhouses also underpinned its national role. By 1771 there were nearly 2,000 workhouses in the country, many the result of the SPCK's initiatives. The Society provided a series of printed rules for the standard operation of the workhouses and circulated accounting practices to each workhouse. From 1720 the Society offered premiums to towns to set up both charity schools and workhouses, and in 1723 published a guide on how to establish parish workhouses. The Society also sponsored the Workhouse Test Act of 1723. For the Society, workhouses were another opportunity to inculcate religion, and they also established another national network for Anglicanism.[54] The behaviour of the poor was modelled by the SPCK through catechising and the medium of Anglican clergy who served on the boards of workhouses.

Anglicanism also contributed to a shared national experience through education, and particularly the charity school movement. Like the SPCK, the charity school movement was a self-consciously national organisation: Queen Anne herself had commended the schools as a means to promote piety 'throughout this kingdom'.[55] The goal of the charity schools' curriculum was 'the education of poor children in the knowledge and practice of the Christian religion as professed and taught in the Church of England.' To that end 'the Master shall make it his chief business to instruct the children in the principles thereof as they are laid down in the Church catechism'.[56] To give effect to this goal, the SPCK circulated James Talbot's *The Christian Schoolmaster* (1707) to charity schools, to guide them in the duty of inducting children into the doctrines of the Church. Huge numbers of children passed through almost 2,000 schools: 20,000 in London between 1700 and 1733, 158,000 in England between 1737 and 1761, and nearly 12,000 in Wales attended circulating schools in 1763 alone. Each child was taught to recite the catechism, the litany and the principal prayers of the Church.[57] The same was true of the hundreds of parish schools, often endowed by parish charities, and sometimes accommodated in the parsonage, church or vestry.

In other ways too the eighteenth-century Church provided a shared national experience. Religious holidays that had formed the core of the leisure time since before the Reformation adapted themselves to an early industrial society; so that, for example, St Blaise's day became one of celebration for woollen workers.[58] It was to the Church also that people looked at moments of great national importance. Coronations and other great national events were the subject of prayers and proclamation. But there were more subtle effects of national events. In 1789 the *Annual Register* recorded that the French Revolution had exerted a profound influence on the minds of rich and poor alike:

> the churches were well attended and sometimes even crowded. It was a wonder to the lower orders to see the avenues to the churches filled with carriages. . . .[59]

By the eighteenth century the Church was also the principal national institution of charity and almonry. The charitable responsibilities of the Church had evolved since the Reformation. Influenced by Protestant individualistic piety, bequests became increasingly focused on secular purposes, such as the relief of poverty, rather than on masses for the souls of the dead.[60] In the parish of St Pancras, London, by the middle of the eighteenth century, the value of charitable bequests had reached almost 3,000 pounds, with some additional income from lands and tenements. The money was devoted to providing food, clothing, coal and shelter for the poor as well as maintaining the vicarage and providing for annual sermons.[61] Indeed even the poorest in society felt the obligation to provide for their fellows. In 1710 James Hocker, a labourer, left his tiny estate to the poor of Lowestoft, and the parish received numerous bequests of small sums for the poor.[62] But such charity was not simple humanism; it was a religious duty and identified as such. A writer in *The Guardian* in 1713 argued that

> as social inclinations are absolutely necessary to the well-being of the world, it is the duty and interest of each individual to cherish, and improve them to the benefit of mankind; the duty, because it is agreeable to the intention of the author of our being, who aims at the common good of his creatures, and as an indication of his will, hath implanted the seeds of mutual benevolence in our souls. . . .[63]

It was on this principle of good works and individualistic piety that Protestantism in general, and Anglicanism in particular, built the national edifice of charity and generosity towards those in distress. Such charity also had a function in drawing people together. In Bristol, Protestants of many complexions were drawn together to support charitable civic institutions, leaving their religious divisions behind. As Mary Fissell has suggested:

> in England, these divisions were cross-cut by the curious role of charity institutions in unifying the deeply divided urban politics after 1688 . . . [charity] provided powerful motives to overwrite differences in emblems of civic unity. Where party politics failed or were irrelevant, movements to reform manners and an interest in primitive Christianity served as sites where difference could be overcome in common cause. . . .[64]

Similar urges encouraged the Church to engage in social reform. In the years during which gin and other liquors were regulated, the anti-gin lobby was dominated by churchmen like Erasmus Phillips, James Oglethorpe, Edmund Gibson, Thomas Wilson and Stephen Hales. Indeed, Bishop Gibson regarded gin as such a social evil that in 1743 he returned to the Lords for the first time in seven years to vote for greater restrictions. Bishop Isaac Maddox, like Hales and Wilson, wrote works of 'pioneering social commentary' on the physical and moral dangers of gin. Similarly the work of the Society for the Reformation of Manners in suppressing vice was also a response to a range of social problems like poverty, crime and social disorder. It is in this light that William and Mary's proclamations against vice should be read.[65]

For much of the eighteenth century, the impact of charity, both as cause and effect, promoted social cohesion. In 1736 Martin Benson suggested that the subscribers for one infirmary were

> men who had been unfortunately divided . . . [but were] with one heart and voice uniting to promote this amiable design; under the auspices of ever-sacred charity; which can still even the noise of party rage, and the madness of the people.[66]

The same view was advanced during the turbulence of 1745. Thomas Holme told the governors of the Northampton Infirmary that

> the pious meetings occasioned for the support of these public charities cannot sure but greatly contribute to heal our pernicious divisions, to reconcile the minds of men, and to allay those fierce hates and animosities which give the greatest encouragement to our enemies, and which have brought us to the very brink of destruction.[67]

By 1771 the idea that charity reconciled men and women to one another was developed into a greater political thesis. In that year, Brownlow North, dean of Canterbury, preaching before the Canterbury Lying-in Charity, suggested that charity was

> a means of sobriety and order among the people, as the ground of their attachment to the welfare and peace of their country, that they may be happy in their submission to government, that they may esteem themselves blessed in a peaceable acquiescence under the necessary laws of subordination. Let us therefore bind them by the strongest obligations, affection to their families and gratitude to their benefactors.[68]

However, Grayson Ditchfield had also argued that by the end of the eighteenth century charity and philanthropy, like education, were increasingly more sharply conceived in denominational terms.[69] Nevertheless, Samuel Glasse suggested social control was the role of charity schools, their purpose was to 'silence the voice of murmuring and discontent, which a series of distress might too probably exact, by instructing them that if they seek the kingdom of God and his righteousness . . . persevering in their course of honest industry, all things will assuredly work together for good to them that unfeignedly love God'.[70] In this way the Church made the soothing balm of charity a national experience and one that connected benevolence with national identity.

One of the mechanisms through which a shared Anglican experience promoted national identity was the attention that the Church paid to history and tradition. Eighteenth-century Anglican clergymen were steeped in a new scholarship that consciously explored British history. Historians of the late seventeenth century hinted at the common religious heritage of England, Wales, Scotland and Ireland in Celtic Christianity.[71] Edmund Gibson's *Britannica* (1695) and John Horsley's *Britannia Romana* (1732) exemplify this attention to the history of Britain among the clergy. It was an interest that spanned the study of Anglo-Saxon, archaeology, ancient history, topography and post-Reformation history.[72] Some of these histories were less scholarly than polemical: Henry Rowlands, vicar of Anglesey, suggested in *Mona Antiqua Restaurata* (1723) that the sons of Japhet were the first inhabitants of Europe, that Welsh was descended from Hebrew and that the original inhabitants of Britain were descendants of Noah and were 'fountains of religion and worship'. Similarly, scholars like William Stukeley were anxious to develop a view of the past that promoted Anglicanism. In his study of Stonehenge in 1740, Stukeley argued that it was built to promote the knowledge of true religion 'which is no where on earth done in my judgement better than the Church of England'. Indeed, Stukeley's decision to enter holy orders in 1729 had been a result of his archaeological studies which led him to a commitment to the Trinitarianism of the Church of England.[73] The interest of the eighteenth-century clergy in history was part of a desire on the part of Britons to locate themselves historically at an uncertain political time and to understand their identity. Anglicans saw themselves as separate from Catholic Europe and from Dissent, and inextricably part of the political and social establishment. The values developed by the Church were consequently the values predominantly of the elite, and of the *Gentleman's Magazine*, which assiduously documented the clergy's appointments, marriages, deaths and activities. Nevertheless, as Gerald Newman asserts, the Church was a means of bridging the cultural differentiation of rich and poor, and thus her values were more universal than those of other institutions.[74]

The third contribution of Anglicanism to national identity was an expression of moderation by the only national institution besides the monarchy. For those men and women of the eighteenth century who looked for models to emulate, the Church provided the principal influences in their lives. Among these was a reverence for the past and a reliance on tradition rather than on novelty, these were born from a Church view of the scriptures and gave rise to a national identity which was dominated by moderation and equanimity. Even *The Independent Whig*, the mouthpiece of commonwealthmen who often denounced the Church for 'priestcraft', proclaimed that Anglicanism was an expression of the 'meekness' and the 'mildness' of Christianity. In February 1720, *The Independent Whig* asserted that the role of the clergyman was 'to promote the welfare of human nature, and to propagate its peace and prosperity'.[75] Another Whig publication, *Cato's Letters*, took up the message of the function of the Church: 'by it men are taught and animated to be useful, assisting, forgiving, kind and merciful to one another.' And in the same issue: 'the moral duties of religion [are] general peace, and unlimited charity, public spirit, equity, forbearance and [to do] good deeds to all men'.[76] Moderation was widely preached from Church pulpits. The congregations of one Hampshire parson, who repeated the sermon on numerous occasions between 1753 and 1792 were told:

> religion doth not design to annihilate and root out passions, but regulate and govern them, it doth not wholly forbid and condemn them, but determine them to their proper objects and appoint them their measure and proportions

The purpose of this moderation, the preacher argued, was 'restraint from sin' and the inculcation of reverence and obedience.[77] Moderation born of Anglican values was a feature of English society observed by Voltaire, who concluded that English politics and values were closely influenced by the Church of England, and this connection was responsible for the mutual forbearance that existed in the mainstream of English culture.[78]

The theme of moderation dominated Anglicanism in the years after the Glorious Revolution. Popular preachers, like John Evans, George Tullie, John Vesey, Henry Dove, Nicholas Brady, Samuel Fuller, James Fall, Henry Nelson, Thomas Rennell, and John Hartcliffe emphasised the importance of moderation in books and sermons.[79] It was this characteristic that was often sought in appointing bishops in the eighteenth century. William III in preparing instructions for Tenison to pass on to the members of the Ecclesiastical Commission for Church appointments included in them that they should seek out as bishops 'men of temper and who join the Church and State together . . .'.[80] Moderation was not simply an end in itself; the avoidance of the dangers of extremism was the guarantee of the success of all the components of the constitution. At the height of the Convocation controversy and the general election campaign of 1705, Gilbert Burnet issued his *Advice to the Clergy*. It was an appeal to set aside the momentary furies:

> what is the meaning of the distinction of High and Low Church; do not both agree in doctrine, worship and government? . . . What means all the anger that some vent at moderation? It is a word of good sound in the world, it signifies a due measure, and is as opposite to a feeble remissness as to excessive rigour. . . .[81]

Moderation was also the touchstone of the new Hanoverian regime. William Burscough in a sermon preached in 1715 before the new King, George I, asserted that the people were

> happily seated between the two extremes of arbitrary power and popular licentiousness, where both the liberties of the subject and the prerogatives of the crown are equally guarded; the one from the ambition of the prince, and the other from the madness of the people . . . as to the Church, a government seated between the follies of superstition and the wildness of enthusiasm, where neither the people are forc'd to submit blindly to the dictates of the priest, nor the priest to submit his just authority to the will of the people. . . .

For Burscough the formula for universal happiness was simple:

of the prince to rule men and not slaves; of the priest, to lead the discerning and not the blind; of the people to follow the gentle guidance of both; to submit to no laws but those of their own making and to no religion but that of their own choosing. . . .[82]

Such high views of the *via media* formed an essentially pragmatic paradigm of the nature of Anglicanism and its social consequences, but one which typified the eighteenth-century view of the effect of the Church's teachings on the minds of men and women. An element in this theme of moderation was aversion to civil strife and division. For, as Francis Atterbury pointed out 'nations are liable to guilt, and consequently to punishment'.[83] Suspicion of those leaders and politicians who led people away from moderation was much in evidence in the sermons of the period. In February 1778, in a sermon to the SPG, Bishop Richard Hurd of Worcester commented on the American War of Independence:

it is much to be lamented indeed that on the continent of America, unfortunate civil disputes have raised difficulties in the way of our endeavours. . . . But it is not the part of Christian ministers, or of a Christian congregation, to complain. I shall pass by the sufferings of both on this occasion, but I must in the spirit of charity, lament the unhappy delusion of the people themselves; whose religious apprehensions have been raised by their political leaders for political purposes; who have been led to fear where no fear was, to suspect the ministers of their peace as the instruments of oppression; and to seek their fancied deliverance where least of all it could be found, in the violence of religious conflict.[84]

In short, while Anglicans in the eighteenth century may have defended the use of force in the Glorious Revolution, in contemporary political matters they tended to inculcate the values not just of moderation, but of stoicism and passivity.

Moderation did not simply mean the maintenance of the *status quo*, it offered a model of a righteous society for which Anglicans should strive. Some clergy made even more sweeping claims for the transforming power of moderation. For Bishop Gilbert Burnet, commitment to the teachings of the Church would

make princes just and good, faithful to their promises and lovers of their people: it will inspire subjects with respect and submission, obedience and zeal for their prince: it will teach masters to be gentle and careful of their servants and servants to be faithful, zealous and diligent in their master's concerns: it will make friends tender and true to one another; it will make them generous, faithful and disinterested it will make men live in their neighbourhood as members of one common body, promoting first the general good of the whole, and then the general good of every particular as far as man's sphere can go: it will make judges and magistrates just and patient, hating covetousness, & maintaining peace and order without respect of persons: it will make people live in so inoffensive a manner, that it will be easy to maintain justice, whilst men are not disposed to give disturbance to those about them. . . . Thus religion, if truly received and strictly adhered to, would prove the greatest of all blessings to a nation. . . .[85]

This was a picture of a moderate nation that Burnet believed adherence to Anglicanism would create. It was a vision of benevolent government, obedient subjects, peaceable families and communities in which all people knew their place. It inculcated the Anglican virtues of deference and diligence and promoted characteristics such as stoicism and phlegm. It rejected strife in all its form: civil war, class antagonism and sectarian conflict.

Moderation was not simply an abstraction; it was an expression of the path that the Church walked between Catholicism and Dissent. But Anglicanism did not squeeze into a narrow theological stream but broadened into a wide river, with eddies and flows that encompassed the view of some of her competitors and enabled her to be tolerant of a shared origin. Francis Atterbury told his congregation at St Bride's in 1698 that

the Church you are of is without doubt the purest and soundest, the most reasonable and moderate Church upon earth; the nearest to the primitive pattern of any, and the most serviceable to our improvement in virtue and godliness. . . .[86]

Indeed it was moderation that underpinned the Church's tolerance of Dissent. When in February 1747 George Benson, the noted Dissenter, dedicated a book of sermons to Archbishop Thomas Herring, the newly appointed primate sent a letter of thanks in which he wrote,

I think it happy that I am called up to this high station at a time when spite and rancour and narrowness of spirit are out of countenance; when we breathe the benign and comfortable air of liberty and Toleration; and the teachers of our common religion make it their business to extend its essential influence and join in

235

supporting its true interest and honour. No times ever called more loudly upon Protestants for zeal and unity and charity.[87]

Assertions of national identity are prone to become stereotypes, but that is not the intention of this chapter. The three-fold contributions of eighteenth-century Anglicanism to national identity are pregnant with historical possibilities. The principle of a government founded on divine sanction undoubtedly spurred British military adventurism in the eighteenth century, and legitimised the sense of election that bore fruit in the development of empire. The shared national experience of Anglicanism provided a cultural, social and intellectual cohesion that transcended class barriers. This cohesion made for greater social unity than the nation might otherwise have enjoyed. The elevation of moderation and restraint to become cardinal teachings of the Church established one of the central features of national identity. It militated against extremes and radicalism in both politics and wider society.

Notes

1 L. Colley, *Britons*, New Haven, 1992, p. 11.
2 T. Claydon, *William III and the Godly Revolution*, Cambridge, 1996, p. 139.
3 J. Black, *Natural and Necessary Enemies*, London, 1986, p. 161.
4 Hampshire Record Office (HRO), W/K5/7, Jacob Scrapbook no. 6.
5 A. A. Sykes, *The Reasonableness of Mending the Executing the Laws Against Papists*, London, 1746. J. White, *New Preservative Against Popery*, London, 1755.
6 J. Black 'The Catholic Threat and the British Press in the 1720s and 1730s', *Journal of Religious History*, 1983, vol. 12, part 4.
7 HRO, W/K5/7, Jacob's Scrapbook no. 6.
8 C. Haydon *Anti-Catholicism in Eeighteenth Century England, c.1714–1780* Manchester, 1993; and *idem*,' "I love my King and my country, but a Roman Catholic I hate" Anti-Catholicism, Xenophobia and National Identity in eighteenth century England', T. Claydon and I. McBride (eds.), *Protestantism and National Identity: Britain and Ireland c.1650–c.1850*, Cambridge, 1998.
9 J. Black, 'Confessional State or Elect Nation? Religion and Identity in Eighteenth Century England' in Claydon and McBride (eds.), *op. cit.*; J. C. D. Clark, *The Language of Liberty, 1688–1832*, Cambridge, 1994; B. Young, 'A History of Variations: the Identity of the eighteenth century Church of England' in Claydon and McBride (eds.), *op. cit.*
10 J. Hoadly (ed.), *The Works of Benjamin Hoadly DD*, London, 1773, vol. 1, p. 662.
11 B. Hoadly, *Serious Advice to the Good People of England*, London, 1710, in J. Hoadly, *op. cit.*, vol. 1, p. 616.
12 *Ibid.*, vol. 1, p. 621.
13 B. Hoadly, *Reasons Against Receiving the Pretender and Restoring the Popish Line*, in J. Hoadly (ed.), *op. cit.*, vol. 1, p. 657. Jeremy Black has questioned whether

the Toleration Act justified claims of *religious* liberty in the eighteenth century; however for Hoadly the Toleration Act was one of a series of rights and liberties that contributed to the whole. J. Black, 'Confessional State of Elect Nation? . . .', *op. cit.*, p. 58.

14 B. Hoadly, *Letter of Advice to the Freeholders of England* . . . in J. Hoadly (ed.), *op. cit.*, vol. 1, p. 670. In a postscript to a letter to James Harris on 5 November 1728, Hoadly wrote 'a joyful day, November 5th forty years ago, even to those who curse it now'. HRO, Malmesbury Papers, 9M73/G15/45.

15 *Ibid.*, vol. 1, p. 670.

16 B. Hoadly, *An Enquiry into the Reasons of the Conduct of Gt Britain, with relation to the Present State of Affairs in Europe*, London, 1727, p. 79.

17 *Ibid.*, p. 91.

18 J. Trelawny, *A Sermon Preached before the Queen and both Houses of Parliament at the Cathedral Church of St Paul's, Nov. 12 1702, being the day of Thanksgiving for the signal successes vouchsafed to Her Majesties Forces by sea and land* . . . , London, 1702, p. 38.

19 *Ibid.*, pp. 41–2.

20 T. S. Hughes (ed.), *The Works of Bishop Sherlock with some account of his life* . . . , London, 1830, vol. 3, p. 320.

21 T. Hayter, *A Sermon preached before the Honourable House of Commons at St Margaret's Westminster, being the anniversary of his Majesty's happy accession to the Throne*, London, 1746, pp. 20, 23, 26.

22 *Seven Sermons by Dr Thomas Herring, Lord Archbishop of Canterbury* . . . , London, 1763, p. xvii. J. Ingamells, 'Hogarth's "Red" Herrings: A Study in Iconography', *The Connoisseur*, January 1972.

23 J. Ayres (ed.), *Paupers and Pig Killers, the Diary of William Holland, A Somerset Parson 1799–1818*, Gloucester, 1984, pp. 62, 127.

24 K. Wilson, 'The Island Race: Captain Cook, Protestant Evangelicalism and the Construction of English National Identity, 1760–1800' in Claydon and McBride (eds.), *op. cit.*

25 O. F. Christie (ed.), *The Diary of The Revd William Jones 1777–1821*, London, 1929, p. 175.

26 Quoted in F. C. Mather, *High Church Prophet: Samuel Horsley*, Oxford, 1992, p. 262.

27 Quoted in W. E. Smith, *The Navy and its Chaplains in the Days of Sail*, Toronto, 1968, p. 100.

28 G. Newman, *The Rise of English Nationalism, A Cultural History 1740–1830*, London, 1997, *passim*. Newman's thesis is flawed by a failure to recognise the critical role of Anglicanism.

29 J. Black, 'The Tory View of Eighteenth-Century Foreign Policy', *Historical Journal*, 1988.

30 J. Brown, *Estimate of the Manners and Principles of the Times*, London, 1757, vol. I, pp. 181–2.

31 S. Mandelbrote, 'The Bible and National Identity in the British Isles *c.*1650–*c.*1750', Claydon and McBride (eds.), *op. cit.*

32 C. J. Stranks, *Anglican Devotions*, London, 1961, p. 275.

33 Quoted in W. Gibson, *Religion and Society in England and Wales 1689–1800*, London, 1998, pp. 225 *et seq.*

34 W. M. Jacob, *Lay People and Religion in the Early Eighteenth Century*, Cambridge, 1996, pp. 64–5.

35 E. H. Pearce, *Hartlebury Castle*, London, 1926, p. 177.

36 J. Bowtell, *A Defence of the LVth Canon . . .* , London, 1710, p. 1.

37 W. Wake, *The Principles of the Christian Religion . . .* , London, 1699, p. 133.

38 T. Moore (ed.), *Sermons on several occasions by the Right Revd Father in God Francis Atterbury DD, late Lord Bishop of Rochester and Dean of Westminster* London 1734, vol. 2, p. 222.

39 T. Bennet, *An Answer to the Dissenters' Plea for Separation*, London, 1699; *A Confutation of Popery*, London, 1701; *A Discourse of Schism*, London, 1703; *A Confutation of Quakerism*, London, 1705; *The Non-jurors Separation from the Public Assemblies of the Church of England*, London, 1716.

40 T. Bennet, *Devotions, Confessions, Petitions, Intercessions and Thanksgivings for every day in the week, and also before, at, and after the Sacrament . . .*, London, 1705; *A Brief History of the Joint Use of Precomposed set forms of Prayers*, London, 1708; and *A Discourse of Joint Prayer*, London, 1708.

41 Bennet was chosen incumbent of Colchester by chance, having stood in as preacher for the deceased parson and so impressed the parishioners that they selected him as a successor; the same occurred at St Olave's Southwark later in his career. *DNB*.

42 C. Oldacre, *The Last of the Old Squires*, London, 1854, p. 102.

43 J. Wickham Legg, *English Church Life from the Restoration to the Tractarian Movement*, London, 1914, *passim*.

44 See, for example W. Gibson review of C. Pickford (ed.), *Bedfordshire Churches in the Nineteenth Century*, Part 2, 1998, Bedfordshire Historical Record Society, vol. 77, in *Archives*, 1999.

45 C. Oldacre, *op. cit.*, p. 65.

46 For visitation queries see W. R. Ward (ed.), *Parson and Parish in Eighteenth Century Surrey: Replies to Bishops' Visitations, op. cit.*; W. R. Ward (ed.), *Parson and Parish in Eighteenth Century Hampshire: Replies to Bishops' Visitations, op. cit.*

47 H. A. Lloyd-Jukes, *op. cit., passim*; J. Gregory, *op. cit., passim* and E. Ralph, *op. cit., passim*.

48 A. Hartshorne (ed.), *The Memoirs of a Royal Chaplain 1729–1763*, London, 1905, p. 109.

49 Hampshire Record Office, Copy/605/116.

50 *Ibid.*, Copy/605/105.

51 M. Clement, *Correspondence and Minutes of the SPCK Relating to Wales, 1699–1740*, Cardiff, 1952, p. 248.

52 W. K. Lowther Clarke, *Eighteenth Century Piety*, London, 1945, p. 5.

53 Smith, *op. cit.*, p. 129.

54 T. Hitchcock, 'Paupers and Preachers: the SPCK and the Parochial Workhouse Movement', L. Davison, T. Hitchcock, T. Keirn and R. Shoemaker (eds.), *Still the Grumbling Hive: The Response to Social and Economic Problems in England, 1689–1750*, Stroud, 1992, pp. 147–61.

55 M. G. Jones, *The Charity School Movement*, London, 1964, p. 28.

56 *Ibid.*, p. 76.

57 *Ibid.*, pp. 23, 51, 407, 351.

58 Jacob, *op. cit.*, p. 67.

59 *Annual Register* 1789, vol. 40, p. 229.

60 C. Litzenberger, *The English Reformation and the Laity, Gloucestershire, 1540–1580*, Cambridge, 1997, *passim*.

61 S. Palmer, *St Pancras; Being Antiquarian, Topographical and Biographical Memoranda* . . . , London, 1870, pp. 271–3.

62 H. D. W. Lees, *The Chronicle of a Suffolk Parish Church*, Lowestoft, 1949, p. 146.

63 *The Guardian*, 5 August 1713.

64 M. E. Fissell, 'Charity Universal? Institutions and Moral Reform in Eighteenth Century Bristol', L. Davison, T. Hitchcock, T. Keirn and R. Shoemaker (eds.), *op. cit.*, p. 139.

65 L. Davison, 'Experiments in the Social Regulation of Industry: Gin Legislation, 1729–1751', and R. Shoemaker, 'Reforming the City: The Reformation of Manners Campaign in London, 1690–1738', L. Davison, T. Hitchcock, T. Keirn and R. Shoemaker (eds.), *op. cit.*, pp. 29–43 and 99–102.

66 M. Benson, *A Sermon addressed to the Lord Mayor, Aldermen and Governors of the several hospitals of the City of London*, London, 1736, p. 15.

67 T. Holme, *A Sermon Preached before the Governors of Northampton Infirmary*, London, 1745, p. 39.

68 Quoted in D. T. Andrew, 'On Reading Charity Sermons: Eighteenth Century Anglican Solicitation and Exhortation', *Journal of Ecclesiastical History*, 1992, vol. 43, no. 4, p. 589.

69 G. M. Ditchfield, 'English Rational Dissent and Philanthropy *c.*1760–*c.*1810', H. Cunningham and J. Innes (eds.), *Charity, Philanthropy and Reform*, London, 1998.

70 *Ibid.*, p. 590.

71 S. Mandelbrote, *op. cit.*, pp. 163 *et seq.*

72 D. C. Douglas, *English Scholars 1660–1730*, London, 1951, *passim.*

73 S. Piggott, *William Stukleley, an Eighteenth Century Antiquarian*, Oxford, 1950, pp. 115, 127.

74 G. Newman, *op. cit.*, p. 7 *et seq.* Interestingly, Newman tends to neglect religion in his work, but concedes that Anglicanism contributed the sort of ideological element to nationalism that raised it above mere patriotism. *Ibid.*, p. 63.

75 *The Independent Whig*, 1720, no. 3, Feb. 3.

76 *Cato's Letters*, 1721, no. 66, Feb. 17. This was the sort of reductionism that Wesley found unacceptable in the Church of England.

77 Hampshire Record Office 35M96/2, unfortunately the identity of the parson is unknown.

78 Voltaire, *Letters from England*, Harmondsworth, 1980, p. 41.

79 J. Evans, *'Moderation Stated' in a Sermon Preached before the Rt Hon. the Lord Mayor of London* . . . , London, 1682; G. Tullie, *Moderation Recommended in a Sermon Preached before the Lord Mayor of York* . . . , York, 1689; N. Brady, *'Let Your Moderation be Known to All Men' in Fourteen Sermons, preached on several occasions* . . . , London, 1704; J. Vesey, *A Sermon Preached to the Protestants of Ireland in and about the City of London*, London, 1689; H. Dove, *A Sermon Preached before the Queen at Whitehall February 5th 1690/1*, London, 1691; S. Fuller, *A Sermon Preached before Her Majesty at Whitehall* . . . , London, 1693; H. Nelson, *Charity and Unity In a Sermon preached at the Hertford School feast, August 19, 1707*, London, 1708; T. Rennell, *A Sermon preached at St Mary's Oxford* . . . *March 8 1708/9 being the Anniversary of Her Majesty's Inauguration* . . . London, 1709; J. Hartcliffe, *A Treatise of Moral and Intellectual Virtues* . . . , London, 1691; J. Fall, *A Preface to Robert Leighton's*

Practical Commentaries upon the Two First Chapters of First Peter . . . , London, 1693.

80 Lambeth Palace Library, Ms. 927, Tenison Correspondence.

81 T. E. S. Clarke and H. C. Foxcroft, *A Life of Gilbert Burnet . . . with an Introduction by C. H. Firth*, Cambridge, 1907, p. 416.

82 W. Burscough, *The Duty of Praise and Thanksgiving in a Sermon Preached before the King at the Royal Chapel of St James . . . May 29th 1715, being the Anniversary of the Restoration of the Royal Family*, London, 1715, pp. 20–1.

83 T. Moore (ed.), *op. cit.*, vol. 2, p. 16.

84 Pearce, *op. cit.*, p. 274.

85 G. Burnet, *History of My Own Time*, London, 1838, p. 923.

86 T. Moore (ed.), *op. cit.*, vol. 2, p. 334.

87 J. Duncombe (ed.), *Letter by Several Eminent Persons, including The Correspondence of John Hughes Esq* . . . , London, 1773, vol. 2, pp. 169–70.

CONCLUSION

Anglican clergy returned to the theme of unity and peace repeatedly in their sermons. One of the most explicit was that of Samuel Bradford in June 1709.[1] Bradford's interpretation of the Glorious Revolution was that William III was the nation's 'deliverer . . . in our day of danger' and therefore the means of 'preserving peace among our selves'. That peace was God's

> singular pledge of his favour toward us; particularly in making this kingdom a place of refuge for so many thousand distressed persons and families, especially Protestants who have suffered persecution in their own countries.[2]

Bradford viewed unity and peace as a feature of primitive Christianity to which his audience should aspire; it was a universalist doctrine that meant that Anglicans

> should be ready to join with each other in all the offices of Christian worship in every other part of the world . . . ; and they should all with one heart and soul endeavour to promote the interest of the whole body.[3]

But Bradford was not blind to the forces of division that were apparent in the early eighteenth century. If God represented peace and unity, 'contention and division are the works of the devil.' Bradford claimed there was

> at this time a loud and just complaint of the abounding of infidelity and iniquity among us: but there is also another and a better spirit moving vigorously at the same time to the great satisfaction and pleasure of all good Christians.[4]

That spirit, claimed Bradford, was expressed in the Societies for the Reformation of Manners, the SPCK, the SPG, parochial libraries and charity schools. Bradford was optimistic:

> we live in an age wherein divisions abound and that not only between persons of different persuasions in religion, but even between those of the same communion. The design which we are here pursuing has a natural tendency to unite the serious and pious of different persuasions.[5]

Bradford's were the views of most Church clergy, both Latitudinarian and High Church, throughout the eighteenth century. In the 1770s William Jones emphasised the vital importance of religious unity to his parishioners:

> how extremely dangerous it is then, to break the order and peace of the Church; even though it be done with a sincere desire to promote faith and piety. . . . Division is not the way to unity.[6]

How should we reconcile the emphasis placed on disunity in the eighteenth-century Church by historians for so long, with the arguments presented here, that Anglicanism was marked by a strong sense of political, religious, cultural and national unity? The explanation lies in the various debates that historians have assumed consumed the eighteenth-century Church. The Convocation debate, the Sacheverell and Bangorian debates, the issue of subscription and most of the other issues that divided opinion among the clergy, were only ripples on the surface of the Church. They did not undermine the consensus that had been established in 1689, indeed they reinforced it. The focus of these debates was on the form, not the fundamental principle, of divinely-ordained government. But they were only marginal to the way in which the Church viewed itself and its role in the eighteenth century. In 1735, Dean Cheyney of Winchester for example lamented the Church's 'divisions and disputes about obscure and unnecessary things'.[7] This was also the view that underlay James Gardiner's *The Duty of Peace amongst Members of the Same State, Civil or Ecclesiastical . . .* (1713).[8] The Convocation controversy and Sacheverell were the 'hot spots' in the Church, but they do not represent the generality of eighteenth-century Anglicanism. Rumbling debates over Methodism, subscription to the Thirty-Nine Articles, Toleration and non-Trinitarian Dissent preoccupied some churchmen, but there were large areas of the country that were untouched by these divisions.[9] Moreover, these issues concerned and engaged only a minority of clergy. After these occasional outburst of division and dispute, there was evidence of an equally strong resurgence of moderation.[10] As one of Viscount Townshend's correspondents recorded in 1716 the clergy had returned to 'preaching and promoting unity, peace and charity'.[11] Perhaps, inevitably, many churchmen, of all sorts, pronounced themselves moderate and reasonable.

Francis Atterbury, one of the principal authors of the ostensible divisions during the first two decades of the eighteenth century, recognised the 'duty of living peaceably' in his farewell sermon at St Bride's in 1698. He advocated that his parishioners should avoid all contention and strife, live peaceably and follow the law. He argued that his parishioners should enjoy their own opinions:

> without arraigning their superiors in Church and State for being otherwise minded and without disturbing the public peace in order to propagate their tenets and make proselytes.

The duty of Christians, argued Atterbury, was to be inoffensive and obliging, to live peaceably with all men, to reign in passions and anger and to 'moderate our desires and shorten our designs'.[12] Atterbury may have broken these tenets, but he understood their power and importance to Anglicans.

Bishop Samuel Peploe of Chester might almost have been addressing posterity in his charge to the clergy of the diocese in 1747. He responded to detractors of the Church:

> they have represented us as useless and burdensome, as idle and superficial in our ministerial performances, which, however true it may be in regard to some particular persons . . . yet surely it is an unjust imputation on the body of the clergy.[13]

The same argument may be advanced regarding the disunity of the Church. Though individual churchmen may have disagreed, the clergy as a whole was a far larger body which was more cohesive and united.

The evidence presented here also suggests that the definition of, and the breach between, High and Low Churchmen has been exaggerated. Our eyes have been dazzled by the glare of individuals such as Atterbury, Hoadly and Sacheverell, and the heat and light that they generated has blinded us to the comparative agreement of High and Low Churchmen on matters of Church doctrine, liturgy, ceremony and pastoralia. The apparent hostility of Anglicanism to Dissent has also been overstated. Hoadly and Burnet's desire for a greater Comprehension was not the eccentric longings of extremists, they represented the main body of churchmen who often co-operated with Dissenters in parishes and in the episcopal hierarchy, who came closer to reunion than at any other time since the Reformation. The wider unity of society was a function of Church participation in culture and in the development of national identity.

The Church's orientation toward unity and accord was one which arose from the context within which it found itself. In a sermon before the House of Commons on the anniversary of the martyrdom of Charles I in 1717, John Hoadly, Benjamin's brother, argued that the English Civil War was God's punishment for godlessness and disunity. This indeed was the evidence of the seventeenth century: disunity and discord had bred profound political upheaval, from which eighteenth-century Britain was still recovering.[14] The Church's swings between Laudianism, Puritanism, the Clarendon Code and the Catholicism of James II in the seventeenth century was a source of its exhaustion with disunity and extremism.

By the early eighteenth century, even the Non-juror, Robert Nelson, who had momentarily separated from the Church asked in *Festivals and Fasts*: 'How ought religious differences to be debated among Christians?' The answer he proffered was:

> without throwing scorn and contempt upon those that oppose us . . . without railing and injurious reflections . . . without detracting from the real worth of our adversaries . . . without ever suffering our passions to vent themselves under a pretence of zeal for God's Glory. . . .[15]

Notes

1 S. Bradford, *Unanimity and Charity, the Character of Christians: A Sermon preached in the parish Church of St Sepulchre, June 16th 1709 . . . at the Anniversary Meeting of the Charity Schools of the cities of London and Westminster*, London, 1709.

2 *Ibid.*, p. 21.

3 *Ibid.*, p. 11.

4 *Ibid.*, pp. 18, 19.

5 *Ibid.*, p. 28. It was a view to which Bradford repeatedly returned, most notably in his sermon *The unprofitableness of external, without internal, religion, A Sermon Preached before the King at St James's January 1st 1715/16*, London 1716, in which he claimed the Church 'was designed to be one body . . .', pp. 11–20.

6 W. Jones, *Sermons: Practical, Doctrinal and Expository*, London, 1829, p. 234.

7 From the 1735 will of Dean Cheyney of Winchester. G. H. Blore, *Thomas Cheyney Wykhamist, Dean of Winchester 1748–1760*, Winchester, 1950, p. 5.

8 Subtitled '. . . or How a man should behave himself as becomes a Christian with respect to High and Low Church; Whig and Tory. A Sermon Preached at the Cathedral Church of Lincoln, July 7th 1713'*, London 1713.

9 W. Gibson, ' "A Happy Fertile Soil which bringeth forth Abundantly": The Diocese of Winchester, 1689–1800', J. Gregory and J. Chamberlain (eds.), *The Church in its Local Identities, 1660–1800*, Woodbridge, 2001.

10 W. C. Watson, 'The Late Stuart Reformation: Church and State in the First Age of Party', PhD thesis, University of California, Riverside, 1995, pp. 179, 264.

11 British Library, Egerton Mss. 3,124, f 52, D'alonne to Townshend, 5 May 1716.

12 T. Moore (ed.), *Sermons on several occasions by the Right Revd Father in God Francis Atterbury DD, late Lord Bishop of Rochester and Dean of Westminster*, London, 1734, vol. 2, pp. 322–34.

13 S. Peploe, *A Charge of the Lord Bishop of Chester on the Occasion of his Visitation, 17th June 1747*, Manchester, 1747, p. 3.

14 J. Hoadly, *A Sermon Preached before the Honourable House of Commons at St Margaret's Westminster on 30th January 1717 . . .* , London, 1717, p. 6.

15 C. F. Secretan, *Memoirs of the Life and Times of the Pious Robert Nelson . . .* , London, 1860, p. 172.

BIBLIOGRAPHY

MANUSCRIPT SOURCES

Bodleian Library, Oxford
  Add. Mss A269.
British Library, London
  Stowe Ms 354.
  Egerton Mss 3,124.
  Add. Mss 5,852 f 119.
  Add. Mss 32,686 f 353.
  Add. Ms 32,717 f 38.
  Add, Mss 32,722 f 5.
  Add. Ms 32,906 f 387.
Brotherton Library, Leeds University
  Anon., *Verse on the defiance of the Seven Bishops, 1688*, Lt q 52, Record No. 4485.
  S. Davies 'Verses on the 29th May, an exercise at King's College, Cambridge, 1731', Ms Lt q19, Record No. 2648.
  Add. Mss 39,311 f 39.
Christ Church, Oxford
  Wake Ms.
Lambeth Palace Library, London
  Ms 927, Tenison Correspondence.
Hampshire Record Office, Winchester
  Malmesbury Papers, 9M73/G15/45.
  35M96/2.
  29M65/2.
  W/K5/7, Jacob Scrapbook No. 6.
  Copy/605.
  31M67 P19.
Harry Ransom Research Center, University of Texas, Austin, USA
  Phillips Mss.
Public Record Office
  SP Domestic, George II, B, 23.

Surrey History Centre, Woking
  G173/2/1, John Butler Mss.

SERMONS AND CONTEMPORARY WORKS

Anon, *A Defence of the Archbishop's Sermon on the Death of her Late Majesty . . .* , London, 1695.

Anon, *A Friendly Conference Concerning the New Oath of Aliegiance to King William and Queen Mary, Wherein the objections against taking the oaths are impartially examined . . .* , London, 1689.

Anon, *Reflections Upon Two Books, the One intitled The Case of Alliegiance to a King in possession, the Other, An Answer to Dr Sherlock's Case . . .* , London, 1691.

P. Allix, *An Examination of the Scruples of those who refuse to take an oath of Alliegiance . . .* , London, 1689.

An Account of the Proceedings of Jonathan, Bishop of Exeter, in his late Visitation of Exeter College . . . , Oxford, 1690.

F. Atterbury, *Letter to a Convocation Man concerning the Rights, Powers and Privileges of that Body*, London, 1697.

  The Wisdom of Providence manifested in the Revolution of Government: A Sermon preached before the House of Commons at St Margaret's Westminster, May 29th 1701, London, 1701.

J. Aycliffe, *Parergon Juris Canonici Anglicani*, London, 1726.

L. Bagot, *A Charge to the Clergy at the Primary Visitation of the Diocese of Norwich . . .* , Norwich, 1784.

S. Barrington, *A Charge delivered to the Clergy of the Diocese of Durham . . . , MDCCXCVII*, Durham, 1797.

A. Bedford, *Evil and Danger of Stage-plays . . .* , Bristol, 1724.

T. Bennet, *An Answer to the Dissenters' Plea for Separation*, London, 1699.

  A Confutation of Popery, London, 1701.

  A Discourse of Schism, London, 1703.

  A Confutation of Quakerism, London, 1705.

  Devotions, Confessions, Petitions, Intercessions and Thanksgivings for every day in the week, and also before, at, and after the Sacrament . . . , London, 1705.

  A Brief History of the Joint Use of Precomposed set forms of Prayers, London, 1708.

  A Discourse of Joint Prayer, London, 1708.

  The Non-jurors Separation from the Public Assemblies of the Church of England, London, 1716.

M. Benson, *A Sermon addressed to the Lord Mayor, Aldermen and Governors of the several hospitals of the City of London*, London, 1736.

T. Birch, *The Life and Works of Archbishop Tillotson*, London, 1753.

E. Bohun, *History of the Desertion*, London, 1689.

J. Bowtell, *A Defence of the LVth Canon . . .* , London, 1710.

S. Bradford, *Unanimity and Charity, the Character of Christians: A Sermon preached in the parish Church of St Sepulchre, June 16th 1709 . . . at the Anniversary Meeting of the Charity Schools of the cities of London and Westminster*, London, 1709.

The unprofitableness of external, without internal, religion, A Sermon Preached before the King at St James's January 1st 1715/16, London 1716.

W. Bradshaw, *A Sermon Preached before the Lords Spiritual and Temporal in Parliament Assembled in the Abbey-church at Westminster January 30th 1729/30*, London 1730.

N. Brady, *'Let Your Moderation be Known to All Men' in Fourteen Sermons, preached on several occasions . . .* , London, 1704.

J. Brown, *Estimate of the Manners and Principles of the Times*, London, 1757.

The English Theological Works of George Bull DD, Oxford, 1844.

G. Burnet, *A Sermon Preached before the King and Queen at Whitehall on the 19th October*, London, 1690.

Reflections upon a Pamphlet . . . , London, 1696.

A sermon preached before the House of Lords November 5th 1689 . . . being Gunpowder Treason Day as Likewise the Day of His Majesty's Landing in England, London, 1689.

Pastoral Letter to the Clergy of His Diocese Concerning the Oaths of Allegiance and Supremacy to King William and Queen Mary, London, 1689.

An Exposition of Church Catechism, London, 1710.

Discourse of Pastoral Care, London, 1713.

History of My Own Time, London, 1838.

W. Burscough, *The Duty of Praise and Thanksgiving in a Sermon Preached before the King at the Royal Chapel of St James . . . May 29th 1715, being the Anniversary of the Restoration of the Royal Family*, London, 1715.

J. Butler, *A Charge to the Clergy of his diocese of Hereford . . . in the year 1792*, Hereford, 1792.

E. Chandler, *A Sermon Preached at the Cathedral Church of Worcester . . . Being the day appointed for the General Thanksgiving for the Glorious Campaign of the Arms of Her Majesty*, Worcester, 1710.

The Works of William Chillingworth M.A., London, 1762.

W. Cleaver, *A Charge delivered to the Clergy of the Diocese of Chester . . . 1799*, Oxford, 1799.

H. Compton, *The Bishop of London's Letter to his clergy . . . 'how they ought to behave themselves under a toleration'*, London, 1692.

H. Consett, *The Practice of the Spiritual Courts*, London, 1700.

D. Defoe, *A Tour of the Whole Island of Great Britain*, London, 1724–6.

The Family Instructor, London, 1722.

P. Doddridge, *Free Thoughts on the Most Probable Means of Renewing the Dissenting Interest*, London, 1731.

H. Dove, *A Sermon Preached before the Queen at Whitehall February 5th 1690/1*, London, 1691

J. Downes, *A Sermon Preached in the Old Chapel in Sheffield . . . 26 August 1742 before the Society of Cutlers*, London, 1743.

J. Duncombe (ed.), *Letter by Several Eminent Persons, including The Correspondence of John Hughes Esq . . .* , London, 1773.

H. Durbin, *A Narrative of some extraordinary things . . . supposed to be the effect of Witchcraft . . .* , Bristol, 1800.

J. Evans, *'Moderation Stated' in a Sermon Preached before the Rt Hon. the Lord Mayor of London . . .* , London, 1682.

J. Fall, *A Preface to Robert Leighton's Practical Commentaries upon the Two First Chapters of First Peter . . .* , London, 1693.

J. Fisher, *A Charge delivered to the clergy of the Diocese of Exeter . . . 1804 and 1805*, Exeter, 1805.

W. Fleetwood, *Essay on Miracles*, London, 1701.

A Letter to an Inhabitant of the Parish of St Andrew's Holbourn about New Ceremonies in the Church, London, 1717.

R. Fleming, *A Discourse on Earthquakes as Supernatural and Premonitory Signs to a Nation*, London, 1692.

J. Fordyce, *Sermons to Young Women*, London, 1766.

E. Fowler, *The Principles and Practices of Certain Moderate Divines of the Church of England . . .* , London, 1670.

S. Fuller, *A Sermon Preached before Her Majesty at Whitehall . . .* , London, 1693.

T. Gent, *Ancient and Modern History of the Famous City of York . . .* , York, 1730.

E. Gibson, *The Sacrament of the Lords Supper Explained: or the things to be known and done to make a worthy communicant . . .* , London, 1705.

Codex Juris Ecclesiastici Anglicani, London, 1713.

A Sermon of the Growth and Mischief of Popery Preached at the Assizes held at Kingston in Surrey, Sept. 5, 1706, London, 1706.

The Charge of Edmund, Lord Bishop of Lincoln at his Primary Visitation in the year 1717, London, 1717.

A Sermon Preached before the Society for the Reformation of Manners 6 January 1723, London, 1724.

The Bishop of London's Third Pastoral Letter to the People of his Diocese . . . , London, 1731.

Observations upon the Conduct and Behaviour of a certain Sect usually distinguished by the name of Methodists, London, 1744.

Bishop Gibson's Three Pastoral Letters to the People of his Diocese; particularly to those of the two great cities of London and Westminster in defence of the Gospel Revelation . . . , London, 1820.

W. Gilpin, *Observations relative chiefly to Picturesque Beauty in the year 1776 . . . particularly in the Highlands of Scotland . . .* , London, 1776.

Observations on the River Wye . . . , London, 1782.

Observations relative chiefly to Picturesque Beauty . . . particularly the Mountains and Lakes of Cumberland and Westmorland, London, 1786.

Observations on the Western Part of England . . . , London, 1798.

Remarks on Forest Scenery . . . , London, 1808.

J. Godolphin, *Repertorum Canonicum*, London, 1680.

S. Gough, *An Enquiry into the Causes of the Decay of the Dissenting Interest*, London, 1730.

B. Gravener, *A Sermon Preached to the Society for the Reformation of Manners*, London, 1705.

J. Hartcliffe, *A Treatise of Moral and Intellectual Virtues . . .* , London, 1691.

T. Haweis, *The Evangelican Expositor; or a Commentary on the Holy Bible . . .* , London, 1765–6.

A Word in Season . . . , London, 1795.

T. Hayter, *Remarks on Mr Hume's Dialogues Concerning Natural Religion*, London, 1780.

A Sermon preached before the Honourable House of Commons at St Margaret's Westminster, being the anniversary of his Majesty's happy accession to the Throne, London, 1746.

Seven Sermons by Dr Thomas Herring, Lord Archbishop of Canterbury . . . , London, 1763.

G. Hickes, *An Apology for a new separation . . .* , London, 1691.

Two Treaties on the Christian Priesthood and on the Dignity of the Episcopal Order, Oxford, 1845–7.

B. Hoadly, *Serious Advice to the Good People of England*, London, 1710.

An Enquiry into the Reasons of the Conduct of Gt Britain, with relation to the Present State of Affairs in Europe, London, 1727.

'Sermon at St Swithin's Church 30 Jan 1702–3 On Christian Moderation . . .', B. Hoadly, *Sixteen Sermons by Benjamin Bishop of Winchester*, London, 1754.

J. Hoadly, *A Sermon Preached before the Honourable House of Commons at St Margaret's Westminster on 30th January 1717 . . .* , London, 1717.

(ed.), *The Works of Benjamin Hoadly DD*, London, 1773.

R. Hodgson, *The Works of the Rt Revd Beilby Porteus DD . . . With His Life*, London, 1811.

T. Holme, *A Sermon Preached before the Governors of Northampton Infirmary*, London, 1745.

G. Hooper, *A Sermon Preach'd before the Honourable the House of Commons at St Margaret's Westminster on Friday the 4th day of April 1701, being the day of publick fast and humiliation*, London, 1701.

G. Horne, *A Letter to the Right Hon. The Lord North, Chancellor of the University of Oxford, Concerning the Subscription to the XXXIX Articles . . .* , Oxford, 1773.

S. Horsley, *A Charge to the Clergy of his Diocese, delivered by Bishop Horsley . . . in the year 1790*, Gloucester, 1790.

T. S. Hughes (ed.), *The Works of Bishop Sherlock with some account of his life . . .* , London, 1830.

J. Jackson, *An Address to the Deists*, London, 1744.

P. King, *The History of the Apostles Creed: With Critical Observations on its Several Articles*, London, 1702.

W. King, *State of the Irish Protestants under James II*, London, 1691.

W. Law, *The Absolute Unlawfulness of the Stage Entertainment fully demonstrated*, London, 1726.

W. Lloyd, *A Discourse of God's Ways of Disposing of Kingdoms*, London, 1681.

H. W. Majendie, *A Charge Delivered to the clergy of the Diocese of Chester in July and August 1804*, London, 1804.

T. Moore (ed.), *Sermons on several occasions by the Right Revd Father in God Francis Atterbury DD, late Lord Bishop of Rochester and Dean of Westminster*, London, 1734.

C. Moss, *A Sermon before the House of Lords on 30th January 1769 . . . on the Anniversary of the Martyrdom of King Charles I*, London, 1769.

T. Naish, *A Sermon Preached at Sarum Cathedral before the Society of Musick Lovers 22 November 1700*, London, 1701.

H. Nelson, *Charity and Unity In a Sermon preached at the Hertford School feast, August 19, 1707*, London, 1708.

B. North, *A Sermon before the Incorporated Society for the Propagation of the Gospel in Foreign Parts . . .* , London, 1778.

J. Norris, *Discourses Concerning Submission to Divine Providence . . .* , London, 1693.

T. Oughton, *Ordo Judicorum*, London, 1728.

The Works of William Paley DD in one volume, London, 1853.

W. Paley, *The Principles of Moral and Political Philosophy*, London, 1785.

S. Patrick, *A Sermon Preached on the 5th November*, London, 1696.

S. Peploe, *A Charge by the Rt Revd Samuel, Lord Bishop of Chester to the Clergy of his Diocese in his Primary Visitation begun at Chester June the 19th 1728*, London, 1728.

A Charge of the Lord Bishop of Chester on the Occasion of his Visitation, 17th June 1747, Manchester, 1747.

B. Porteus, *A Review of the Life and Character of Archbishop Secker*, New York, 1773.

A Letter to the Clergy of the Diocese of Chester Concerning Sunday Schools, London, 1786.

A Letter to the Clergy of the Diocese of London . . . , London, 1789.

A Charge delivered to the clergy of the Diocese of London . . . , MDCCXC, London, 1790.

A Charge delivered to the Clergy of the Diocese of London . . . , London, 1793.

G. Pretyman, *A Charge delivered to the Clergy of the diocese of Lincoln . . . in May and June 1794*, London, 1794.

A Charge delivered to the Clergy of the Diocese of Lincoln . . . in June and July 1800, London, 1800.

The Life of The Revd Humphrey Prideaux DD, London, 1748.

J. Randolph, *A Charge delivered to the Clergy of the Diocese of London . . . , MDCCCX*, Oxford, 1810.

T. Rennell, *A Sermon preached at St Mary's Oxford . . . March 8 1708/9 being the Anniversary of Her Majesty's Inauguration . . .* , London, 1709.

H. Sacheverell, *The Loyal Catechism*, London, 1710.

In Perils among False Brethren: A Sermon preached before the Lord Mayor of London . . . , London, 1710.

T. Secker, *Lectures on the Catechism of the Church of England with a discourse on Confirmation*, London, 1826.

G. Sewell, *The Clergy and the Present Ministry Defended Being a Letter to the Bishop of Salisbury, occasioned by his Lordship's New Praface to his Pastoral Care*, London, 1713.

W. Sherlock, *A Resolution of Some Cases of Conscience Which Respect Church Communion . . .* , London, 1683.

A Short Summary of the Principal Controversies between the Church of England and the Church of Rome, London, 1687.

The Case of the Allegiance due to Soveraign Powers, London, 1691.

W. D. Shipley (ed.), *The Works of the Right Reverend Jonathan Shipley DD, Lord Bishop of St Asaph*, London, 1792.

R. Smallbrook, *A Charge to the clergy of the Diocese of St Davids*, Carmarthen, 1726.

M. Stanhope, '*The Sinfulness of Separation*' *from the Establish'd Church of England in a Sermon Preached in the Parish Church of St Clement Danes . . .* , London, 1710.

E. Stephenson, *The Beginning and Progress of a needful and hopeful Reformation*, London, 1691.

A. A. Sykes, *The Reasonableness of Mending the Executing the Laws Against Papists*, London, 1746.

J. Talbot, *The Judicial Powers of the Church Asserted in a sermon at All Saints Pavement . . .* , York, 1707.

W. Talbot, *The Bishop of Sarum's Charge to the clergy of his Diocese at his Primary Visitation, 1716*, London, 1717.

T. Tenison, *A Discourse on Idolatry*, London, 1687.

'*Concerning Discretion in Giving Alms*' *A Sermon Preached before the Lord Mayor of London . . .* , London, 1681.

The Works of the Most Revd Dr John Tillotson, Late Lord Archbishop of Canterbury, London, 1720.

E. Timberland, *The History and Proceedings of the House of Lords*, London, 1742.

J. Trelawny, *A Sermon Preached before the Queen and both Houses of Parliament at the Cathedral Church of St Paul's, Nov. 12 1702, being the day of Thanksgiving for the signal successes vouchsafed to Her Majesties Forces by sea and land . . .* , London, 1702.

The Tryal of Dr Henry Sacheverell before the House of Peers for High Crimes and Misdemeanours . . . , London, 1710.

J. Tucker, *An Apology for the Present Church of England as by law Established occasioned by a Petition laid before Parliament for Abolishing Subscriptions in a Letter to one of the Petitioners . . .* , Gloucester, 1772.

G. Tullie, *Moderation Recommended in a Sermon Preached before the Lord Mayor of York . . .* , York, 1689.

J. Vesey, *A Sermon Preached to the Protestants of Ireland in and about the City of London*, London, 1689.

W. Wake, *An Exposition of the Doctrine of the Church of England*, London, 1686.

A Sermon Preached before the House of Commons . . . 5 June 1689, London, 1689.

The Principles of the Christian Religion . . . , London, 1699.

R. Warner, *A Tour Through the Northern Counties of England . . .* , London, 1802.

Walks Through Wales . . . , London, 1798.

R. Watson, *A Charge Delivered to the Clergy of the Diocese of Llandaff at the Visitation of Richard, Lord Bishop of Llandaff . . .* , London, 1791.

    A Charge delivered to the clergy of the Diocese of Llandaff in June 1809, Bristol, 1809.

W. Whiston, *Memoirs of the Life and Writings of Mr William Whiston*, London, 1749.

D. Whitby, *A Dissuasive from Enquiring into the Doctrine of the Trinity . . .* , London, 1714.

J. White, *New Preservative Against Popery*, London, 1755.

W. Wilberforce, *A Practical View of the Prevailing Religious System*, London, 1797.

J. Wilmot, *The Life of the Revd John Hough DD, Bishop of Oxford, Lichfield and Coventry and Worcester*, London, 1812.

T. Wilson, *Parochialia*, Oxford, 1840.

BOOKS

C. J. Abbey and J. H. Overton, *The English Church in the Eighteenth Century*, London, 1878.

G. W. O. Addleshaw and F. Etchells, *The Architectural Setting of Anglican Worship*, London, 1958.

J. Addy, *Sin and Society in the Seventeenth Century*, London, 1989.

C. Annesley and P. Hoskin (eds.), *Archbishop Drummond's Visitation Returns, 1764*, 1997, vol. 1, Yorkshire A–G, Borthwick Texts and Calendars, vol. 21.

A. Armstrong, *The Church of England the Methodists and Society 1700–1850*, London, 1973.

P. Avis, *Anglicanism and the Christian Church*, Edinburgh, 1989.

J. Ayres (ed.), *Paupers and Pig Killers, the Diary of William Holland, A Somerset Parson 1799–1818*, Gloucester, 1984.

S. Baring-Gould, *The Church Revival*, London, 1914.

V. Barrie-Curien, *Clerge et Pastorale en Angleterre au XVIIIe siècle, Le diocese de Londres*, Paris, 1992.

A. Barrow, *The Flesh is Weak*, London, 1981.

J. Barry and K. Morgan (eds.), *Reformation and Revival in Eighteenth Century Bristol*, Bristol Record Society, 1994, vol. XLV.

R. A. Beddard (ed.), *The Revolution of 1688*, Oxford, 1991.

G. V. Bennett, *White Kennett, 1660–1728*, London, 1957.

    The Tory Crisis in Church and State, 1688–1739, Oxford, 1975.

    and J. Walsh (eds.), *Essays in Modern Church History in Memory of Norman Sykes*, London, 1966.

J. Black, *Natural and Necessary Enemies*, London, 1986.

    An Illustrated History of Eighteenth Century Britain, Manchester, 1996.

    (ed.), *Culture and Society in Britain 1660–1800*, Manchester, 1997.

    The Politics and Culture of an Aristocratic Society, Charlottesville, VA, 1999.

P. Bliss, *Reliquiae Hearnianiae*, London, 1869.

P. Borsay, *English Urban Renaissance: Culture and Society in the Provincial Town 1660–1770*, Oxford, 1991.

J. Bossy, *Peace in the Post-Reformation*, Cambridge, 1998.

J. E. Bradley, *Popular Politics and the American Revolution in England*, Macon, 1986

J. Bramston (ed.), *The Autobiography of Sir John Bramston*, Camden Society, 1845, vol. 32.

P. Brassley, A. Lambert and P. Saunders (eds.), *The Accounts of the Revd John Crakanthorp of Fowlmere 1682–1710*, Cambridgeshire Records Society, 1988, vol. 8.

T. Bray, *Bibliotheca Parochialis*, London, 1697.

J. Brewer, *The Pleasures of the Imagination*, London, 1997.

R. L. Brown, *Llandaff Figures and Places*, Gwasg Eglwys Trallwng, 1998.

R. Browning, *The Political and Constitutional Ideas of the Court Whigs*, Baton Rouge, 1982.

T. L. Bushell, *The Sage of Salisbury, Thomas Chubb 1679–1747*, London, 1967.

L. A. S. Butler (ed.), *The Archdeaconry of Richmond in the Eighteenth Century*, 1990, Yorkshire Archaeological Society, vol. CXLVI.

E. Cardwell, *Synodalia . . .* , Oxford, 1842.

Documentary Annals of the Church of England, London, 1844.

E. Carpenter, *Thomas Tenison*, London, 1948.

The Protestant Bishop, London, 1956.

R. T. Carroll, *The Common-Sense Philosophy of Bishop Edward Stillingfleet, 1635–1699*, The Hague, 1975, International Archives of the History of Ideas, vol. 77.

O. Chadwick, *The Secularisation of the European Mind*, Cambridge, 1975.

J. S. Chamberlain, *Accommodating High Churchmen: The Clergy of Sussex, 1700–1745*, Chicago, 1997.

C. R. Chapman, *Sin, Sex and Probate*, Dursley, 1997.

O. F. Christie (ed.), *The Diary of The Revd William Jones 1777–1821*, London, 1929.

C. Clair (ed.), *John Nichol's Literary Anecdotes*, Carbondale, Ill, 1967.

J. C. D. Clark, *English Society 1688–1832*, Cambridge, 1985.

Revolution and Rebellion: State and Society in England in the Seventeenth and Eighteenth Centuries, Cambridge 1986.

The Language of Liberty, 1688–1832, Cambridge, 1994.

Samuel Johnson: Literature, Religion and English Cultural Politics from the Restoration to Romanticism, Cambridge, 1994.

B. F. L. Clarke, *The Building of the Eighteenth Century Church*, London, 1963.

T. E. S. Clarke and H. C. Foxcroft, *A Life of Gilbert Burnet . . . with an Introduction by C. H. Firth*, Cambridge, 1907.

T. Claydon, *William III and the Godly Revolution*, Cambridge, 1996.

and I. McBride (eds.), *Protestantism and National Identity: Britain and Ireland, c.1650–1850*, Cambridge, 1998.

M. Clement, *Correspondence and Minutes of the SPCK Relating to Wales, 1699–1740*, Cardiff, 1952.

L. Colley, *Britons*, New Haven, 1992.

J. Collier, *Vindicae Juris Regii*, London, 1689.

H. and P. Coombs (eds.), *The Journal of a Somerset Rector 1803–1834*, Oxford, 1984.

R. Cornwall, *Visible and Apostolic: The Constitution of the Church in High Church Anglican and Non-Juror Thought*, London, 1993.

(ed.), *Bishop Burnet's Discourse of the Pastoral Care*, Lewiston, 1997.

D. Cressy, *Bonfires and Bells: National Memory and the Protestant Calendar in Elizabethan and Stuart England*, London, 1989.

E. Cruiskshanks (ed.), *Ideology and Conspiracy: Aspects of Jacobitism 1689–1799*, Edinburgh, 1982.

H. Cunningham and J. Innes (eds.), *Charity, Philanthropy and Reform*, London, 1998.

G. C. B. Davies, *The Early Cornish Evangelicals 1735–1760*, London, 1951.

L. Davison, T. Hitchcock, T. Keirn and R. Shoemaker (eds.), *Still the Grumbling Hive: The Response to Social and Economic Problems in England, 1689–1750*, Stroud, 1992.

D. C. Douglas, *English Scholars 1660–1730*, London, 1951.

D. Eastwood, *Government and the Community in the English Provinces, 1700–1870*, London, 1997.

E. J. Evans, *The Contentious Tithe, the Tithe Problem and English Agriculture 1750–1850*, London, 1976.

G. N. Evans, *Religion and Politics in Mid-Eighteenth Century Anglesey*, Cardiff, 1953.

K. Fincham (ed.), *The Early Stuart Church 1602–1642*, London, 1993.

H. Fishwick (ed.), *The Notebook of the Revd Thomas Jolly 1671–1693, Extracts from the Church Book of Altham and Wymondhouses . . .* , Chetham Society, 1894, vol. 33, new series.

W. K. Ford (ed.), *Chichester Diocesan Surveys 1686 and 1724*, 1994, Sussex Record Society, vol. 78.

L. Fox, *The Correspondence of the Revd Joseph Greene 1712–1790*, London, HMC, 1965.

H. C. Foxcroft, *A Supplement to Burnet's History of My Own Time, derived from His Original Memoirs, His Autobiography, His Letters to Admiral Herbert and His Private Meditations, all hitherto unpublished*, Oxford, 1902.

J. A. Froude, *Short Studies on Great Subjects*, London, 1878–83.

J. Garnett and C. Matthew, (eds.), *Revival and Religion Since 1700*, London, 1993.

J. Gascoigne, *Cambridge in the Age of the Enlightenment: Science, Religion and Politics from Restoration to the French Revolution*, Cambridge, 1989.

W. Gibson, *Church, State and Society 1760–1850*, London, 1994.

The Achievement of the Anglican Church, 1689–1800: The Confessional State in Eighteenth Century England, Lewiston, 1995.

A Social History of the Domestic Chaplain, 1540–1830, London, 1996.

Religion and Society in England and Wales, 1689–1800, London, 1998.

A. D. Gilbert, *Religion and Society in Industrial England 1740–1914*, London, 1976.

W. Gladstone, *The Gleanings of Past Years*, London, 1879.

(ed.), *The Works of Joseph Butler*, Oxford, 1897.

I. M. Green, *The Christians ABC: catechisms and catechising 1530–1740*, Oxford, 1996.

D. Greenwood, *William King, Tory and Jacobite*, Oxford, 1969.

J. Gregory (ed.), *The Speculum of Archbishop Thomas Secker*, Church of England Record Society, vol. 2, 1996.

M. I. J. Griffin and L. Freedman, *Latitudinarianism in the Seventeenth Century Church of England*, Brill's Studies in Intellectual History, vol. 32, 1992.

J. R. Guy, *The Diocese of Llandaff in 1763*, South Wales Record Society, 1991.

R. Haakonssen (ed.), *Enlightenment and Religion: Rational Dissent in Eighteenth Century Britain*, Cambridge, 1996.

P. Hair (ed.), *Before the Bawdy Court*, London, 1972.

A. T. Hart, *The Life and Times of John Sharp, Archbishop of York*, London, 1949.
William Lloyd 1627–1717, London, 1952.
The Eighteenth Century Country Parson, Shrewsbury, 1955.
The Country Clergy in Elizabethan and Stuart Times, 1558–1660, London, 1958.
The Country Priest in English History, London, 1960.
Country Counting House, London, 1962.
The Man in the Pew 1558–1660, London, 1966.
Clergy and Society 1600–1800, London, 1968.
The Curate's Lot, Newton Abbot, 1971.
Some Clerical Oddities in the Church of England from Medieval to Modern Times, Bognor, 1980.
Ebor, York, 1986.

A. Hartshorne (ed.), *The Memoirs of a Royal Chaplain 1729–1763*, London, 1905.

C. Haydon, *Anti-Catholicism in Eighteenth Century England, c.1714–1780*, Manchester, 1993.

P. Hazard, *The Crisis of the European Mind, 1680–1715*, London, 1953.

W. G. Hiscock, *Henry Aldrich Christ Church 1648–1710*, Oxford, 1960.

R. T. Holtby, *Daniel Waterland 1683–1740. A Study in eighteenth century Orthodoxy*, Carlisle, 1966.

C. Howse (ed.), *AD: 2,000 Years of Christianity*, London, 1999.

E. Hughes (ed.), *The Letters of Spencer Cowper, Dean of Durham 1746–1774*, Surtees Society, 1956, vol. 165.

J. Hunt, *English Religious Thought from the Reformation to the End of the Last Century*, London, 1873.

K. Hylson-Smith, *The Churches in England from Elizabeth I to Elizabeth II*, London, 1997.

J. Ingamells, *The English Episcopal Portrait 1550–1835*, London, 1981.

W. M. Jacob, *Lay People and Religion in the Early Eighteenth Century*, Cambridge, 1996.
and N. Yates (eds.), *Crown and Mitre*, Woodbridge, 1993.

J. Jago, *Aspects of the Georgian Church: Visitation Studies of the Diocese of York 1761–1776*, London, 1997.

F. G. James, *North Country Bishop*, New Haven, 1956.

A. P. Jenkins (ed.), *The Correspondence of Bishop Secker*, 1991, Oxford Record Society, vol. 57.

G. H. Jenkins, *Literature, Religion and Society in Wales 1660–1730*, Cardiff, 1978.

J. G. Jenkins, *The Dragon of Whaddon, The Life of Browne Willis*, High Wycombe, 1953.

M. G. Jones, *The Charity School Movement*, London, 1964.

W. Jones, *Sermons: Practical, Doctrinal and Expository*, London, 1829.

W. K. Jordan, *Philanthropy in England 1480–1660 . . .* , London, 1955.

J. P. Kenyon, *Revolution Principles: the Politics of Party, 1689–1720*, Cambridge, 1977.

P. Langford, *A Polite and Commercial People*, Oxford, 1989.

H. D. W. Lees, *The Chronicles of a Suffolk Parish Church*, Lowestoft, 1949.

S. E. Lehmberg, *Cathedrals Under Siege 1600–1700*, Philadelphia, 1996.

C. L. S. Linnell, *Some East Anglian Clergy*, London, 1961.

H. A. Lloyd-Jukes (ed.), *Bishop Secker's Visitation Returns, 1738*, Oxfordshire Record Society, vol. xxxviii, 1957.

W. K. Lowther Clarke, *Eighteenth Century Piety*, London, 1945.

R. Lund (ed.), *The Margins of Orthodoxy: Heterodox Writing and Cultural Response 1660–1750*, Cambridge, 1995.

A. M. Lyles, *Methodist Mocked*, London, 1960.

M. W. McCahill, *Order and Equipoise: The Peerage and the House of Lords, 1783–1806*, London, 1978.

J. S. Macauley and R. Greaves, *The Autobiography of Thomas Secker, Archbishop of Canterbury*, Lawrence, Kansas, 1989.

C. E. Mallett, *A History of the University of Oxford*, London, 1927.

F. C. Mather, *High Church Prophet: Bp Samuel Horsley*, Oxford, 1992.

J. H. Monk, *The Life of Richard Bentley DD*, London, 1833.

J. H. Moorman, *The Curate of Souls 1660–1760*, London, 1958.

G. Morgan, *Circulating Schools in Cardiganshire 1738–1777*, Occasional Papers in Ceredigion History, no. 1.

The Newgate Calendar, London, 1997.

G. Newman, *The Rise of English Nationalism, A Cultural History 1740–1830*, London, 1997.

P. B. Nockles, *The Oxford Movement in Context: Anglican High Churchmanship, 1760–1857*, Cambridge, 1994.

J. E. Norton, *The Letters of Edward Gibbon*, London, 1956.

C. Oldacre, *The Last of the Old Squires*, London, 1854.

R. O'Day, *The English Clergy 1558–1640*, London, 1979.

S. L. Ollard, *The Six Students of St Edmund Hall, Expelled from Oxford in 1768*, London, 1911.

and P. C. Walker (eds.), *Archbishop Herring's Visitation Returns, 1743*, Yorkshire Archaeological Society, vol. LXXVII, 1930.

J. H. Overton, *William Law: Non–juror and Mystic*, London, 1881.

Life in the English Church 1660–1714, London, 1885.

A. Pagden (ed.), *The Languages of Political Theory in Early Modern Europe*, Cambridge, 1987.

S. Palmer, *St Pancras; Being Antiquarian, Topographical and Biographical Memoranda* . . . , London, 1870.

S. Patrick, *Autobiography of Symon Patrick*, Oxford, 1839.

W. B. Patterson, *James VI and I and the Reunion of Christendom*, Cambridge, 1997.

E. H. Pearce, *Hartlebury Castle*, London, 1926.

A. L. Peck, *Anglicanism and Episcopacy*, London, 1958.

T. C. Pfizenmaier, *The Trinitarian Theology of Dr Samuel Clarke (1675–1729). Context, Sources, and Controversy*, New York (Studies in the History of Christian Thought), 1997.

S. Piggott, *William Stukleley, an Eighteenth Century Antiquarian*, Oxford, 1950.

A. Plummer, *The Church of England in the Eighteenth Century*, London, 1910.

C. Podmore, *The Moravian Church In England, 1728–1760*, Oxford, 1998.

R. Porter and M. M. Roberts (eds.), *Pleasure in the Eighteenth Century*, London, 1996.

W. S. Powell, *Discourses on Various Subjects*, London, 1776.

M. Ransome (ed.), *The State of the Bishopric of Worcester 1782–1808*, 1968, Worcestershire Historical Society vol. 6.

(ed.), *Wiltshire Returns to the Bishop's Visitation Queries, 1783*, 1972, Wiltshire Record Society, vol. XXVII.

N. Ravitch, *Sword and Mitre*, The Hague, 1966.

F. Renaud (ed.), *The Fellows of the Collegiate Church of Manchester*, 1891, Chetham Society, Part 2.

I. Rivers (ed.), *Books and their Readers in Eighteenth-Century England*, London, 1982.

Reason, Grace and Sentiment: A Study of the Language of Religion and Ethics in England 1660–1780, Cambridge, 1991.

C. Robbins, *The Eighteenth Century Commonwealthman*, New York, 1968.

K. Robbins, *Great Britain, Identities, Institutions and the Idea of Britishness*, London, 1998.

R. E. Rodes Jr, *Law and the Modernization of the Church of England: Charles II to the Welfare State*, Indiana, 1991.

A. W. Rowden, *The Primates of the Four Georges*, London, 1917.

G. Rowell (ed.), *Tradition Renewed*, London, 1986.

J. T. Rutt (ed.), *An Historical Account of my Own Life by Edmund Calamy* . . . , London, 1830.

C. F. Secretan, *Memoirs of the Life and Times of the Pious Robert Nelson* . . . , London, 1860.

R. Sedgwick (ed.), *Some Materials toward Memoirs of the Reign of King George II*, London, 1931.

H. S. Skeats, *A History of the Free Churches in England*, London, 1869.

D. Slatter (ed.), *The Diary of Thomas Naish*, Wiltshire Archaeological and Natural History Society, 1965, vol. 20.

M. G. Smith, *Pastoral Discipline and the Church Courts: the Hexham Court, 1680–1730*, 1982, Borthwick Paper, no. 62.

Fighting Joshua, Sir Jonathan Trelawny 1650–1721, Redruth, 1985.

W. E. Smith, *The Navy and its Chaplains in the Days of Sail*, Toronto, 1968.

J. Sommerville, *The Secularisation of Early Modern England: From Religious Culture to Religious Faith*, Oxford, 1992,

W. Spellman, *The Latitudinarians and the Church of England 1660–1700*, Athens, Georgia, 1993.

T. Simpson Evans, *The Life of Robert Frampton, Bishop of Gloucester*, London, 1876.

C. J. Somerville, *Popular Religion in Restoration England*, Gainsville, FL, 1977.

V. Staley (ed.), *Hierurgia Anglicana*, London, 1902–4.

G. T. Stokes, *Some Worthies of the Irish Church*, London, 1900.

M. Storey (ed.), *Two East Anglian Diaries 1641–1729*, Suffolk Record Society, 1994, vol. 36.

G. M. Straka, *The Anglican Reaction to the Revolution of 1688*, University of Wisconsin, Madison, 1962.

C. J. Stranks, *Anglican Devotions*, London 1961.

R. N. Stromberg, *Religious Liberalism in eighteenth century England*, Oxford, 1954.

N. Sykes, *Edmund Gibson*, Oxford, 1926.

Church and State in England in the Eighteenth Century, Cambridge, 1934.

Old Priest and New Presbyter, Cambridge, 1956.

William Wake, Cambridge, 1957.

From Sheldon to Secker, Cambridge, 1959.

W. E. Tate, *The Parish Chest*, Cambridge, 1946.

T. F. Thistleton-Dyer, *Old English Social Life as told by Parish Registers*, London, 1898.

J. E. Thorold Rogers, *A Complete Collection of the Protests of the House of Lords . . .* , Oxford.

G. M. Trevelyan, *The English Revolution 1688–1689*, London, 1956.

R. Trumbach, *Sex and the Gender Revolution, vol. 1: Heterosexuality and the Third Gender in Enlightenment London*, Chicago, 1998.

E. S. Turner, *Unholy Pursuits: the Wayward Parsons of Grub Street*, London, 1998.

A. Urdank, *Religion and Society in a Cotswold Vale, Nailsworth 1780–1865*, Los Angeles, 1990.

E.A. Varley, *The Last of the Prince Bishops*, Cambridge, 1992.

J. E. Vaux, *Church Folklore*, London, 1894.

J. Venn, *Annals of a Clerical Family*, London, 1904.

P. Virgin, *The Church in an Age of Negligence*, Cambridge, 1989.

Voltaire, *Letters from England*, Harmondsworth, 1980.

J. Walsh, C. Haydon and S. Taylor (eds.), *The Church of England c.1689–1833*, Cambridge, 1994.

W. R. Ward, *Georgian Oxford*, Oxford, 1958.

Religion and Society in England, 1790–1850, London, 1972.

(ed.), *Parson and Parish in Eighteenth Century Surrey: Replies to Bishops' Visitations*, Surrey Records Society, vol. XXXIV, 1994.

(ed.), *Parson and Parish in Eighteenth Century Hampshire: Replies to Bishops' Visitations*, Hampshire Records Series, vol. 13, 1995.

A. Warne, *Church and Society in Eighteenth Century Devon*, Newton Abbot, 1969.

W. B. Whitaker, *The Eighteenth Century English Sunday*, London, 1940.

C. E. Whitting, *Nathaniel Lord Crewe, Bishop of Durham*, London, 1940.

A. Whyte, *Characters and Characteristics of William Law . . .* , London, 1893.

J. Wickham Legg, *English Church Life from the Restoration to the Tractarian Movement*, London, 1914.

A. J. Willis (ed.), *Winchester Ordinations, 1660–1829*, Folkestone, 1964.

A. S. Wood, *Thomas Haweis 1734–1820*, London, 1957.

The Inextinguishable Blaze, London, 1960.

D. H. Woodforde (ed.), *The Woodforde Diaries*, London, 1932.

D. K. Worcester, *The Life and Times of Thomas Turner of East Hoathly*, New Haven, 1948.

C. Wordsworth, *Social Life at the English Universities in the Eighteenth Century*, Cambridge, 1874.

Scholae Academicae: Some Account of Studies at English Universities in the Eighteenth Century, Cambridge, 1877.

C. E. Wright and R. C. Wright (eds.), *The Diary of Humphrey Wanley 1715–1726*, London, Bibliographical Society, 1966.

B. W. Young, *Religion and Enlightenment in Eighteenth Century England: Theological Debate from Locke to Burke*, Oxford, 1998.

ARTICLES

P. Adman, W. A. Speck and B. White, 'Yorkshire Election Results 1734 and 1742: a computer analysis', *Northern History*, 1985, vol. 21.

D. T. Andrew, 'On Reading Charity Sermons: Eighteenth Century Anglican Solictation and Exhortation', *Journal of Ecclesiastical History*, 1992, vol. 43, no. 4.

A. Ashley, 'The Spiritual Courts of the Isle of Man especially in the seventeenth and eighteenth centuries', *English Historical Review*, 1957, vol. 72.

N. Aston, 'Horne and Heterodoxy: The Defence of Anglican Belief in the Late Eighteenth Century', *English Historical Review*, 1993.

'The Limits of Latitudinarianism: English Reaction to Bishop Clayton's *An Essay on Spirit*', *Journal of Ecclesiastical History*, 1998, vol. 49, no. 3.

'From a Deanery Window: An Eighteenth Century View of Lincoln Cathedral', *Archives*, 1998, vol. xxiii, no. 98.

J. C. Baily, 'Bishop Lewis Bayly and His *Practice of Piety*', *Manchester Quarterly*, 1883, vol. 2.

L. W. Barnard, 'Thomas Secker and the English Parliament', *Parliaments, Estates and Representation*, 1992, vol. 12, no. 1.

D. Barnes, 'The Duke of Newcastle, Ecclesiastical Minister, 1724–54', *Pacific Historical Review*, 1943, vol. 3.

S. W. Baskerville, 'The Political Behaviour of the Cheshire Clergy 1705–1752', *Northern History*, 1987, vol. 23.

G. V. Bennett, 'The Convocation of 1710: An Anglican Attempt at Counter-Revolution', *Studies in Church History*, 1971, vol. 7.

J. Black, 'The Catholic Threat and the British Press in the 1720s and 1730s', *Journal of Religious History*, 1983, vol. 12, part 4.

'The Tory View of Eighteenth-Century Foreign Policy', *Historical Journal*, 1988.

G. H. Blore, 'An Archdeacon of the Eighteenth Century, Thomas Balguy DD 1716–1795', *Winchester Cathedral Record*, 1951, vol. 20.

J. E. Bradley, 'The Anglican Pulpit, Social Order and the Resurgence of Toryism During the American Revolution', *Albion*, 1989, vol. 21, no. 3.

J. C. D. Clark, 'The Decline of Party, 1740–1760', *English Historical Review*, 1978, vol. 93.

'A General Theory of Party, Opposition and Government, 1688–1832', *Historical Journal*, 1980.

'The Politics of the Excluded: Tories, Jacobites and Whig Patriots, 1715–1760', *Parliamentary History*, 1983, vol. 2.

'Eighteenth Century Social History', *Historical Journal*, 1984.

'England's Ancien Regime as a Confessional State', *Albion*, 1989, vol. 21, no. 3.

R.. D. Cornwall, 'Advocacy of the Independence of the Church from the State in Eighteenth Century England: A Comparison of a Non-juror and a Nonconformist View', *Enlightenment and Dissent*, 1993, vol. 12.

R. S. Crane, 'The Diffusion of Voltaire's Writings in England 1750–1800', *Modern Philology*, 1923, vol. 20.

G. M. Ditchfield, 'The Subscription Issue in British Parliamentary Politics, 1772–9', *Parliamentary History*, 1988, vol. 7, no. 7.

'Anti-trinitarianism and Toleration in Late Eighteenth Century British Politics: The Unitarian Petition of 1792', *Journal of Ecclesiastical History*, 1991, vol. 42, no. 1.

'English Rational Dissent and Philanthropy, *c.*1760–*c.*1810' in H. Cunningham and J. Innes (eds.), *Charity, Philanthropy and Reform*, London 1998

E. Duffy, ' "Whiston's Affair": The Trials of a Primitive Christian 1709–1714', *Journal of Ecclesiastical History*, 1976, vol. 27, no. 2.

'Pudding Time', P Cunich *et al.* (eds.), *A History of Magdalene College, Cambridge, 1428–1988*, Cambridge, 1994.

P. Elmer, 'Richard Allestree and *The Whole Duty of Man*', *The Library* 1951, fifth series, vol. 6.

V. Gammons, ' "Babylonian Performances": The Rise and Suppression of Popular Church Music, 1660–1870', E. Yeo and S. Yeo (eds.), *Popular Culture and Class Conflict, 1590–1914: Explorations in the History of Labour and Leisure*, Sussex, 1981.

J. Gascoigne, 'Anglican Latitudinarianism and Political Radicalism in the Late Eighteenth Century', *History*, 1986, vol. 71.

W. Gibson, 'Somerset Evangelical Clergy', *Somerset Archaeology and Natural History*, 1986, vol. 130.

'A Hanoverian Reform of the Chapter of St David's', *The National Library of Wales Journal*, 1988, vol. 25, no. 3.

'An Eighteenth Century Paradox: The Career of the Decypherer-Bishop Edward Willes', *The British Journal for Eighteenth Century Studies*, 1989, vol. 12, part 1.

'Disraeli's Church Patronage 1868–1880', *Anglican and Episcopal History*, vol. 61, no. 2, 1992.

' "A Great Excitement": Gladstone and Church Patronage', *Anglican and Episcopal History*, Sept. 1999.

' "A Happy Fertile Soil which bringeth forth Abundantly": The Diocese of Winchester, 1689–1800', J. Gregory and J. Chamberlain (eds.), *The Church in its Local Identities, 1660–1800*, Woodbridge, 2001.

D. Green, 'Augustinianism and Empiricism: A Note on Eighteenth Century Intellectual History', *British Journal for Eighteenth Century Studies*, 1967, vol. 1.

'Latitudinarianism and Sensibility: The Geneaology of the "Man of Feeling" Reconsidered', *Modern Philology*, 1977, vol. 75.

'How "Degraded" was Eighteenth Century Anglicanism?', *Eighteenth Century Studies*, 1990, vol. 24, no. 1.

M. Grieg, 'The Reasonableness of Christianity? Gilbert Burnet and the Trinitarian Controversy of the 1690s', *Journal of Ecclesiastical History*, 1993, vol. 44, no. 4.

D. Hempton, 'Evangelicalism and Reform *c.*1780–1832', J. Wolffe (ed.), *Evangelical Faith and Public Zeal: Evangelicals and Society in Britain, 1780–1980*, London, 1995.

B. Hilton, 'Apologia pro Vitis Veteriorium Hominum', *Journal of Ecclesiastical History*, 1999, vol. 50, no. 1.

N. W. Hitchen, 'The Politics of English Bible Translation in Georgian England', *Transactions of the Royal Historical Society*, 1999, sixth series, vol. IX.

J. Ingamells, 'Hogarth's "Red" Herrings: A Study in Iconography', *The Connoisseur*, January 1972.

B. H. Kelly, 'Some Reflections on Church and State relations in the Time of Bishop Wilson', *Proceedings of the Isle of Man Natural History and Antiquarian Society*, 1963, n.s., vol. 6.

T. Kendrick, 'Sir Robert Walpole, The Old Whigs and the Bishops, 1733–36: A Study in Eighteenth-Century Parliamentary Politics', *Historical Journal*, 1968, vol. 11, no. 3.

M. Kinnear, 'The Correctional Court in the Diocese of Carlisle, 1704–1756', *Church History*, 1990, vol. 59.

D. Lemmings, 'Marriage and the Law in the Eighteenth Century: Hardwicke's Marriage Act of 1753', *Historical Journal*, 1996, vol. 39, part 2

J. Marshall, 'The Ecclesiology of the Latitude-men 1660–1689: Stillingfleet, Tillotson and Hobbism', *Journal of Ecclesiastical History* 1985, vol. 36, no. 3.

F. C. Mather, 'Georgian Churchmanship reconsidered: some variations in Anglican Public Worship', *Journal of Ecclesiastical History*, 1985, vol. xxvi.

J. Nankivell, 'Edward Stillingfleet, Bishop of Worcester 1689–1699', *Worcester Archaeological Society*, 1945, vol. XXII.

F. O'Gorman, 'J. C. D. Clark *English Society 1688–1832* . . . Reappraised' in *Reappraisals in History* Institute of Historical Research, London web-site 1998, http://www.ihr.sas.ac.uk/ihr/reviews/frank.html

J. A. Phillips, 'The Social Calculus: Deference and Defiance in Later Georgian England', *Albion*, 1989, vol. 21, no. 3.

J. E. Pinnington, 'Anglican Openness to Foreign Protestant Churches in the Eighteenth Century', *Anglican Theological Review* 1969, vol. 51.

R. Porter, 'Georgian Britain: An *Ancien Regime*?', *British Journal for Eighteenth Century Studies*, 1992, vol. 15.

G. F. Scholtz, 'Anglicanism in the Age of Johnson: The Doctrine of Conditional Salvation', *Eighteenth Century Studies*, 1988–9, vol. 22, no. 2.

J. A. Sharpe, ' "Such disagreement betwyx Neighbours": Litigation and Human Relations in Early Modern England', J. Bossy (ed.), *Disputes and Settlements: Law and Human Relations in the West*, Cambridge, 1983.

K. Sharpe, 'Symposium: Revolution or Revisionism', *Parliamentary History*, 1988, vol. 7, no. 2.

C. J. Somerville, 'Religious Typologies and Popular Religion in Restoration England', *Church History*, 1976, vol. 45.

'The Destruction of Religious Culture in Pre-Industrial England', *Journal of Religious History*, 1988, vol. 15, no. 1.

J. Spurr, 'Latitudinarianism and the Restoration Church', *Historical Journal*, 1988, vol. 31.

N. Sykes, 'Benjamin Hoadly', J. F. C. Hearnshaw (ed.), *Social and Political Ideas of Some English Thinkers of the Augustan Age*, London, 1928.

'Bishop Gibson and Sir Robert Walpole', *English Historical Review* 1929, vol. xliv.

' "The Buccaneer Bishop": Lancelot Blackburne 1658–1743', *Church Quarterly Review* 1940, April–June.

'The Duke of Newcastle as Ecclesiastical Minister', *English Historical Review*, 1942, vol. 57.

'Archbishop Wake and the Whig Party 1716–1723: a study in incompatibility of temperament', *Cambridge Historical Journal*, 1945, vol. 8, no. 2.

'Bishop Butler and the Church of His Age', *Durham University Journal*, 1950, XLIII, No. 1.

S. Taylor, 'Sir Robert Walpole, the Church of England and the Quaker Tithes Bill of 1736', *Historical Journal*, 1985.

'William Warburton and the Alliance of Church and State', *Journal of Ecclesiastical History*, 1992, vol. 43, no. 2.

' "The Fac Totem in Ecclesiastical Affairs"? The Duke of Newcastle and the Crown's Ecclesiastical Patronage', *Albion*, 1992, vol. 24, no. 3.

'Whigs, Bishops and America: the Politics of Church Reform in Mid-Eighteenth Century England', *Historical Journal*, 1993, vol. 36, no. 2.

' "Dr Codex" and the Whig "Pope": Edmund Gibson, Bishop of Lincoln and London, 1716–1748', R. W. Davis (ed.), *Lords of Parliament, 1714–1914*, Stanford, 1995.

'The Government and the Episcopate in the Mid-Eighteenth Century: The Uses of Patronage', C. Giry-Deloison and R. Mettam (eds.), *Patronages et Clientelismses, 1550–1750*, London, 1995.

G. M. Townend, 'Religious Radicalism and Conservatism in the Whig Party under George I: The Repeal of the Occasional Conformity and Schism Acts', *Parliamentary History*, 1988, vol. 7, pt 1.

P. J. Wallis, 'Book Subscription Lists', *The Library*, 1974, vol. XXIX.

A. M. C. Waterman, 'A Cambridge "Via Media" in late Georgian Anglicanism', *Journal of Ecclesiastical History*, 1991, vol. xlvii.

A. C. Wood, 'Nottingham Penances, 1590–1794', *Transactions of the Thoroton Society of Nottinghamshire*, 1944, vol. 48.

B. W. Young, ' "The Soul-Sleeping System": Politics and Heresy in Eighteenth Century England', *Journal of Ecclesiastical History*, 1994, vol. 45, no. 1.

THESES

J. M. Albers, 'The Seeds of Contention: Society, Politics and the Church of England in Lancashire, 1689–1790', Yale University, PhD thesis, 1988.

A. E. Doff, 'Social Conditions in the Cuckmere Valley 1660–1780: the influence of Church and Dissent', Open University, PhD thesis, 1986.

D. R. Hirschberg, 'A Social History of the Anglican Episcopate, 1660–1760', Michigan University, PhD thesis, 1976.

W. Jacob, 'Clergy and Society in Norfolk, 1707–1806', Exeter University, PhD thesis, 1982.

W. Marshall, 'The Administration of the Diocese of Oxford and Hereford 1660–1760', Bristol University, PhD thesis, 1978.

R. J. Pope, 'The Eighteenth Century Church in the Wirral', University of Wales, Lampeter, MA thesis, 1971.

D. A. Spaeth, 'Parsons and Parishioners: Lay-Clerical Conflict and Popular Piety in Wiltshire Villages', Brown University, PhD thesis, 1985.

S. Taylor, 'Church and State in England in the Mid-Eighteenth Century: The Newcastle Years 1742–1762', Cambridge University, PhD thesis, 1987.

W. C. Watson 'The Late Stuart Reformation: Church and State in the First Age of Party', University of California, Riverside, PhD thesis, 1995.

INDEX